ATTITUDES
TOWARD HISTORY

KENNETH BURKE

Third Edition
With a New Afterword

University of California Press
Berkeley • Los Angeles • London

This book is a print-on-demand volume. It is manufactured
using toner in place of ink. Type and images may be less
sharp than the same material seen in traditionally printed
University of California Press editions.

University of California Press
Berkeley and Los Angeles, California

University of California Press, Ltd.
London, England

Library of Congress Cataloging in Publication Data

Burke, Kenneth, 1897–
    Attitudes toward history.
    1. History—Philosophy. I. Title.
D16.8.B83   1984   901   80–51234
ISBN 0–520–04148–8 (alk. paper)

Printed in the United States of America

ATTITUDES TOWARD HISTORY

TABLE OF CONTENTS

INTRODUCTION

PART I

ACCEPTANCE AND REJECTION

ATTITUDES TOWARD HISTORY

PART III

ANALYSIS OF SYMBOLIC STRUCTURE

INTRODUCTION

THOUGH the tendency is to pronounce the title of this book with the accent on *history*, so far as meaning goes the accent should be on *attitudes*. And by "history" is meant primarily man's life in political communities. The book, then, deals with characteristic responses of people in their forming and reforming of congregations. You might call it "Attitudes Toward the Incessant Intermingling of Conservatism and Progress." Or, translating into expressions now often encountered, we could entitle it "Statements of Policy on Problems of Organizational Behavior." Or, one more try: "Manual of Terms for a Public Relations Counsel with a Heart" (we shouldn't overlook the cardiac touch).

It operates on the miso-philanthropic assumption that getting along with people is one devil of a difficult task, but that, in the last analysis, we should all want to get along with people (and do want to).

To this end, the book makes three main inroads into its material, and then proceeds to a summary that, in discussing the terminology we had developed as analytic instruments for the first three inroads, becomes in effect a fourth (and longest) inroad.

The first section, on "Acceptance and Rejection," deals with those most basic of attitudes: Yes, No, and the intermediate realm of Maybe. To consider, as succinctly as possible without loss of depth, the various typical ways in which these attitudes are both subtly and grandly symbolized, this section inquires into the spirit of such literary genres as tragedy, satire, fantasy, comedy. For such expressive forms are viewed as recordings on the dial—and we aim to get our accuracy by the inspecting and charting of their accuracy.

Our second section, "The Curve of History," seeks to chart the over-all problems of merger and division (with corresponding confusion and profusion of orthodoxy, heresy, sect, and schism) that marked our particular Western culture. Dramatistically inclined, we conceive of these developmental stages after the analogy of a five-act play, thus:

Act I. Evangelical Christianity emerging out of dying, pagan Rome.

Act II. Mediaeval Synthesis.

Act III. Protestantism.

Act IV. Early Capitalism.

Act V. Collectivism, as imposed in some form or other by the conditions of modern technology and accountancy, encompassing such a variety of polities as Fascism, "Police States," socialism, communism, the "Welfare State," and the giant industrial corporations which are typical of our own nation at the present time (and which have aptly been called "business governments," as distinct from strictly "political governments").

The third section, on "The General Nature of Ritual," is necessary because of the ironies whereby a group's routines can become its rituals, while on the other hand its rituals become routines. Or, otherwise put: poetic image and rhetorical idea can become subtly fused—a fusion to which the very nature of poetry and rhetoric makes us prone. For the practised rhetorician relies greatly upon images to affect men's ideation (as with current terms like "power vacuum" and "iron curtain"), and a poet's images differ from sheerly sensory images precisely by reason of the fact that a poet's images are saturated with ideas.

Throughout these three sections we have gradually worked up a terminology, some terms of which recur quite frequently. These are our "attitudinal" terms for confronting kinds of quandary that *mutatis mutandis* recur under various historical conditions. That is, though every historical period is unique as regards its particular set of circumstances and persons, the tenor of men's policies for confronting such manifold conditions has a *synthesizing* function. For instance, if we feel happy on three different occasions, these three occasions are in a sense *attitudinally united*; they are *one in spirit*, regardless of how different they may have been in their particulars. And in this sense, history "constantly repeats itself."

One now sees the importance of our stress upon the term *attitudes* in our title. For all the terms which we consider alphabetically in our fourth section are of a strongly attitudinal sort. Even when they name a process or a condition, they name it from a meditative, or moralizing, or even hortatory point of view. And saturating the lot is the attitude of attitudes which we call the "comic frame," the methodic view of human antics as a comedy, albeit as a comedy ever on the verge of the most disastrous tragedy.

If "comedy" is our attitude of attitudes, then the process of processes which this comedy meditates upon is what we call the "bureaucratization of the imaginative." This formula is designed to name the vexing things that happen when men try to translate some pure aim or vision into terms of its corresponding material embodiment, thus necessarily involving elements alien to the original, "spiritual" ("imaginative") motive.

We could best sum up this view of history by a story, an anecdote presumably invented by the late Lincoln Steffens. It is so basic, if there were such a thing as a Comic Book of Genesis surely this story would be there:

Steffens, as the story goes, was entering the New York Public Library when a friend of his came stumbling out. The man was obviously in great agitation. "I've found it!" he shouted. And he clamorously called for Steffens to go with him and listen while he told of his discovery.

Steffens obliged. The two bumped along Forty-Second Street and turned down Fifth Avenue while the friend somewhat incoherently explained.

Gradually, despite his excitement, his words began to make sense—and Steffens realized that his friend had found a plan for saving the world. And the more the outlines of the plan began to emerge, the better the scheme sounded.

Then Steffens became aware that someone was walking along beside them, listening to the account. And finally, turning, he saw a very distinguished-looking gentleman—then, looking again, he realized that it was the devil.

Steffens: "You seem to be interested in my friend's plan."
The Devil: "Decidedly!"
Steffens: "What do you think of it?"
The Devil: "I think it's an excellent plan."
Steffens: "You mean to say you think it would work?"
The Devil: "Oh, yes. It would certainly work."
Steffens: "But in that case, how about you? Wouldn't it put you out of a job?"
The Devil: "Not in the least. I'll organize it."

That is: As regards our notion of the "Bureaucratization of the Imaginative," the friend's plan would be the originating spiritual vision (the "Imaginative") ; and the organizing of it, its material embodiment or reduction to utilitarian routines, would be its "Bureaucratization." Such would be the mildly Machiavellian nature of this key formula.

In the twenty some years between the first edition of this book and its present reprinting, a momentous quantitative difference has entered the world; and as the Hegelians and their offshoots might say, this particular change in quantity has produced a critical change in motivational quality. It is almost as great as the change from No to Yes that struck down the thirteenth apostle, Saul-become-Paul, on the road to Damascus.

We refer to the invention of technical devices that would make the rapid obliteration of all human life an easily available possibility. Up to now, human stupidity could go to fantastic lengths of destructiveness, yet always mankind's hopes of recovery could be born anew. Indeed, had you reduced the world's population to but one surviving adult, in time all the continents could again be teeming with populaces, if that one hypothetical survivor were but fairly young, and pregnant with a male child. But now presumably a truly New Situation is with us, making it all the more imperative that we learn to cherish the mildly charitable ways of the comic discount. For by nothing less than such humanistic allowances can we hope to forestall (if it can be forestalled!) the most idiotic tragedy conceivable: the willful ultimate poisoning of this lovely planet, in conformity with a mistaken heroics of war—and each day, as the sun still rises anew upon the still surviving plenitude, let us piously give thanks to Something or Other not of man's making. Basically this book would accept the Aristophanic assumptions, which equate tragedy with war and comedy with peace.

Also, perhaps in another respect we should invoke the charity of the comic discount. For despite some revisions in this tiny Universal History, the work still clearly reveals its origins in the conditions and temper of the thirties (both the century's and the author's). So, let us hope that the reader, comically inspirited, will forgive the author those occasions when the author's efforts to transcend a local situation drastically tossed him back into the very midst of it.*

K. B.

ANDOVER, NEW JERSEY
AUGUST, 1955

---

* When this book first appeared, one reviewer objected to the profusion of footnotes. We grant that they are a blemish. But they were necessary. For the material "radiated" in various directions, and these "radiations" could not have been traced in any other way.

Another reader, who preferred the footnotes to the text, suggested that we should try writing a book that was nearly all footnotes, with but the barest minimum of central text.

Of the two extremes (either no footnotes or all footnotes), the second would certainly be the better suited to this material. And, looking again, perhaps we might discover that the last and longest section, on the "pivotal terms," is in effect one continuous series of footnotes alphabetized.

The problem of "radiations" forced us to consider repeatedly the labyrinthine way in which one term involves others. And after all, as you progress along a traffic-laden avenue, sometimes it's easier to see down the side-streets than up and down the avenue. Nor should we forget that all those side routes have their ways of connecting with one another, in the labyrinthine city of a terminology.

PART I

ACCEPTANCE AND REJECTION

CHAPTER ONE

WILLIAM JAMES, WHITMAN, AND EMERSON

TO "accept the universe" or to "protest against it."
William James puts them side by side, as *"voluntary
alternatives"* between which "in a given case of evil the
mind seesaws." And: "The second not being resorted to till
the first has failed, it would seem either that the second
were an insincere *pis aller,* or the first a superfluous vanity."
Characteristically, James looks for a way of avoiding both.
He will be neither an optimist nor a pessimist, but a "meliorist." "The solution can lie only in taking neither absolutely."
Where resignation *must* be, it will be "provisional." It will
afford "ground and leisure to advance to new philanthropic
action." And he will situate the worth of an action in the
"attempt to improve . . . rather than the result." The speculation was written in 1869, many years before James's philosophy of pragmatism was given form. Yet the definitive
doctrine should be approached with this early *moralistic*
proviso always in mind. Actions and results, in James's
scheme, were never purely utilitarian. To choose the lesser
evil was also an act, if it could be seen as an eventual opportunity to choose a still lesser evil.

"Acceptance" and "rejection" (Schopenhauer's *Bejahung
und Verneinung*) then, start from the problem of evil. In
the face of anguish, injustice, disease, and death one adopts
policies. One constructs his notion of the universe or history,
and shapes attitudes in keeping. Be he poet or scientist, one
defines the "human situation" as amply as his imagination
permits; then, with this ample definition in mind, he singles
out certain functions or relationships as either friendly or

3

unfriendly. If they are deemed friendly, he prepares himself to welcome them; if they are deemed unfriendly, he weighs objective resistances against his own resources, to decide how far he can effectively go in combating them.

"Action" by all means. But in a complex world, there are many kinds of action. Action requires programs—programs require vocabulary. To act wisely, in concert, we must use many words. If we use the wrong words, words that divide up the field inadequately, we obey false cues. We must name the friendly or unfriendly functions and relationships in such a way that we are able to do something about them. In naming them, we form our characters, since the names embody attitudes; and implicit in the attitudes there are the cues of behavior. If your naming is of such a sort, for instance, that you place your hope of salvation in a church, even a corrupt church, and if that church is on the side of great wealth in social issues, your very character is enlisted in the cause of wealth. You personally may never be called upon to "act," in the brute sense of the word. You may act, a generation later, in the names and attitudes you bequeath to your children.

Hence, it is an act for you to attempt changing your attitudes, or the attitudes of others. Our philosophers, poets, and scientists act in the code of names by which they simplify or interpret reality. These names shape our relations with our fellows. They prepare us *for* some functions and *against* others, *for* or *against* the persons representing these functions. The names go further: they suggest *how* you shall be for or against. Call a man a villain, and you have the choice of either attacking or cringing. Call him mistaken, and you invite yourself to attempt setting him right. Contemporary exasperations make us prefer the tragic (sometimes melodramatic) names of "villain" and "hero" to the comic names of "tricked" and "intelligent." The choice must be weighed with reference to the results we would obtain, and to the resistances involved. By "frames of acceptance" we mean the more or less organized system of meanings by which a thinking man gauges the historical situation and adopts a role with relation to it.

Perhaps the three most well-rounded, or at least the most picturesque, frames of acceptance in American literature are those of William James, Whitman, and Emerson. All three had mystical, or transcendental, hankerings. James leaned towards the Manichaean heresy: his "pluralism" allowed for a good God still struggling to dominate the universe. It allowed for "free will," in that the individual could deliberately decide to enlist his services in this struggle. Any pious or consolatory belief was legitimate unless scientific evidence proved its falsity. For his philosophic trinity he proposed "rationality, activity, faith." Faith invigorates the power of action; rationality provides method for the act. And since by rationality is meant a willingness to consider all available evidence, it should shape the act by tests of completeness and consistency. All of his fundamental assertions were designed to equip him and others for living. He "accepted" the universe by admitting any faith (in progressive evolution, in God, in the benefits of prayer) that enabled him to have the sense of moving towards something better. In an early letter to his brother Henry we find him selecting to admire in Swinburne the expression "compromise with the nature of things" and a remark on the presence of "air" in the work of Matthew Arnold. The two details characterize James perfectly. They were pivotal co-ordinates of his reformism. And so strongly did he need the concept of *Better* rather than the concept of *Best,* as a way of equipping himself for action, that he rejected absolutism always, preferring even the asymmetry of "pluralism," a doctrine that outraged his form-loving colleagues.

Professor Ralph Barton Perry's remarkable volumes on *The Thought and Character of William James* provide us amply with the material for understanding how James shaped his philosophic frame of "acceptance." Let us try to summarize its wealth of evidence briefly, making a selection in accordance with our particular purposes.

Logical specialists, experts in a vast impersonal system of checking (learning to "think forwards" with an equipment essentially "backwards," as we check addition by subtraction, or multiplication by division) had reason to be annoyed with him. And realizing (in the words of Professor Perry) that a man must *earn* his assertions instead of *helping himself* to them as the elder Henry James had done, James was humble about his methodological laxity. The morality of his craft, he admitted, required that all assertions should be checked, insofar as the resources for checking were available. Hence, he was apologetic for dealing in a philosophic method that the boisterous mystic, Blood, who had found God in a dentist's chair, could salute as "poetry in overalls and blouse." Not until the close of his life was James able to forswear "his *Sturm und Drang* propensities forever in order that he might satisfy his intellectual scruples and the 'respectable academic minds' of his colleagues." But having reached this decision, he died. His biographer notes the coincidence without irony, though irony might be justified. Perhaps, having resolved to "be good," he had nothing more to live for. Maybe the prospect was not enticing enough, for a temperament such as his, to keep his bad heart going.

Besides, Professor Perry shows how much painstaking study went into James's books, even while the man with characteristic humbleness was bemoaning his ignorance.

JAMES, WHITMAN, EMERSON

And above all, we are made to feel how profoundly James earned everything he wrote. For he wrote what was *necessary to sustain* him. Like Socrates, he had to name relationships a certain way, in order to be a moral man. Without this secular kind of prayer, he could not have lived and acted.

Not that the naming could be of too readily consolatory a nature. We find him admiring the attitude of tragic resignation in the *Iliad*; but he adds important qualifications:

"Resignation should not say, 'It is good,' 'a mild yoke,' and so forth, but 'I'm willing to stand it for the present.' . . . Three qualities to determine. (1) how much pain I'll stand; (2) how much other's pain I'll inflict (by existing); (3) how much other's pain I'll 'accept', without ceasing to take pleasure in their existence."

His father had said disapprovingly of Emerson: "He found that certain transcendentalist and platonic phrases *named* beautifully that *side* of the universe which for his soul . . . was all-important." And whatever the father was shrewd in, he bequeathed to the son. Similarly William resented in Hegelianism a verbalizing device that "encouraged men to *see* the world good rather than to *make* it good." Hence, the business of naming, and of making the names congruous with one another, was no mere trick of euphemism. But name he did—with names sound enough to make a naturally weak man strong, a naturally sick man healthy, a naturally morbid man competent and inspiring in human relations. In the process, he built himself a character: this was his "vocation"—and Professor Perry's documents and commentaries provide invigorating testimony as to the nature of such construction.

The issue moves us into the matter of style. James was a stylist, in a family of stylists, and surrounded by stylists.

7

Nowhere will you observe the esthetic and the ethical more clearly intertwined than in these accounts of James's encounters with "truthfulness." Perhaps his somewhat opportunistic shift from "truth" to "truthfulness" (that led Peirce to rebuke him for taking as a metaphor what Peirce took as rock-bottom reality) was due in large part to the kind of extra-curricular education he derived from conversations with his father. "The literal played in our education," Henry writes, "as small a part as it perhaps ever played in any. And we wholesomely breathed inconsistency and ate and drank contradictions." The man who could say of Carlyle's humility that it was "his way of distinguishing himself from the vulgar herd of literary men" (an observation made despite the fact that Carlyle was one of the family idols) could offer substance for a moral sense subtle and complex enough. No pursuit could be pursued in its simplicity, without his badgering; thus the father's comment on Emerson: "He has no sympathy with nature, but is a sort of a police-spy upon it, chasing it into its hiding places, and noting its subtlest features, for the purpose of reporting them to the public." There seems always to have been a slight distinction that made all the difference in the world.

The father's zeal was such as to teach while forcing the taught to be independent. "The sect to which he belonged, and of which he was the head," Professor Perry writes, "may be said to have consisted of himself alone." His extremes required him to fight for whatever authority he wielded. We discern the resistance behind one family friend's recollection: "It was not unusual for the sons to invoke humorous curses on their parent, one of which was, that 'his mashed potatoes might always have lumps in them.' " As so qualified, "father rejection" could be humane, without the distortions of brash antithesis (such as Samuel Butler seems to have suffered). The father's influence, which made it natural for James to write a book "too biological for the religious, too religious for the biologists," is well indicated by Professor Perry's statement: "Having committed no excesses of credulity in his youth, there was nothing to repent in his maturity or old age. There was nothing to drive him by reaction into intellectual asceticism." The result was even a willingness to take "excursions to the scientific underworld"; for

"He grew up in a circle in which heresies were more gladly tolerated than orthodoxies. Men like his father and his father's friends, who were attracted to Fourierism, communism, homeopathy, women's rights, abolition and spiritism, were not likely to have any prejudices against mediumship, clairvoyance, mesmerism, automatic writing, and crystal gazing. From his youth James contemplated such 'phenomena' without repulsion and with an open mind."

He was not conditioned to "know" in advance, once and for all, who the "cranks" were. Without snobbery, he was "one who welcomed light from any quarter."

Those are really poignant pages that indicate the part played by Peirce in the sharpening of James's understanding. "Perhaps," in Professor Perry's diagnosis, "it would be correct, and just to all parties, to say that the modern movement known as pragmatism is largely the result of James's misunderstanding of Peirce." Stressing the *public* nature of truth, Peirce writes to James: "I say to people—imaginary interlocutors, for I have nobody to talk to . . ." and "Come up and see our waterfalls, therein is peace."

Peirce was James's gadfly, forever making it difficult for James to indulge his weaknesses for resonance. Thus we find him reproaching James for his generous use of terms, and even being led to these uncomfortable rigors:

"It is an indispensable requisite of science that it should have a recognized technical vocabulary, composed of words so unattractive that loose thinkers are not tempted to use them; and a recognized and legitimate way of making up new words freely when a new conception is introduced; and that it is vital for science that he who introduces a new conception should be held to have a *duty* imposed upon him to invent a sufficiently disagreeable series of words to express it. I wish you to reflect seriously upon the moral aspect of terminology."

When James had written that the Kantian "I think" could be reduced to the experience of breathing, the gadfly answered:

"I call your attention to the circumstance that many people, of whom I am one, involuntarily hold their breath while thinking. . . . If I have got to believe that I think with my lungs I will take as my equation: *Ich denke*   I don't breathe."

In reading the interchange between them, in the light of what we know of their contrasted destinies, we feel the greater rigor of Peirce's methods, but we also recognize that his muscles were beyond his management. Because *he* held his breath, *others* may breathe more easily. And if James was never forced so cruelly into a corner as Peirce was (finally being led by division to decide: "my style of 'brilliancy' consists in a mixture of irony and seriousness— the same things said ironically and also seriously"), James did unquestionably master his own brand of terminological proficiency.

JAMES, WHITMAN, EMERSON

Perhaps the most picturesque·instance is in his caricature of Spencer. Spencer had written:

"Evolution is an integration of matter and concomitant dissipation of motion; during which the matter passes from an indefinite, incoherent homogeneity to a definite, coherent heterogeneity; and during which the retained motion undergoes a parallel transformation."

James translates this into:

"Evolution is a change from a no-howish untalkaboutable all-alikeness to a somehowish and in general talkaboutable not-all-alikeness by continuous sticktogetherations and somethingelseifications."

James's constant bursting into metaphor was not a mere trick of embellishment for popular consumption. It arose from the fact that he lived very close to an awareness of the emotional overtones associated with his ideas. Thus, he could not accept absolute idealism, because it *really meant* to him the same thing as "an aquarium, a crystal globe in which goldfish are swimming." And he had to make his own revisions of empiricism because the doctrine in its simplicity was *exactly* "one of those dried human heads with which the Dyaks of Borneo deck their lodges." In calling his work on psychology an "enormous *rat*" he implicitly announced an intention of moving into other fields. Much of his inability to abide by the accepted rules of the game, his tendency to "disregard the boundary between philosophy and psychology" (Perry), his "intellectual larking" (Henry), his writing as "an impressionist in psychology . . . a veritable storm-bird" (G. Stanley Hall) arose from his unusual artistic sensitivity, forcing him to a concern with wayward manifestations that are, in their extreme aspects called "mystical."

Abstractions are but fossilized metaphors—and even the man who deals in them habitually will often, in strategic moments (such as the exaltedness of an "In Conclusion") tend to break the frame and burst into metaphor pure and simple. And such metaphors at strategic places may reveal the essence or temper of a man's work, the core of its unification, something like a "motive for philosophizing." James was always saying in effect that denotations, when pursued with engrossment, must by the very nature of the case have emotional connotations that determine the engrossment. Feeling the pressure of this free imagery, this "fringe," he could not keep himself from treating it as part of the total situation to be handled. Such openness explains his great sympathy with Bergson.

"As life closes," James said, when his father died, "all a man has done seems like one cry or sentence." Approaching the same matter from another angle, Professor Perry paraphrases James as holding that "All views of the universe as a whole are based on the analogy of one of its parts." Were we to seek the sentence for James's work we might, borrowing a cue from Fritz Mauthner (who suggests that empiricism is "adjectival") characterize his method by an analogy from grammar: we could call him an expert in the *comparative degree* of adjectives of value. Distrusting absolutism (which is really the *superlative*, identifying the One as the Best) he thought in terms of *more* rather than *all*. Hence his dislike of monism, authority, the rationally finished. To optimism or pessimism, he preferred "meliorism." His assertion of free will, that played so important a part in his moral rehabilitation, owed its shape to similar notions of partiality. Even God was on the make, not a Completed Best but a Candidate for Better, as he wrote to Davidson:

"I can sympathize perfectly with the most rabid hater of

him and the idea of him when I think of the use that has
been made of him in history and philosophy as a *starting-
point*, or premise for grounding deductions. But as an ideal
to attain and make probable, I find myself less and less able
to do without him. He need not be an *all*-including 'subjective unity of the universe,' as you suppose."

It was this *comparative* pattern of thought that could lead
him to the amusingly ingenious observation on Bradley:
"He is, really, an extra humble-minded man, I think, but
even more humble-minded about his reader than about himself, which gives him that false air of arrogance." There is
something of the same genius in his remark to a friend concerning Royce: "You make some pointed objection to him
which needs a definite reply, and his invariable reply is
simply to restate the whole system." It promoted a kind of
any-port-in-a-storm attitude, annoying perhaps to lovers
of the symmetrical when it takes the metaphysical guise of
pluralism, but extremely helpful for the moral jugglings
we must manage in this imperfect world: "One can meet
mortal (or would-be mortal) disease," he writes to his dying
friend Davidson, "either by gentlemanly levity, by high-
minded stoicism, or by religious enthusiasm. I advise you, old
T. D., to follow my example and try a playful *durcheinan-
der* of all three, taking each in turn *pro re nata*." The same
distinctions in schematic form seem implicit in his rule-of-
thumb kind of trinity, "Rationality, activity, faith." And
if, in his preference for the comparative, his world became
pluralistic, it followed that as a thoroughly sincere man he
would even buy a pluralistic house. His sister Alice reports
him as saying: "It's the most delightful house you ever saw;
it has fourteen doors, all opening outwards." (We may add,
for the sake of the record, that James credits it with but
eleven.)

Much of James's resistance to the procedures of his "respectable" colleagues seems to have come from his conviction that they were in danger of dealing with too restricted a world. He hated the *"streng wissenschaftlich"* not merely because he was too restless or too physically ill to persist in minute measurement. He also felt that too much of vital importance might, by the nature of the method, necessarily be left out of account. Here we see James spontaneously obeying his father's injunction, striving to maintain the widest notion of *vocation,* vocation not as a *specialist,* but as a *man.*

Is not Whitman the poetic replica of James? His "Song of the Open Road" preaches "the profound lesson of reception." He would phrase a *"Salut au Monde,"* welcoming "all the inhabitants of the earth." He would be as promiscuous as Blake in universal love. Where things looked bad on the surface, he would discern "unseen existences" ("objects gross and the unseen soul are one"). He matched James's pluralism by the vision of himself "disintegrated," ecstatically asserting: "I will scatter myself among men and women as I go." Like James, he resorted to pluralism as a way of seeing an organized unity of purpose behind diversity:

> Every existence has its idiom, everything has an idiom
>   and tongue,
> He resolves all tongues into his own and bestows it
>   upon men, and any man translates, and any man
>   translates himself also,
> One part does not counteract another part, he is the
>   joiner, he sees how they join.

Were some things repellent? He would make himself the universal maw nonetheless, the all-consuming appetite.

(And there the limitations of acceptance suggest them-selves. If a whole people perfected his ways, building his frame of acceptance into a collective poem as vast as that of the mediaeval church, we can imagine someone saying in effect: "You would digest everything? Very well, here is a diet of sawdust and nails. Try casting that into your belly.")

By inhaling "great draughts of space," he owned the four horizons. He would not ask for good-fortune; "I myself am good-fortune." Hurrying along the open road, with a haste that troubles the thoughtful (why hurry so, if there were so many invitations to tarry?), he sensed in himself "the past, the future, majesty, love." Challengingly: "The earth, that is sufficient." Yet he carried his "old delicious burdens." He could not deny "the felon, the diseas'd, the illiterate person"; he promised that "if you become degraded, crimi-nal, ill, then I become so for your sake"; yet in the exalta-tion of his "Allons!" he votes for "defiance, gaiety, self-esteem, curiosity," and warns that his companions must have "the best blood, thews, endurance . . . courage and health." In sum, when considering both the "accepted by men" and the "rejected by men," he solves the problem by fiat:

> I know not where they go,
> But I know that they go toward the best—toward
>   something great,

his "*toward* the best" doing with a preposition what James's "meliorism" does with the comparative degree of an adjec-tive. Noting a *bad-good tangle*, he transcends the contra-diction by a synthesizing attitude, whereby the good ele-ment is taken as the *essence* of the pair.

As James located value in the *attempt* to improve, so

Whitman contrives, by a prestidigitation of accent, to convert a very discouraging possibility into something almost like a promise:

"It is provided in the essence of things that from any fruition of success, no matter what, shall come forth something to make a greater struggle necessary,"

a statement he can smuggle in, under good auspices, because he has been talking of his great happiness, that goes simultaneously in opposite directions, since it "flows unto us" and is "the efflux of the soul." This gorgeous subterfuge is repeated in "Sea-Drift," where we are told *with joy* how the sea whispered "the low and delicious word death," and how his own songs, his "thousand responsive songs at random," had "awaked from that hour." The rhapsodic style thereby turns a disturbing thought (that his poems were motivated by a vision of death) into a delightful one. In "Crossing Brooklyn Ferry," he seems to be crossing the bar, merrily, as he is dictating his testament, for people like him to read after he is dead; and he suggests that he may be watching them as they read.

The mode of thought is necessary to his logic; he can only affirm "the certainty of the reality and immortality of things, and the excellence of things," by a transcendental bridging. On the open road, he had delighted in "air-sweetness." In "The World Below the Brine" he imagines the life submerged in the "thick-breathing air" of the ocean. Out of the contrast he shapes a pattern: as life in that "thick-breathing air" is to our earthly life of "air-sweetness," so the life of air-sweetness is to "that of beings who walk other spheres."* We might round out the picture by noting the

---

* The pattern suggests somewhat the "ideal" that has been "implemented" in the eye-formation of a certain fish: Anableps anableps; family

succession of events in his "Song of the Broad-Axe": a "weapon shapely, naked, wan," its "head from the mother's bowels drawn." This axe is procreative of many things— and in the end, surprisingly, we come upon the narrative of a son returning home, to be received by the mother, whereat

> The main shapes arise!
> Shapes of Democracy total, result of centuries,
> Shapes ever projecting other shapes,
> Shapes of turbulent manly cities,
> Shapes of the friends and home-givers of the whole earth,
> Shapes bracing the earth and braced with the whole earth.

---

anablepidae; habitat, Central, and northern South America. "The eyes of these fish are divided horizontally so that the upper part is adjusted to vision above the surface of the water and lower part to vision below it."

Seeing a specimen in the New York Aquarium, we recalled a passage in a fiction we once wrote, *Towards a Better Life*, where the protagonist says: "I can remember stepping slowly into a lake, until my eyes were even with its surface, the water cutting across the eye-balls." In the light of Whitman's ratio, we realize that, as placed in the story, the passage symbolized not emergence, but submergence. It was Whitman's pattern in reverse.

A famous variant, stressing submergence rather than emergence, is found in Matthew Arnold's "The Forsaken Merman," constructed about the theme:

> Down, down, down!
> Down to the depths of the sea!

It also appears in Malcolm Cowley's poem, "Leander," where the waves *persuade* the swimmer to surrender and drown.

We shall later discuss the ways in which such symbols of emergence or submergence serve as rituals of rebirth. They are magical incantations whereby the poet effects a change of identity, killing some portion of himself as a technique of initiation for membership in a new situation.

In Whitman we find, as a cluster: immortality, brother-hood, work, I, democracy, "answering," air-sweetness, life-in-death—and, in other pivotal poems, the Union (the corporate *reintegrating* symbol for his sympathetic *disintegration*), and Lincoln (the "Captain" that is the Union's *personal* counterpart). The whole is Whitman's "frame of acceptance."

Perhaps the genius of Emerson's enterprise finds its most thorough expression in his essay on "Compensation." The technical problem that Emerson confronts can be easily stated: by affirming a doctrine of "polarity," he is able to confront evil with good cheer. In all evil, there is inevitably some compensatory good. "For everything you have missed, you have gained something else." A bad government creates the resistances that cure its badness. The swindler swindles himself. And so on, ingeniously, for many pages, with examples from physics, biology, and human history.

"All things are double, one against another.—Tit for tat; an eye for an eye; a tooth for a tooth; blood for blood; measure for measure; love for love,—Give and it shall be given you.—He that watereth shall be watered himself.— What will you have? quoth God; pay for it and take it.— Nothing venture, nothing have.— . . . If you put a chain around the neck of a slave, the other end fastens itself around your own.—Bad counsel confounds the adviser.— The devil is an ass."

But this theory of ambivalence cannot be entrusted to bungling hands. If "every excess causes a defect; every defect an excess," and "every sweet hath its sour; every evil its good," we might resign ourselves to the conclusion: "Thus do all things preach the indifference of circumstances. . . .

Everything has two sides, a good and an evil. Every advantage has its tax. I learn to be content."

Emerson skirts this difficulty by introducing at this point his transcendental doctrine of the soul. "The soul is not a compensation, but a life. The soul *is*." There is no part to counterbalance it, since it is not a part. It is Being, and Being is good, and whole. "Being is the vast affirmative, excluding negation, self-balanced, and swallowing up all relations, parts and times, within itself. Nature, truth, virtue are the influx from thence." This shift in strategy enables him to assert: "There is no penalty to virtue; no penalty to wisdom; they are proper additions of being. In a virtuous action, I properly *am*; in a virtuous act, I add to the world; I plant into deserts conquered from Chaos and Nothing, and see the darkness receding on the limits of the horizon." Hence, in another form, we arrive at the *meliorist* emphasis, in a project for living by the extending of cosmos farther into the realm of chaos, the reclaiming of chaos for cosmic purposes. His device prepares him for new and better things. He warns that "we are idolaters of the old," that "we cannot let our angels go." And while we are tempted to grow sluggish, the nature of life itself forces us to exert ourselves "up and onward." Calamities arise, and by compensation, they force us to turn them into benefits, lest we perish. As a transcendentalist, he employs a variant of the same device that Hegel developed, and that Marx proposed to secularize. The pressure of good-evil conflicts on "one" level brought forth the necessity for a solution, and this solution moved the issue to a "higher" level.

"Acceptance" and "Passivity"

So much by way of general illustration. Could we not say that all symbolic structures are designed to produce such "acceptance" in one form or another? In its most trivial form (where a good device is made sentimental by over-simplification) we get the Pollyanna solution: If you break your leg, thank God you didn't break your neck. We see it in the attitude behind the vulgar assurance that it always rains when you forget your umbrella. We have it when the fox, unable to reach the grapes, decided they were sour. We find it in the jokes whereby men, in the face of danger, dwarf the danger ("trench humor" that maintains "trench morale"). It is said of Democritus, that when he imagined a universe made of tiny atoms bumping and combining with one another, he *laughed*. Why did Democritus laugh? Perhaps he laughed because, by his materialist doctrine, he had "debunked" the gods. He "accepted" the world by ruling out the threats of ghostly vengeance. He was in the trenches of metaphysics, and materialism was the humor for his trench morale.

"Frames of acceptance" are not the same as *passiveness*. Since they name both friendly and unfriendly forces, they fix attitudes that prepare for combat. They draw the lines of battle—and they appear "passive" only to one whose frame would persuade him to draw the line of battle differently. Aquinas was as realistic as Marx, for instance, in recognizing the existence of social classes. It was the bourgeois interregnum that tried to eliminate them by fiat, in treating the bourgeois class as universal mankind. The difference between Marx and Aquinas is in the attitude (incipient program of action) taken towards the existence of classes. Since Aquinas, following Augustine, looked upon classes (with attendant phenomena of government, property, and slavery) as punishment for the fall of man, his frame was designed to accept the inevitability of classes, and to build a frame of action accordingly. Marx, on the other hand, accepted the *need of eliminating classes*, hence drew the line of battle differently.

It was the bourgeois attitude that came nearest to passivity in this respect, because of an understressing that was often purely sentimental. In its heyday, following comparative victory over the nobility, the bourgeois frame simply smeared the issue out of mind. It "rejected" class morality by "accepting" the doctrine that the resources of private initiative were equally available to all. And many centuries elapsed before people's characters were molded in accordance with this frame.*

All three frames would be active with relation to the line between "friendly" and "unfriendly" that each drew in its own way. Those who call it "passive" usually mean that they would draw the critical line of action elsewhere.

Rejection

"Rejection" is but a by-product of "acceptance." It involves primarily a matter of emphasis. It takes its color from an attitude towards some reigning symbol of authority, stressing a *shift in the allegiance* to symbols of authority. It is the heretical aspect of an orthodoxy—and as such, it has much in common with the "frame of acceptance" that it rejects. It somewhat robs a thinker of his birth-right, his

* The maximum development from a subsistence economy to a money economy was not attained until the period just preceding the rise of Fascism with its great hordes of state laborers that show a marked analogy to the feudal ideal. The peak was probably reached when the genius of capitalism had become sufficiently implemented by the money market and the private control of credit (the symbolic medium of exchange) to force the "money crop" idea upon the agrarians, the group that clung most tenaciously to the vestiges of a purely subsistence economy, and hence were the last to adopt a *purely financial* concept of efficiency in living and producing.

right to "consume" reality without regurgitation. If the king is well thought of in many quarters, the man who would build his frame to accept the necessity of *deposing* the king is almost necessarily, by the tactics of the case, shunted into a negativistic emphasis. Such rigors may explain the fact that the Communist Manifesto begins with a terroristic metaphor. At this strategic point (for beginnings and endings are particularly strategic, the first setting the tone for the reception of one's message, the second clinching the thesis before a final parting) the authors were presumably led by the power of the orthodox authority to depict their project for redemption, in negativistic terms, as a *specter that haunts*; and in parting they address themselves to the *anger of slaves*. This polemic, negativistic genius (stressing the *no* more strongly than the *yes*) throws the emphasis stylistically upon the partiality of rejection rather than the completeness of acceptance.

The relation that frames of acceptance bear to symbols of authority inevitably puts the symbolist of change at this tactical disadvantage, warping somewhat the perfect roundness of his utterance. There is no "no" in music—and educators of children have also suggested the possibility that there is no "no" in the psychology of attention. The full strategy for saying *"don't* do that" is *"do* do this." The issue may throw light upon the resistances of our countrymen, who were long trained in the Emerson-Whitman-James mode of emphasis, and constructed their notions of sociality upon it.

The preference is grounded in Christian apologetics. Thus, when the increasing economic strain of late feudalism was making men restless and bellicose, when their growing "mobility," under the stimulus of economic frustration, manifested itself first in pilgrimage and eventually took the form of militant crusades, the Church quickly put forward beneficent fictions of penance and indulgence whereby the mounting pugnacity could be "saved" as far as possible. The blood that was let was let for God and personal salvation. The churchmen were saying, in effect: "Where there is unseemly work to be done, let us at least do it in a seemly vocabulary."

As a given historical frame nears the point of cracking, strained by the rise of new factors it had not originally taken into account, its adherents employ its genius casuistically to extend it as far as possible. Thus the Churchmen invented peaceful fictions for war, in their simplicity probably hoping that, if and when the wars abated, the genius inherent in the pacific terms could again express itself in less imperfect modes. (This casuistic stretching, incidentally, is to be noted also in the judicial interpretations by which the American Constitution has been expanded to permit a freedom for corporations not foreseen at the time of its adoption. The stretchers pre-empt the "acceptance" emphasis. thus forcing the "rejection" emphasis upon the opposition.)

We find the "rejection" feature arising with Machiavelli, who crystallized the shift to civil co-ordinates of authority, and whose *"Realpolitik"* laid the foundations for the ma- terialistic emphasis, in putting forward the *cult of power* as the basis of human motivation. It is present in Hobbes, with the picturesque *homo homini lupus* and *bellum omnium contra omnes* formulae as the groundwork of his monarchic system. In the realm of paradox, it gains ground in Mandeville's "Fable of the Bees," whose clever subtitle, "Private vices public virtues," is well on the road to the commercialist "transvaluation of values." The new economic structure has, by this time, revealed its outlines with sufficient clarity to necessitate a new code of morals—and Mandeville's fable radically reverses the Church's attitude towards a key value, personal ambition. In the Church's moral scheme, ambition had been a major vice. Mandeville playfully speculated upon the possibility of enshrining it as the major virtue. He fabulously suggested that if people were greedy and pushing enough in personal enterprise, they would produce an abundance of commodities whereby the whole community would profit.

In the spirit of high comedy, Mandeville dealt with the same shift in values that Shakespeare had considered tragically in *Macbeth*. Macbeth is the poetic adumbration of the "Faustian man," who would fulfill his destiny at all costs. He stands at the turning point between the feudal attitude towards ambition, as *punishable pride*, and the commercial attitude towards ambition, as the *essence of vocation*. Shakespeare heralds the new, while fearing it in terms of the old. In Mandeville the conflict is considered less drastically, though he still draws upon it for his literary effects.*

By the time we get to Adam Smith, the new code has gained sufficient authority to be framed as *orthodoxy*. Smith proceeds simply by rationalizing Mandeville *without* the paradox; ambition becomes a private virtue because it is a public virtue. The utilitarians completed his theory. Thus, in England the "transvaluation of values" had gained codification and authoritative backing long before Nietzsche,

---

* Though this lineage makes no attempt to be complete, perhaps we should also include Marlowe's *Dr. Faustus*, where the new values (of "power-knowledge") are introduced with fearsome connotations. The drama itself shows closer connections in form with the church "morality play" out of which secular tragedy developed. Marlowe's ambiguity, in confronting the new bourgeois standards from the old feudal point of view, is even greater than Shakespeare's, as was his personal irritability.

in more feudalistic Germany, began to put it forward challengingly and confusedly. And Marx, whose English training had shown him its ascendancy, laid out the frame for its *rejection.* Ironically, he came before Spencer, whose *optimistic* picture of disintegration (epitomized in his definition of "progress" as a development from homogeneity to heterogeneity) completed the intellectual architecture of Adam Smith's economics.

The Changing Emphasis of Frames

When surveying the historic curve on the graph of Western culture, we can better understand what was accomplished by the shift from the classical emphasis upon resignation to the liberal ("Faustian") emphasis upon freedom. The revolutionary philosophy of business enterprise served to democratize a sense of personal mastery hitherto reserved to but a few—and even they, with their stress upon pre-established *status,* had not generally thought of their privileges in terms of *advancement.* Machiavelli provided the turbulent Renaissance "prince" with the beginnings of "success" co-ordinates. The later, more exclusively commercial focus, seems to have been sharpened by the text-books on accountancy that began gaining attention shortly after him. Particularly, as Sombart has observed, the perfection of double-entry bookkeeping, with its clear visualization of profit and loss in monetary terms, prepared the way for the abstract concepts of "production for gain" that rationalized investment and efficiency in accordance with purely capitalist criteria. Here began the attempt to shift from the "prosperity of poverty" to the "economy of plenty."

The earlier tests of human effort had been *qualitative*— and when you organize a mode of operation about qualities (standards of "good living," mainly grounded in the authority of custom), your policies cannot readily meet the requirements of discursive reason. You become entangled in blunt assertions of the *de gustibus non disputandum est* variety. Accountancy offered a *quantitative* device for making action rational. The merchant did not have to juggle tenuous notions of vice and virtue when judging his plan of action. He simply consulted his ledgers, and the plan proved "good" if his balance at the end of the year showed income outweighing costs. The "rational" henceforth ceased to be the mere "handmaiden of faith"—it became the very essence of method. There is no point in either saluting or regretting the shift. Here we need but observe it.

And we may further speculate upon the great *relief* that the liberal doctrine must have brought to men, made restless by the Church's organized attempts to legislate against the genius of the glandular system, and by the extent to which the privileged had "moved in on" the people's attitude of obedience until acceptance of the *status quo* had become almost physically impossible. The psychological equivalent of the attempt to "resign" oneself under such conditions was neurosis. The religious rationalization could provide a vent for an incredible amount of neurotic agitation—but in time these resources also were strained to their breaking point.

At such a critical juncture, the commercial, quantitative tests for rationalizing conduct were a very happy invention. They opened up a new field of effort, further widened by the discovery of America and the development of technology. For several centuries, they made a population of Fausts *possible*, by providing the historical environment in which such a "culture" (in the bacteriological sense) could grow and multiply. The range of *opportunity* for individualistic assertion was widened, permitting a percentage of individualism that, in any other setting, would probably have led to chaos.

Instead of leading to chaos, the new material and moral resources were eventually able to adapt the notions of "profit" so completely to the secular frame that the zeal of the religious wars abated. There resulted several centuries of fairly rational *organization*. But now, after nearly half a millennium, these new resources seem to have been exploited to the point where they in turn are nearing their "Malthusian limits." The liberal habits of private enterprise "proliferated," like yeast in the mash, until they could not proliferate much further. The by-product of their activity (the "alcohol" they generated) now threatens their extinction (a metaphorical way of rephrasing the thesis that liberalism, like *any* cultural trend long followed, must produce its "inner contradictions").

Any organized mode of understanding and acting offers its own possibilities of laxity. In time, there occurs a proliferation of the habits that take advantage of these opportunities. The exploitation of such habits will itself become organized, "bureaucratized," until the given mode of understanding and acting has been stretched to its "Malthusian limits." A culture then faces a crisis, the need for a "revolution" of sufficient scope to make new opportunities for exploitation possible. Insofar as the new opportunities are not provided, we get decadence, neurosis, anger (expressing itself in either external war or internal antagonisms, the devices whereby a people "projects" its uneasiness upon a scapegoat).

Many have charted the difficulties of such a critical period, as they apply to "frames of acceptance." The ideal conditions for thought arise when the world is deemed about as satisfactory as we can make it, and thinkers of all sorts collaborate in constructing a vast collective mythology whereby people can be at home in that world. Conflicts are bridged symbolically; one tries to mitigate conflict by the mediating devices of poetry and religion, rather than to accentuate the harshness. Such is man's "natural" vocation. It makes for the well-rounded philosophy of an Aristotle, who contributed much to the Summa of Aquinas. It seeks to develop attitudes of resignation whereby we may make the best of things as they are.

But the inexorable workings of the "neo-Malthusian" principle eventually make such frames drastically inadequate. New material arises, if only as "by-products" of the cultural pattern. Marx has shown the effects of new productive techniques in this respect. While the frame centers the attention upon some relationships, by this very thoroughness it obscures the perception of new factors that are of critical importance. Or it may induce thinkers to damn the new factors as *symptoms*, without disclosing the *causes* of the symptoms. We note this tendency towards sermon and invective particularly in the thinking of the Church, where men trained in prayer are particularly prone (under the promptings of their "occupational psychosis") to handle all untoward issues verbally, by benediction or anathema: they would "legislate" a disorder out of existence. But the tendency is not unknown even to secular thinkers. Note, for instance, the proliferation of laws under parliamentary governments, where the ready availability of law-making has invited people to "move in on" this convenience to such an extent that legislation often becomes hardly more than a kind of public prayer.

Frames stressing the ingredient of *rejection* tend to lack the well-rounded quality of a *complete* here-and-now philosophy. They make for fanaticism, the singling-out of

28

one factor above others in the charting of human relationships. Their simplest caricature is the "money crank," who would shape all life's purposes around some project for tinkering with the *symbols* of exchange without concern for the underlying economic factors and psychological attributes that go with them. Marx, being born into the great century of rejection philosophies, discloses the scars of his environment; nevertheless he did unquestionably lay the foundations for a vast public enterprise out of which a new frame of acceptance could be constructed. Arising among idealists, he caught the genius of realism. His project, we might say, was pre-realism or pro-realism, a here-and-now philosophy designed mainly for action during the late-capitalist interregnum, but containing some ingredients for a post-capitalist reintegration.

The romanticism that is contemporaneous with Marx, and left its imprint upon his writings (particularly in his stressing of antithesis) is cluttered with rejection frames having varying degrees of accuracy and thoroughness. Goethe had both welcomed and feared his Faust, the man of driving personal ambition who would assert his genius even at the risk of partnership with the devil. This "tragic ambiguity," whereby a growing trend is at once recommended and punished, is present also in Shakespeare's treatment of Macbeth, who represents the new bourgeois concepts of ambition in grotesque guise. In confronting the emergent capitalist standards, Shakespeare retained many conservative, feudal norms of value. The result, made by the incongruous juxtaposition of both conservative and revolutionary frames, was a "tragic ambiguity" whereby he gave expression to the rising trends, but gave them the forbidding connotations of criminality.

Byron, admired by Goethe, gave us "Faustian" heroes

who were the lineal descendants of Milton's Satan (the creation of a man whose political allegiances made him a symbolic regicide). As a whole, those who had religious leanings, but were sufficiently affected by science to become skeptical of the Church's dogmas, tended to "reject" the world symbolically by entering the monastery of art. Wagner's "temple of art" stretches before him and after him. A kind of "two-world" scheme arose, the antithetical worlds of the practical and the esthetic, with a few writers like Mann trying, by mixture of irony and melancholy, to mediate between them. Such frames can be labeled, as you prefer, either by their "acceptance" of the esthetic or their "rejection" of the practical.

Sentimental Acceptance in Futurism

The "futurists" occupy an important place in this trend. For although a writer like Marinetti never gained wide popularity, he is a concentration point, a summing-up, of movements that occurred in less "efficient" form all about him—and nearly all of his proposed innovations have since been introduced, in fragments or attenuations, by typical contemporary writers. Nietzsche, a kind of incipient futurist, seems to have forced himself to welcome developments that he did not really like. He saw the world going in a direction basically abhorrent to him—but his cult of optimism and historicism made him want to salute his times, to be a "yea-sayer," an "answerer," to make his peace with the *Zeitgeist*. The result was a kind of *brutality* that is also apparent in his disciple, Spengler. We may note a strong ingredient of such brutality in the futurists' frame of "acceptance."

Marinetti became remade, he tells us, during a trip in an airplane, an event that seems to have startled him by a secular vision of "the pit."* Since we shall later make much of such symbols, we note that on at least three occasions Marinetti attributes this genesis to his perspective, whereby there would be a violent *break* in the continuity of culture. Everything preceding futurism would be like Homer—and with futurism would begin the abruptly new. Zealous in his "liberal" apostasy, he advocated not merely free verse, but *free words*:

"an absolutely free expression of the universe beyond the limits of prosody and syntax—a new way of feeling and seeing—a measuring of the universe as the sum of forces in movement."

"The *mots-libristes* orchestrate colors, noises, sounds, they form suggestive combinations with the materials of language and slang, arithmetical and geometric formulae, old words, words distorted and invented, the cries of animals and the roar of motors."

He and his school would "abolish the cult of proportion"— they would be "drunk on life," a life which they would eagerly depict by the metaphors of "revolution, war, shipwreck, earthquake"—they would stress verbs, since adjectives and adverbs were not strong—they would seek for analogies without the restrictions of good taste:

"For instance, some people have compared an animal to

* The airplane symbol figures similarly in Muriel Rukeyser's *Theory of Flight*. It pilots the poet above the modern Chamber of Horrors, as Virgil guided Dante through hell, and finally returns to firm earth. Contrast this symbolism with the related symbolism of Faulkner's novel, where the airplane falls with its human burden into the "lake." . . . "Truth lies at the bottom of a well," a "pit mood" that Thomas Mann expands novelistically through the opening hundred pages of *Joseph and his Brothers*.

man or to other animals, which is almost photography. Others, more advanced, might compare a fox-terrier to a gun. But I compare it to boiling water."

They are for a "maximum of disorder"; a "lyric obsession with matter"; the abolition of sentiment; for the "telegraphic," the "vibratory," the "cult of speed, the new." For the ugly, the "reign of machinery," "imagination unchained," the glorification of industrial and financial nationalism. They are "against the harmonious," against "moonlight, reminiscence, nostalgia, eternity, immortality."

"Instead of humanizing, let us animalize, vegetalize, mineralize, electrify, or liquefy our style."

A recent manifesto in glorification of war shows how well the futurist mode of acceptance was adapted for recruiting in the service of Mussolini. The futurist, to praise war, needed only to recite its *horrors*, and call them *beautiful* (somewhat as the ancient Greeks had considered the left side ill-omened, and had made up the difference euphemistically by calling the left flank of their armies the "well named").

One need not read the statements of Marinetti without making allowances for a certain operatic posturing (*"qu'-importe la victime si le geste est beau!"*). Furthermore, Marinetti's manifestoes *promised* too much. His attempts to embody them in artistic products are necessarily a letdown. Perhaps the most charitable thing we can say is that his manifestoes were themselves the works of art they proposed to herald. Though pleading for syntactical confusions (of the sort that Joyce subsequently perfected?) they were themselves phrased in keeping with the orthodox tenets of syntax. Hence, whatever the "chaos" in their "clear ideas," they conveyed their attitude more forcefully in the planning than in the execution. A call to disorder can be stronger when it can draw upon the cumulative force of order. Thus, the *manifestoes* could profit by the effectiveness of form (a "public grammar") whereas the works written in response to the manifestoes could not.

Marinetti contrived to attain "yea-saying," at whatever cost. Like a cruel caricature of Whitman, he would be the omnivorous appetite. By a cult of the picturesque, his project categorically silenced objections. To any who might say, "This modern world is disease," it could answer, "But what a *perfect* example of disease!" Its affinity with the antics of our recent "hard-boiled" school is apparent. We may also note (unruly thought!) the *sentimental* aspect of both. Futurism, so cast, could provide the most rudimentary kind of solace. Were the streets noisy? It could counter by advocating an uncritical cult of noise. Might there be stench? It would discuss the "beauties" of stench. *Apparently* active, it was in essence the most passive of frames, an elaborate method for feeling *assertive* by a resolve to drift with the current. Its incompleteness, or partiality, as a frame was drastic. A well-rounded frame of acceptance involves constant discrimination. But this was a project for gluttony, a blanket endorsement of historic trends as they were. As a cult of yea, it would say yea to the reigning symbols of authority at all costs. We cite it because of its "chemical" purity. It has exploited a trend so thoroughly that there is no possible step in the same direction beyond it.

CHAPTER TWO

POETIC CATEGORIES

OUR way of approaching the structures of symbolism might be profitably tested by the examination of various literary categories, as each of the great poetic forms stresses its own peculiar way of building the mental equipment (meanings, attitudes, character) by which one handles the significant factors of his time.

We shall begin with the epic, as a typical frame of symbolic adjustment under primitive conditions. We do get sophisticated imitations of the epic, such as the *Aeneid*, in highly "enlightened" eras. But the form arises under primitive, non-commercial, conditions. Writers have remarked on the *deliberately* archaic quality of the Homeric poems, which may suggest a certain nostalgia behind their composition, as though the new ways had already begun to make themselves felt while the materials of primitive living were still largely present, there being just enough of the new to make appreciation of the old more poignant.

In the case of Virgil, the prestige of Homer might be enough to account for his choice of form. Also, he wrote to celebrate the rise of Augustus, who marked the turn away from the *laissez-faire* period in Roman enterprise, and founded the bureaucratic modes of governmental administration, under central imperial authority, that would eventually lead to the crystallization of the Roman state. From the time of Augustus, "prosperity" in the business sense of the term was on the wane. Roman efficiency, backed by bureaucratic organization, and possessing such valuable granaries as Egypt, could garner much material wealth; and agricultural science, perfected during Hellenism, could increase and regularize productivity; but the heyday of private investment, that had "flowered" just before the rise of Caesar, was over. Under the, emperors, the speculations of the *equites*, who had mulcted the Roman provinces, were radically curbed. *Public* enterprises again came to the fore. Even at the time of imperial decay, when one soldier after another seized power at Rome, advancement for the great bulk of the army was as regular as among the underlings of a modern insurance company. Soldiering eventually became a trade, and on the whole a very stable one, without great risks. The empire built an invisible Chinese wall about its borders, and perfected an internal network of communications that long made it able to resist the sporadic, unorganized pressure at the frontiers. Business slowly abated to a standstill—the *novus homo* of Cicero's day no longer (as Belloc would say) gave the "tone" to the state—the fixation of class status became the rule.

This trend began with the reforms of Augustus, and Virgil was his poet. As such, he may have been sensitive to the course of events in their incipient form, a frequent characteristic of great poets. By this interpretation, it would be not merely the prestige of Homer that prompted Virgil to select the epic form. It would also be the fact that the epic is indigenous with the period *preceding* commercial enlightenment, and Virgil's position is somewhat analogous since he was writing to celebrate the *close* of commercial freedom.

The epic is designed, then, under primitive conditions, to make men "at home in" those conditions. It "accepts" the rigors of war (the basis of the tribe's success) by magnifying the role of warlike hero. Such magnification serves two purposes: It lends dignity to the necessities of existence, "advertising" courage and individual sacrifice for group advantage—and it enables the humble man to share the worth of the hero by the process of "identification." The hero, real or legendary, thus risks himself and dies that others may be *vicariously* heroic (a variant of the symbolic cluster in Christianity whereby the victim of original sin could share vicariously in the perfection of Christ by his membership in the Church, the *corpus Christi*). The social value of such a pattern resides in its ability to make humility and self-glorification *work together*: the sense of one's limitations (in comparison with the mighty figure of the legend) provides one with a realistic attitude for gauging his personal resources, while his vicarious kinship with the figure gives him the distinction necessary for the needs of self-justification.*

The thought suggests what psychological devastation would follow from a complete adherence to the "debunking" school of biography whereby, in destroying the dignity of great legendary or historical characters, we automatically destroy ourselves. The heroic legend is saying, in effect, as Goethe said to Schopenhauer: "We can only get from life what we put into it"; and if we are greedy, we had better put in a great deal. Since the epic heroes mediate between men and gods, having the qualities of both, their divinity is generally "humanized" (being given, as James would say, "cash value") by the presence of a flaw, as the one vulnerable spot on Siegfried or Achilles, or Christ's pre-

---

* Insofar as the tragically and epically heroic approaches a purely non-religious emphasis, it approaches the risks of coxcombry. The proper ingredient of humility is retained only when one's identification with the godlike hero is discounted by the realization that one is *not* the hero. A religious concept of the hero's *divinity* induces this discounting. But insofar as the hero becomes purely secular, it is easier for the non-hero to make his identification with the hero *complete*.

destination for the cross. The process of identification thus becomes more accessible, and incidentally dignifies any sense of persecution that may possess the individual, who may also feel himself marked for disaster. This sense of a flaw serves happily to promote an openness to realistic admonition—the invitation to seek the flaw in oneself promotes in the end the attitude of *resignation* (which, when backed by a *well-rounded* symbolic structure, is nothing other than the inventory of one's *personal* limits).

Tragedy

The resignation of tragedy is based upon this same sense of personal limits; but the cultural materials with which the tragic playwright works are much more urban, complex, sophisticated than those that prevailed at the rise of the primitive epic. Though the same magical patterns of fatality, magnification, and humility are present, they are submerged beneath a more "enlightened" scheme of causal relationships. Greek tragedy flowered when the individualistic development of commerce had been strongly superimposed upon the earlier primitive-collectivist structure. The fear of self-aggrandizement was strong, as is shown in the fact that commercial enterprise was mainly entrusted to the "metics," foreigners who were imported to manage the interchange of goods for profit.

The period of human relationships *preceding* the rise of trade is close to the psychology of the "potlach," where goods are distributed by promiscuous *giving* rather than by *getting*; the shift from one attitude to the other is a basic "transvaluation of values." In the Greek cities, the shift of attitude is revealed in the changing uses to which the institution of the "guest-friend" was put, as commerce gradually expanded to confuse the bearings of the earlier culture.

The visiting trader enjoyed rights of protection only by coming as a "friend" of a local citizen. Eventually, with the spread of trade, the fiction was expanded casuistically until we find some prominent citizen acting as "guest-friend" for a whole city (the original magic of an intimate guest-relationship thus being obliterated by an enlightened extension into "quantity production" of impersonal guest-friendships).*

However, the greater complexity of relationships that went with the development of trade and urban living led to a proliferation of the *forensic*, as exemplified in the law courts and in parliamentary procedure. Out of legal sophistication there grew the vast *metaphysical* structures, that eventually imposed *scientific* concepts of causality upon the earlier patterns of magic and religion. The new attitude reached its culmination *explicitly* in Aristotle, but we find it *implicitly* in the great writers of tragedy that preceded him. Their plays, we might say, are complex trials by jury, with plaintiff, defendant, attorneys, judges, and jury all rolled into one—or, otherwise stated, we get in one piece the offence, the sentence, and the expiation. The magical concepts of fatality remain (the *participation mystique* whereby divine dispositions are concerned with human destinies), but they must be fused with the new forensic materials. Hence, the events of a tragedy are made to grow

---

* We may note a similar trend in the Egyptian "democratization" of Osirianism, whereby the sale of priestly incantations, first confined to the immortalizing of the Pharaoh, gradually spread to all the people, with a corresponding drop in quality, or in Europe when, as Strachey observes in his *Coming Struggle for Power*, the sale of indulgences was finally organized on a business basis. "Demoralization" always occurs when commercial rationalism seeks to retain the co-ordinates of magic or religion out of which it developed.

out of one another in keeping with the logic of scientific cogency, the Q.E.D. of Euclid and the political oration.

The rise of business individualism sharpened the awareness of personal ambition as a motive in human acts, but the great tragic playwrights were pious, orthodox, conservative, "reactionary" in their attitude towards it; hence they made pride, *hubris*, the basic sin, and "welcomed" it by tragic ambiguity, surrounding it with the connotations of crime.* Their frame of acceptance admonished one to "resign" himself to a sense of his limitations. They *feared* good fortune, as the first sign of punishment from the gods. Among contemporary psychologists, schooled to the norms of bourgeois thought, this attitude is usually considered as an aspect of pathology.

Comedy, Humor, the Ode

Comedy, Meredith has said, is the most civilized form of art. What reason is there to question him? The class that can produce good comedy is about as happy as can be. True, the adjustment, though admirable in itself, is often shown by subsequent events to have been a very dangerous one, as though a contented village were to have evolved its culture at the edge of a sleeping volcano that is already, in its "subconscious" depths, preparing to break forth and scatter destruction.

---

* This statement of the case might be a partial answer to those who ask whether a given writer of tragedy is "progressive" or "reactionary." Tragedy deals in crime—and any incipient trend will first be felt as crime, by reason of its conflict with established values. But tragedy deals *sympathetically* with crime. Even though the criminal is finally sentenced to be punished, we are made to feel that his offence is our offence, and at the same time the offence is dignified by nobility of style.

Caroline Spurgeon notes the great part that the imagery of *ill-fitting clothes* plays in giving the tone of *Macbeth*. And ill-fitting clothes

We should account for this dramatic irony, that subsequent history adds to our interpretation of the happy time, by suggesting that the materials incorporated within the frame are never broad enough to encompass all the necessary attitudes. Not all the significant cultural factors are given the importance that a total vision of reality would require. Class interests provide the cues that distort the interpretative frame, making its *apparent* totality function as an *actual* partiality. From the organization of class interests there inevitably follow over-emphases and under-emphases: favorable factors are seen too favorably, unfavorable factors are neglected. While the thinker trains himself and his audience to balance on one tightrope, history is stretching a tightrope elsewhere. Hence, as regards *all* the necessities, the very glories of the frame become its menace.

"Class morality" functions as "cultural lag," insofar as another class of people arises whose situation is not accurately located by the attitudinizings of the frame. And insofar as those for whom the frame is comparatively adequate are kept by their own material emphases from noting its limitations, it is the "culturally dispossessed" whom they accuse

---

are *grotesque*; they *caricature* a man. Shakespeare's stressing of a grotesque ingredient in the offender might suggest that in this case the weight of the stylistic admonitions *against* the crime is stronger than in most cases of tragic sympathy with crime. The ambiguous endorsement by dignification is much weaker than, let us say, the treatment of Brutus and Cassius, offenders against "ambitious" Caesar. Again: Macbeth's thoughts are *witches*—these subhuman creatures are the dramatic objectification of his subjective state (a modern Expressionist dramatist might have shown them coming out of his head, as Strindberg made his characters walk through walls). Like the ill-fitting clothes, they caricature his destiny.

of "attitudinizing" (the new attitudes, not being their attitudes, are felt as attitudes, rather than as "truth"). So, for instance, Samuel Johnson's aptnesss at purveying comic humanism of the sort desired by his employers, led him to misgauge the significance of the incoming romanticism. And Pope, for all his incipiently romantic insistence that great art over-rides established rules, tended to excoriate the new emphasis as bad taste (*whose* bad taste?), without concern for the necessities that stimulated writers to outrage the established canons of taste. A frame becomes deceptive when it provides too great plausibility for the writer who would *condemn symptoms* without being able to gauge the *causal pressure* behind the symptoms.

Like tragedy, comedy warns against the dangers of pride, but its emphasis shifts from *crime* to *stupidity*. Shakespeare, whose tragedies gravitate towards melodrama (notably in a work like *Othello*) required *villains* to make his plot work. Henry James made an essentially comic observation when saying that his plots required the intervention of *fools*. Antony, in becoming the active agent of the plot after the murder of Caesar, suggests a third instrument: the "good" character activated by motives of justifiable vengeance.

The progress of humane enlightenment can go no further than in picturing people not as *vicious*, but as *mistaken*. When you add that people are *necessarily* mistaken, that *all* people are exposed to situations in which they must act as fools, that *every* insight contains its own special kind of blindness, you complete the comic circle, returning again to the lesson of humility that underlies great tragedy. The audience, from its vantage point, sees the operation of errors that the characters of the play cannot see; thus seeing from two angles at once, it is chastened by dramatic irony; it is admonished to remember that when intelligence means *wisdom* (in contrast with the modern tendency to look upon intelligence as merely a *coefficient of power* for heightening our ability to get things, be they good things or bad), it requires fear, resignation, the sense of limits, as an important ingredient.

Comedy requires the maximum of forensic complexity. In the tragic plot the *deus ex machina* is always lurking, to give events a fatalistic turn in accordance with the old *"participation"* pattern whereby men anthropomorphize nature, feeling its force as the taking of sides with them or against them. Comedy must develop logical forensic causality to its highest point, calling not upon astronomical marvels to help shape the plot, but completing the process of internal organization whereby each event is deduced "syllogistically" from the premises of the informing situation. Comedy deals with *man in society*, tragedy with the *cosmic man*. (This emphasis, after the organized documentation that followed Darwin, eventually led to Hardy's kind of tragedy, *man in nature*. In classic tragedy the motivating forces are superhuman, in romantic-naturalist tragedy they are *inhuman*.) Comedy is essentially *humane*, leading in periods of comparative stability to the comedy of manners, the dramatization of quirks and foibles. But it is not necessarily confined to drama. The best of Bentham, Marx, and Veblen is high comedy.

In contemporary drama we find it revealed effetely in a play like Coward's *Bitter Sweet*, where the very title suggests a rudimentary kind of comic ambivalence: we must take the bitter with the sweet. The playwright exemplifies this lesson none too maturely in a plot where the heroine, unable to choose between two lovers, ends by taking both. Undecided whether to order sherbet or cake, she "resigns herself" to the necessity of ordering sherbet *and* cake. The "curative value" of such a happy thought seems to have been appreciated by the public, ever in search of artistic inventions whereby redemption comes easy.

We might, however, note an important distinction between comedy and humor, that is disclosed when we approach art forms as "frames of acceptance," as "strategies" for living. Humor is the opposite of the heroic. The heroic promotes acceptance by *magnification*, making the hero's character as great as the situation he confronts, and fortifying the non-heroic individual vicariously, by identification with the hero; but humor reverses the process: it takes up the slack between the momentousness of the situation and the feebleness of those in the situation by *dwarfing the situation*. It converts downwards, as the heroic converts upwards. Hence it does not make for so completely well-rounded a frame of acceptance as comedy, since it tends to gauge the situation falsely. In this respect it is close to sentimentality, a kinship that may explain why so many of our outstanding comedians (who are really humorists) have a fondness for antithetical lapses into orgies of the tearful. Their customary method of self-protection is the attitude of "happy stupidity" whereby the gravity of life simply fails to register; its importance is lost to them. The mimetics of this role is often completed by some *childish* quality of voice, as with Joe Penner, Gracie Allen, Eddie Cantor, the burbling Ed Wynn, the stutterers and the silent.

In the epic, the tragic, and the comic frames the element of *acceptance* is uppermost. We might also include here work in the spirit of the Horatian ode, the *carpe diem* attitude, which invites us to snatch whatever mild pleasures may be at hand, and call it a day. The lyric tends to fall into this bin, though often we may consider it with relation to the broader frames of adjustment, according to the ingredient it stresses in any particular case. As we turn towards the plaint or elegy, satire, burlesque and the grotesque, the element of *rejection* comes to the fore.

Negative Emphasis: the Elegy, or Plaint

Even here the distinction cannot be clearly maintained. William James, for instance, complained that Schopenhauer was *content* with his pessimism. He wanted a world that he could bark at. And unquestionably, once a man has *perfected* a technique of complaint, he is more at home with sorrow than he would be without it. He has developed an equipment, and the integrity of his character is best upheld by situations that enable him to use it. Otherwise, he would have to become either disintegrated or reborn. As a child, Augustine said, one learns to "avenge oneself by weeping" —and if one matures the same device by the use of adult material, one may paradoxically be said to have found a way of "accepting" life even while symbolizing its "rejection." In such cases, "acceptance" does come very close to "passiveness." The elegiac, the "wailing wall," may serve well for individual trickeries in one's relation to the obligations of struggle—but if it becomes organized as a collective movement, you may feel sure that a class of people will arise to "move in on" it, exploiting it to a point where more and more good reasons for complaint are provided, until the physical limits of the attitude are reached. Like humor, it is a frame that does not properly gauge the situation: when under its spell, one does not tend to size up his own resources accurately—but in contrast with humor, it really *spreads* the disproportion between the weakness of the self and the magnitude of the situation.*

* We should also note, in the protectiveness of the plaint, an ingredient of "homoeopathy," in the most literal sense of the term. One seeks to

44

POETIC CATEGORIES

In *Some Versions of Pastoral*, a work that should be coupled with I. A. Richards' *Principles of Literary Criticism* and Caroline Spurgeon's *Shakespeare's Imagery* as the

---

develop tolerance to possibilities of great misfortune by accustoming himself to misfortune in small doses, administered stylistically. We may note the broad difference between homoeopath and allopath in stylistic treatments by noting the difference between the man who "coaches" good health by asserting that he "never felt better in his life" (the "allopath") and the man who, though he might be equally healthy, "protects" himself by conceding: "I feel well enough, if only things keep up as they are."

The "allopathic" style of treatment confronts the threat of danger with an antidote of assurance—hence, the stronger the antidote the better. The "homoeopathic" style is based, rather, on the feeling that danger cannot be handled by head-on attack, but must be *accommodated*. Benjamin Franklin's lightning rod was a "homoeopathic remedy" for lightning, as it sought to *attenuate* a risk (to control by channelization) rather than to *abolish* it (to control by elimination).

There is an intermediate territory of stylistic prophylaxis, notable in its simplest form among those who, when there is talk of some illness going around, will tell you, "So far, nobody in *our* family has been hit," whereupon they knock on wood, sometimes literally, sometimes in unnoticeable mental reservations they make while speaking. They are responding to the essentially "homoeopathic" feeling that "pride goes before a fall," a feeling that leads them to a gesture of "protective humility." Yet their act of knocking on wood tends to become an "allopathic" antidote, a spell *antithetical* to the threat of danger.

Insofar as a danger *can* be eliminated, the stylistic homoeopath tends to become "psychologically unemployed," since his strategy becomes a bad fit for the situation at hand. Insofar as a danger *cannot* be eliminated, those who have invested too heavily in the allopathic antidote are the ones to be disorganized.

Western optimism, that began its formal career with the attacks made by the bourgeoisie upon the style of the church (based homoeopathically on the "prosperity of poverty") was superbly direct in the development of allopathic hygiene. The change had much to do with the rationalization of the revolutionary attitude, as it stimulates people under disaster

most important contributions to literary criticism in contemporary England, William Empson proposes a definition

---

to begin grumbling *early*. Particularly in America, where we have been trained to take prosperity as the *norm*, any interference with the acquisition of commodities creates immediate resentment (a response further stimulated by the fact that "justification by the acquisition of commodities" has been written into the whole texture of the productive-distributive mechanism). Hence, our "conscientious" business leaders are up against a basic contradiction. To uphold a structure based upon sales and advertising, they would coach a return to religion. When the "economy of plenty" cannot abide by its own norms, they would "take up the slack" by restoring the "prosperity of poverty." They can recommend the church's homoeopathy with some plausibility because it is adequate *insofar as disease, sorrow, frustration, and death are ineradicable.* And they would try to extend the area of such plausibility so that men would resign themselves even to situations for which the remedies must be sheerly "economic."

We might analyze Shakespeare as a writer who, in his stylistic inheritance from feudalism, had invested thoroughly in the homoeopathic remedy, inducing him to evolve a set of solaces that "made the best of things" (as in his "sweet are the uses of adversity" formula, the formula that we consider as the "essence" of the *feudal* Shakespeare). But the incoming "economy of plenty," with its shift to the cult of acquisitions, and a corresponding shift from "wisdom" to "power-knowledge," threatened to destroy his homoeopathic co-ordinates (whereby one developed "tolerance" to misfortune by "stylistic dosage").

Incidentally, we may note in religion itself the tendency to move towards the hygiene of allopathic science. It would employ rituals or prayers as antidotes (the only difference between its antidotes and the antidotes of science residing, for our present purposes, in the fact that the latter are usually more accurate in their choice of means). "Tragic" religion has almost dropped out of consciousness, except in the case of secular artists, who seek to make their misfortunes the basis of their insights, thereby attempting to *transcend* a misfortune rather than to *eliminate* it. Their "neurosis" being essential to their "genius," they begin to fear that a "cure" would rob them of their working capital.

Magic was based on the homoeopathic principle ("*similia similibus*

of "pastoral" that would seem to fall on the bias across our categories of humor and elegy, with important ingredients

---

curentur"). But in proportion as its rituals became bureaucratized, they shifted towards the "allopathic" category of spell, antidote. Hence, magic became simply *bad* science—thereby forming the basis for development into *good* science. Frazer has pointed out that, during the hegemony of religion in the middle ages, "magic" meant "black magic," as the early alchemic experimentalists were distrusted. Religious emphases were closer to the "pure" homoeopathic impulse that underlay magic but was obscured in proportion as magic led to the "pure" incantatory antidote (the "attack" on natural forces, flowering in Dewey's "conquest" of nature).

It is relevant to note that Hahnemann, the propounder of modern homoeopathic medicology, tried also to deduce all diseases from three principal stocks, psora (the itch), syphilis, and sycosis (fig-wart disease). This "integrative" zeal, seeking for a kind of "nosological trinity," seems to have caused his followers much embarrassment, since it left them with much to defend that cannot be defended by modern experimental evidence. They ended by retaining his theories of dosage (whereby you cured a sick man by giving him such medicines as would cause similar symptoms in a well man) while abandoning his genealogy of disease. But though the two may be dissociated in practice, they seem to be both modes of the same substance; each embodies the same *attitude towards life*, an *integrative* attitude much akin to the "tragic integration" in Mann's assertion that one must "contain his enemies." We question whether Hahnemann could have made his admittedly valid contributions to medicine without his admittedly invalid vision of nosological genesis. Whatever their differences in practical serviceability, they are parts of the same "work of art."

One may note subtle shifts from the similar to the antithetical in a word like "counterpart," which may mean *replica* (homoeopathic), *complement* (intermediate), and *opposite* (allopathic). We believe that in *Permanence and Change* we employed the concept of "recalcitrance" thus ambiguously. It refers to the factors that *substantiate* a statement, the factors that *incite* a statement, and the factors that *correct* a statement. In medicine, we come fully upon the homoeopathic-allopathic ambiguity in the routines of inoculation, "tragic cure" by the "containing of one's enemies," the systematic pollution of the blood stream.

of the heroic. Gray's "Elegy in a Country Church Yard," *The Beggar's Opera*, *The Vision of Piers Plowman*, and *Alice in Wonderland* are all analyzed as aspects of "pastoral." The heroic device operates, paradoxically, in the sympathetic treatment of *humble* people (like the Christian transvaluation of the pagan Percival legend whereby the "fool" becomes the "saint"). The lowly are pictured as the bearers of the true nobility, by the revolutionary "first shall be last and last shall be first" paradox. Children, fools, criminals, rogues, and simple rustics "turn slowly into Christ and ruler," as Empson says of the sorrowing Piers Plowman.

Empson's remarks on "ironic humility" are particularly relevant to our purposes:

"Ironic humility, whose simplest gambit is to say, 'I am not clever, educated, well born,' or what not (as if you had a low standard to judge by), and then to imply that your standards are so high in the matter that the person you are humbling yourself before is quite out of sight. This has an amusing likeness to pastoral; the important man classes himself among low men, and the effect is to raise his standards, not to lower them."

This is the "gentleman's" subtle form of boasting. He practices long and hard, he becomes an adept, he assures you that he is a veritable tyro—and then you play, and he beats you. In case you win, that also has been taken care of.*

---

* One is reminded of the anecdote about the British prime minister. A member of his party, with a young son, asked the minister to find the son a position. The minister asked about the son's qualifications. "Well, he is very modest," said the father. "Modest!" exclaimed the minister; "What has he done to be modest about?" The anecdote draws its logic from the springs of "ironic humility."

POETIC CATEGORIES

Empson's analysis of Gray's reference to the flower

> born to blush unseen
> And waste its sweetness on the desert air

discloses the ways in which the poet, confronting the rise of the get-ahead philosophy that went with the mounting industrial-commercial pattern of England, provides resignation for the man who has not found a *carrière ouverte aux talents*, and yet would feel himself of good quality. It is "Marxist criticism" of a sort that few of our professional Marxists have discovered, though they may claim the virtue of having pressed Empson to break the confines of his earlier volume, *Seven Types of Ambiguity*, where the psychologism was of a different sort.

Satire

Satire is as confusing as the plaint. For the satirist attacks *in others* the weaknesses and temptations that are really *within himself*. The satiric projection could be charted roughly as follows: A and B have a private vice in common (both are cleptomaniacs, homosexuals, sadists, social climbers, or the like, in varying degrees of latency or patency). At the same time, on some platform of the public arena they are opponents (they belong to clashing forensic factions). A is a satirist. In excoriating B for his political views, A draws upon the imagery of the secret vice shared by both. A thereby *gratifies* and *punishes* the vice within himself. Is he whipped with his own lash? He is.

One cannot read great satirists like Swift or Juvenal without feeling this strategic ambiguity. We sense in them the Savonarola, who would exorcize his own vanities by building a fire of other people's vanities. Expertness in satiric practice makes good inventory almost impossible. Swift's aptitude at "projection" invited him to beat himself unmercifully, eventually with drastic results.

Wyndham Lewis, the compleat satirist of our day, would define satire as an approach "from without." To which we should agree, if we are permitted to add the reservation, "an approach *from without* to something *from within*." In Lewis's case, there are symptoms to indicate that his excoriations arise from a suppressed fear of death, or, in other words, from religiosity frustrated by disbelief, though it must be admitted that our reasons for such diagnosis are tenuous. They are offered here for what they may be worth:

In Spender's book, *The Destructive Element*, you will find a comment on the analogy Lewis uses when advocating his thesis that satire is "from without," and that all good art is satire. Lewis says that art should not deal with the "intestines," but with the "ossature." Spender observes that even the "ossature" is internal, hence the very analogy that Lewis selects, with a whole world of examples to pick from, is unfit. Now, if there is any justification to our contention that one may get cues about a writer's motives by noting the quality of the imagery he employs at strategic points, would there not be even greater justice in attributing significance to an image that bursts forth by an actual *discontinuity* in the logic? Lewis would observe "from without"—and illogically he picks something to observe that is *within*; namely: the skeleton. Our test might indicate the kind of drive behind his "eye-mindedness" and his hatred of "time-mindedness." For "eye-mindedness" enables him to *project* "the enemy," to look at it by subterfuge; but "time-mindedness" requires either the frank acceptance of death or the belief in immortality. To make the speculation a little less tenuous, recall that Tarr, when embracing a woman, is said to draw her "skull" to him, the quality of the imagery here suggesting a furtive linkage between heterosexual love and death.*

True, there are other important ingredients here. The "opposite" of the ossature is the intestines, which gets us close to Swift's disgust with the excretions of the body—a disgust, as a significant quotation from Swift in Empson's *Some Versions of Pastoral* makes clear, that was also linked with sex, because of the way in which the body has economized in localizing the channels of these two functions. This sense of a union between love and filth was the

---

* The strategy, good and bad, accurate and inaccurate, involved in the *necessary* rejection of authoritative symbols need not, of course, encompass the whole issue. The synthetic nature of every symbol would require a doctrine of "multiple causation" (since the statement that a symbol unites many ingredients can often be translated into "scientific" as the statement: "An event is the summation of many different causes"). Since the rejection of authority is "symbolic parricide," and the rejected authorities have often made themselves "the owners of God the Father," such rejection stimulates atheism. And atheism in turn involves the denial of *immortality*.

Now, if one denies the existence of life after death, he can only face death with some variant of *defiance*. Donne was possibly at the turning point, halfway between the religious and the secular, when he challenged, "Death, thou shalt die." He still relied upon the religious affirmation of immortality—but his attitude was different in quality from that of a Kempis, who *wanted* to "live a dying life." Donne was enlisting religion on his side *against an enemy*, whereas the man who is fully entrenched in religious belief does not consider death as an "enemy." Rather, it is a "stage in one's development."

Hence, even if the patterns of defiance were not made necessary by bureaucratic disorders (the dispossession of "rights"), they could arise from the denial of immortality. And one might then carry his defiance "creatively" into other areas, transferring them by covert "metaphorical extension" to his treatment of purely social relationships. Which is to say that the man who began by "defying death" could end by "defying his neighbor." The thought would suggest the possibility that insofar

essence of his working credo, that "everything spiritual and valuable has a gross and revolting parody, very similar to it, with the same name." If the "life within" equals the intestines, and the "life without" equals a deceptive projection of the skeleton, and the man's love of woman is secretly tied to both, maybe there *is* no way of making peace with the state of things. One is on the run, like Whitman, but without the "salute."

Burlesque

We might add one justification for externality that Lewis does not offer. Namely: if the state of the world and the criteria of art have gone to such a point that we are con-

---

as a Communist Society becomes established, hence requiring emphasis upon *acceptance*, the attitude of defiance (grounded in defiance of death) will require abatement. Thus, in Russia we note a tendency for God to return (first perhaps in the form of Santa Claus).

Usually, the "scientific" mind prefers simply to truncate its thinking on the subject. It "suspends judgment." "Maybe there is immortality, and maybe there isn't." At least, if science abides by its rules, adopting a conviction only when it can be "proved by the evidence," it would not seem possible for the "scientific mind" to go beyond this agnostic position. Atheism (and, in keeping, a categorical denial of immortality) is a statement of *faith* that necessarily cannot be substantiated by a "weighing of all the evidence."

When you find a man who is exceptionally eager to deny the possibility of immortality (as though he "could not rest" without a constant "secular prayer" to the effect that death is absolute) you may legitimately grow quizzical of his intensity. Why such zest? Might it not come from a fear of *punishment* after death? For it is obvious that, if the possibility were either death or heaven, there would be no incentive for a man to become engrossed in the denial of immortality. He would let the matter slide, content to await his sojourn in paradise when it came, and to go about his business in the interim. If, on the other hand, the possibility of immortality contained for him the likelihood of his taking up permanent residence in hell, he would have "good emotional reasons" for wanting to

cerned primarily with the depiction of very despicable, forlorn, and dissipated people, the writer might very well protect himself by not imagining them with too great intimacy. For to picture them intimately, he must be one with them. Goethe has suggested that he was equipped as a writer by his ability to imagine himself committing every crime. Similarly, a writer who could imagine himself in the many humiliating roles that are in fashion today would, by this very ability, open himself to great risk. A purely *external* approach to such characters would protect him greatly. If he

---

"pray" immortality out of existence. Hence, when we see a man who goes out of his way to amass evidence that "proves" mortality, we should take his engrossment as a somewhat unwieldy and roundabout way of cancelling guiltiness. The man who says "perhaps not" abides by the truly "scientific" mode of truncation; but the man who says "absolutely not" is driven by an emotional necessity, such as the *fear* of immortality (which could only derive from a latent fear of hell that stimulated him thus indirectly to "legislate" the possibility out of existence).

It is also a paradoxical possibility that the tendency to "ease away" from considerations of death has an effect upon the birth rate among those financially able to raise children. The "pattern of mortality" *depersonalizes* the notions of continuity. One does not think of self-perpetuation in terms of progeny, turning instead to a more "spiritual" identification, such as may be found in a purely abstract concept of historical development. The "mortalist" lives on vicariously, in the life of his movement, cause, class (a notion somewhat akin to the Roman-Stoical secularization of immortality through "fame"). The "symbolic suicide" of childlessness is even more accentuated when one identifies himself with a class or movement that he considers to be dying.

We are not here trying to "vote for" immortality. The belief in immortality has always been "moved in on" by the priesthood, who found it an excellent way for "implementing" their threats against the champions of necessary social change. We do feel it necessary, however, to note the ways in which liberalism distorted the "psychological function" of death (as liberalism always distorted the meaning of everything). It simply put the Pollyannic in place of the messianic. And in all sorts of

merely described their *behavior*, without depth in imagining the state of their *minds*, his superficiality would contribute to his comfort.

But that gets us to the matter of *burlesque*. It is our contention that Lewis's plea for the external is carried out, not in the satiric form, but in burlesque (and such related forms as polemic and caricature). Here the attack really is external —and for that reason, though we enjoy burlesque as an occasional dish, no critic has ever been inclined to select it as the *pièce de résistance* for a steady diet.

The writer of burlesque makes no attempt to get inside the psyche of his victim. Instead, he is content to select the externals of behavior, driving them to a "logical conclusion" that becomes their "reduction to absurdity." By pro-

---

devious ways, it managed to convey the notion that a "dying life" was "defeatist" and "escapist" (gloriously oblivious of the fact that, precisely while its "scientific enlightenment" flourished, practically every sincere artist was organizing vast esthetic monuments in accordance with the "dying life").

We should also recognize that, as finally worked out, the religious pattern also contained its expressions of "symbolic suicide." We refer to the "religious athleticism" of the monks (who called upon an influx of "grace" to assist them in their competitive efforts to "legislate" against the genius of the glandular system). This tendency, vigorously manifested in the *thébaïdes* of northern Africa long before the church was wealthy, was unquestionably bureaucratized under the further pressure of property (as childless priests left the "dead hand" of the church estates intact). And the childless priest could be named a "father" because he had "spiritual" progeny, the "children" of the church. He was "perpetuated on earth" by the "eternal" nature of the church. We are suggesting that there is a modern secular equivalent to this attitude, in the "secular monasticism" of those who identify themselves with "history" rather than with "God." And we are suggesting the possibility that a lack of interest in progeny (generally rationalized as a matter of income alone) is related to one's attitudes on the question of death.

gram, he obliterates his victim's discriminations. He is "heartless." He converts every "perhaps" into a "positively." He deliberately suppresses any consideration of the "mitigating circumstances" that would put his subject in a better light. If the victim performs an act that would appear well when done slowly, he performs the same act at top speed; if the act is more appropriate for speed, he portrays it in slow motion. Hilariously, he converts a manner into a mannerism. The method of burlesque (polemic, caricature) is partial not only in the sense of *partisan*, but also in the sense of *incompleteness*. As such, it does not contain a well-rounded frame within itself; we can use it for the ends of wisdom only insofar as we ourselves provide the ways of making allowances for it; we must not be merely *equal* to it, we must be enough *greater than* it to be able to "discount" what it says.

An enormous amount of early liberal pamphleteering was done within this mode. In fact, the very basis of classic liberal apologetics, the over-emphasis upon freedom, was but a sober way of carrying out the burlesque genius. It *stressed* freedom, and sought to *smuggle* in restrictions. It cried for "rights," enjoying the strategic advantage of this invitation, without considering the corrective feature of ambivalence whereby "rights" also require their unpleasant reverse, "duties" or "obligations."

At the time of the French Revolution, when a "bill of rights" was being drawn, some members of the Assembly suggested that a "bill of obligations" be included to match them. The proposal was voted down by an overwhelming majority. Here the genius of neither tragedy nor comedy was at work, but the genius of burlesque.

The mediaeval scheme, so well-rounded *on paper*, had been made to *function* as the most *partial* of schemes, hence giving rise to a partial antithesis. But this burlesqued over-emphasis has remained to plague us ever since, as we note to-day in the discomfitures of such a liberal as John Dewey who, in following the cues of classic liberalism, is still trying to introduce a plea for collective elements without admitting that a collective frame requires us to stress the *ambivalence* of rights and obligations (which would require a *formal admission* of strictures). A kindred hankering to preserve the liberal one-way system of apologetics is to be noted among the Southern agrarians, who want to make men "free" by making private property *inalienable*, ignoring the fact that the history of emancipation in Europe shows the *integral relation between freedom and alienation*. In "binding" the serf to the soil, feudalism also bound the soil to the serf, matching his "duties" with "rights" that were protected by custom. The liberal revolution "freed" him of his "duties" by alienating him from his "rights." Hence, for great numbers of the people, "freedom" functioned simply as "dispossession." Conversely, you cannot "repossess" without a corresponding pattern of obligations. "Freedom" is a truncated concept, an unintended *caricature* of human relations. Hence, the liberal who rates social organisms by its test alone is vowed to disillusionment. He will find that his ideals are too good for this world.*

---

* Significantly, it is the theoreticians behind Lewis's C.I.O. who are re-introducing into America the concept of ambivalence in property relationships. They are proceeding, roughly, as follows: Beginning with the recognition of the worker's obligations, they are insisting that these obligations be matched by rights. Hence, under the stimulus of their thinking, an economist writing in the daily press said recently: "Labor has a property right in skill, an ownership right in the job, an investment interest in income." Extend the concepts of property and ownership in

POETIC CATEGORIES

The Grotesque

None of these poetic categories can be isolated in its chemical purity. They overlap upon one another, involving the qualitative matter of emphasis. One could with justice divide the field differently, as we have noted in the case of Empson's remarks on "pastoral." Our distinctions are offered only for their suggestive value, the primary purpose here being simply to indicate that, whatever "free play" there may be in esthetic enterprise, it is held down by the gravitational pull of historical necessities; the poetic forms are symbolic structures designed to equip us for confronting given historical or personal situations.

Though "acceptance" and "rejection" cannot be sharply differentiated (the "acceptance" of A involving the "rejection" of non-A), it could be said approximately that the epic, tragedy, and comedy gravitate towards the positive side, while elegy, satire, and burlesque stress the negative. The distinction suggests two other modes, preponderantly transitional, the grotesque and the didactic. The grotesque focuses in mysticism; the didactic to-day is usually called propaganda.

The isolated mystic may appear at any time in history, since one man's experiences may be unique enough, sufficiently a "sport," to engross him with transitional concerns even in an era that has great fixity for most people—but mysticism *as a collective movement* belongs to periods marked by great confusion of the cultural frame, requiring

this way, with institutions in keeping, and the classical co-ordinates of private ownership are automatically dissolved—somewhat as Schoenberg dissolved modulation in music by making compositions that were in *constant* modulation.

a radical shift in people's allegiance to symbols of authority. Thus, it flourished during the Hellenistic period, when philosophic thought, as shaped by the philosophers of the Greek *polis*, was readjusting itself to the rise of Oriental despotism.

At the very time when Aristotle was putting the final touches to his forensic pattern, his former pupil, Alexander, commissioned him to write two tracts, one on *monarchy*, and the other on *colonization*. A practical administrator laid out for him the path of the future, while in works of his own choosing he completed the ideological architecture that belonged to the fast receding democratic past. The thinkers that followed him had to reshape Greek independence to the form of cosmopolitan absolutism. Slowly, mystics and saviors came to the fore. A collective mystical movement also arose to adumbrate the counter-shift from theocracy to national absolutism that went with the rise of the Protestants. Such correspondence should justify us in looking for strong mystical ingredients to-day. Since other critics have found them, and expatiated on their find, we shall attempt here merely to make a few incidental additions to the discussion.

Humor specializes in incongruities; but by its trick of "conversion downwards," by its stylistic ways of reassuring us in dwarfing the magnitude of obstacles or threats, it provides us relief in laughter. The grotesque is the cult of incongruity *without* the laughter. The grotesque is not funny unless you are out of sympathy with it (whereby it serves as unintentional burlesque). Insofar as you are *in* sympathy with it, it is in deadly earnest. Thus, the strange lonely landscapes of the Superrealists (there are some impressive examples in James Johnson Sweeney's *Plastic Redirections in 20th Century Painting*, a brief book full of sharp formulations) are frightfully sober matters.

POETIC CATEGORIES

The incongruity of the grotesque-mystical comes to a focus in the oxymoron: one hears silence, peoples loneliness, feels distance, and sees in the dark. James felt that Hegel's key concept, the synthesis of contradictions, was essentially a mystic insight, and he preferred the insight to the logical frame by which Hegel strove to make it rationally negotiable. Applying "metaphorical psychoanalysis," we should note that Hegel likened his philosophy to the "owl of Minerva that sets forth at nightfall." And we might contrast the subdued glow implicit in this attitude with the revealing metaphor of Nietzsche, who likened his philosophy to the flash of lightning that flares up for an instant in the night, to reveal the unseen landscape. Robert Cantwell has recently remarked on a passage in Joyce's *Portrait of the Artist as a Young Man*, where the line "Brightness falls from the air" is wrongly remembered by Stephen as "Darkness falls from the air." Perhaps Joyce's later concern with twilight states is foretold here, in this mystic reversal of the customary meanings for dark and light. Cantwell himself, who doubtless selected this passage out of all Joyce's work because of some deep-lying sympathy with it, could be said to enroll himself on the fringes of mysticism in the symbol by which he introduces his "proletarian" plot in *The Land of Plenty*. At the very start of the story, the lights of the factory go out—and he proceeds to portray the ways in which a deeper understanding among the workers arises while the lights are out. He tells us in effect that they are seeing in the dark.

The analysis of grotesque symbolism is admittedly a very weedy garden. As yet there is no Occam's razor for us to use as a hoe, nor even a criterion for distinguishing the flowers from the weeds. We might say here, in quick summary, that the grotesque comes to the fore when confusion in the forensic pattern gives more prominence to the subjective elements of imagery than to the objective, or public, elements. One could probably analyze any art, even the most classically clear, and find there such motives as the pit, symbolic castration, rebirth, the *mystic* awe of light.* But when the public frame erected above these primitive responses is broken, the essence stands more clearly revealed. The symbolic quality is revealed more clearly, precisely because the forensic superstructure erected above it is less firm.

An electrician, for instance, may be led to choose his trade rather than some other because of "deeper meanings" that electricity has for him. This choice may go back to very early childhood impressions, as an awe of lightning— and he may choose the trade of electrician because it "symbolically" enables him to triumph over this awe. In the course of perfecting his skill as an electrician, he leaves the symbolic incentive far behind, developing instead a vast "superstructure" of non-symbolic interests and techniques. Confront him with an electrical problem that he cannot solve, however, or let the frustration of a bad economic system deprive him of his practical outlet, and the symbolic motive may again come to the fore. The "public" aspect of his trade falls to a minimum, whereat the subjective aspect may become hypertrophied. In this way confusions of the superstructural, or objective, lead to the stressing of symbolic ingredients in human acts.

* The stories in the New York papers last year, after the failure of the power plant in one portion of the city had caused several hours of total darkness, were written in a tone of awe. Reading them, one felt that if some new cosmic radiation entered the solor system, to make the performance of electricity a bit irregular, as with the weather, urban populations would start praying for electricity as farmers pray for rain.

Might it not be the call for a revolutionary shift in our attitude towards the symbols of authority, for instance, that has given such voice to homosexual patterns in current literature? The homosexual is involved personally in a "bipolar" conflict between the symbols of father and mother, usually the most important *pre-political* symbols of authority, established as such during childhood. And this pre-political pattern is paralleled in socialized maturity by a pattern of political strife. The homosexual thus finds a perfect match between his private situation and the public, historical situation.

Such superstructural fluctuancy may promote not only the homosexual, but even the androgynous, beginning with Blake's discovery that, if the universe, a universe of promiscuous love, contains a male and a female principle, it is in its totality hermaphrodite—and the thinking of one who "identified himself" with such a universe would manifest a similar convergence of sexual opposites. (Let us recall in passing that Yarmolinsky, on noting Dostoievsky's treatment of "double thoughts" in *The Idiot*, speaks of the novelist's "psychic hermaphroditism.")

Blake was grotesque. If we would not be, and there is enough public business to be done, we may leave the ultimate issue merely *implicit*. That is, someone might discover that his way of dealing with everyday events would, if carried through to its metaphysical conclusions, pledge him to Blake's philosophy—yet if the public frame is rich enough, not only in *details*, but in *satisfactions*, he may not have the incentive to become so engrossed in the issue as to make it the all-important ingredient of his concerns. Or, if the satisfactions *are* slight, he can solve the matter in the usual way, that has its points: by becoming *trivial*. A vast entertainment industry has been erected for those who prefer the last solution, asking that "distraction" be converted from ill-omened to good-omened connotations. Others solve the problem, like Democritus, by materialism. Others, like James with his pluralism, prefer to leave the universe in pieces.*

Anyhow, what we get, is people atop magic mountains, or poets clambering over mother-mountains (Baudelaire's *"La Géante"*) or being drawn towards magnetic mountains (which are as lonely and severe as any Superrealist land-scape, even though a socialist society is said to await us there). We get the symbolizing of parallels, "correspona-ences," whereby simple notions of identity become con-fused, as *one thing* is seen in terms of *something else*—Joyce

---

* With James, of course, there was no overt sexual antinomy that needed to be "synthesized" as Blake could synthesize universal male and female principles in the imagery of collective intercourse. There was a "class struggle" between good and evil, requiring him to choose his side (and requiring a doctrine of free will to make his act of choice possible). His father, the Swedenborgian author of *Substance and Shadow*, would appear (by "metaphorical analysis") to have confronted the universe as something much like the problem of *food vs. excrement*. Basing his thought on a distinction between morality and religion (the latter ap-parently being his variant of motives "beyond good and evil," "beyond the opposites"), "Conscience," he wrote, "is purgative, not nutritive." Which we might rephrase by saying that *morality* has connotations in a higher synthesis beyond good and evil whereby the excremental-evil is purified. The genius of the metaphor is apparent at the two most critical moments of his life: his rebirth (religious conversion) and his death. Of his conversion, he writes:

"It was impossible for me . ... to hold this audacious faith in selfhood any longer. *When I sat down to dinner* on the memorable chilly afternoon in Windsor, I held it serene and unweakened by the faintest breath of doubt; before I rose from the table, it had *inwardly shrivelled to a cinder.*

charting modern life as a parody of the *Odyssey*; Lawrence reading pansexuality into the non-sexual; Eliot expressing the mystic's sense of "drought" by borrowings from the lore of primitive magic; Yeats sharpening his realism by reference to a reservoir of fanciful correlations; Pound working with a concept of the "contemporaneous" very much like Spengler's, as he interprets a present situation by classing it with analogous situations taken from any point in time. Perhaps Thomas Mann, in his Joseph novels, has gone farthest of all in such speculations, involving an almost forgotten notion of identity. He takes the Biblical roles as eternally recurring roles; hence if one is now cast as Jacob, or as Joseph, or as Rebecca, the forms of history evolved in

---

One moment I devoutly thanked God for the inappreciable boon of self-hood; the next, that inappreciable boon seemed to me the one damnable thing on earth, seemed a literal nest of hell *within my own entrails*." (our italics)

When he died, Henry writes to William of ". . . a gradual refusal of food, because he *wished* to die. There was no dementia except a sort of exaltation of belief that he had entered into 'the spirit of life.' Nothing could persuade him to eat."

Of his theology, Prof. Perry writes:

"There are two and only two movements, down and up, or alienation and return. The fall is the beginning of creation, for a mere passage from perfection to perfection would be a meaningless repetition. And it is God himself who has fallen: God become ignorant and depraved, or God undone, in the illusory, carnal, and selfish moments of actual human experience."

Prof. Perry also comments on the fact that so much of the conversational brilliance in the James household took place at table. The stress suggests a kind of secular *agape* (and, in the offing, the miracle of transubstantiation, with the heretical scruples of the Stercoranistae who held that, the blood and body being consumed by mortal things, the processes customary to digestion should follow). The quotations are from Ralph Barton Perry's *The Thought and Character of William James*.

the collective legend enable him to *foretell* his destiny; in living *like* the Biblical character, he *is* that character, so his "number" is already written down, along with the fate that goes with this particular number.

We get changes of identity, often symbolized—in strict obedience to the rules of magic—by the changing of one's name, as the new synthetic character is felt to require a corresponding verbal change; or there is a formal choice of "ancestors," as one in meeting the exigencies of his *present*, proposes to coerce the *future* by a quasi-mystical revising of his *past*. Looking over the titles of the books written by Huysmans, who went *from* naturalism, *through* Satanism, *to* Catholicism, we find that his titles of the naturalistic period are with one exception nouns, all those of the transitional period are prepositions actually or in quality (*A-Vau-l'Eau, En Rade, A Rebours, Là-bas, En Route*) and all in his period of Catholic realism are nouns.

We get people in airplanes above the pit, people having (as Cowley says of *The Big Money*) the brittle life of glass, travelers who see eyeless in Gaza, and those who, like Eliot in his *Murder in the Cathedral*, have gone from negation to the "negation of the negation" (as the saint, with the same name as Eliot, recognizes the "tempter" in his own words, and must admonish himself lest he make martyrdom a *career*). We might also note fixed clusters or amalgams that amount in the end to oxymorons, as you find that the poet had fused, by interacting associations, symbols logically at odds: life, death, eternity, mother, sexual desire, castration, health, disease, art, forests or the sea, all linked indiscriminately together, so that he can only talk of one by talking of the others, and when he centers upon one, the others flicker about the edges of his imagery. Perhaps eventually, by charting these clusters, and noting how many of them

a writer or thinker works with, we may be surprised to find
that even a lyric poet embodies in his work several characters, maybe as many as there are in a novel by Dickens.
There may be a character that shouts (i.e., a certain limited
cycle of thoughts always couched in a ranting tone of
voice), a conversationalist (who speaks in the tone of the
essayist), a whisperer, an utterer of asides, and so forth,
each with his proper domain of "associations."* And there
may even be animals among them, a latent jungle-book,
with lion-thoughts, dog-thoughts, horse-thoughts, cow-
thoughts, jackal-thoughts, old-hen thoughts, and the like,
revealing (by the use of imagery that is felt to be akin) the
quality that such animals possess for him (as when, in the
citation from James already given, we find James associat-
ing pessimism in Schopenhauer with a dog's bark—and in
the paintings of Chirico strange horses play an important
part, being presumably related to oddities of perspective,

---

* Recall the scheming young man who was in this predicament: There
was a dowager, wielding influence, and very susceptible to flattery. He
needed her influence, and in payment was willing to flatter her atrociously. But:

The dowager was somewhat deaf. And to the scheming young man,
such words of flattery as he would address to her seemed to require the
tone of half-whispered confidences. Result:

He did not flatter her enough, and so did not win her favor. He was
willing to say anything, however false, but he could not bring himself
to say it in a "false" tone of voice. He could not *shout* flattery. So he was
sincere in spite of himself.

It is these deeper tests of propriety and sincerity that are revealed in
poetry. A writer may *profess* allegiance to a certain cause, for instance,
but you find on going over his work that the *enemies* of this cause are
portrayed with greater vividness than its advocates. Here is his "truth"
about his professions of belief.

unusual juxtapositions of light and shade, and deathlike statues-in-place-of-people).* Districts (the town or the

* Perhaps our scientists take their Jungle Book much more seriously than do our poets and novelists. Thus with the strangely feudalistic mode of thought that survives so profoundly in nineteenth-century liberalism. We refer to the century's extreme emphasis upon *genesis, origin.* The feudalist attacked a man by attacking his *whole family.* His corruption was the corruption of his entire tribe. He was identified as member of a bad corporation. Or, when he was attacked as an individual, the strategy most natural to the feudalistic dramatist was to picture him as a bastard—hence, a kind of one-man enterprise.

Those who applied the Darwinian formula of the "descent of man" as their cue for the charting of human motives might thus be said to have preserved a feudal mode of thought at the core of a philosophy nominally the opposite of feudalism. They analyzed *what man is* by reference to his parentage: *what he was.* Hence, he is an animal because he comes of animal progenitors. The genealogical ingredient in Darwin's formula is revealed in his very choice of title, naming as *descent* a process that later "progressive evolutionists" would tend rather to name as *ascent* (thereby shifting from family-tree connotations to commercial connotations of "success").

The effect of the Darwinian bar sinister upon poets is perhaps best exemplified in Ibsen's *When We Dead Awaken,* where the artist Rusbeck, having abandoned his ideals, becomes a successful society painter, getting high prices for his portraits because he sees the traits of animals in the faces of his subjects. This is the *secret* of his success, since he keeps his mode of interpretation hidden. He organizes his portraits about animal metaphors, but he leaves the metaphors lurking in the background. Hence, his customers are really his victims, but they do not know it. They admire him, paying him good prices for his interpretations, while he is really slandering them—and they recognize his covert slander as the "truth."

He himself, however, is punished for the slander. For the sharpness of his vision derives precisely from his own surrender. He has "sold out"—and in his bitterness, he sees his whole society as "sell-outs."

Scientists, meanwhile, continued their strange caricature of feudalism undisturbed. Finally we come to the behaviorists, who felt that you can learn everything there is to be learned about man by watching animals

country) may be assigned appropriate voices, as also machines (the airplane spoke stridently for Marinetti, but

---

in a maze. They paint without bitterness, and with total frankness, the
same portraits that Rusbeck had painted bitterly and furtively. They
make public what Rusbeck had kept private. There is unquestionably
a tremendous difference here, since their statement has been "socialized,"
whereby its guilt is largely cancelled. They say in effect: "I am lost, so
let's socialize my loss—let's all go down together, which makes us brothers in adversity."

In Ibsen's case, however, the discovery that he had been a "Darwinian"
dramatist seems to have been a tremendous shock. After this play, he suffered a collapse. And there are indications that, had he been able, he would
have reverted to the poetic mode of drama preceding his turn to prose
naturalism. In some devious way, he must have felt that he himself was
a Rusbeck, despite his life-long attacks upon Rusbecks.

Might we, at this point, go back to the sixth century before Christ,
observing, in the light of what we have said, the fables of Aesop? Was
not the moralist Aesop also saying, in effect, that men are animals? In
notable respects, Aesop was like Ibsen. He even lost his life in opposing
human greed. "Having been sent to Delphi with a large sum of gold for
distribution among the citizens, he was so provoked at their covetousness
that he refused to divide the money, and sent it back to his master. The
Delphians, enraged at this treatment, accused him of impiety, and executed him as a public criminal." Whereat "the blood of Aesop" became
an adage, in the same category of events with the hemlock of Socrates.

Yet Aesop was a moralist, not a scientist. He obviously "discounted"
his own metaphor, as the Darwinian did not. His animals were members
of a polity, not simply competitors in a jungle. They were ironists, like
Socrates. They could betray virtue, they could "cash in on" virtue—but
at least they knew of virtue.

Aesop did not leap from the extremes of sentimental euphemism to the
antithetical extremes of cynical debunking. He did not conceive of idealism in a way that made for disillusioned brutality. The point is made here,
in passing, as preparation for subsequent development, in our advocacy of
the "comic frame."

seems to speak as a kind guardian for Muriel Rukeyser).
Capitalism shouted to Marx until the annoyance gave him
a diseased liver, but it seems to sing a cradle song for some.
(Cf. 1955, the "power of positive thinking.")

The charting of such territories may not be worth the
while, except perhaps for therapeutic purposes, when we
seek to repair a man's equipment for living by discovering
which of his clusters draw the lines at the wrong places. In
any case, the matter cannot be handled properly unless a
collective enterprise is organized about the search. One
man's guesses are too erratic, and too much distorted by his
own idiosyncrasies of emphasis. But if we are ever to recover
a world of nouns, going from a philosophy of *processes* to a
philosophy of *categories* (perhaps to something like "pro-
cess-categories") without merely dismissing by snobbery
and legislative fiat all the enlightenment that process-think-
ing has brought with it, such analysis of associational clusters or constellations may have to be undertaken. A felici-
tous frame of acceptance would seem to be one in which
the subjective firmament is in stable order, so that its astrono-
mers can proceed at leisure to draw the lines between its
stars, discovering the belt, the crown, the great bear and
the little bear, and similar logicizing marvels. And the
approach to these inner constellations through the discussion of their external counterparts (where one, on noting
elements *a*, *b*, and *c*, should be able to test his chart of interrelationships by *predicting* element *d*, and seeing whether
his prediction was borne out) should give us a *phenomeno-
logical* science of psychology, rather than the tenuousness
of the purely introspective or the impoverishment of the
purely behavioristic.

The grotesque-transitional appears in varying degrees;
concerning its use as a *passive* "frame of acceptance" when

it emerges in all its purity, we might cite the closing lines of Sweeney's volume on the gargoyle art of the Superrealists:*

"The Superrealists' dissatisfaction with the existing state of things no longer leads to a mere nihilism; they have found life worth living but feel it must be lived on entirely different grounds. The richness of life, according to them, lies in the subconscious. They feel the only true enjoyment of it can come from free expression of the subconscious. For them art has become the means to that end."

Monasticism and the Transitional

Monasticism has a peculiar place in the expression of transitional thought. At times when monastic orders are sincere, and have not degenerated into opportunities for business men in a theocratic state, they tend to enlist their members at a *point of crisis* (which is to say, a point of transition). Such a state of anguish quite regularly includes thoughts of self-punishment that lead to overt or symbolic castration. With the passing of the crisis, this mood would naturally

---

* We have speculated elsewhere on the possibility that the impulse behind Joyce's work resides in his "criminality" in rejecting the Catholic frame of his childhood. He is our greatest modern heretic, the contrast between his childhood and his maturity necessarily causing him to *reject with intensity* modes of thought that writers trained in Protestantism or agnosticism simply *neglect*. This shift in allegiance manifested itself as a cult of incongruity, made by the "impious" impact of two frames upon each other. Such is the "technical" or "formal" impulse behind his enterprising puns.

The punning game of "knock, knock," that gained great popular favor in the United States precisely at a time when there was widespread indecision with relation to the business symbols of authority (so central to our notions of purpose) might throw exegetic light upon his psychology.

Further to document this exegesis, we recall DeQuincey's comments on the way guilt was symbolized in *Macbeth* by the knocking at the

abate—but the monastic order *institutionalizes the mentality prevailing at the point of crisis*. It fixes the transitional, makes permanent the *status evanescentiae*. Suspended between heaven and earth, like Mohammet's coffin, it confronts a neither-here-nor-there; and in the name of *there*, organizes it as *here*. Finding a man who stands between two worlds, it offers him a world formed of this midway state. And since the spiritual features are given their material grounding in a collective technique of living (the "imaginative" ingredients being "bureaucratized" by the economic order) the "grotesque" becomes "natural," with conventional norms. The subjective state is embodied in a public order, a society-within-a-society. And by reason of this *public* element, the original private ingredients become socially negotiable. They may even provide such *material, objective* cues for living that Luther, it has been said, proposed to resolve the two-worlds antinomy by making all the world a monastery.

Eventual developments in Russia should provide us an opportunity to discover whether the sense of two-worldliness arises from social causes only, or derives from a subjective dualism inherent in man's "glassy essence." At present we may see signs of an inherent dualism among those in Russia who choose remote Arctic regions as the

---

gate. Recall also the variant in the Negro spiritual, "Somebody's Knocking at Your Door." We should also recall the "tapping," "gentle rapping" of Poe's raven.

In the case of *Macbeth*, the knocking called forth a passage of *lewdness*, an expulsion of filth. Sometimes it seems to have frightened Joyce similarly. One finds a kindred manifestation in the naive expulsion of filth in many of our so-called "realistic" novelists. Might there be lurking behind this literary symptom something like the fear that in the child causes evacuation?

scene of their practical activities. It may be found in time that for such people the psychology of science merely duplicates in new guise the psychology of religion—and as the churchman, in accordance with the mediaeval frame of values, put himself apart from the market place to *pray* for the good of mankind, so these rigorous explorers may be putting themselves apart to *study* and *search* in behalf of their fellows.

It has even been noted how, in such thoroughly capitalist countries as the United States, scientists have tended to resist proposals for banding themselves together as corporations that commercialize their discoveries for their own benefit. This observation does not apply to the general run of laboratory technologists, the hoard of wage-minded myrmidons whose application converts the astounding *poetry* of the pivotal scientific discoveries into the deadly efficiency of a Detroit factory or the noise and stench of a traffic-laden New York street. But it does apply to the imaginative men who formulated the basic inventions out of which this clutter has been built. They seem to have something of that tragic awe that makes them unwilling to look a gift horse in the mouth—like Cezanne, they want to abandon their canvases and hurry on.

And it might be relevant to note some analogy between their hesitancy to "cash in on" their genius, in a society that invites us even to capitalize on the affections, looking for their quantitative equivalent (in the fixed sums for alimony, or in the salesman's cultivation of a good-will presence for better success in wheedling customers)—to note an analogy between this resistance, with its attendant feeling that the pure scientist should leave his formulae for others to apply, and the earlier religious theorizing in behalf of a "poor church." At the time of Protestantism's emergence, earnest men proposed that the church should renounce its earthly wealth. Christ was poor—and the church, being the "body of Christ," should be poor also. The notion had its value, particularly in view of the fact that the church's enormous material wealth had led to the organization of business within its anti-business fictions, beginning with the popes themselves, who turned over their revenues for Italian bankers to invest (the Thomist proscriptions against usury being casuistically stretched by legal fictions to make allowance for the laxity and keep it *formally* inside the earlier frame). At a time when this degeneration was thorough, and Calvin had not yet arisen to produce a new morality by *changing the rules of the game* (so that the taking of interest, prohibited by the church, was admitted only by the spread of face-saving fictions, whose trickery amounted in the end to decay), heretics began pleading that the church should be as humble as the Christ-child in the manger. It was proved in time, however, that this pious doctrine could also be capitalized: the "poor church" was eventually, by organized effort, made equivalent to the *rich individual*—and the steady progression, from Piers Plowman's mystic vision of the moral value in toil to the private accumulations of a Rockefeller or Ford, was on. We are simply suggesting here that there is a doctrine of "poor science" to match the doctrine of the "poor church," and that the same process is under way whereby this essentially non-capitalist insight is made to serve capitalist ends.

A philosophy of force, vengeance, polemical compulsion ("cogency") would appear to be a reversal of the monastic solution. Here the sense of guilt that goes with "two-worldliness" is met, not by a ritual of contrition, as in the monastic response, but by such explicit rejection of contrition as we note in "gang morality."

POETIC CATEGORIES

We presume a "gang morality" to arise as follows: The orthodox values are no longer adequate to handle the situation; and this inadequacy manifests itself in the "dispossession" of individuals (who are removed from its spiritual and/or material benefits by their inability or their unwillingness to accept its code of effort). This dispossession manifests itself, in the minds of individuals, as negativism— a negativistic attitude that tends to reject much in rejecting a little, in accordance with the "all-or-none rule," while this negativism is further coached to extremity by the counter-invective of orthodox priests (either the churchly kind, or their secular counterparts, the educators and publicists). The individuals finally are able to "transcend" this sense of guilt by forming a band of their own. This band, a new collectivity, converts the old negatives into new positives— and by *its* values the deviations of the individuals (with relation to the orthodox frame) are "justified."

"Gang morality" is thus a "Lumpenproletarian" form of "sect." Marx's "class morality" is a dignified variant of the same process, organizing the individual mind to confront a present imperfect world by the co-ordinates of a subsequent better world. But until the day of redemption arrives with the establishment of a socialist state, it is essentially ideal rather than realistic. For like the church in its early evangelistic period, it confronts the *here-and-now* with a concept of a *beyond*.

In proportion as it becomes organized, we note a reverse counterpart to the monastic arrangement. As its scheme is completed with respect to all necessities, its "informing essence" becomes obscured. In the monastic pattern, this obscuring took place when the "spiritual" attained its "material" correctives, as when the artist "bureaucratizes" his imaginative vision in the objective, social materials of his product. And in the secular pattern, the "material" attains its "spiritual" correctives. Thus, though the movement takes its origins from such negative emphases as force, vengeance, compulsion, it can develop its own positives, such as "comradeship," "party discipline," "solidarity," thereby restoring the ingredient of charity necessary for co-operative enterprises.

In sum: the monastic order begins with "spirituality," and in the course of "implementing" it with relation to all human necessities, arrives at "material" organization. The treatment of the transitional emphasis in Marxist "class morality" begins with materiality, and in the course of implementing it, arrives at "spiritual" organization, or "consciousness."

Our resistance to a purely "debunking" vocabulary of motives is made clear if we imagine a thinker who chose to "debunk" such a motive as "solidarity." There are unquestionably ways in which one may "cash in on" it, in the purely selfish sense of the term—but if *all* acts of "solidarity" were interpreted in the light of this possibility, its "reality" would be dissolved out of existence quite as Democritus' atomism resolved the gods out of existence; and anyone who thought of it as real would be a fool. Those who co-operate with the help of this concept must leave its "euphemistic" nature as a motive intact. And they must frame a vocabulary of motives accordingly. However, euphemism alone would not be enough, since it would provide a "eulogistic covering" for acts in which "cashing in on" really was identical with "selling out." Without the resources of comic ambivalence, one is not equipped to gauge the full range of human potentialities.

POETIC CATEGORIES

The Didactic

We have noted, as many others have noted, how too thorough a cult of the mystical-grotesque makes for passivity in the frame of acceptance. The active frame to match it is the didactic (propaganda, rhetoric, "applied" art).

In the *spontaneous* unfoldings of history, the imaginative expression of a trend precedes its conceptual-critical counterpart—as Greek tragedy went before its essayistic formulation in Aristotle's *Poetics*; or as the imaginative symbolization of individualist enterprise appeared (theologically) in *Pilgrim's Progress*, (secularly) in *Robinson Crusoe*, and (fantastically) in the lonely travels of Gulliver before its conceptual symbolization in *The Wealth of Nations*; or as the organized literary movement of symbolism preceded its corresponding critical formulation in psychoanalysis. The didactic would attempt to reverse this process, by *coaching* the imagination in obedience to critical postulates.

Insofar as the imagination cannot be coached, insofar as the full poet must draw upon all his resources (sincerity thus being both a technical and moral necessity), the attempt to coerce the imagination leads to the problems of "will" that are bothering such contemporary critics as Allen Tate. The issue may also explain what Trotsky is aiming at when he denies the possibility of a "proletarian" literature. (The literature of the revolution would, by our interpretation, more properly be sought in the imaginative works of Dostoievsky than in anything that followed the organized activities of critics after 1917, where the so-called "revolutionary" literature really is analogous to our stories of fights between patriots and Tories that were written *after* the Revolutionary War, while the *incipient* or *emergent* elements implicit in this literature are still to be disclosed by critical formulation.) *

However, the matter is not so simple as all that. For since Descartes' formulation of "organized doubt" as a creative method, and the integration of experiment, induction, and skepticism in technological advance, criticism has become a more positive factor, with the result that some measure of reversal in the imaginative-critical order is inherent in our productive modes. It could also be pointed out that Marx, with his sharp critical formulations, was *contemporary* with Dostoievsky, though we should counter by noting that Marx offered no conceptual psychology to match Dostoievsky's imaginative processes. By the concept of antithesis Marx schematized the psychological issue, pitting one "morality" against another, without analyzing the possibility that the imaginative writer tends to *"adumbrate" the eventual synthesis*, hence confusing the simple for-or-against attitude that prevails in lawyer's-brief polemic.

Dostoievsky's tragic ambiguities of crime and punishment were not considered by Marx; as a barrister, he was not "exposed" to them. But the poet, whose clusters led

---

* Though our categories do not lay claim to be complete, we might note the relation of the *essay* to didactic patterns. Often we might also note in the essay a paradoxical kinship with the elegy, or plaint. Thus, there is a kind of transcended hypochondriasis in the "scientific" writer who says: "I am not proposing a remedy; I am simply telling you the nature of the problem." We have characterized the grotesque as something like humor-with-the-laughter-omitted. The essay of "impartial diagnosis" might be likened to a plaint-with-the-tears-omitted. Hamlet caught a glimpse of the method, but in his day it lacked the vast body of thought that has since been developed to "implement" it. Hence, the plaintive ingredient in his diagnoses is stressed—and, though relying upon words almost as much as did his author, his exigencies of living made him poor workman enough to quarrel with his tools.

him by identification to make the "little father" and the people synonymous, was dealing with issues that could not be solved by essayistic legislation. In Russia after the revolution, Stalin and the people were viewed as synonymous, in accordance with a general tendency towards such identification (between the people and a personal symbol of authority). And the necessity of wrenching apart such associations where the Marxist doctrine of class morality was concerned, created great difficulties for the imaginative writer who, using all of himself, felt the need of a personal apex for his pyramidal edifice.*

Democracies, with their attempt to put a *delegated* authority at the head of the state, and their play of factional, debunking devices whereby the chosen symbol is constantly attacked by slander, cannot permit the full expression of this integrative impulse. And if, as we have said, one lifts up *himself* by erecting a hero, factional mud-slinging must always interfere with the completion of legendary magic. It is admittedly a grim thought: how parliaments tend to protect us by releasing modes of thought that restrict the

---

* The structure is paralleled in Egypt by the fiction that all men were tenants of the Pharaoh; in Rome by the integration about the symbol of the emperor, who was divine; in Catholic feudalism by the theocratic hierarchy culminating in the Pope, perhaps an exceptionally cunning design in that, if there is any truth to Freud's concept of the sexual rivalry between father and son that goes with the bourgeois-patriarchal family, the papal father-symbol could reassure the many sons by being institutionally castrated. This tendency to complete the integration by a personal figure is revealed in the British use of their king as a symbol for consolidating an empire faced with dismemberment. We have noted it in Whitman's attitude towards Lincoln. We note it as the sole magical device that now [1937] holds the Japanese together despite their tense internal discords. And in Germany, though the people have built roads for many centuries, when they build a road after 1933, *Hitler* builds it.

possibilities of self-respect (in cutting off the heroic fountain-head); while "totalitarian" orders, in providing the necessary opportunities for myth-making, thereby stifle the protective resources of criticism, as we observe so tragically to-day in Germany, where the myth contrives to make the people's major virtues function as the most ominous of vices.

The magic of authority (which, in the relations of child to parent, is not *delegated*, but just *is*) may account in part for the tendency in democracies to select heroes from the "other worlds" of science or art, or even from technology and business (figures whose authority is not delegated by the avalanches of factional suffrage). In the bourgeois body politic, even *politicians* damn an opponent's motive by calling it *political*; and professional partisans like to advocate their measures as *transcending* factional antitheses. Candidates for office say, in effect: "Vote for our faction, which is more able to *mediate between the factions*." The delegation of authority is, by the very nature of the case, the popular selection of a puppet to act as a public convenience. It *votes* its man an identity, a dramatic role in regulating the traffic of the state. And astute "debunkers" continually arise to discover that the puppets are puppets.

The truncated nature of a frame lacking its culmination in an absolute may explain the disturbing willingness, on the part of so many people "trained" in democracy, to entertain favorable thoughts of some eventual apocalyptic man on horseback who will come to make "tyranny" and "good tyranny" synonymous. Nothing less than the most mature and comprehensive of critical frames would seem capable of competing against this tendency, as the irregularities of liberal democracy increase. Otherwise, the Scramble must lead to the Smash, with no assurance that the Smash will lead to the happy outcome Marx consolingly called scientifically inevitable.*

The didactic poet, as his detractors are eager to point out, attempts to avoid the confusions of synthesis by a schematic decision to label certain people "friends" or "enemies." Hence, the didactic poet is headed towards allegory, as revealed in the work of the young English communist group. His procedure also leads naturally to oversimplifications of character and history that can, by the opposition, be discounted as "sentimentality" (writers who can escape the charge, as Malraux does in *Man's Fate*, must draw upon a *cult of tragedy* that is not "politically enlightened"). The poet is born to be "naive," but critical exigencies make him "sentimental" (a state of affairs considered over a century ago by the didactic author of *William Tell*). So we shall close our discussion of literary categories by an examination of the sentimental, which is the weak side of didacticism.

Sentimentality is an *act of will* in this sense: Suppose that, in confronting life, one found, inextricably interwoven, some trends which he considered desirable and others which he considered undesirable. And suppose that he simplified the logic of existence for himself by deciding that the desirable feature was the "essence" of the lot. He found, like

---

* Perhaps it requires more astute self-consciousness than people are capable of, if they are to retain their appreciation of democracy while the disorders of capitalism discredit it by "contagion." Particularly since there are so many channels of education that explicitly discourage the spread of such criticism. Nonetheless, critics must persist in their attempts to spread and perfect a "comic" interpretation of human motives, aware that, whatever avalanches of heroic euphemism of the Hitler or Mussolini variety may fall upon the world at times, the movement towards the humane and civilized is maintained precisely insofar as the astute self-consciousness of comedy is "implemented" by the accumulated body of comic shrewdness.

Emerson, that every good had its bad and every bad its good; but he voted the *good* as the "true meaning" of the pair. Or, to bring the analogy nearer home, the writer finds that there is good and bad in everybody, but for hortatory purposes he divides people into *classes*—and by treating them *as members of these classes*, he tries to coach his "human" attitude in accordance with his philosophy of classes, thereby schematically dividing the good from the bad, the vital from the decadent, the rising from the dying, etc. He thereby tends to "transcend" his earlier position, to "reconcile opposites" by a concept of a "higher synthesis." Specifically, in the case of the propagandist, his theory of classes *transcends* his ambivalent notion that "there is good and bad in everybody." Though bourgeois critics rail at this "sentimental" simplification without sympathy, the literature of bourgeois apologetics is full of it. For a whole century we got books where the honest commoner triumphed over the vicious aristocrat, as dramatic roles were assigned to the figures of fiction on the basis of their class function.

The problem comes close to the basic devices of character-building, as character-building is accomplished in the "secular prayers" of art. It is Hegel's *"Aufheben"*—and by the time this process is rounded out, we find it allied with Goethe's *"Entsagen."* Let us illustrate by improvising a psychology for an early didactic poet, Hesiod.

Didactic "Transcendence" in Hesiod

The plaints of this old Greek poet were the obverse of Homer's "air-sweetness." In contrast with the "receptive" realism of Homer, Hesiod's realism was of the sort that "indicted." Or else it was "compensatory." Hesiod seemed to love nature, not like a man who "owned" it, but like a man who, threatened with pauperdom, clung to the little that he had. So he wrote a naturalistic account of the gods that "debunked" them, and he expressed his plaintive hedonism in the "indictments" and "compensatory" realism of *Works and Days.*

Hesiod had quarrels with his brother. Hesiod felt that the brother had mistreated him. Hesiod tried to forgive. That is, the quarrels led him to the "negation" of the fraternal ties—but Hesiod, being scrupulous in the manner of Eliot (*Murder in the Cathedral*), tries to "negate the negation." He will adopt a wider and subtler perspective, wherein the earlier resentment is "transcended," being assigned its place as a minor incidental. Thus Hesiod would "purify" himself of a simple desire for vengeance: he would not merely suppress his hatred, he would outgrow it. In sum: he is willing to write off the past, to cancel the debt, if the brother, after this voluntary bankruptcy, will enter a *new* partnership, signing a contract with much subtler clauses. However, in this new contract there will also be a *"hodie mihi, cras tibi"* element, regardless of the intensity with which Hobbes abominates the thought. It will not be a one-way system, a giving-out of affection and forgiveness on the part of Hesiod, and a mere receiving on the brother's part. It will be a two-way interchange.

At this point, Hesiod unquestionably "feels better," having recovered the right to be affectionate. Though an humble man, he is "nearer to the gods," and doubtless enjoys a sense of relief, and outwardness, that is "divine" in its freedom. And, as we have said, prosperity being the visible testimony of God's pleasure (the Protestant emphasis, that subsequently did much for private enterprise), Hesiod waits to see his moral improvement matched by a material counterpart.

Instead, the ironical occurs. The brother continues as unpartnerlike as before. Hesiod has gone through his private revolution, prepared himself for reconciliation with his brother on a "higher level of abstraction" (as Korzybski might put it)—and the brother remains unmoved.

Crisis. Would Hesiod advance to a still more exacting perspective, so transcendent, so "purified," that he could forgive his brother not only past injustice, but even present persistence in injustice? Or would Hesiod "freeze"? Would he cease his attempts to "spiral," stopping at his present level of development, and converting his prayers into their simple reverse, invective? Humble Hesiod is no Christ, for all his pastoral qualities. He cannot turn the other cheek (perhaps, since he is in bad straits, the economic pressure sharpens his impatience). His mind becomes organized, bureaucratized, at this second level. Attempting no further transcendence, he seeks to exploit this level as it is, to find whatever limited "cash value" it may have to offer.

Shift in the focus of battle. Note first that Hesiod cannot be vengeful with wholeheartedness, for he has already attained a level sufficiently complicated to stimulate a categorical distrust of vengeance. So if his brother's unresponsiveness makes him vengeful nonetheless, in being vengeful he must turn not only against his brother, but also against himself. "Introversion"—concern with the *diable au corps*, the "enemy within." A fight on two fronts; on *three* in fact, for the economic pressure continues.

What to do? Hesiod goes sour. He breaks. In moments of discouragement, he becomes angry with the entire complexity of his concerns; he turns against his "method" itself. He becomes enraged at the whole business of transcendence, which in his case does not reach its full culmination in *Entsagen*. And being a very thorough, conscientious fellow, he goes to the roots of the matter: he rejects the very gods, who are the ultimate concretion of the transcendental process.

Whereat we get: Hesiod, the dissolver of the cosmogonic myths. He will dissolve them, in thoroughly resenting the process by which they arose. He will choose atheism, and the plaint.

Still, there is a *faute de mieux* available. His negation has its own positive counterpart. He can "cash in on" *naturalism* and *work*. The work presumably acts somewhat as penance; it pays his debt for the sin against himself, the unpardonable sin of interrupting the transcendental spirals of his moral growth. And we may assume that the toil serves to meet his material obligations somewhat (hence has a "synthetic" function in easing moral and material pressures simultaneously). And naturalism provides the *level of satisfaction beneath which he cannot sink*; he will have his taste buds, and kindred sensory channels, that provide him with an humble, or rather humiliated, version of the Horatian *"carpe diem"* attitude. But since, as a farmer, he *works* with nature, nature is linked with the *penitential* aspect of his toil. Hence, he not only enjoys nature, but suffers it.

Adding up, we get as the sum of his character: hardworking, complaining, resentful and resentful-of-resentment, pious, free-thinking, enjoying-and-suffering simultaneously — and expressing the whole moralistically, didactically.

Didactic Transcendence in Eliot

We have mentioned Eliot's *Murder in the Cathedral*. It also illustrates the didactic - sentimental - transcendental nexus. Improvising a psychology for Eliot:

A work on Thomas the Saint, by Thomas the Poet, the Saint Louis boy who was too good for Saint Louis (why shouldn't he be!). Concerned with the royal road to God.

Stages: The author leaves the old locale behind to go in search of its antithesis. He will abandon the inelegancies of Missouri for the elegancies of upper-class England. By antithesis, he builds up a concept of elegance—and then he goes in search of it *geographically*. He tries to find a place here-and-now that will give sufficient bodily substance to the structure of his imagination. For a time he thinks he has found it in England. But eventually it occurs to him that England is moving towards Saint Louis. Life becomes a waste land at the thought. England is not elegant enough. And eventually the poet meditates upon God, the only symbol elegant enough. But:

Being a profound and imaginative man, being perhaps our most accomplished poet, Eliot knows very well that there is no slogan: *per elegantiam ad astra*. He questions the validity of his way. He knows that he must get to God by humbleness, so he must "transcend" his elegance, building atop it a new structure of humility. The God of elegance being the negation of Saint Louis, he must round out his development by "negating the negation." *Murder in the Cathedral* is the symbolic solution of this problem in spiritual tactics.

The crux of the matter comes with the role of the fourth tempter, who disturbs the Saint by tempting him with his own words. Sainthood must not be a career. The poet, in the persona of the saint, eventually "transcends" this problem. Saint Thomas's quiet sermon, delivered to his flock prior to the assassination, attests his moral victory. It is as calm as *The Tempest* which, in the magician's final release of Caliban, symbolizes Shakespeare's "transcendence" beyond the melodramatic antithesis of good and evil. The Saint, having exposed himself to the warning, is prepared to welcome a martyrdom purified of *arriviste* connotations.

However, the drama has only begun. For when Thomas the Poet is symbolically slain in the role of Thomas the Saint who deputizes for him, a surprising thing takes place. The poetic frame is shattered, and there step forth the four murderers, who presumably deputize for Thomas the Critic, and entertain us with the most biting critical prose. These breaks in continuity are always of great significance in a writer's work (as we pleaded when analyzing the broken logic of Lewis's "ossature" metaphor). In Eliot's play, they seem to symbolize a change in the identity of the author, whose critical self slays his poetic self. However, the Saint in his opening speech had told us that we

> are fixed
> In an eternal action, an eternal patience
> To which all must consent that it may be willed
> And which all must suffer that they may will it,
> That the pattern may subsist, for the pattern is the
>   action
> And the suffering, that the wheel may turn and still
> Be forever still.

So the plot is a wheel, an *aria da capo*, a rondo form, closing on a resumption of the poetic mode. In this progression from poetry, to polemic prose, back to poetry, the author probably states stylistically what the speech of Thomas had stated philosophically: That the turning of the wheel goes on, that in turning it remains where it was, that each morning the poet will arise, will slay himself, the critic will step forth, towards nightfall the Phoenix-poet will rise again, and this procession will continue, being forever new and forever the same, and the writer, in affirming it by the activity of his work, is being at once active and passive—hence *"Entsagen,"* the Goethean resignation.*

Other Instances of Transcendence

Admittedly, this business is elusive. We must ask the reader, if he can, merely to consider it as being on the track of something. We are trying to bring up an issue, rather than to persuade anyone that we can make it crystal-clear. The point to be stressed is that the process of transcendence, basic to thought, is revealed most simply in didactic-moralistic literature. There must be many ways by which "transcendence" takes place.

Thales presumably was attaining some such triumph for himself when, looking at the "four elements," earth, fire, water, and air, he decided that they were all "in essence"

* Could we not apply a similar exegesis to Milton's "Lycidas"? Is not Mr. Paul Elmer More too literal in his account of a possible origin for Milton's "inspiration"? He says that Milton was contemplating a sea voyage, that the risks of shipwreck were great, and that the drowning of his "learned Friend" made him fearful enough for his own safety to express it in his sorrow for the death of another.

"Lycidas" was written in 1637. Milton traveled in 1638 and 1639. And for the next twenty years thereafter, with the exception of an occasional sonnet, he devoted all his energies to his polemic prose.

These dates, coupled with the contents of the poem, would justify us in contending that "Lycidas" was the symbolic dying of his poetic self. It was followed by a period of transition (the "random casting" of travel). And then he focused upon the work of his "left hand." During this prose period, except for the occasional sonnet, he hid "that one talent which it is death to hide."

Ever since his schooldays, however, he had planned to write a poem vast in scope. The idea never left him. During the greatest intensity of his pamphleteering, he continued looking for a suitable theme (at one time deciding upon the fall of Adam). And in "Lycidas" he testifies that

water. We have no body of his writings to help us in con-
jecturing, by metaphorical analysis, how many practical,
non-metaphysical relationships he incidentally located for
himself by his cosmic symbolism (of how much it was a
"vessel"), though we were happy to read in Zeller: "We find
him in the train of the Lydian king on his expedition against
Persia, when he made possible the crossing of the Halys by
diverting the course of the river," which would suggest that
his metaphysics was a fit with his acts as a patriot. He likewise offered a theory to explain the inundations of the Nile
—and "after the defeat of Croesus he advised the Ionians
to join in a close political combination against the threaten-
ing peril of Persia," again manifesting his "synthetic" tendencies. Holding that "earth floats on the water like a piece
of wood," and having the typical Greek notion of cosmos
as an area of order roped off from a wider area of chaos, he

---

he is holding his dead self in abeyance, and that it will rise again. For after
the funereal solemnities of his catalogue of flowers, he adds a coda:

> Weep no more, woeful shepherds, weep no more,
> For Lycidas, your sorrow, is not dead,
> Sunk though he be beneath the watery floor;
> So sinks the day-star in the ocean bed,
> And yet anon repairs his drooping head,
> And tricks his beams, and with new-spangled ore
> Flames in the forehead of the morning sky:
>   So Lycidas. . . .

So the poet remained, for all his dying; and at the Restoration, after
the political interregnum of Cromwell, he would be reborn. *Paradise Lost*
is the fulfilment of his contract, though he returns to the poetic matrix
as one of the "blind mouths" he tells about in "Lycidas."

May we not also see the pure poet continuing to exist beneath the prose?
Notably in the "Areopagitica," when the Luciferian eagle of freedom
stares into the blinding glare of the sun, the "day-star" of "Lycidas," and
sees nonetheless.

probably loved Hellas as a piece of wood that he would keep afloat upon the barbarian seas of Persia.*

A variant of the Heraclitan transcendence may be noted today in Lola Ridge's *Dance of Fire*, constructed about the image of a universal burning, life as a process of combustion. There is trial by fire, when the burning is too intense— and there is a transcendent burning, light. But this "synthesis" becomes finally the basis of a new antithesis, as we find the poetess apostrophizing the "ice-heart," where all will "congeal in harmony." Perhaps the reader will think we are cheating if we suggest that this antithesis in turn is resolved by a device of a different order, not capable of statement in the forensic language of "excluded middle."

---

* The ways in which such symbolic patterns behave when released into a socio-economic texture may take surprising twists. That is: we must not expect a simple one-to-one correspondence whereby a doctrine of unity functions unifyingly, or vice versa. Marxism, for instance, makes it clear how the Catholic unification eventually behaved in a disintegrative manner, as privileged groups organized with increasing efficiency and proliferation their ways of "moving in on" its resources.

German historicism, beginning with collectors of the Germanic incunabula like Vom Stein, and culminating symbolically in Hegel's picture of integration through the hegemony of Prussia, probably served as the cultural basis for the political implementation supplied by Bismarck and Hitler. Here we find something like a one-to-one correspondence. But in England, we note how the upbuilding of the world's vast empire drew upon a strongly *atomistic* trend in the symbolism of its thinkers. This atomism may have served for the imperialistic kind of integration by suggesting a strongly *relativistic* attitude whereby no over-zealous attempt would be made to "co-ordinate" all the cultural pattern of the conquered areas in conformity with the patterns of the conqueror. Hence, this atomism is tied with the genius of "muddling through," rationalizing a relativistic opportunism, of the serviceable "let well enough alone" variety. And since this atomism attained much of its rationale through the quantitative tests of "good business," it stimulated an attitude of "tolerance" towards any aspects of the local *mores* that did not radically

POETIC CATEGORIES

The over-all unification is, in this interpretation, accomplished by ritual, by tone, by the poet's *music* (for in music, themes can be *different* from each other, but they cannot *contradict* each other). Similarly, the Saint's speech in Eliot's play would appear to equate the *active* voice (we act upon) with the *passive* voice (we are acted upon) by proclaiming both in the same *poetic tone* of voice:

> They know and do not know, that acting is suffering
> And suffering is action. Neither does the actor suffer
> Nor the patient act.

We can note another aspect of transcendence in Wagner's *Tristan und Isolde*, a bit of magic whereby the composer transcendentally puts life and death together. After the taking of the potion, Tantris dies for Isolde and is reborn as Tristan. Their duet celebrates their death as individuals and their birth as a corporate identity. The equations are: love = life and love = death. And, since things equal to the

interfere with the demands of business, which "transcends" the dislike of selling to an infidel.

But though this solution may have had its advantages, from the standpoint of an exploiting imperial core, it meant "alienation" for the local cultural integers. Their cultural patterns, like a low animal with much of its activity directed through the spinal column, bunglingly survived in a state of *decapitation*, as the ultimate tests of *success* (by which the natives felt their culture's "fullness") necessarily shifted to the conqueror's symbols of authority (as backed by the bureaucratic embodiment of commercialism and technology). We make the observation here, to adumbrate some later remarks on "alienation," the kind of material and spiritual dispossession that requires a new concept of social purpose if people are to be spared the rigors of nostalgia and emptiness. Tactically, such changes in emphasis attain their focus in changes of allegiance towards the symbols of authority.

same thing are equal to each other, it follows that life =
death, whereupon the tragic rejoicing of the *Liebestod*.
Of course, there are many other factors involved here (for
instance, the tragic ambiguity whereby illicit love is at once
gratified and punished, and the elation of the close arises
from the symbolic solving of this problem also). We should
also note the similarity in musical texture between the love
duet and Isolde's love-death soliloquy.

Hegel "transcended" by using a dialectic of *historic* process as a way of resolving metaphysical opposites. Our review of the way in which Emerson handled the problem of
ambivalence indicates a kindred solution. Marx secularized
the Hegelian pattern (though retaining unavowed vestiges
of godhead, a covert "god-function," in the idea that social
antitheses would be reconciled by a "higher" synthesis). His
attacks upon the established symbols of authority seem likewise to have stimulated some sense of guilt, for he identifies
himself in "pastoral" fashion with a suffering proletariat,
who must redeem the world by a blood-sacrifice. (For further morphological parallels, indicating correspondences
between the Hebraic-Christian patterns of redemption and
Marx's secularized equivalents, the reader is referred to the
relevant chapter in Louis Rougier's *Les Mystiques poli-
tiques*.) Materialism pure and simple contrives a kind of
"inverted transcendence," or "transcendence downwards,"
resolving the contradictions between mind and matter by
voting that the *essence* of the duality is matter.

Such considerations may offer reasons why, when a problem is handled in too simple a frame, as the needs of propagandistic exhortation are often felt to demand, critics are
led to attack the didactic as "allegory," "literature of the
will," and "sentimentality." One may even discern the didactic sentimentality in Whitman when, looking at a real

estate boom, he sees there a mystic reaching-forth of hands (to abide by his program as "answerer," he "salutes" the materialistic reality in terms of "unseen existences").* It is questionable, however, whether historical issues can be handled in any other way. All we can ask is that the modes of "prayer" employed (with their reverse, invective) shall be sufficiently mature and complex to take the key factors of the situation properly into account.

* "As Neccho Allen saw and suspected the tremendous Unseen Value of anthracite, so to-day thousands of car-owners are discovering the meaning and importance of Unseen Value in motor cars.

"The Chrysler Corporation has made America definitely aware of Unseen Value. It is not something you can see or feel. It is not a tangible thing like beauty, power or safety. Yet Unseen Value is far more real and far more vital to the car-owner than the iron, rubber, steel, glass of which a car is made."

We quote from an advertisement in *Nation's Business*. It tells us further that, to "see the Unseen Value of the car you are buying," you must "look beyond the assembling line and search for the impelling aims and *ideals* of the organization." Advt-writing here moves into the sphere of the mystical. We had previously thought that Whitman attained his social substantiation (the "bureaucratization" of his "imaginative") in Kiwanis and the Rotary Clubs, who "transcendentally" erect good-fellowship upon a basis of sales rivalry. But in this piece of "applied art," we are taught that the transubstantiation, the business parallel for the Church as the "body of Christ," arises when Unseen Value is incorporated in the body of a Chrysler car. Our visionary turner-out of copy has evidently brought his religion to market—and our concern with linguistic analysis leads us to wonder whether the cunning idea might, after all, have been suggested to him by the genius of the Christ-Chrysler pun.

CHAPTER THREE

THE DESTINY OF ACCEPTANCE FRAMES

PLAY, love, war, work—these are the names for the ways in which a man is engrossed. The putting of them all together, the "allocating" of them, is "religion," leading to some manner of transcendence or other.

One confronts contradictions. Insofar as they are resolvable contradictions he acts to resolve them. Insofar as they are not resolvable, he symbolically erects a "higher synthesis," in poetic and conceptual imagery, that helps him to "accept" them. Thus, Thomism defined certain important contradictions of ownership as *unresolvable*, and erected a series of transcendental bridges, poetic and critical fictions, for producing a synthesis atop the antithesis by the organizing of a unifying *attitude* (backed by logic, ritual, and economic patterns). Marx defined these same contradictions of ownership as *resolvable*; hence his modes of symbolic transcendence were manifested by a different "pontifical" structure (based on the assertion of a synthesizing function in history). Each frame enrolls for "action" in accordance with its particular way of drawing the lines.

Out of such frames we derive our vocabularies for the charting of human motives. And implicit in our theory of motives is a program of action, since we form ourselves and judge others (collaborating with them or against them) in accordance with our attitudes.

A supernatural scheme of motives too quickly misleads the social critic by serving as a "eulogistic covering" for utilitarian interests. But the antithetical scheme, of purely "debunking" motives, makes co-operation difficult, since it sees utilitarian motives everywhere. The "debunking" frame of interpretation becomes a colossal enterprise in "transcendence downwards" that is good for polemical, *disintegrative* purposes, but would make that man a fool who did anything but spy upon his colleagues, watching for the opportunity when he himself may "sell out" and "cash in."

There are various ways of "cashing in on" a given historical situation. If a writer's audience believes that it is wrong to murder a friend, the poet can "cash in on" this belief, as Shakespeare did with great subtlety in depicting the relations between Brutus and Caesar. And, probably without great cunning, the mediaeval moralist "cashed in on" the contemporary belief in the authority of custom when he propounded a philosophy of status that kept the lines of status intact. Accordingly, if you will imagine such a term being used with both connotations at once, putting together both the poet's way and the swindler's way of "cashing in on" our confidence, you will grasp the distinction we would make between a wholly "debunking" (polemical, burlesque) scheme of motives and the motives of comic ambivalence. The methods of caricature do not equip us to understand the full complexities of sociality—hence they warp our programs of action and, by identification, humiliate the manipulator of them, thereby making cynical self-interest the most logical of policies.

But once the comic proviso is added, the whole terminology of capitalism is found remarkable for its clear simplification of social processes. All the time that savants were concerning themselves with child psychology, abnormal psychology, primitive psychology, and animal psychology, and out of them inventing one-man vocabularies of motivation to chart human complexities with the help of simplifying laboratory conditions, we were ignoring the most ingenious and suggestive vocabulary of all, the *capitalist*

vocabulary of behavior. It is *collective* in origin, it arose by
the "dialectic" interaction of mental and material factors;
and at best it *was* comic, in that it gave the human, social
equivalents for concepts previously handled in superhuman
terms. Thus, "providence" became "investment for profit";
the processes of "justification" took the simple form of "advertising," "salesmanship," and "success"; the close relationship between morality and utility came to a head in
the "gospel of service"; the devices of perfidy were exposed
in the legal manipulations of contract; the synthesizing
tendencies of man were manifest, as they could never be
by experiments with decerebrated frogs, in the growth of
holding companies; corporate identity itself was shorn of
its unwieldy mysticism when the member of the church, as
the "body of Christ," became simply the holder of non-
voting stock. And so on; the morphological parallels could
be piled up endlessly. It would be cultural vandalism to
leave this field unused, and not to borrow its "cues." But
the truly comic use of them cannot confine itself to the
"debunking" mode alone. The ways of advertisers may help
us to understand the ways of pure poetry, but they do not
"dissolve" the dignity of poetry as Democritus with his
atoms dissolved the dignity of the gods. A properly comic
use of ambivalence will not pledge us to "debunking" as
the only alternative to indiscriminate euphemism.

When the genius of pure debunking prevails, the qualifications of comic charity drop away. It is then that the invitation to "cash in" becomes identical with the invitation
to "sell out." And the man imbued with such a scheme of
motives is as embittered when he *does* sell out as he is when
he *can't*. His own *self*-indictment is implicit in the thumbs-
down system of motives by which he indicts all mankind.

Marx felt this atomistic, disintegrative genius in the utilitarians' theories of motivation. It should be said, in Bentham's defense, that he was trying the old liberal trick of founding "virtue" upon "vice." The tactical problem was like this: Self-interest being everywhere, and even altruism being capable of interpretation, by transcendence downwards, as an aspect of self-love, if you could found *virtue* upon so ubiquitous a base, you had a firm foundation indeed.

Marx's collectivist emphasis even introduced the possibility of self-sacrifice, as the conduct of the individual was located with reference to the requirements of his *group*. Marx could restore the possibility of the hero as a function of his group, with all the enrichment of the individual that such a possibility contained. A similar attitude could only be smuggled into utilitarianism, at least as interpreted by Carlyle in his opposition to the "pig-sty philosophy."

We have already discussed, in connection with Dostoievsky, the psychological problem that, by our view, the Marxist vocabulary slighted. That is: should not the *synthetic* future already make itself felt *incipiently* in the minds of poets confronting the *antitheses of the present?* By Marx's schematization as a barrister, this confusion could be exorcized. The rational symmetry of his frame could persuade him that the pacific norms of a future "classless" society need not muddle the simplicity of "class war" here and now. He seems to have relegated the business of *mediation* to a historical process alone. But when this same act of mediation is done, not by "history," but by *people*, the sharpening of class lines tends to be obliterated.

For this mediating function is performed by *politicians* among others, whose *first* obligation is to keep their party in power. True: They are indebted to their *employers*, the people of wealth who finance their political campaigns.

They will repay this debt as far as possible. But there is a partial contradiction, since the party must get *votes*, and it cannot get enough votes to hold office unless it does obtain some concessions for the masses. To a degree, therefore, the party makes itself a good investment for its financial backers by obtaining concessions (such as doles, better working conditions, or the exposure of business frauds) which do not fully satisfy the "ideals" of its backers. If it did not obtain these concessions it could not permanently enlist votes enough to make itself a good investment for these same backers. So the pulling and tugging goes on—and in bourgeois democracies the enlistment of political parties in behalf of the big propertied interests can never be complete. Insofar as politicians, owing their *first* loyalty to their party rather than to their employers, really do act as mediators, "histo.·y" is prevented from producing its "new synthesis" out of an aggravated "antithesis." Political parties, however grudgingly, must either themselves introduce "reforms" or accept reforms that their opponents have introduced. And insofar as these reforms quiet a large majority of the people, there is a postponement of "Der Tag."

In such a situation, where material resources are ample, where a state's productive plant is highly developed along modern lines, and where rich men can only make their profits by selling goods (i.e., *distributing* goods) to the people, the pressure for mediation by reform is great. An economic order that lives by sales ("the citizen as customer") supplies its own incentives to make "good" customers, incentives contradicted by the incentives to despoil, but present nonetheless. Perhaps an antithesis would be aggravated to the breaking point only were a national war to occur, with its organized destruction of goods. Or the rise of Fascism would produce the same result, since under

Fascism political authority is divorced from the tests of the ballot that so quickly reveal the need of further mediatory measures.

Fascist countries appear to be solving the problem temporarily by enrolling the dispossessed as wards of the state, quite as our liberal democracies are doing; this group is recruited in a special *subsistence* economy (backed, in Fascist countries, by a propaganda technique that spreads a "morale" of collective symbolism, for "armies" who march with shovels as well as armies with guns). Others are kept in orthodox *capitalist* economy by employment in munitions factories. But since this unproductive activity is, in the last analysis, an economic drain on the state (obtaining a mountain of bullets by a shortage of butter), it could be made to pay only in the old feudalistic sense: an investment in ammunition must be an investment in the prospects of "booty."

At present, the big industrialists and financial interests are standing the costs of this investment (in the sense that they must take much of their profits in *paper*, the interest on this paper is paid with more paper, and the compounded debt is discharged with still more paper). The present German inflation, by this concealed pyramiding, must be fabulous; and there is no reason to believe that the powers behind Hitler are delighted with the nightmare, caused by "capitalist contradictions." There could be no adequate "return on the investment" unless the fighting machine, whose costly upbuilding gives the workers some measure of wages, were permitted to "turn out its product. And the only product that such a factory could produce is *booty*, the taking of rich resources from *foreign* territory. Then there could be the customary feudal disposition of the spoils: a little to the masses, who did the fighting, a lot to the Fascist nobility, who came forward to redeem their paper. If the foreign territory resists for long, and the prospects of profit are not great enough to attract foreign credit, the fighting factory must collapse—and if the nobles are left at all, they are left with their unredeemable paper.*

In our liberal democracies, the processes of political mediation *have* been leading towards socialism, *via* a policy which has been named (accuracy making for irony) the "socialization of losses." One group after another draws upon the *collective* credit of the government for support of its *private* fortunes, as when our federal treasury comes to the rescue of the private banks. This policy for "socializing" losses has been creeping into favor for many decades. It took a significant step forward with Hoover's Reconstruction Finance Corporation. And the tendency towards the *quantity production* of a good thing led to a greater democratization of this salvation device under Roosevelt. We are still far behind England in the extent to which the "socialization of losses" has been democratized, in the organization of federal doles to the people at large—but perhaps we have been slower only because we could *afford* to be; and as the situation demands, the necessities of political mediation may carry us further in this comically inverted

---

* Unfortunately, there are factors that make the foreign credit a likelihood. For there is a minor "class war" between security-sellers and security-buyers, and under some conditions the former "class" can "exploit" the latter for sizable profits. If the bankers see a way of underwriting a loan to a Fascist state and unloading it on the general investment public, they would get their commissions, and these profits would be "real" enough, no matter how worthless the securities would be to the holders. (Addendum, 1955: The same result could be got more roundabout, but with less risk, if a government made purchases abroad or advanced foreign credits, and to meet these costs made loans through its own investment bankers.)

approach towards "socialism," unless the cataclysms of war intervene to arrest it. (In the less than 20 years since this observation was written, the nation has gone beyond "social security" to the "guaranteed annual wage.")

Discomfitures of Rejection

The various poetic categories we have analyzed illustrate some major psychological devices whereby the mind equips itself to name and confront its situation. They provide in miniature the cues for us to follow when considering the broad course of Western civilization with reference to its "collective poems," the total frames of thought and action, roughly classifiable under the heads of primitive evangelism (in the midst of Hellenistic decay), mediaeval theocracy, Protestantism, capitalism, and socialism.

The difficulty with any such terms arises from the way in which economic patterns overlap upon one another. Sometimes we use our terms to designate the *distinctive* features of a pattern, sometimes we include features that it has in common with other patterns. Thus, when an average compatriot expresses his allegiance to *capitalism*, he is not considering merely the things that make it *different* from other economic systems. The symbol also includes for him such notions as family, friendship, neighborliness, education, medicine, golf, tools, sunlight, future, and endless other such sundries. When the orator shouts "Down with capitalism!" the auditor often resists because he is countering in secret, "I love the memory of the river bank where I lolled in the sun as a boy."

This problem of dissociation always arises to make trouble when conditions require a shift in our patterns of allegiance. Many men, attempting to reject a given symbol of authority, eventually get shunted into all sorts of "anti-social" attitudes, as they are sidetracked by the impact of social material adhering to this authoritative symbol. The better rounded a frame of acceptance is, the more such distortions tend to arise in those who would question it. Even Luther, whose Protestant frame is closely analogous to the Catholic pattern it replaced, could only prepare himself to admit his German princes by a psychology of satanism, which he solved very happily for himself by "projecting" his devil and throwing a bottle of ink at him. Milton's association with the anti-monarchist faction seems to have produced a similiar effect upon him, if his sympathetic portrait of Satan may be taken as evidence of the poet's "identification" with his subject. Nineteenth-century rejection frames abounded in satanistic elements. And many of our contemporary agitators, in their bellicose zeal that so obviously defeats its propagandist purposes, seem similarly affected, particularly when they seem to be inviting persecution, as a way of absolving them from some unavowed sense of guilt.

The endless "splintering" to which radical factions are subject may also at times derive from such irrational causes, no matter how thoroughly the impulse may be rationalized. If our conjecture is correct, it should be revealed in the tenor of the metaphors, which would show an hypertrophy of the defensive, with a tendency to cultivate the polemical for its own sake, even when the polemical defeated its propagandist purposes by stimulating in the audience resistance rather than compliance. Pseudonyms may also put us on the track of something, even when they are justified by practical necessities—for the man who must bear two names is also a man of two identities; and insofar as they are antithetical identities (one for a "capitalist" role and one for an "anti-capitalist" role) they make for a state of internal war, with one identity "rebuking" the other. A mere profession of rationalism cannot exorcise the issue, pride not being the mature attitude with which to confront a situation demanding humility.

When those patterns of thought are organized that give full body to the sectarian emphasis (as such opportunity is provided by the bodies of both theological and secular law, the first laying the grounds for "heresy," the second for "parties"), we may expect a tendency to "cash in on" such opportunities. Sectarianism is made negotiable by logic (and logic, as Marx says, is "the legal tender of the mind"). Hence, the bureaucratization of the imaginative possibilities, in the frame of orthodoxy, automatically invites an extension into the "polar opposite," heterodoxy. In the end, the organized and implemented pursuit of such thinking as can produce a catholic faith, continues until it has produced a sect; and so, as men further "move in on" these opportunities, in accordance with our "neo-Malthusian principle," they arrive at a sect-within-a-sect-within-a-sect. Which may be merely a technical way of saying that a historic trend, in developing the power to go *far enough*, by the same token develops the power to go *too far*. At this point it confronts its physical limits; and it tries to reverse the process of "splintering" (whereat you get the call for a "united front"). But:

The solution is not wholly a happy one. In men who have been trained to sectarian thought, too simple an attempt to reverse the direction of their thought becomes confusing. They are threatened with demoralization, in that the simple reversal of sectarianism is *opportunism*—and opportunism arises when the man schooled in sectarianism is dispossessed of his sect. In breaking down the clear lines of demarcation by which his character has been formed, the dispossessed sectarian is in danger of losing his character. In these pages we are trying to suggest that only by the adoption of a wider frame (essentially "comic") can this problem be met *actively, positively*. The comic frame relieves the pressure towards opportunism by a broadening, or maturing, of sectarian thought.

The proliferation of Protestant "splintering" goes naturally with the attempt to break a well-rounded frame of authority already established. Anthropologists have noted a similar phenomenon among savages, where the attempt to remove one feature of the cultural pattern (like head-hunting) tends to bring in its train the disintegration of the whole cultural pattern, even in areas where Western economic practices have not spread sufficiently to account for the disintegration, as with sea-coast tribes in Africa whose subsistence-economies have been destroyed by the Western imposition of the hut tax). In the Protestant countries, the atomistic, disintegrative tendencies that go with the breaking of a frame made eventually for business individualism. In the Catholic countries, where agrarian patterns interfered with the development of technology, the opportunities for business expansion were more restricted, and we got instead an emphasis upon anarchism. The business pattern sought a way back to synthesis in evolving the corporate identity of nationalism—and out of the humanitarianism that went with it, the outlines of socialism gradually emerged. The anarchist emphasis seems to have been working towards its way back in evolving the corporate identity of syndicalism. The Fascist state is another attempt to reestablish an integrative process by reference to corporate thought; insofar as its frame is erected upon the flat denial of economic contradictions, attempting to exorcise a bitter reality by a secular prayer, we should call it "sentimental," though the term is not usually applied to things so menacing.

THE DESTINY OF ACCEPTANCE FRAMES

A well-rounded frame serves as an amplifying device. Since all aspects of living tend to become tied together by its symbolic bridges, each portion involves the whole. Hence, the questioning of a little becomes amplified into the questioning of a lot, until a slight deviation may look like the abandonment of all society. This deceptive kind of magic also figures largely in the thinking of children (hence, applies to adults insofar as they are merely children-plus). A slight offense blackens the whole character; a "good deed" makes one "good all through." When there is a priesthood at hand, to exploit this "all or none" principle, a partial offense against a symbol of authority may be imaginatively aggravated, to make sure that, as the twig is bent in one matter, so it will be inclined in all matters.

Often, the defense against this is "dissociation," which in time leads to "atomism," "splintering." There is another strategy, however, which we might call the "stealing back and forth" of symbols. A sect maintains its integrative identification with the orthodoxy by insisting that it alone truly embodies the orthodox principle. The history of European apologetics thus shows the constant taking and retaking of strategic ideological redouts by rival factions. Thus, at one period you find the doctrine of the "divine right of Kings" being invoked *against* the church (on the plea that the secular sovereign, and not the theocracy, was entitled to represent "the people") ; and at another period you find the churchmen themselves appropriating the doctrine to justify their allegiance to the secular authority in power. Similarly, Marxism remains orthodox by "taking over" many slogans that derived their power from the prestige of bourgeois commercialism—and even the church, for all its "timelessness," now seems willing to forget its past, and to draw upon appeals to nationalism and "liberty."

(Incidentally, this stealing back and forth of symbols makes it difficult for the critic to disclose the *future* implications of a doctrine by merely noting to what use the doctrine had been put in the *past*.) *

The church has been pulled so far outside the framework of Thomist economics that some of the faithful can make proposals typical of the liberal distintegrative genius. Hilaire Belloc's project of "distributism," for instance, reveals its atomism in the quality of the very word he selects to call it by. As outlined in his recent book, *The Restoration of Property*, it offers an incongruous pastiche of protectionism and *laissez-faire*. The author would have the government (preferably a monarch) deliberately plant a lot of petty bourgeois seedlings, *independent* property owners, admired in the Adam Smith code. It takes us far from the heyday of Catholic theory when, as Croce has observed, "liberal" had the connotations of "licentious" and "servile" had the connotations of "loyal." Belloc is so far from the mediaeval connotations of the word "servile" as to call his picture of the bad state the "Servile State" (generously lumping Communist and Fascist states together under this heading). A writer in the *Commonweal*, when reviewing the book of his disciples in America, the Southern agrarians, suggests that an economic scheme should stress not *inde-*

---

* The "classical" procedure is for one faction to say, "This great thinker of the past is *ours*." And the opposition counters, "No, he is *ours*." But apologists sometimes make a surprising reversal, saying to the enemy, "*We* don't want him; *you* take him." Thus recently we saw a logomachist of the Left *insisting* that the enemy take Plato. We prefer the less generous procedure, since it gets us farther from a "symbolic burning of the books." One must learn *how to read* books, not *how to fear* them.

pendence, but *interdependence.* In this, the reviewer was nearer to Catholic origins than was Belloc, who is a convert.*

---

* Might the atomistic aspect of Belloc's proposals be linked, once more, to his concern with *shifts* in the symbols of authority? For he likens monopoly capitalism to a great tree, which he would kill; but having no instrument strong enough to fell it, he proposes to kill it by cutting off its leaves one by one. And his plan for the planting of petty bourgeois seedlings is called a plan of "re-afforestation." The metaphor suggests symbolic parricide: the author would slay the monopolist partriarch, planting his own little small-enterprise children in its stead. And the government (preferably a monarch) would seem to be his adoptive father, who remains aside from the childish squabbles, however, and merely intervenes now and then to protect the small children from the roughness of their big brothers.

CHAPTER FOUR

CONCLUSION

WE HAVE attempted, in the foregoing pages, to illustrate some of the major factors involved in the "strategy" of writing and thinking. We have tried to reveal the subterfuges to which the poet or thinker must resort, as he organizes the complexity of life's relationships within the limitations imposed by his perspective. He begins, we have said, with the "problem of evil." He finds good and evil elements intermingled. But he cannot leave matters at that. Exigencies of living require him to choose his alignments, by the devices of formal or "secular" prayer.

He builds his frames of acceptance or rejection by overt or covert acts of "transcendence." He coaches his set of meanings by an "act of will" that opens him to the charge of "sentimentality" on the part of those who would coach their meanings differently. He must choose his notions of essence, by either "transcendence upwards" or "transcendence downwards." And his symbols contain many "overtones"—they are "mergers"—they are "vessels"—they are acts of synthesis, capable of infinite analysis.

Hence, we next proceeded to discuss the broader aspects of symbolism, by noting some of the principal processes involved in political relationships (problems of synthesis and sect).

We hope, incidentally, to have so weighted our discussion that the comic frame will appear the most serviceable for the handling of human relationships. It avoids the dangers of euphemism that go with the more heroic frames of epic and tragedy. And thereby it avoids the antithetical dangers of cynical debunking, that paralyze social relationships by

CONCLUSION

discovering too constantly the purely materialistic ingredients in human effort.* The comic frame is charitable, but
at the same time it is not gullible. It keeps us alive to the ways
in which people "cash in on" their moral assets, and even
use moralistic euphemisms to conceal purely materialistic
purposes—but it can recognize as much without feeling
its disclosure to be the last word on human motivation.
Dealing with man in society, it requires maximum awareness of the complex forensic material accumulated in sophisticated social structures. By astutely gauging situation
and personal resources, it promotes the realistic sense of one's
limitations, hence has a proper ingredient of *"Entsagen,"*
yet the acceptance is not passive.

To say as much is not to imply that the other frames do
not have their uses. We should test the value of literature
as a *body*; we must not fall into the error of considering the
requirements of literature as though there were only one
book. Works vary in their range and comprehensiveness.
One man's character is but another man's mood. We are
simply suggesting that, when you lump the lot, discounting
each poetic category according to its nature, they seem to
add. up nearest to comedy. Which might be a roundabout
way of saying: whatever poetry may be, criticism had best
be comic.

* A reviewer recently cited with approval Chamfort's epigram:
"Whoever is not a misanthrope at forty has never loved mankind." That
is fair enough. We should add merely that the process of development is
not ended when the "thesis" of illusion has become the "antithesis" of
disillusion. A philosophy is an "entelechy," its "final cause" being something far more complex than either "goodwill advertising" on one hand
or "indictment" on the other, either "hagiography" or "iconoclasm."

PART II

THE CURVE OF HISTORY

CHAPTER ONE

CHRISTIAN EVANGELISM

IN OUR previous chapter we discussed "frames of acceptance and rejection" as exemplified primarily in various poetic categories. Here we shall center attention upon those "collective poems" evolved by the widest group activities. Our emphasis is not upon individual strategy, but upon the productive and mental patterns developed by aggregates. The two emphases are not mutually exclusive, since the individual's frame is built of materials from the collective frame, but the change from one to the other shifts the emphasis from the *poetic* to the *historical*.

As an agent organizes the logic of action with reference to the period in which he writes, the drama of the past must frequently be rewritten—and the last act in one version may even become the first act of a later version. The version of the early Christian poet Prudentius ended with God's establishment of the Roman Empire. Upon this sound material base, he felt, the complex superstructure of Christian symbolism could be erected. The doctrines that Constantine had legitimatized (in terms made ironical by subsequent etymological developments, since he had saluted the new religion as the "Christian heresy") were felt by Prudentius to be implemented by the communicative, productive, and military network of Rome. The last act of Prudentius' historical drama closed on this spectacle of invincibility—and a few years later, the barbarians were over-running the peninsula. We might conveniently begin where Prudentius ended.

In Act I of a drama we get the situation out of which the action will arise. It presents in a lump a myriad of prior dramas. We are shown the *gist* of these prior dramas—not their particularities. The opening situation for the drama of Western history, as written to-day, must take in a lump the accumulation of Mediterranean lore. The play begins with an intermixture of Hellenistic decay and Christian evangelism triumphant.

Past empires had built up much public equipment, that could be taken over by any co-operative enterprise. The new enterprise could take over a roadway that other enterprises had constructed, an established trading route by sea, a methodology of agricultural efficiency, a chart predicting eclipses, a belief in the divinity of a ruler (the identification of a king with "the people"), a structure of property relations, a grammar of thought. In short, a great many spiritual factors are "bureaucratized" in an objective, material order—and any new cultural enterprise must be built of this material. The resources perfected by previous empires, as those of Egypt, Babylon, Persia, and the Macedonians, were available to Rome. A roadway constructed by a power expanding westward could be retrod by a western power expanding eastward. The same applies to the habits of thought that are the spiritual counterpart of roadways.

For our Act I, we take all these resources as "the given." The great immobility of Egypt, constructed to utilize the periodicity of the Nile, was an important part of the given. And particularly as you moved towards the East, you found a similar condition. The literate culture was a crust, capable of crumbling, of shiftiness. The vocal documents that have survived mislead us somewhat, as we tend to feel that this voice was the representative voice of the times. A dance step is lost, the posture of men at work in the fields is lost—and insofar as this language was a different language from that of the Alexandrian library, the most important thing of all is lost; namely: the *percentage* of different cultural ingredients. The records that survive give disproportionate representation to the mobile crust, which was antithetical or compensatory rather than typical. That is: It utilized the *mobile opportunities* made available to the sophisticated few by the *immobility* of the unsophisticated many.

Change the underlying percentages, and you get a different cue for interpreting a voice. If a philosopher of Periclean Athens, for instance, speaks of man as the measure of all things, and means thereby the *individual* man, you must discover how many *collective* ingredients, how much deference to custom, was *assumed* in his statement before you know whether his words are representative or compensatory. That is, one may call individual man the measure of all things precisely because he *isn't*, precisely because one may be using a collective grammar that *permits* this luxury.

Thus, in the nineteenth century, our grammar permitted considerable vocalizing on the subject of "anarchism." One would not understand the statements in their full cultural bearing if one did not know that they coexisted with extreme regularity in the co-operative organization of railroad schedules. Printing, mails, education, bookstores—an enormous amount of such equipment had to be "taken for granted" by the speaker. And the horror of a non-anarchist, when the anarchist spoke, arose from the fact that the speaker made other allowances than the auditor. The anarchist generally used the word to designate an emphasis made *atop* this organization; the auditor resisted because, for him, the word designated organization *per se*, and he knew that you can't get a world *without* organization.

Act I confronts this problem. We suggest that the issue comes to a head in the ratio of mobility to immobility. The utterances of the forensic crust, during the period of Hellenistic decay, were mobile. Towards the end, the shifts in imperial authority were mobile. But there seems to have been a profound reserve of immobility, which conquerors usually left intact.

The Persian empire seems to have set the style. When including a new area, the Persian rulers did not attempt to revolutionize its internal order. They supplied as much new bureaucratic organization as would assure the collecting of revenues, and left the rest of the customary arrangements intact. Foreign invaders of Egypt acted much as a group of modern bankers might who, by the assistance of the "credit squeeze," were able to dispossess an industrialist and take over his factory. Some officials at strategic points might be replaced, but the general "customs" of the factory would be left as they were. Even innovations in method would be introduced by the customary technique. And when the Macedonian rulers, halfway between Greek and Persian thought, conquered the Greek city-states, they did not alter the form of Greek parliamentary practices. True, they meddled in the local political battles, backing one faction rather than another; they "exploited" local autonomy for monarchic ends; but they did not revolutionize the parliamentary pattern itself.

We have such situations in mind when we speak of "immobility," which is not radically impaired unless a conquered area is actually repeopled, as when Rome during its period of upbuilding cleared out the old inhabitants and settled its army on the appropriated lands. To-day, imperialism makes for revolutionary mobility by introducing a new technique of production, and recruiting in its service natives whose minds were formed by an older technique of production. But as regards our Mediterranean background in general, the outlying provinces were not subjected to such mobilization. They tithed for Rome, thereby producing the excess of commodities that (a) put Roman citizens out of work, and (b) supported them on the dole (the only mitigating arrangement possible to the given system of property relations).

Some measure of Hellenistic efficiency was introduced, to replace with new "scientific" methods earlier productive patterns grounded in custom. But most of this mobilization, that went with the rise of big plantations, occurred in the Latin peninsula itself, and in regions near the Latin peninsula. The outlying areas tended to persist in the productive order upheld by custom, providing the reserve of immobility that underlay the mobility of the Hellenistic cultural crust.

When beginning this book, we tended to resist the purely "economic" interpretation of history. We felt that the rise of great imperial integers could only be explained by reference to some "spiritual" force. But as we proceeded, we found the economic emphasis inescapable. For even if you assume that there is some "spiritual" factor operating at the imperial "core," the enterprising area from which the whole organization radiates, it still seems that the upbuilding of an empire as a whole can only be explained by economic factors.

Let us call it the "bandwagon" theory of history. A candidate for nomination appears strong—but he is not strong enough. The first several ballots disclose a deadlock. Then, of a sudden, something happens. There have been negotiations behind the scene; on the next ballot, the delegates of three more states are found to have switched their votes to this candidate. And on the following ballot, that process known as "climbing on the bandwagon" takes place. Delegates from other states, seeing how things are going, switch their votes (there are local plums to be picked, if you switch in time). The candidate gets a sweeping majority—and a few weeks later you find the very politicians who were opposing him so bitterly, now hurrying about the country to argue for his election.

You might say that the candidate's value as a "core" was "spiritual" (in the technical sense: for the word must be used to designate the "spirituality" of a Harding). But the bandwagon process as a whole is "economic," to be explained by one's apprehension lest he lose his political hide. Similarly when a state has become strong enough to be a candidate (as Rome did by her Latin coalitions), the adjacent areas have a choice between very risky resistance and the bandwagon. And once the bandwagon process is under way, its strength makes it stronger (so that the king of Pergamum "voluntarily" bequeaths his territories to Rome). Weak areas that would resist cannot attract the allies that would make their resistance effective.

We are *only now* ready for the "spiritual." The bandwagon has brought the group together—and on the basis of their togetherness they evolve, or seek to evolve, the appropriate co-operative slogans.

These slogans were perfected by Stoicism, the Roman theory of *"Weltbürgertum,"* the intellectual counterpart to the vast practical network of communications perfected by the early emperors. Piracy abated (both on the high seas, and among the knighted Roman business men, the *equites*, the *"novi homines"* who owned the voice of Cicero). A variant of the collective emphasis returned (the collective emphasis that had prevailed in primitive Rome when greater wealth "entitled" one to serve in the first line of battle, as it later entitled one to make money by selling supplies to hired armies).

It was undeniably erected above a non-collective system of ownership—but even here we must make a reservation. There *was* one notable respect in which the emperor's interests, as representative of the collective empire, militated against the interests of the other owners. It was "the emperor's" treasury that paid out the large sums needed to uphold the communicative network (its trade channels, its governmental bureaucracy, its army). The owner of latifundia could not completely identify his interests with the emperor's. Some of the largest proprietors were able to do so, but not the lesser proprietors. If the emperor confiscated a plantation, its revenues went to "him" (and "his" treasury really was the "public" treasury). Hence, as financial conditions became tighter, there was a growing tendency for the emperors to seek pretexts whereby these proprietors could be dispossessed, particularly if, when some darling of the army seized power, they had been slow in climbing on the bandwagon.

So the theory of state collectivism, in the Stoics' frame of acceptance, was not a mere sentimental fraud. We can say merely that it centered about a "contradiction" throughout the imperial era. As a representative of monopoly, the emperor was the upholder of property rights—but since "he" paid the expenses of running the empire, he did come into conflict with lesser monopolists, other owners of latifundia. Financial necessities prompted him to seize wealth wherever it was available, as a steel trust might now seek favorable legislation at the expense of cotton merchants. The costs of maintaining his major political monopoly often induced him to confiscate the revenues of the minor monopolists.

It has even been suggested that much of the moralistic vilification attached to such characters as Nero arose from this conflict. Imperial policies for the architectural development of Rome were not wholly in keeping with the ideals of the speculators in real estate. And the literary voices employed by this outraged class, and using its stylistic insignia, paid for their keep in the customary currency of moral indignation. (We can understand the situation somewhat by recalling the contemporary resistance, on the part of business interests, to governmental housing projects. Nor have the documents of moral indignation been lacking.) It is interesting to note, incidentally, how closely the moral imagery employed, even by such pagans as Suetonius, reflected the moral patterns of emergent Christianity. Because of this close fit, when Christian values triumphed, the "permanence" of the imperial portraits followed as a matter of course. They were painted in the "fast colors" of the rising Christian morality.

Since the public buildings were the emperor's buildings, much of his "personal" squandering necessarily had a collectivist feature, as with the great baths and amphitheaters erected throughout the empire. Before the period when this mighty bureaucratic pyramid had crystallized, and there was still a large measure of private business enterprise, the taxes became regularized, so that communities could plan on a basis of steady expectations. As things became tighter, there was a tendency, like the earlier practice in Greece, to meet public expenses by putting wealthy citizens in office, and requiring munificent outlays from them in exchange for the "honor." Ironically, as the financial situation tightened, we see a subtle reversal in the connotations of this practice, until public honor became a form of punishment, visited upon wealthy Christians and Jews.*

---

* Such shifts in the connotations of a practice are always of great importance in providing us with cues for the interpretation of a curve in history. The classic example, noted by anthropologists, is the shift in

CHRISTIAN EVANGELISM

Stoic cosmopolitanism was developed by those who were most concerned with the communicative aspects of the Roman economic integer. In other words, it was a state philosophy; and humane, humanistic, in laying its main stress upon *man in society* (rather than upon man in nature, or man as a future citizen of heaven). It even served to mitigate the rigors of slavery, which it never "justified," but looked upon as a condition requiring improvement. In the end, of course, the Stoic frame of acceptance "resigned" itself to slavery, since it was developed for the consumption of a literate class who were not slaves, so that even educators who were or had been slaves formed their stylistic identity by adopting the insignia of the privileged. It taught that man was too limited, and the problem was too big, for a complete remedy to be possible. But it looked *in the direction* of slavelessness, since the co-ordinates of Stoicism were essentially humane.

Today, we are impressed, and depressed, by its nostalgic quality. The economic integer seems to have been too big

---

the meaning of the service exacted of males at marriage. Originally, presumably in a matriarchal stage of property relationships, it was customary for the male to pledge so many years of servitude to the bride's family as part of the marriage contract. But the rise of stock-breeding (carried on by the males, who had originally been the hunters in the primitive division of labor along lines of sexual differentiation, with agriculture mainly plied by women) changed the connotations of such service by putting the male line in possession of "money."

The "ox" became the normative unit of exchange—and we might say that the first "inflation" took place when a real ox was replaced by a symbolic ox, a coin having the nominal value of an ox. Here we get the first working of Gresham's Law, according to which, when there are two kinds of money, the "baser" drives the "sounder" out of circulation. Hence, the symbolic ox replaced the real ox as the unit of exchange, to establish a pecuniary basis for commerce (Latin: *pecus*, cattle). By this development, when hunting became "bureaucratized" as stock-breeding, the

for a *positive* communicative frame that would match the communicative network of commerce. Confronting the subjectivism that went with the jumble of distinct cultural integers (all brought together into one economic frame) it could only assimilate the confusion negativistically, by agnosticism and eclecticism. The emperor might solidify his relations with each conquered tribe by bringing images of the local gods to Rome—but such a mechanical transference of the pivotal religious symbols did not integrate the deeper aspects of the local *mores*.

Thus the communicative frame developed by the Stoic crust was abstract and superficial. It was more like the co-ordination that we get by a telephone exchange than the co-ordination of intimacy, as in the *rapport* between Shakespeare and his audiences. It communicated by semaphore signals, rather than by the subtleties of intonation that go with the language of a tribal integer. It was an *official* phi-

---

property of money" shifted to the male line. But the social order was still based on the matriarchal system, organized about the forms of property that preceded stock-breeding. In this matriarchal system, the male "earned" his bride by servitude in the wife's family. The new order, by providing him with money, enabled him to hire someone else for his service. In time, this practice came to mean simply that he "paid" for his woman. Hence, a custom that began with connotations of male servitude ended with connotations of male superiority, as the male simply *bought* a woman The process is charted in Briffault's *The Mothers*—and though some may hold that he is excessive in seeing evidences of a primitive matriarchate everywhere, none could deny that his testimony applies on many occasions.

We have elsewhere noted the shift in the connotations of "liberal" and "servile," as the revelation of a historic curve. We might here note another variant, in the fact that, even in the late nineteenth century, "servitude" meant to the Polish peasant the "right" to take firewood from the lord's estate. In denying him this right, one denied him his "servitude," because of the ambivalence latent in such concepts. Perhaps these

losophy, designed for broad, administrative ends—its literate adherents were either managers, or purveyors of ideas for the consumption of the managerial class.

Divorced from the humbler forms of personal exoneration, or "justification," that went with physical toil, it was also divorced from the physical vitalizing to be derived from such modes of effort. Its "work" was not in lifting things, but in *overseeing* the lifting of things. Some of its nostalgia must have been quite like that of those to-day in sedentary occupations, or sedentary leisure, who develop strange discomfitures simply because the physical resources of their muscles and organs are denied expression (and in the economy of the body, any capacity that is not given expression is "frustrated"). All these minus signs were canceled by a bowing of the head before the abstract plus-sign of serviceability to the needs of the state.

For the soldiers, the slaves, the illiterate, the passionate

---

subtle shifts are the most important thing of all, for historic analysis.

The shift most germane to our present disord〔 〕s is the one whereby the "right" to sell one's services has become the *need* to have one's services sold. This ironic turn was implicit in the beginnings of bourgeois liberalism, when one "freed" the serf of his bondage to the soil by *alienating* his customary rights to the use of the soil. Eventually we get to Anatole France's parable, where the homeless man sleeping under the bridge is as "free" as the man of great wealth. It is the basis of the comic ambivalence in Marx's interpretation whereby the "freedom" obtained through wages became "wage-slavery."

Such ambivalence is obscured in contemporary liberal apologetics (of the American Liberty League sort) by the campaign to make collective security look like individual slavery. It is made possible by the fact that liberal thinkers, of even the best sort, have usually been sublimely impervious to the problem of ambivalence. They talked enthusiastically of "rights," without much concern for the *obligations* that were their counterpart.

(those who could not be content with the nostalgia of abstraction, inanition, "alienation") its doctrine was not enough. Hence, the rise of Christianity, another universalizing doctrine, among such people. It had gained favor in the smaller trading centers, where the confusions of cultural interchange were felt, but where the peculiarly Roman attitude towards the problem of integration was necessarily weak. In place of the abstract Stoic absolute, the cult of the state, it proposed an "intimate" absolute, a single personal god with whom one could carry on the subtlest kind of commercial transactions, wheedling and haggling and bargaining for relief. In rites like the love-feast, the *agape*, it developed a deeper, positive magic that the Stoic philosophy of administrative co-ordination ignored. Here, in one ceremony, there was put together: collective communion with other men and supernatural power, the purification of guilt, and the gathering of strength by the symbolic eating of the god (a ritual that all of the tribal integers had utilized in one form or another). Again, the many burial societies of late Rome were a good field for recruiting, since Christian evangelism had much to tell those who had banded together, in a primitive kind of insurance brotherhood, to make financial arrangements with regard to death.

Act I of our historical drama must stress these two themes. Hellenistic Stoicism in decline, Christian evangelism emergent, each of them a *world view* to match the Roman cosmopolitan *orbis terrarum*, as developed by the *pax Romana*. And the Stoic forensic patterns schematized the legalistic material which the evangelical doctrine could eventually borrow when its somewhat vague promises of a better day had to be fitted into the practical requirements of a going concern. If you would end Act I on a strong curtain, you may restate Prudentius' picture, of the divine and worldly interweaving, and then shift abruptly to the barbarians' sack of Rome. For a quiet curtain, we propose two other events:

One, Constantine's official recognition of the "Christian heresy." The other, the imperial edicts *fixing* the status and location of workers. It had been found that the burdens of taxation were leading to mobility among the populace. This made the problem of taxation difficult, since a high tax on workers in a given trade led them to change their trade or to move elsewhere. The needs of immobilization were met by legislative decree. But with immobility established by fiat at a time when drastic economic pressure stimulated mobility, people had to "take up the slack" somehow. There had to be a differential. This was supplied by Christianity, which offered a "spiritual freedom" to compensate for the deprivation of much-needed material freedom. By it, a man could be tied to one place, and yet range far.

CHAPTER TWO

MEDIAEVAL SYNTHESIS

THERE is no unearned increment in living. Each man, in whatever situation he is placed, must undergo an extra-curricular education. It is no mere pious fraud, for making a man content with adversity, to say that privileges also can be an impoverishment unless the privileged can prod themselves to the kind of exertion necessary for surmounting the handicaps of privilege. By the economy of the body, people are endowed for struggle. If they do not struggle, they rot, which is to say that they struggle in spite of themselves. Give them "leisure," and unless they transcend it by supplying new forms of effort, they suffer the recondite neuroses of the "psychologically unemployed." Let them go where they want on wheels, and they discover new forms of uneasiness through not using their legs.

This need of struggle, this physically grounded commandment that the resources of strain be utilized, can be linked with the human need for *justification*. One must "prove himself right," by some form of practical or esthetic composition. One must acquire ways of making himself at home in his situation (the lowest form of such mastery being, perhaps, the moral obligation to accumulate commodities, as developed under bourgeois criteria of advancement). People buy refrigerators, not merely to keep their butter hard, but to show that they "belong." And the writers of advertising copy consistently play upon this hunger for "justification," no matter how "enlightened" their notions of human motivation may be.

An interview with Malraux, recently published in *The New Republic*, deals explicitly with this problem of "earning." If a man tells you that he loves the people, Malraux says, the declaration means nothing. But if Krupskaya, at Lenin's death, says "Lenin loved the people," the statement moves him profoundly. For here, what "comes after" gets its meaning from what "goes before." This relation between the "goes before" and the "comes after" is at the basis of cultural issues.

An inventor, for instance, makes some momentous discovery. It is the subtle synthesis of countless unchartable factors in his personal life. In putting together this instrumentality, he incidentally puts together many aspects of his life that are wholly lost upon those of us who, approaching the invention from without, as a mere material contrivance, the mummification of a life purpose, simply "use" it, in the bare utilitarian sense. In time, a great many such contrivances accumulate, and we "use" them. All that "went before," in the personal drama of the inventor, who is giving us his version of a profoundly intimate poem, is ignored, leaving us solely with what "came after." In using such contrivances, without having "earned" them as their inventor did, we may become much like barbarians among monuments of a culture to which they are alien.

There is but one way of avoiding such impoverishment, such *inanition*. We must *earn* an inheritance by taking it as the basis of a new problem. Confronting it as the "goes before," we must train ourselves to develop a new "comes after." If we do not, if the clutter becomes greater than we can creatively assimilate, if we merely squander our inheritance rather than making it the basis of a new "job," the process of "alienation" is under way. Life becomes "empty." A man may devote twenty years to the invention of some new labor-saving device. Its psychological value to him resides precisely in the amount of labor it *caused*, not the amount it *saved*. His individual salvation is our collective damnation, unless we erect a new logic of effort atop its performance. Otherwise, we are emptied, that he may be full.

The Christian frame of acceptance, that arose from the cluttered accumulations of Rome, and finally attained its completion in the Summa of Aquinas, dealt explicitly with this problem of guilt, justification, earning and alienation. Herein lay its appeal—and herein lay the poignancy that went with the need of renouncing it, when a class of people had "moved in on" its opportunities, stretching them to their "Malthusian limits," so that the whole course of history had to be altered, if people were actively to earn their world anew.

We see the whole curve, by merely charting the sequence in which the great monastic orders were established. First came the Benedictines, groups of loosely federated monks who spread the knowledge of the humanities. Next arose the orders devoted to hospitality, that indicate the beginnings of a new mobility. In time we come to the *fighting* orders whose pugnacity, for all the face-saving fictions of penance and indulgence, revealed dissatisfaction with the growing economic pressure. And significantly, the last order before the Protestant crash was that of the Franciscans, who sought to make a vocation of the *mendicant*, thereby turning the passivity of the beggar into a positive purposiveness. And *after* the Reformation you get the propagandists, the relativistic Jesuits, who sought to reclaim Europe for Catholicism by translating old doctrine into the new terminology. (Addendum, 1955: Clearly, the recent rise of the "worker priests" in France reflects the influence of Marxism, by seeking more direct ways of proselytizing among the industrial workers.)

126

We might consider the monastic orders, paradoxically, as "incipient heresies." Each of them, in obedience to the historical emphases of its time, stressed some *particular aspect* of the faith, endangering the symmetry of the whole by making it the *all-important* aspect. The orthodoxy managed to reshape its frame so as to admit the order, thus inoculating the incipient heresy by finding a place for it in the bureaucratic totality. But the order of Saint Francis came near the breaking point; for a long time there was doubt whether it would be proclaimed a heresy or a new order. It was probably admitted because it arose in Italy, and so was able to commend itself in terms closest to the thinking of the central authorities. Similar movements further North, such as the Waldenses, lacking this strategic advantage, the incipiently heretical became the out-and-out heretical.

As for the Jesuits, they disturbed the orthodox as much as they disturbed the Protestants. Attempting to reclaim Protestantism for Catholicism by recommending Catholicism in Protestant terms, they developed a relativistic technique wholly alien to Catholic absolutism in its heyday—and insofar as Catholic thinkers remembered their heyday, they resisted it, quite as Catholic thinkers to-day *should* be against nationalism and business enterprise, if they remembered their heyday.

But the church does move, for all its timelessness—and we may even imagine some eventual day in the future of Russia when thinkers will find it necessary to make radical changes in the nature of socialism; and we may imagine the Greek Orthodox church re-established, accepted by the political authorities because all its officials are staunch Communists; and, if this time comes when important shifts in the patterns of effort are found necessary, we may imagine the church itself rising up to excommunicate, condemn, and mark for slaughter those earnest men who would explain why and how the necessary changes should be made.

Act II of our historic drama is concerned with the frame of mediaeval feudalism, so thoroughly interweaving a vast symbolic architecture with the concomitant patterns of production that the confusions arising from our attempts to reshape it are with us still.

With astounding exactitude, as we have said, it built upon the foundations of human guilt, subtly contriving both to intensify people's sensitivity to the resources of guilt (making two opportunities for guilt grow where but one had grown before) and to allay this guilt by appropriate rituals and by acts of loyalty to the social status established by custom.

Following Augustine, Thomist thought attributed government, property, and slavery to the judgment of God, as penalty for the fall of Adam. The established order was thus God's order—and in questioning it, one questioned God himself. Churchmen were admittedly not perfect, but the Church, as the earthly incorporation of the body of Christ, *was* perfect. Hence by membership in the church, one shared perfection vicariously, so that the incentive to "justify" oneself by extreme individual initiative ("ambition") was sidetracked.

There was an "organic" theory of society: it was not asked that people be all alike, as in the later Protestant communities; there were those who fought, those who worked, and those who prayed, each kind of effort contributing its part to the general welfare. (Its organic theory "transcended" the discordancies of noble and serf by a "synthesizing" reference to their common citizenship in heaven.) The whole made a building, a piece of cultural architecture comprising both practical and spiritual materials (methods of production and symbolism)—and the *static* implications in the architectural metaphor were stressed.

The other key metaphor was that of the family. Sociologists have said that we should consider primitive tribes, not as small communities, but as large families. The Thomist frame developed this *familial* perspective to universal limits. The church bureaucracy was pictured as a large-scale replica of family relationships, with "fathers," "mothers," "brothers," "sisters," "Father," and "Mother" (a particularly serviceable pattern in that it readily shunts the erring son into the role of symbolic parricide). From this metaphor there flowed the need of obedience to authority, as embodied in custom. In families one does not "vote." Authority does not arise by deputation, as in parliamentary procedure—it just is where it is, being grounded in the magic of custom. And family affections cannot find their exact quantitative equivalent in money.

Any resistance to this frame, at any point, was necessarily felt as "guilt," hence the frame tended to be self-sustaining. Guilt is misery, and misery loves company—and so the impulses of guilt could reenforce collectivistic effort. In joining with other men, a man absolved himself.

The earlier evangelical frame had lacked finish. It had not become interwoven with the productive pattern in its broadest aspects. It was *extreme* in ways that the Thomist pattern was not. For Thomism, like all complete orthodox faiths, had developed the *compromises* required to fit a theory of spiritual perfection into a material "imperfect world." It is the heretics who get themselves driven into a corner, forced by a mixture of logical consistency and social pressure to distort the percentage of the cultural ingredients. The heretics will decide *either* that there is free will *or* there is determinism—the orthodoxy, by manipulating some intermediate passes with a doctrine of grace, will decide that there is free will *and* determinism. Heretics will decide that, if the body is sinful, we should humiliate the body, even by indulgence in all manner of evil. The orthodoxy, while maintaining that the body is prone to sinfulness, will also admonish that life in the body prepares for eventual citizenship in heaven, with a purified body. Hence, whereas the earlier evangelical frame was uncompromising in its genius (leaving a man with a flat choice between saintliness and corruption), the Thomist frame introduced gradations. There were "stages," there was a "graded series," there were mitigating fictions whereby a man poor in religiosity could yet consider himself religious.

We have noted how the roads built for expansion westward could also be used by a power expanding eastward. The church's mitigating fictions were also of this sort. They helped to eliminate the "either-or" by a theory of "both-and." One need not be either saintly or corrupt: one could be both saintly and corrupt. (Specifically, one could be evil by inheriting Adam's fall, and good by vicariously sharing Christ's perfection through membership in the church, the *corpus Christi*.) Such mitigating fictions made it possible to go far along the road towards corruption without abandoning the sense of reclamation. But like the eastward-westward road, this device was ambivalent. For it made compromise easy; a saving grace could be found for any policy. Naturally, there was a tendency to exploit such an excellent device to its Malthusian limits.*

---

* Aesop takes the adage, "Persuasion is better than force," and expands it into the fable of the contest between the north wind and the sun. "The North Wind first tried his power, and blew with all his might: but the keener became his blasts, the closer the Traveller wrapped his cloak

MEDIAEVAL SYNTHESIS

It is doubtful whether all heresies can be explained "economically." The mind is enterprising—it will "earn" the world for itself by making its own inventions atop the inventions of others—and this pressure might be enough to account for heretical emphases. But when a heresy recruits a large group, and leads to active resistance, and even the use of force, on the part of the orthodoxy, *here* we may look for economic factors.

The economic factor enters when different factions have "moved in on" the resources afforded by the orthodoxy and the resources afforded by the heresy, so that clashing modes of life are organized about the symbolic differences. (The symbols of controversy, in other words, become "vessels" containing more than is made apparent by their "labels" alone, as Darwinism in nineteenth-century Germany was not merely an issue in pure science, but a vessel of bourgeois protest against the survivals of feudalism.) This process would occur even without the rise of new cultural materials

---

around him; till at last, resigning all hope of victory, he called upon the Sun to see what he could do. The Sun suddenly shone out with all his warmth. The Traveller no sooner felt his genial rays than he took off one garment after another, and at last, fairly overcome with heat, undressed, and bathed in a stream that lay in his path."

The institution of the confessional was an ingenious variant of this story. The church's poets and psychologists well understood the disastrous accumulative power of silence. They knew that speech is curative. And they invented the kinds of philosophic sunning that could induce one to strip himself bare.

In fact, they made a man act as his own detective. "Of his own free will" he made confessions that would otherwise have remained inaccessible to his spiritual overseers.

A hypothetical case might illustrate the ways in which this resource could be misused. Imagine a company union that hired psychologists to "cure" the workers of "neuroses." The workers' confessions must be

(new instruments of production and defense, or the increase of money that imperiled the rationale of the mediaeval subsistence economy, or the plagues that gave workers better bargaining power in their demand for more of this money.) But it is made more acute when new factors further bewilder the old frame, which is not designed to encompass them.

If the frame of acceptance makes for obedience (as with the family metaphor of feudalism), you may expect the gradual organization of people who "tap" this vein until it is exhausted. It is a resource for exploitation, as any frame is—and the particular opportunity it offers will eventually be seized upon with "efficiency," until the "Malthusian limits" of the opportunity are reached. This process endangers the serviceability of a frame. And of course, the rise of new material, which it had not been designed to handle, endangers the frame still further.

---

wholly frank, otherwise they are not effective. They must, for instance, confess each occasion on which they felt "tempted" to join an outside union, a union beyond the jurisdiction of the company.

We do not mean to imply that the confidences of the confession were divulged, as if the psychologists of the company union were to hand on these important tips to their employers. If you defined the temptation to join an outside union as being in itself "neurotic," it would follow "by strict logic" that a worker could only hope to be "cured" if he and his father confessor collaborated in "freeing" him of this "temptation." Hence, so long as he accepted the premises, he himself was doing the detective work that kept him "in line."

The church's frame was adapted to the maintenance of the established property relationships. Hence, in questioning it at any point, you were automatically "being tempted with the thought of joining an outside union." And in being "cured" of this "temptation," you automatically did all in your power to preserve the established property relationships.

In the end, however, this very perfection aggravated the disorder, as

MEDIAEVAL SYNTHESIS

For a time the frame will be extended to meet the new necessities by casuistic stretching. We note the element of casuistry in the Thomist doctrines of compromise, made necessary as the church developed from the Platonic, otherworldly emphasis of the evangelical period to the Aristotelian realism of a worldly, going concern. We have noted it in the devices whereby incipient heresies were often reclaimed for the orthodoxy as monastic orders. And we may note it in the legal fictions by which the mediaeval proscriptions against the taking of interest were ingeniously nullified to allow for the investments of the popes and for the borrowings of ambitious sovereigns. Whereas originally *all* interest was usury, these fictions gradually made for a subtle distinction between usury and interest.

But there comes a point when casuistry no longer serves. Its ambivalent method of reclamation is carried too far. Itself a way of stretching the frame, it in turn is stretched,

---

the higher authorities "moved in on" it, exploiting to the breaking point its resources as a promoter of obedience.

We note a similar manifestation lurking in the South's distinction between "good niggers" and "bad niggers." The "good nigger" is one who accepts his inferior status and makes the best of it. His "social superiors" do often reward him for his phenomenal gentleness. But also they "move in on" it, by permitting conditions among Negroes as a whole to increase in wretchedness. Finally, there are some Negroes who simply cannot get the rewards of obedience and subjection. There is not enough charity to go around. And the Negroes that show resentment at this are punished, in one way or another. They are thus "driven into a corner." Their resentment, by the operation of the vicious circle, becomes "creative," as their superiors match it by further punishments or withholding of rewards. In the end, these Negroes who have "dropped through the bottom," become the "bad niggers." And so you are told simply that there are good niggers and bad niggers—and you are shunted away from an accurate criticism of the economic factors, with their psychological counterparts, aggravating the distinction.

until in the end it is felt, not as reclamation but as demoralization. Some of us, for instance, feel demoralization rather than reclamation in the casuistic stretching to which conservative members of the Supreme Court have subjected the original frame of the Constitution, as they supply new legal fictions to encompass new material arising since the Constitution was framed.

So a frame will be stretched until it breaks. And as it nears this breaking point, we find three important symptoms: Besides casuistry and force, we note increased reliance upon whatever resources for *prayer* the frame may provide. The mediaeval frame offered exceptional resources in this respect, owing to the great body of men whose vocation made them specialists in prayer. So they met the stringencies of the "moving in on" process, in its most aggravated phase, by petition and invective. In short, they threatened to force the recalcitrant beyond the pale of the orthodoxy's "graded series" for salvation. The period of Protestantism was at hand.

CHAPTER THREE

PROTESTANT TRANSITION

ACT III is our "peripety," with a radical turn in the arrows of the plot. Here is the act of marked transition, the "watershed" of the historic drama. Renaissance and Reformation. At this point, a *negativistic* emphasis becomes organized, both in the materials of pure thought and in economic implementation. Beginning with a plea for the separation of the church and state, we formally inaugurate the dissociative process that will end with the theoretical separation of everything—a few centuries later, religion will be in one bin, politics in another, art in another, science in another, business in another—and there will be subdivisions, each in its own separate bin. We have even wondered whether the ideal might have attained its ultimate symbolization in the modern physiologists' dream of bearing children outside the mother, so that even mother and embryo are separated." Keep the government out of business." "Keep business out of the government." Keep the judiciary independent of the administrative and legislative functions. Keep the educators out of public affairs. Keep everything out of everything else—and then complain that things are in pieces, that there are "no longer any great men" who see the situation in its entirety. Yearn to put Humpty Dumpty together again—and at the same time be askance at the integrative trend in Russia.

Every period in history is transitional, but the period intermingling Renaissance enlightenment with Protestant fanaticism and emergent bourgeois enterprise is exceptionally so. We could never chart the bewildering ways in which one man's intelligence became another man's stupidity, as the anti-religious and non-religious speculation of abstract thought finally filtered down until, among less accomplished minds, it manifested itself in the vicious Wars of Religion. Or the ways in which individualistic enterprise, stimulated by colloquial translations of the Bible, whereby every man could become his own interpreter without training in the collective body of interpretation accumulated by the church, served to intermingle material ambition with high moral motives (an integrative structure that was not dissociated until we reach the "economic psychoanalysis" of Bentham's utilitarianism in the nineteenth century, with its doctrine that moral motives were a "eulogistic covering" for material interests).

Sincerity and guile were as hopelessly interwoven as enlightenment and stupidity. The men who enunciated the doctrine of the "poor church" probably meant just what they said: that the church should not be rich, like a Babylonian whore, but poor, like Christ—but their doctrine became "economically implemented" when ambitious sovereigns used the doctrine to justify the appropriation of church lands for themselves and their clique, thereby upsetting the feudal ties and eventually taking from the peasants whatever collective property rights they did possess.

In the feudal pattern, the casuistic fictions had tended to confine "investment for profit" to a comparatively small class of rulers and big churchmen. In Calvinism, this "salvation device" was "democratized"—as Calvin discarded the legalistic subterfuges and placed a positive sanction upon the taking of "interest" in general. His notions of Providence "transcended" the conflicting clutter, that amounted to demoralization, since the reality of a monetary practice was being sentimentally denied. And his spiritual symbol was "economically implemented" by the ambivalence whereby the spiritual futurism of "providence" could be equated with the worldly futurism of "investment."* This move, so necessary to the development of business enterprise, was further backed by a new philosophy of justification, with more modern connotations of "ambition."

In the church pattern, the priestly role alone had been a "vocation." And one who got too far from thoughts of it, devoting too great attention to practical enterprises, was rebuked as being "idly solicitous" of worldly goods (the congruity of this to us discordant pair that makes "idleness" synonymous with "busyness," being perfectly apparent to one trained in the feudal frame, with its particular notions of "vocation"). But Calvinism found that one could make profits for the glory of God—every trade was a "vocation" —and if one worried lest, by Calvinist doctrine, he was one predestined by God for damnation, let him attain material prosperity as the visible sign of God's favor.

There was the negativism of the "inductive method," Descartes' doctrine of "organized doubt" that proposed to convert the state of uncertainty into a positive, creative principle. It has since shown its fertility, in technological advance—but among simpler souls, the entertaining of even a partial "suspended judgment" must have led to the impatient reconstitution of certainty, *any* certainty. And the non-transcendental theory of motives, inaugurated with Machiavelli's discourse on worldly power, provided a rationalization of acts in frank accordance with criteria of

* The reversal is not complete until in the early nineteenth century we arrive at Bentham. Whereas the scholastics had condemned all interest categorically as "usury," and Calvin introduced a nice distinction between interest and usury, Bentham justified the taking of interest in a formal "Defence of Usury."

material aggrandizement (an attitude that was at first confined to high places, but eventually became more "democratized" as resources for private enterprise became progressively organized, beginning largely with the development of businesses for equipping the sovereigns' armies).

As we have noted elsewhere, the ambiguities of "alienation" played an important role here. Bourgeois "freedom" was no greater a boon for many people at the start of its career than it appears to be at the finish. In England, thousands of the "freed" seem to have simply starved as the new proprietors who took over the land frequently abandoned farming for the financially more profitable raising of sheep for wool. Less hands were required for this work, and the people who were dispossessed of the old economy were without sustenance, except those who could migrate to the factory towns and be absorbed by the rising industries. Those caught in a "stagnant pool of unemployment" midway between the two economies were further handicapped by the fact that the charitable institutions of the church had been greatly crippled. This whole process of alienation, and changing productive methods, was "rationalized" by the quantitative tests of profit which the increased use of money and the development of accountancy made possible.

But while it is hard to discuss the rise of Protestantism without considering it as the adumbration of the capitalistic frame (an intermingling of Catholic orthodoxy, misused science, and quantitative, monetary norms for the guiding of human effort by a shift from "Mystery to Mathematics," to borrow a formula from the magnificent close of Pope's *Dunciad*) we should be wrong in approaching it from this angle alone. In many ways the Protestant community had much the same mystical homogeneity as the early Christian sects. Nevertheless, here also we get a paradox: How, in contrast with the church's "organic" theory, whereby one put a going social concern together by the toleration of *differences*, the Protestant sects stressed the value of *complete uniformity*. Each time this uniformity was impaired, the sect itself tended to split, with a new "uncompromising" offshoot reaffirming the need for a homogeneous community, all members alike in status. Yet from this doctrine of homogeneity there arose the greatest heterogeneity of occupations the world has ever known. The Protestant doctrine of secular vocations stimulated technological developments that led far beyond the ideals of uniformity inherent in Protestant sectarianism.

The thought suggests another important co-ordinate for the charting of a historical curve. We must note how a given frame tends to develop by-products. In aiming at one thing, we incidentally bring about something else. Such cultural by-products are of many sorts—and they lead to the full range of "alienation," as regards the people's participation in both material and spiritual properties.

When "by-products" have accumulated to the point where they are more important as cultural factors than the historic emphasis out of which they arose, a new shift in the methodology of purpose is necessary. Unfortunately, the old purpose has, by this time, attained its full bureaucratic embodiment throughout the legislative, educative, and constabulary functions. People are *taught* adherence to the older system of authority; political mechanisms are organized to enact laws in accordance with its spirit; and there is an efficient hierarchy of police to coerce those whom the cultural misfit compels to be "criminals."* "Cultural lag,"

---

* The constabulary function gains greater prominence in proportion as the state of misfit is aggravated. We now take a vast constabulary structure as "normal," considering only the ways for making it most

"class morality," and "inner contradictions" thus become interchangeable terms, as a special group becomes organized whose mode of prosperity *requires* the retention of the alienating by-products. They may not want the by-products, as they may not want slums. But they do want the rationale of purpose that produces these by-products, as they want the system of profits that makes for slums. And by utilizing their control upon the channels of authority, they "train" the mind and force the mind to want the "right" things.†

Insofar as these things are *not* the "right" things, insofar as they are not framed to take the "unintended by-products" properly into account, we get "alienation." To avoid this "inanition" or "emptying" *("Entfremdung")*, a new frame of acceptance is required that "transcends" the older scheme of purposes, quite as Calvinism's sanctioning of in-

---

"honest" and "efficient," generally unmindful of the fact that the proliferation of constabulary functions follows the same curve of development as the proliferation of habits involving a "stake in" capitalism.

† Is our concept of the "neo-Malthusian principle" still vague? This principle names the process whereby a certain set of habits, in attaining its full bureaucratic embodiment, proliferates to its physical limits. In a sense it is another word for the "vicious circle," since the proliferation gives rise to arrangements that call for still further proliferation, as capitalism generated modes of work that required one to be intensely capitalistic in equipping himself for them. The rise of Protestantism, coupled with technological advance and the bourgeois system of ownership, made an exceptional amount of individual enterprise both possible and necessary. The possibilities were necessarily utilized, until in time the whole social order became organized about the efficient utilization of these possibilities. This efficiency, as backed by the material order, equals "bureaucratization." And as such bureaucratization matured, the corresponding set of habits proliferated toward its "Malthusian limits." At this point, we find "class privilege" functioning as "cultural lag," since there is a group profiting by precisely the extreme bureaucratization that

vestment transcended the mediaeval theories in which investment had arisen as a by-product. But since the older frame has implicated itself in all the symbols of authority, which is itself a *social* manifestation, a shift of authority may drive its earlier prophets into a corner, leading to "antisocial" emphases. This manifests itself psychologically as "negativism," "dissociation," "disintegration," "sectarianism," "splintering." Or else it is compensated by a strategic solution, the "stealing back and forth" of authoritative symbols. When advocates of the old order have built up the prestige for such symbols as "liberty, justice, fraternity," a proponent of the new order may frame his apologetic so as to "take them over." Particularly in America to-day, there is much strategic maneuvering for the possession of the symbol "liberty," as the representatives of the dispossessed and the representatives of the big possessors both lay siege to it in the battle of words, the monstrous and strident "logomachy" that accompanies the "stealing back and forth" of symbols.

---

causes suffering to another group, and the profiting class utilizes its hold on the bureaucratic resources to maintain the disturbing set of habits to the breaking point.

The function of the neo-Malthusian principle, as backed by the "bureaucratization of the imaginative," may be illustrated by a simple ratio comparing the mediaeval church with modern art: church (bureaucratization) is to religion (imaginative) as academy is to art.

Bureaucratization equals the tendency to "move in on" and "cash in on." As this tendency advances toward the breaking point, indicated by casuistic stretching, we get a maximum reliance upon "prayer." Prayer has its obverse in "invective" (a "sailing into"). Its secular, forensic equivalent is *legislation*, which utilizes the bureaucratic organization of the law to exorcise evil symptoms, not removing the causes, but by acts of verbal excommunication. Verbal excommunication may, in turn, be given "reality" as the legislative pronouncers of anathema "implement" their "prayers" by drawing upon the resources bureaucratized in the constabulary order.

CHAPTER FOUR

NAIVE CAPITALISM

WE now come upon the period in which the negativistic feature of the Protestant dissociation contrives to take on positive ingredients, the old abnormality having become the new norm. The battle, a long one, required considerable coaching, backed by strong economic compulsion, to "democratize" the new ambitiousness. The people had been trained in a subsistence economy. They asked at most for full bellies and the barest comforts; for further riches they should turn to "laziness," art, the rituals and the festivals. This "immoral" attitude had to be "educated" out of them, so that they would bring their sturdiest energies to the running of their employers' enterprises. It was further grounded in a whole system of attendant moral evaluations. The humble qualities by which one had judged a man "good" were out of keeping with the new necessities.

We note an analogous situation in Japan to-day, where the social norms of feudalism (with an emphasis upon *status* that interferes with a morality of *advancement*) are not adjusted to the philosophy of business. The qualities that make a man admirable are still those of the self-effacing sort, stressing obedience and resignation. Hence, the humbler classes, who retain the older values, are confused (psychologically dispossessed, confronted by inanition, "alienation"). And those of privilege, who can seize the new resources, are "demoralized"—the older vocabulary of self-effacement becoming simply a "eulogistic covering" for norms of a totally different sort. (As when one *says* "I do this for the good of society or the glory of God" and *knows* that he is not doing anything of the sort. This device for making up the difference by "secular prayer" is sentimental when it convinces and hypocritical when it doesn't convince.) The misfit, in its totality, makes for the customary symptom of misfit: aggravated pugnacity. Since Japanese "Fascism" is really but a survival of "feudal socialism" in a modern setting, this pugnacity can be organized about the psychology of the *samurai*, requiring self-sacrifice with relation to the ancient unifying symbol of authority, the mikado. He himself has apparently joined forces with the rising industrial leaders, hence adding to the confusion by functioning for business aggrandi. .ment under the aegis of a feudal, anti-business morality. The confusion, further sharpened by economic pressure, stimulates the naive militaristically, as they project the enemy-within to an external symbol, and so attack it "integratively" as an enemy-without, a foreign foe, while the "logic" of business expansion provides the leaders with "rational guidance" for charting a course through the labyrinth of confused *qualities* by the *quantitative* tests of profit.*

* The mikado is the magical, divine, fatalistic, non-delegated symbol of authority, enjoying his prestige, like the authority symbols in Western feudalism, by drawing upon the deep, familial responses formed during the "pre-political" period of infancy and childhood. The rising class of liberal businessmen show him a new vision of profitable purpose, to be extracted from a vein which no one trained in the purely feudal frame could see unless he were able to "transcend" the frame's limitations.

We may assume that, along with the most modern of Western material apparatus, the Japanese have also imported some of our comparatively recent legalistic improvements. Hence, we may assume that Japan now has its variant of modern corporation law. If we are right in this, the ease with which partnerships are contracted by the distribution of stock would help the mikado all the sooner to identify his interests with the interests of the rising industrial leaders. He would thus be spared the many incentives to resistance that European monarchs often showed, as

In Europe, the "re-education" of the people away from "subsistence" criteria of living was by no means confined to the feeble resources of moral exhortation. The turn from illiteracy to literacy, for instance, was an imaginative move that could be "cashed in on" by appropriate bureaucratic implementing. The new emphasis flowers in the English "Statute of Frauds," which celebrated the turn from "status" to "contract" (i.e., from unwritten custom to written legality) by holding that a man was not entitled to retain his property unless he could show a *deed* for it. Since the old feudal rights to the use of the "lord's" acres had arisen purely by the authority of custom (a man's heirs being entitled to certain rights "because" his ancestors had been so entitled), it followed that the very lineage of a right was grounds for its retraction. The longer it had prevailed, the less likely was there to be a written document, attesting it (except in the case of the lord's grants, attested by royal records).

Another great help came in 1688 with the Parliamentary "Acts of Enclosure," whereby means for the private appropriation of communal areas were regularized. Much had already been done along these lines by the decisions of the

---

their stubborn failure to gauge the trend of events correctly even sometimes cost them their heads.

The structure of corporate partnerships was only perfected in Europe after the struggle between feudal rulers and business upstarts had been settled by the victory of business. But if it were introduced in its full development *along with* the rise of commercialism, it should clarify the problem of interests for the mikado considerably—and he could identify himself with the "liberals" at the very start, encouraging their work and sharing as a stockholder in its profits. He could pool his "symbolic assets" with the new class's industrial assets, as the Emperor of Ethiopia finally became "enlightened" enough to propose a similar partnership with agents of an American oil firm.

judiciary, who proved themselves as "revolutionary" in England as they did later in America, with their helpful decisions on matters of corporate law (whereby corporations can contrive to escape legislative regulation by being legally considered as "persons," and as such entitled to the personal protection guaranteed by the Constitutional Bill of Rights). By the explicit Parliamentary act, the work of the judges was merely perfected, given maximum "efficiency."

It is possible that England's leadership in the industrial revolution could be traced back to the work of William the Conqueror, who bluntly imposed upon the island a pyramidal structure of rights and obligations headed in the King. On the continent, monarchic feudalism arose slowly out of more primitive patterns. There it never attained the rational perfection that the same institution enjoyed in England, where a conqueror simply wiped the slate clean and organized the new hierarchy from the top down, allotting lands to his underlings, who in turn allotted subdivisions to their underlings, and so on—and as these various rights became crystallized by custom, the monarch remained the pyramidal head of the total structure.

On the Continent, the monarchs gradually obtained their monopoly by the crowding out of other monopolists; they developed their legal structure atop the earlier primitive structure—hence the rational perfection was much less precocious than in England, where it was imposed by the efficient organizing act of a conqueror, who even scattered the lands allotted to his immediate underlings, lest they become too powerful by holdings concentrated in one area.

Thus, though capitalistic practices first clearly emerged in the *southern* regions of Europe, where the combination of Mediterranean trade and papal finances gave the incentive, it was England that eventually proved herself able to provide the maximum resources for the bureaucratization of capitalist possibilities. Nor must the feudal structure of England be considered merely as a "spiritual" asset, a "favorable state of mind." In Nussbaum's summary of Sombart's *Der Moderne Kapitalismus,* we are told that "The English crown was by far the most effective financially of the secular governments of the Middle Ages. William the Conqueror had about $2,000,000 a year at his death; a century later Richard Coeur de Lion had nearly twice as much."

Later, we note a similar phenomenon in America, which eventually outstripped England, so that the cultured English could condemn the Anglicizing of America in a way more comforting to their national pride, when the movement westward came back eastward as the "Americanization of Europe." We too had imposed a rationally perfect frame, in slaughtering the Indians instead of making a new cultural amalgamation with their non-commercial collectivities. Here, however, it was not a feudal conqueror, but the capitalist system that imposed its flat decree. The capitalist pattern could develop with maximum efficiency, because there was little of anything else. In England, capitalism had grown out of feudalism as on the continent feudalism had grown out of Roman and primitive mixtures. Hence, it was not so "chemically pure" there as it could be here.

In America, whatever resistance arose from local communities, could be obliterated by the unifying devices of abstract finance, which could control the destiny of the frontier (the periphery) by controlling the organizing resources of the political center. The rationale of abstract finance served as a kind of smear that could be washed over the genius of particular localities, greatly obscuring the particular characteristics that might have developed as the result of geographic factors or racial tradition. This rationale provided the mould to shape the cultural mass poured from the "melting pot." Encountering the theocratic genius of New England, the feudal genius of the South, and the populist genius of the West, it could reshape them all by the super-genius of capitalism.

In England, the monarchic pyramiding of the feudal structure laid the best basis for a quick start, as the nationalist emphasis got under way. It is also possible that the blunt imposition of the new legal frame, with its affronts to a more primitive order, produced some measure of "alienation" on the part of the people. The frame being somewhat superficial, "abstract," they were more ready to tinker with it (by substituting tests of "rationality" for tests of "custom"). For it had an ingredient more like the rationality of traffic regulation than the pure magical authoritarianism of custom.

William did, it is true, largely leave intact the structure of rights already prevailing among the people. But in the legal apparatus he imported, he introduced new categories of property that overlapped the older categories on the bias. The earlier basic distinctions between "movable" and "immovable" goods gradually gave way to the Norman distinctions between "personalty" and "realty." We may be justified in looking for the grotesqueries of alienation in the interregnum of moral confusion during which the new order of legality was making its encroachment felt but had not yet prevailed.

We should also suspect an important ingredient of alienation in the corresponding status of language, at a time when the speech of the Norman overlords was "antithetical" to the speech of the Anglo-Saxon underlings. With the Norman speech lay the resources of "salvation"—the ownership of it, as insignia, was confined to a few—and there was an intervening period of "sloth" before this "salvation device" became "democratized" by its gradual incorporation in the speech of the populace.*

By the time the new structure had itself gained the sanctions of custom, its pyramidal regularity made it the handiest kind of social instrument to seize for new exploitive purposes. As the disintegration of catholic symbolism threatened, it offered the best opportunity for a new integration, through a nationalist synthesis, with a king at the head.

The shift was assisted, both in England and on the continent, by a group of statesmen and economic philosophers, the mercantilists, putting forward a theory of national prosperity that turned the mediaeval logic upside down. Before these enlightened thinkers arose, it was customary, if one mentioned a "favorable balance of trade" at all, to mean that a locality had a favorable balance of trade when more goods were coming into it than went out of it. If you could, in effect, give away one good ox and get back two oxen equally good, you were enjoying a "favorable balance of trade." That would seem reasonable enough—and the economic theories of the scholastics, who for some reason are usually considered "irrational," started from this axiom.

---

* The democratization of Norman speech (a "salvation device" because of its associations with the symbol of authority) was marked by a corresponding "deterioration in quality." But "deterioration" is not an absolute category. The "deterioration" of the Norman speech, that went with its democratic incorporation in the speech of the populace, was synonymous with the *rise and perfection* of English.

NAIVE CAPITALISM

But the mercantilists as a group hit upon a more advanced notion. For them, a nation had a favorable balance of trade when more goods were going out of it than came into it. And they "transcended" this confusion by recourse to a matter of symbolism; namely: "bullion." The preponderance of exports became "profit" rather than "loss" because it was matched by a preponderance of *symbolic imports*. For the symbol by which exchange was carried on was bullion, money—and the nation most successful in tossing real goods beyond its borders got back, in payment for its superiority, the inflationary symbolic equivalent, money.

We note this paradox not merely for its picturesqueness. Rather, we hold it to be at the very center of capitalist difficulties (nor is the issue solved when, at a further stage, the preponderance of exports is matched by a still more inflated symbolism, the importation of *debts*, as managed through internal loans which are made to foreign countries and are eventually repudiated). We are trying to point out the essentially *anti-patriotic* nature of this mercantile doctrine, even though the anti-patriotism arises merely as an unintended by-product, while the attention of the patriots is directed elsewhere, and they are "patriotically" calling upon their government to assist them, in every possible way, to toss goods beyond the national borders, *forcing* upon alien peoples such products of the mines, forests, and farms as all the combined armies and navies of the world could not manage to capture.

For the fact is that, although this paradoxical mercantilist theory of the favorable trade balance acts *against* the welfare of the nation *as a whole*, it acts *for* the welfare of *a special group* (until the time when the "efficient" depletion of a country's resources is great enough to partially deplete

149

them also).* An international banker may, by floating a foreign loan among his compatriots, thereby promote greater activity in the tossing of goods beyond our borders. And the compensatory symbols that we get in exchange, the written document attesting foreign indebtedness, may eventually have to be repudiated. But the banker can buy himself real goods with symbols that *he* gets for manipulating the tossing-forth. So that, although the country is poorer to the extent of the mineral and agricultural wealth and human labor hours that have been thrown away, tossed

---

* Samson was not the only strong man who pulled down a temple upon himself. Technology, as driven by the necessities of capitalism, can be a vast transmogrification of Samson, amplifying the scope of his act by all the bureaucratic resources of our institutions, the total organization of our productive technique. There is the dubious kind of "profit" that exports two-dollar wheat and gets in exchange a Dust Bowl.

Among the sciences, there is one little fellow named Ecology, and in time we shall pay him more attention. He teaches us that the *total* economy of this planet cannot be guided by an efficient rationale of exploitation alone, but that the exploiting part must itself eventually suffer if it too greatly disturbs the *balance* of the whole (as big beasts would starve, if they succeeded in catching *all* the little beasts that are their prey—their very lack of efficiency in the exploitation of their ability as hunters thus acting as efficiency on a higher level, where considerations of balance count for more than considerations of one-tracked purposiveness).

So far, the laws of ecology have begun avenging themselves against restricted human concepts of profit by countering deforestation and deep plowing with floods, droughts, dust storms, and aggravated soil erosion. And in a capitalist economy, these trends will be arrested only insofar as *collectivistic* ingredients of control are introduced, as with the comparatively insignificant efforts that have already been organized by our state and federal governments.

beyond the national frontiers, the banker is richer to the
extent of his profits for engineering this fabulous effort.*

* You may note an analogous contradiction in the clearing arrangements which the governments of several Balkan countries have contracted with Nazi Germany. The individual who exports agricultural
goods to Germany, from, let us say, Yugoslavia, receives his payment in
the currency of Yugoslavia. And a corresponding sum is credited by
Germany to the *government* of Yugoslavia. Similarly, an exporter of
German manufactured goods to Yugoslavia receives payment in German
currency, and the treasury of Yugoslavia credits the government of Germany with a corresponding sum. Germany's imports have tended to ex-
ceed considerably her exports to these Balkan countries, with the result
that a large credit balance has accumulated in Germany. Until redeemed
by an increased purchase of German goods, this credit is a *national* loss
to the Balkan government. But the *individuals* who sold their products
to Germany made a *private* profit. The exports also enabled them to sell
in the home market at a higher figure, thus further swelling their profits
as individuals at the expense of their countrymen *as a whole.*

As with the bankers, the contradiction in the end catches up with the
particular group that profits at the nation's expense. It has, for instance,
deprived the Balkan governments of free money (such as they could have
got, for instance, had they exported the same goods in a free market to
England or France). In place of money, they simply amass frozen credits
in Berlin; and this withdrawal of money from the local markets tends to
freeze other areas of trade proportionately. And as this process of freez-
ing spreads throughout the national economy, the group that profited
at first comes to feel the cold also.

Nor are matters helped much when Germany proposes to rectify the
balance by large shipments of arms and munitions. For such goods are
outside the *productive* economy. Cannon are a poor economic *Ersatz* for
food, houses, railway equipment, and the like; and only large shipments
of *constructive* goods could really ease matters. So far as the needs of a
peace-time economy are concerned, the German proposal to restore the
balance by shipments of such purely "spiritual" wealth as war equipment would be equivalent to a proposal that Germany cancel the credits
by dumping a corresponding tonnage of steel into the ocean.

(In the brief interval between the writing of this note and its publication, the contradictions have made themselves sufficiently felt to wreck
this practice.)

Indeed, let us add in his defense: So thoroughly is capitalism geared to this paradox, that he is actually entitled to feel "virtuous" for the part he plays in the act of national depletion. If we cannot toss at least ten percent of our productivity beyond our borders, in exchange for inflationary bullion (or even more inflationary paper) "hard times" befall us, manufacturers "retrench," workers are discharged, the internal purchasing power drops accordingly, and it becomes "impossible" to produce and distribute internally the remaining nine-tenths that could be turned out by our farms and factories. Things go "spiraling down," until ways are found for a resumption of the "tossing-forth," that things may "spiral up" again. If someone induces the Hottentots to buy cars and (since "at present" they have no money), if he can float a loan among us to help the Hottentots buy the cars, then our factories start going, and with our wages we all can buy cars—and prosperity is with us, until it becomes apparent that the damned Hottentots can't pay the interest on the loan—whereat the few books that are sold in large numbers picture the glory of life in some earlier century, and the many books that are sold in small numbers picture the end of the world.*

It must be admitted that mercantilism was not so illogical as the paradoxes that later developed from it. The resources of bullion enabled the monarch to equip predatory

---

* Since the expedient of promiscuous foreign investment is temporarily discredited, the usual substitute is a deliberate depreciation of the currency, whereby foreign buyers are enabled to get more for their money, export trade being "stimulated" to a corresponding degree. Hence, we see capitalist countries actually *competing* in a race to make their currencies lower in the international market.

An internal variant of such depreciation is to be seen in the special inducements (such as tax exemptions) that localities offer to attract the migration of industries at the expense of other localities.

armies, and hence by indirection could "buy" him an empire. It served its day adequately enough. The rigor of its basic inconsistency, its full contribution to the aggravation of "class struggle," developed later, as we began to see that the term "favorable balance of trade" must be qualified by a question, "favorable *for whom?*"

Mercantilism was half-way between scholastic theory and the economics that flowered in Adam Smith's *Wealth of Nations*. It manifested the paternalistic emphasis that went with feudalism and its monarchic variant. This same feudalistic-paternalistic tendency remained through the early stages of business enterprise, where merchants and manufacturers still tended to think of themselves as heads of families, and where the business line itself descended with strong connotations of family tradition. The quality of this attitude is well conveyed in Thomas Mann's *Buddenbrooks*, which depicts the earlier paternalistic enterprise (centered about the *Patrizierfamilie*) being elbowed out by the completely modern executive, with a purely abstract view of profit (Germany being nearly a century behind such developments in England).

Among the crafts, this employer-paternalism was matched by the partial survival of the old mediaeval guilds, which had aimed at the standardization of quality through a moralistic, or non-mechanical conception of the "just price," an attitude which Smith proposed to depersonalize by attributing a mechanistic action to the market, holding that a "just price" could be obtained by non-moral mechanism through the self-regulating "laws of supply and demand." The craft guilds had manifested a "reactionary" tendency, being more eager to maintain the status quo of productive methods than to welcome kinds of technological progress endangering the privileges of accomplished craftsmen. Their members were incipient Luddites, retaining old methods as long as possible, since their security was founded upon these older methods. But there was the increasing economic pressure of the market, to force their "education," which could not be called complete (from the standpoint of their own welfare) until the half-way stage between mediaeval guild and modern craft union was surmounted by industrial unionism.

Adam Smith's optimistic version of fatality, with the general scramble of self-interests cancelling one another off as collective welfare, was enunciated just at the time when the shift to a new pattern was taking form. His scheme was, in one respect, merely a secularized version of the mediaeval situation. Whereas the many independent feudal localities were held together by the catholicizing symbolism of the church, we now had, as our somewhat dingy vision, independent local enterprises held together by the laws of the market. Immutable laws of exchange, by this new-found scheme of beneficence, replaced the immutable laws of God; or, otherwise stated, market law replaced "natural law." We got a mechanical Providence.*

---

* As we glance back through various periods of history, we find no justification whatever to attack business enterprise *per se*. In fact, the best fruits of enlightenment seem to occur precisely at those times when the opportunities for individualistic expression are emerging from a collectivistic texture. The question of *percentage* seems to be the most important consideration. Such enterprise functions best, for cultural purposes, when it is strong enough to act as critical stimulus, but has not yet, by the operation of the "neo-Malthusian principle," attained its full proliferation, or bureaucratization. Hence, the argument for a *little* is not an argument for a *lot*. The same consideration applies to a related phenomenon, the town, which is most valuable as a small "enfranchised" island in a sea of immobility, but destroys the "ecological balance" when it becomes the commercial "megalopolis" and is able to impose its standards too thoroughly upon the rural periphery.

NAIVE CAPITALISM

Precisely at this point, the new resources of impersonal relationship, making for the development of monopoly, began to emerge. Men had been members of a religious corporation, a civic corporation, and a vocational corporation. They now had a chance to become members of a financial corporation, that emerged from the proliferation of partnerships until many members were included (significantly, they were called "brothers")—and you finally arrived at the "joint stock company." All that was needed was for earnest-minded judges to endow these strange creatures with a legal "personality," and their future was assured.

Nay more: they were endowed with personality on some counts, and on other counts they were not (for sometimes they could flourish better as persons, as when they required the "freedom" of persons—but at other times they could flourish better as non-persons, as when you tried to imprison them; or again, as persons, if they were venturing abroad, they might be called home when there was danger, their government refusing to guaranty their safety if they insisted upon tarrying, but as non-persons they could remain there, calling upon their government to protect them).

There followed several decades of this "heads I win, tails you lose" strategy in judicial interpretation, culminating in the usual paradox of capitalism: in America the trusts took one of their greatest steps forward during the presidency of the "trust-buster" Theodore Roosevelt, as the Sherman anti-trust law was invoked by the most powerful trusts to prevent the formation of rival combines; and when the courts dissolved the Standard Oil Company, the insiders made more money than they had ever made before, by dividing up the properties in enigmatic ways, spreading rumors that worthless shares were highly valuable, whereupon they could sell at great profit, and spreading rumors that valuable shares applied to companies without assets, whereupon they could buy these shares for a pittance.

Add the "holding company," the corporation-atop-corporations, whereby financial engineers can get hold of *real* operating companies in exchange for *paper*; add all the "ladling devices" whereby the director of one corporation can shunt its profits to himself and his cronies as heads of a little private corporation; add the "credit squeeze" whereby, the medium of exchange having been graduated from money to credit, men can pick off choice properties cheap by getting a strategic hold on the channels of this symbolism—and you have Adam Smith's mechanistic Providence (operating through a multitude of mutually cancelling and mutually beneficial small enterprises) converted into the great economic empires of to-day, their rivalries assuaged by interlocking directorates, and their influence made efficient by their grip upon the legislative, educative, and constabulary functions. Nor need this grip always be direct, though it often is direct. Most of its power derives from *indirectness*, from the fact that it is *implicit* in the frame of acceptance, not *explicitly* aggressive. It gets its much by the same devices that humble men use in the attempt to get their little. And since the humble fear the loss of their little, as a by-product of their fear they protect these corporations' much.

But even this state of affairs, bad as it is, presses on to further problems. For what else can these corporations still get but that little? And if they get it, how can they go on getting more? To an extent, the problem is solved for them despite themselves. They put it in their private pocket as *income*; some of it is taken out by the government as *taxes*, and these taxes are employed in part to support those who have lost their little. Or else, the government does not tax, but borrows—but that process in the end endangers the structure of credit, and private wealth is involved in the structure of collective credit. If you force an increasing percentage of people into a purely subsistence economy, you don't sell to them. If you would retain them in the economy of plenty, you must—either directly, or by governmental indirection—give them the money to buy with.* If you let them buy shoes, the turn-over may enable you in the course of things to buy a yacht. If you try to make profits by cutting down the wages they have for buying shoes, the speed of the turn-over money is slowed, and you must do with less sumptuous a yacht. It is a confusing situation

* We are simply saying that insofar as radical inequalities of distribution become systematized, as they do under private ownership of the productive plant (i.e., "business"), various *redistributive* stop-gaps must be periodically introduced. At the time of the Roman republic, for instance, periodic redistribution of ownership was effected by the settling of Roman armies on newly conquered areas. After such a governmental manufacture of small Roman landowners, some time would be required before the channelization of profits had led to the dispossession of these new proprietors. And the conquest of another area could start the same process again, until the new proprietors in turn were gradually deprived of their holdings by the monopolistic laws of finance.

There was also the redistributive stop-gap of the dole. But Rome always thought predominantly in terms of land and corn. Our modern, more "spiritual" concepts of property place the emphasis more upon money than materials. Hence, we redistribute by a mixture of taxation and inflation, rather than by the reapportionment of physical properties (though the progressive settlement of the Indians' lands during the nineteenth century was our "peaceful" equivalent of the Roman method.) When asking for a reward in money, rather than a share in the productive plant, our own unemployed showed how well they had been trained as *privates* for the regiments of capitalist enterprise. In effect, all they were demanding was *free wages*. They asked only for that "nomadic" kind of rights that goes with "the speed of the circulation of money."

worth getting pugnacious about—and the pugnacity is with us too.*

* The romantic, 'Faustian" concept of effort that went with the rise of business enterprise must have had one great advantage over the feudal and classical concepts of "balance." In contrast with the classical notion that one developed himself by the harmonious apportionment of many different ingredients, you got the notion that development meant the intensification of some one peculiarity or aptitude. Hence, one did not have to feel as though he were holding himself down, or "sitting on the lid." There might be *external* resistances to his self-assertion, but "internally" he was "free" to yearn for as much as he wanted. Henceforth there was great opportunity for those warped by inordinate hungers. In the older frame, they might have tried to *restrain* these hungers—in the new frame, they sought only to *embody* them in material attainments.

We have seen rubbings of bas-reliefs in a Chinese temple, depicting a group of "saints." All these saints were grotesque, with strangely twisted faces and odd bumps all over their heads. And we have wondered whether these "saints" may have been simply incipient businessmen in a cultural setting that denied them full expression. Lacking the resources of a "Faustian frame," as implemented by the capitalist order, they possibly tried to restrain their hungers, to "sit on the lid." And they felt very "good" for doing so, but the effort warped them egregiously, even to the extent of giving their bodies grotesque bumps.

Possibly these frustrated talents could not restrain themselves, in keeping with the norms of effort then current, except by becoming nothing less than "sages" and "saints." Perhaps in a frame where the one-track efficiency of "Faustian" business romanticism prevailed, they would simply have sought their "vocational number," and proceeded to train themselves in its direction, with untroubled zeal, until they had produced the maximum hypertrophy of their special aptitudes. Then, by a vicious circle, these "experts" would have compensated for attendant atrophies by giving all the more attention to ways of making their hypertrophied trait more efficiently itself. Until they all, as actors, would be fit for "type-casting"—none for repertoire. Yet there would be two "super-types": one the specialists in overwork, the other the specialists in forced or voluntary idleness.

CHAPTER FIVE

EMERGENT COLLECTIVISM

ACT V of one's historic drama should be left partly unfinished, that readers may be induced to participate in the writing of it. And one tries to arrange his scenario of the first four acts in such a way, so "weighting" his material and "pointing" his arrows, that the reader will continue in the same spirit. A history of the past is worthless except as a documented way of talking about the future. Our incidental remarks about "secular prayer" might bring up an unintended by-product of resistance, however. You may be led to object that we are "merely praying," attempting to coerce reality by "word magic," by incantation (as Communist audiences show a liking for dances in which the future is mimetically forced, *made* to assume the desired shape, by rites dramatizing the proletarian victory.)

On the contrary: our attitude towards "secular prayer" is too "ambivalent" for such a cursory dismissal. In "secular prayer" there is *character-building*, the shaping of one's individual character and role with respect to a theory of collective, historic purpose. The contemporary symbols of authority being in disarray, one forms his mind with relation to an "ideal" concept of authority, still to attain its total bureaucratization, its embodiment in the totality of institutions, productive methods, and property relations. One constructs his "frame of acceptance" for the present by reference to these futuristic norms.

We have tried, then, to organize the first four acts of our historic drama in such a way that the emergence of collectivism becomes the *logical* content of Act V. Schematizing the whole curve, we get:

Act I. The opening situation. Hellenism on the decline. Christian evangelism emerging.

Act II. The plot under way. The feudal-mediaeval synthesis, with its symbolic culmination in the Summa of Thomas Aquinas. Plea for the maintenance of the status quo, in the static implications of the architectural metaphor. Plea for magical, non-parliamentary concepts of authority, in the family metaphor stressing obedience and custom.

Act III. The "peripety," or transition. Protestantism. Renaissance and Reformation. Concern with the "unintended by-products," generated in Act II. Negativism. Enlightenment. Rationalism. Individualism. Implementation of sectarianism. Quantitative tests of profit, to substitute for the confused qualitative tests grounded in custom.

Act IV. "Flowering" of the new emphases. Naive capitalism, with its symbolic culmination in Adam Smith's rationale of the market. "Virtue" made automatic, as the "laws of supply and demand" operate like a beneficent Providence, to convert individual greed into collective wealth.

Act V. Emergent collectivism. First revealed in Act IV, when the growth of monopoly and the financial corporation began to threaten the symmetry of Adam Smith's rationale. Perplexities of the "favorable balance of trade" (as regards either a nation or groups within a nation).

We prefer to be somewhat shrewd in our notion of the way in which collectivism must emerge. Primarily, we feel that it may enter "by the back door," as signalized in that highly ironic term of modern economists, the "socialization of losses." The tendency to "socialize losses" begins with the largest financial interests, as in times of adversity they call upon the government to protect their private holdings by drawing upon the collective medium of exchange, the national credit. Slowly this handy "salvation device" becomes "democratized," as one group after another arises to claim its benefits (beginning in America with the bonus granted the war veterans, a minor "financial resettlement" that corresponded to the Roman resettlements on conquered land).

One may question the doctrine that each period of depression under capitalism is more intense than the preceding, until a breaking point is reached. One may hold that the manic-depressive alternations of inflation and collapse are "normal" to the capitalist modes of distribution, that there is a "natural" periodicity of fat years and lean years, and that in the fat years the wide distribution of commodities is helped by investors who hope to get more than they do get (each bad investment being in effect a "redistribution of wealth," as it provides work and wages in the interim). Perhaps this fantastic repudiation of "national planning" can continue—particularly since the symbolic structure of money seems capable of endless manipulation. But one must recognize at least that, with each successive depression, there is an increased demand for the "socialization of losses," as the resources of the national credit are drawn upon to cushion the deflation of private properties. In this sense, "by the back door," cyclical depressions bring capitalism progressively closer to socialism.*

* In keeping with such covert processes of socialization, there must now be under way the most fabulous processes involving the manipulation of monetary symbolism (and thus, in the end, making invisibly for changes in the property relationships). They have already come to the surface in a few unmistakable manifestations, such as the equalization

For local purposes, let us note even the socializing tendencies in the official sloganizing of the commercial philosophy, which reached its culmination in the "gospel of service." By this formula, liberal apologetics covertly restored favorable connotations to the idea of the "servile."

By the "gospel of service" one refers to *social service*. One is commending an activity by reason of its *community* value. It is a *collective* attribute.

---

funds used by the governments of Britain, France, and the United States, and the clearing arrangements and variously discounted currencies employed by Fascist countries in the promotion of foreign trade.

But they must be here in much greater profusion than we have yet been able to detect, because the nature of our financial symbolism makes them so possible as to make them necessary. In particular, the ease with which symbols can be manipulated offers inflationary possibilities (necessities). Hence, the "neo-Malthusian principle" would lead us to assume that the proliferation of habits would invite the increasing encroachment of financial laxities that casuistically destroyed the basis of money out of which they arose. Hence, covert inflation. Nor would it be necessary to abandon this belief on being shown that the price of commodities had not greatly risen. For we might hold that the price should properly have *fallen*, and would actually have done so, in direct ratio to increased productivity, had it not been bolstered by *covertly* inflationary processes.

There are uncharted and unchartable confusions of interlocking debts (contracted by political and commercial corporations, and by the individuals' variants of "instalment buying," and in particular involving an unnamed future in the devices whereby *public* credit resources are exploited to stimulate or protect *private* holdings). This bewildering network of debt has completely obliterated the reality of a material basis for money. Money is "backed" not by a material, but by a function, a *social* function. This observation applies even to bullion; and it applies all the more to the fabulous symbolic superstructure fictitiously erected upon bullion, and still vaguely tied to gold by casuistic stretching.

Orthodox economists, who would confine their study of monetary symbols to the interrelationships of the symbols themselves (as if they had been asked to make an analysis of finance by analogy to the perpetual motion machine) will doubtless perform a service to their employers

EMERGENT COLLECTIVISM

And what is behind a psychology of service? A social service is a way of *paying* something to society. It is the discharging of a *debt*. The church, as we have noted, was exceptionally cunning in founding its collectivist structure on the foundations of guilt. It formulated a doctrine of "original sin," holding that the individual could not be saved until he had been socialized. But liberals proclaimed the "innate goodness of man" (possibly a denial by senti-

---

(thereby earning their keep in the endowed chairs of capitalistically orthodox universities). But they serve by contributing to mystification, not clarification. On the other hand, by considering money as a *sociological* phenomenon, rather than as a specifically financial phenomenon, we are better provided with cues for examining the fabulous ways in which Fascist countries have managed so far to counteract the "laws" that would expose their inflation. The admission of socio-political factors is implicit in democratic equalization funds; it is thoroughly explicit in the more "efficient" embodiments of the same managerial principles in the contrivances of Fascist dictators.

But socialism via the "socialization of losses" equals "demoralization." For it involves the demoralizing effect of accumulated legal fictions in quite the same way as we got demoralization from the legal fictions that *permitted* usury atop the scholastic principle that *condemned* usury. Rescue from this corruption was obtained by the "new start" of Calvinism, which changed the rules of the game, making the negativistic stopgaps positive by explicitly sanctioning usury (with the euphemistic name of interest). The attempt to uphold the stop-gaps by making them *look like* an affirmation, is completed in Fascism, which Palme-Dutt, in a superb "perspective by incongruity," has tellingly named "the organization of decay." That in time leads to another incongruity, when we find German and Italian nationalism embodying their principles in upholding a "nationalist insurrection" against the Spanish nation. The Spanish people thereupon were quick to invent their own "perspective by incongruity" in naming the German invaders "Aryan Moors."

Socialism would scrap all these covert, casuistically engendered processes of socialization-via-the-back-door, and put a positive rationale of socialization in their place.

mental transcendence on the part of its originator, Rousseau, who gives evidence of a strong underlying guilt sense, and broke many human relationships because he suffered intensely from feelings of persecution). In any case, liberal apologetics finally gets back to "social service" as the "justification" of business enterprise. We need not here concern ourselves with the way in which service, as so contrived, turns out to be disservice. We are simply pointing out that, at its most "enlightened" stage, a business enterprise directly or indirectly hires apologists to celebrate its prowess, and these apologists must covertly revert to the notion of "paying off guilt" by service (*bondage*) to the collectivity.*

---

* At various points in this work, we suggest strains that may figure in a naturalistic genealogy of guilt. Might not the above remarks on the justification of private enterprise suggest a "formal" genesis of guilt, implicit in the nature of "reason" (insofar as reason is a verbalized social product in which the individual has a property)? That is: the only way in which one *can* rationalize a private act is by reference to a public effect (showing that it is "good" for someone beyond the self, that it is to be tested by reference to a field varying in scope, such as family, class, or nation). And since the individual mind is formed by incorporating such social materials, the social rationalization induces a sense of individual shortcomings, leading to a sense of guilt insofar as his private act is felt as a departure from its ideal.

In this way, there is implicit in reason the need for "justification" (which is *per se* the evidence of guilt). In the esthetic sphere, the same tendency is manifest in the individual's manipulation of the public materials for purposes of appeal ("style" and "form").

The church developed a rationalization of reason. The "debunkers" developed a rationalized critique of this rationalization. That is, the church built on the foundations of guilt, and the rationalism of the anti-church debunked the guilt. Hence, since the church rationalization was collective in its emphases, the critique of it became individualistic (finally attaining its reduction to absurdity in the thinking of Max Stirner). Accordingly, we hold that one cannot "debunk" guilt completely without arriving at a disintegrative, anti-social philosophy (which is always

EMERGENT COLLECTIVISM

We would begin with that, since it enables us, even in a society where talk of "freedom" is being so steadily "cashed in on" for apologetic purposes, to point out that the individual is a bondsman, who "justifies" himself by paying tribute to the norms of his society. The issue then ceases to be a squabble over "freedom vs. bondage"; it becomes a weighing of various frames in which a *bondage-freedom ambivalence* can express itself.

------

formally impaired by the fact that the thinker attempts to *recommend* his thoughts, to "appeal" while formally eschewing appeal as a motive).

The collective emphasis in Hegel is derived from his "theologizing." And Hegel, as the "goes before" for Marx's "comes after," was retained in Marx, lurking behind his secularized vocabulary. There is a point beyond which a *collectivist* debunker cannot go (if you test his act by the co-ordinates of the complete individualist debunker—whose own position is impaired in turn as soon as he attempts to use the public grammar of thought in order to *convince* people).

In sum, then: The "autistic" individual becomes "socialized" in forming his mind by the incorporation of public materials. This public, "forensic" material is formed about strategies of "argument," "evidence," "plea." It is a way of "checking" an assertion. We "live forward" in making assertions—and we "think backwards" insofar as we "check" (like checking addition by subtraction and multiplication by division). In time, we have so thoroughly incorporated this "backward-thinking" in our consciousness that we use it "spontaneously," and can make new "forward" assertions beyond it (seeking to check them in turn by supplying new rationalizing evidence, the organization of the evidence arising largely as a by-product of the assertion, as a mathematician may first glimpse the result he wants, and may then retrace his steps to supply a public argument "justifying" his ways of arriving at his result). And insofar as this use of "evidence" (logical or factual) is not only public property but the property of the private mind employing it, "justification" becomes a *private motive.* Hence, "freedom" from guilt would be "freedom" from public reference, from sociality.

CHAPTER SIX

COMIC CORRECTIVES

THIS notion of *ambivalence* gets us to our main thesis with regard to propagandistic (didactic) strategy. We hold that it must be employed as an essentially *comic* notion, containing two-way attributes lacking in polemical, one-way approaches to social necessity. It is neither wholly euphemistic, nor wholly debunking—hence it provides the *charitable* attitude towards people that is required for purposes of persuasion and co-operation, but at the same time maintains our shrewdness concerning the simplicities of "cashing in." The mystifications of the priestly euphemisms, presenting the most materialistic of acts in transcendentally "eulogistic coverings," provided us with instruments too blunt for discerning the play of economic factors. The debunking vocabulary (that really flowered with its great founder, Bentham, who developed not merely a *method* of debunking but a *methodology* of debunking, while a group of mere epigones have been cashing in on his genius for a century, bureaucratizing his imaginative inventions in various kinds of "muck-raking" enterprises) can disclose material interests with great precision. *Too* great precision, in fact. For though the dcotrine of *Zweck im Recht* is a veritable Occam's razor for the simplification of human motives, teaching us the role that *special material interests* play in the "impartial" manipulations of the law, showing us that law can be privately owned like any other property, it can be too thorough; in lowering human dignity so greatly, it lowers us all.

A comic frame of motives avoids these difficulties, showing us how an act can "dialectically" contain both transcendental and material ingredients, both imagination and bureaucratic embodiment, both "service" and "spoils." Or, viewing the matter in terms of ecological balance (as per footnote, page 150), one might say of the comic frame: It also makes us sensitive to the point at which one of these ingredients becomes hypertrophied, with the corresponding atrophy of the other. A well-balanced ecology requires the symbiosis of the two.*

The comic frame of reference also opens up a whole new field for social criticism, since the overly *materialistic* co-ordinates of the polemical-debunking frame have unintentionally blinded us to the full operation of "alienating" processes. Historians become indignant, for instance, when reviewing the ways in which private individuals were able, in nineteenth-century America, to appropriate "legally" large areas of the public domain. (The most astounding instance being the subsidizing of the railroads, where the government *gave* private promoters the land on which to

---

* The incentives to take Fascism as a way out of the bourgeois-commercialist confusions, and the anti-heroic difficulties that go with the *delegated* authority of parliamentary procedure, may be revealed in the attitude which even men as complex as Goethe had towards Napoleon. In Napoleon they saw the unifier of Europe, by conquests of the *pax Romana* sort whereby, once an area was subdued, it was admitted to the advantages of the imperial communicative network. Napoleon was to be the new Augustus, by establishing a complete "political monopoly" that would force into line the clashing minor monopolies. And though an "upstart," he was not a "delegated authority." He was the "man of destiny," hence his rule would be sanctioned by the same divinely fatalistic arrangements that sanctioned the "rights" of hereditary kings. Not human voting (which leads to polemical debunking) but the balloting of the heavens, would establish his appointment to the role of leader. With so many instrumentalities now on the side of privilege, we hold, a comic frame must detect the lure of such incentives, must make people conscious of their operation, if they are not to be victimized by such

build the road, and then—with this same land as collateral for a loan—advanced the promoters, from the public treasury, the money with which to build the road.) But "public property" extends into much subtler areas than this. A social organization is also public property, and can be privately appropriated.

For instance, our network of roadways increases the hazards of travel. There thus arise both the obligation and the opportunity to insure those exposed to these hazards. This *increased insurability* is a *public liability*. But *private* insurance companies are organized to exploit it as a *private asset*. Thereby they privately appropriate a portion of the "public domain" quite as effectively as those nineteenth-century promoters who, by manipulating the center of coordination in Washington, got personal possession of public resources, in lands, timber, and mineral wealth. By this grip, they can exact a private toll for the performing of a public

---

magic. It is because people must respect themselves, that the cult of Kings is always in the offing. Democracy can be maintained only by *complete sophistication*, once we near the "Malthusian limits" of its opportunities. The sense of frustration that accompanies the narrowing of these opportunities leads to a naive sense of guilt, for which a *Führer*, made "heroic" by the tremendous resources of modern propagandist organization, is the simplest remedy.

The anti-Semitic element that arises in Christian nations at such a critical juncture, might be explainable as follows: Historians have long noted the correlation between economic frustration and actual or symbolic pogroms. Jews are hated most actively in periods of depression. The steps are these: Economic depression means psychologically a sense of frustration. The sense of frustration means psychologically a sense of persecution. The sense of persecution incites, compensatorily, a sense of personal worth, or goodness, and one feels that this goodness is being misused. One then "magnifies" this sense of wronged goodness by identification with a hero. And who, with those having received any Christian training in childhood, is the ultimate symbol of persecuted goodness?

service. And as their interests become organized, they can fight any attempts of the government to provide such services less expensively (as they could be provided less expensively, were the private toll eliminated). And in their charges for insurance they can include the amounts required for lobbying and goodwill advertising, to keep this exploitation of a public domain in private hands. The comic analysis of exploitation prompts us to be on the lookout also for those subtler ways in which the private appropriation of the public domain continues. It admonishes us that social exigencies and "goodwill" are as *real* a vein to be tapped as any oil deposit in Teapot Dome. (Addendum, 1955: Radio and T.V. channels, and the private use of nuclear resources developed by the government, would also be obvious examples.)

The Church thought of man as a prospective citizen of heaven. In time, the critical inaccuracy that such transcen-

---

"Christ." And who persecuted Christ? The Jews. Hence, compensatorily admiring oneself as much as possible, in the magnified version of a hero (the hero of one's first and deepest childhood impressions) the naive Christian arrives almost "syllogistically" at anti-Semitism as the "symbolic solution" of his economically caused frustrations.

True, this process may not be undergone by all men who show obedience to its results. It may fully apply only to the pivotal, the "leaders" and "prophets," the "conscientious"; and many may accept their judgments mainly by inertia, as social conveniences rather than as intensely felt assertions. They may merely "climb on the bandwagon," with material and mental rewards in keeping.

Perhaps we may clarify the significance we attach to the "comic" frame by stating our belief that the comic frame is best suited for making disclosures of this sort, which are necessary to counteract the dangers of "mystification," so momentous in their tendency to shunt criticism into the wrong channels.

dental emphasis brought to the gauging of material relationships became bureaucratically exploited to its limits.
Out of this over-emphasis, a purely antithetical over-
emphasis developed. Against man as a citizen of heaven,
thinkers opposed man in nature; and with the progress of
efficiency in reasoning, we got simply to *man in the jungle*.
A comic synthesis of these antithetical emphases would
"transcend" them by stressing *man in society*. As such, it
would come close to restoring the emphasis of Aristotle,
with his view of man as a "political animal."

In the motives we assign to the actions of ourselves and
our neighbors, there is implicit a program of socialization.
In deciding *why* people do as they do, we get the cues that
place us with relation to them. Hence, a vocabulary of
motives is important for the forming of both private and
public relationships. A comic frame of motives, as here conceived, would not only avoid the sentimental denial of
materialistic factors in human acts. It would also avoid the
cynical brutality that comes when such sensitivity is outraged, as it must be outraged by the acts of others or by
the needs that practical exigencies place upon us.

And one is exposed indeed to the possibilities of being
cheated shamelessly in this world, if he does not accumulate
at least a minimum of spiritual resources that no man can
take from him. The comic frame, as a *method of study*
(man as eternal journeyman) is a better personal possession,
in this respect, than the somewhat empty accumulation of
facts such as people greedily cultivate when attempting to
qualify in "Ask Me Another" questionnaires, where they
are invited to admire themselves for knowing the middle
name of Robert Louis Stevenson's favorite nephew (if he
had one). Mastery of this sort (where, if "Knowledge is
power," people "get power" vicariously by gaining pos-

session of its "insignia," accumulated facts) may somewhat patch up a wounded psyche; but a more adventurous equipment is required, if one is to have a private possession marked by mature social efficacy.

The comic frame, in making a man the student of himself, makes it possible for him to "transcend" occasions when he has been tricked or cheated, since he can readily put such discouragements in his "assets" column, under the head of "experience." Thus we "win" by subtly changing the rules of the game—and by a mere trick of bookkeeping, like the accountants for big utility corporations, we make "assets" out of "liabilities." And can we, in our humbleness, do better than apply in our own way the wise devices of these leviathans, thereby "democratizing" a salvation device as we encourage it to filter from the top down?

In sum, the comic frame should enable people *to be observers of themselves, while acting.* Its ultimate would not be *passiveness,* but *maximum consciousness.* One would "transcend" himself by noting his own foibles. He would provide a rationale for locating the irrational and the non-rational.*

---

* "The irrational and the non-rational." Many of our rationalists have made things more difficult and forbidding by confining us to a choice between two only, the "rational" and the "irrational." But if a tree puts out leaves in the spring and drops them in the autumn, its act is neither rational nor irrational, but non-rational. And so it is with many human processes, even mental ones, like the "identification" that the non-heroic reader makes with the hero of the book he is reading. To call such processes "irrational" is to desire their complete elimination. But we question whether social integration can be accomplished without them. If we consider them simply as "non-rational," we are not induced to seek elaborate techniques for their excision—instead we merely, as rational men, "watch" them, to guard ourselves against cases where they work badly. Where they work well, we can salute them, even coach them.

The materials for such a frame by no means require a new start. They are all about us. (We should question the proposal drastically, were it otherwise, for a man is necessarily talking error unless his words can claim membership in a collective body of thought.) The comic frame is present in the best of psychoanalytic criticism. It is highly present in anthropological catalogues like that of Frazer's *Golden Bough* which, by showing us the rites of magical purification in primitive peoples, gives us the necessary cues for the detection of similar processes in even the most practical and non-priestly of contemporary acts. It is to be found, amply, in the great formulators of "economic psychoanalysis," writers like Machiavelli, Hobbes, Voltaire, Bentham, Marx, Veblen. Yet, while never permitting itself to overlook the admonitions of even the most caustic social criticism, it does not *waste* the world's rich store of error, as those parochial-minded persons waste it who dismiss all thought before a certain date as "ignorance" and "superstition." Instead, it cherishes the lore of so-called "error" as a *genuine aspect of the truth*, with emphases valuable for the correcting of present emphases.

Often, we can reapply, for incorporation in the "comic" frame, a formula originally made in the euphemistic or debunking modes of emphasis, by merely changing our *attitude* towards the formula. We "discount" it for comic purposes, subtly translating it, as Marx translated Hegel, "taking over" a mystificatory methodology for clarificatory ends. This strategy even opens us to the resources of "popular" philosophy, as embodied not only in proverbs and old saws, but also in the working vocabulary of every-day relationships. Thus we can incorporate the remarkable terms of politics and business, two terminologies which quickly chart and simplify constantly recurring relationships of our society. The vocabulary of crime is equally valuable, in such ingenious shortcuts as "ganging up on" and "putting on the spot."

You have heard tributes to "folk art." You should also give thought to "folk criticism." We are not here proposing to cultivate such terms "esthetically," for their purely "picturesque" value. We are considering them as a collective philosophy of motivation, arising to name the relationships, or social situations, which people have found so pivotal and so constantly recurring as to need names for them. The metaphorical migration of a term from some restricted field of action into the naming of acts in other fields is a kind of "perspective by incongruity" that we merely propose to make more "efficient" by proposing a *methodology* for encouraging still further metaphorical migrations. And this efficiency, while open to distrust, is to be tested in turn by tests of "ecological balance," as we extend the orthodox range of a term by the perspective of a totality.

The comic frame of acceptance but carries to completion the translative act. It considers human life as a project in "composition," where the poet works with the materials of social relationships. Composition, translation, also "revision," hence offering maximum opportunity for the resources of *criticism*.

The comic frame might give a man an attitude that increased his spiritual wealth, by making even bad books and trivial remarks legitimate objects of study. It might mitigate somewhat the difficulties in engineering a shift to new symbols of authority, as required by the new social relationships that the revolutions of historic environment have made necessary. It might provide important cues for the composition of one's life, which demands accommodation to the structure of others' lives.*

It could not, however, remove the ravages of boredom and inanition that go with the "alienations" of contemporary society. The necessities of earning a living may induce men actually to compete "of their own free will" to get the most incredible kinds of jobs, jobs that make them rot in the dark while the sun is shining, or warp their bodies and their minds by overlong sedentary regimentation and grotesque devotion to all the unadventurous tasks of filing and recording that our enormous superstructure, for manipulating the mere abstract symbols of exchange, has built up. The need of wages may induce men "voluntarily" to scramble for such "opportunities," even plotting to elbow themselves into offices which, in earlier economies, would not have been performed at all except by slaves and criminals under compulsion. For alienations of this sort (the

---

* Tactics of the intellectuals: Intellectuals as "advance guard." Nor is there anything particularly noble or distinguished about that—since it is, by the very nature of the case, *easier* for the intellectuals to advocate ideals on paper, in the "perfect world" of blueprints, than it is for those completely implicated in the "imperfect world" of the practical. Intellectuals must bargain for a lot, in order that there still be something left after the inevitable discounting that occurs when a society attempts to carry out their policies. "Oriental bargaining." The seller asks ten, the buyer offers two—they finally agree on five. Had the seller asked five, they would have agreed on three.

However, the intellectuals must advocate their extreme policy in such a way that they do not organize a counter-extreme. The seller must not ask so much that the buyer simply will not bargain.

The comic frame, we submit, offers the best cues for the embodiment of this policy. For one thing, it warns against too great reliance upon the conveniences of moral indignation. Nothing organizes a counter-morality more efficiently than do the intellectuals who promiscuously "move in on" the resources of secular prayer open to the morally indignant.

stifling of adventure that, as a by-product, has come with the accumulations of the venturesome) the comic frame could not, and should not, offer recompense. Its value should only reside in helping to produce a state of affairs whereby these rigors may abate.

PART III

ANALYSIS OF SYMBOLIC STRUCTURE

CHAPTER ONE

GENERAL NATURE OF RITUAL

EVEN in the "best possible of worlds," the need for symbolic tinkering would continue. One must erect a vast symbolic synthesis, a rationale of imaginative and conceptual imagery that "locates" the various aspects of experience. This symbolism guides social purpose: it provides one with "cues" as to what he should try to get, how he should try to get it, and how he should "resign himself" to a renunciation of the things he can't get. We have tried to show how groups tend to "move in on" such symbolic structures, profiting by the areas of resignation until people are asked to tolerate the intolerable (whereas, if a different symbolism of purpose and necessity were adopted, the intolerable conditions could be eradicated). A complex symbolism is a kind of "spiritual currency"—and a group of "bankers" may arise who manipulate this medium of exchange to their special benefit. Their efforts need not even be consciously directed to this end. The superstructural frame may so *function* regardless, producing dispossession and alienation largely as an "unintended by-product." All such eventualities lead to the necessity of symbolic tinkering.

The stimulus towards transcendence, or symbolic bridging and merging, arises from the many kinds of conflict among values implicit in a going social concern. Such conflicts are heightened to the point of crisis, necessitating scrupulous choices between acceptance and rejection of the authoritative symbols, in proportion as a given order of rights and purposes attains efficient bureaucratic embodiment. Or we may find simply transcendence on the part of an individual who attempts by his enterprise as symbolist

179

to bridge the gap between his private impulses and the social norms (his individual work becoming "universal" insofar as his audience shares his deviational trend) .*

There is another possibility, implicit in the doctrines of the psychoanalysts, and in the proposals of the surrealists to "integrate" the rational experience of waking life with the incongruous perspectives of sleep. Man is "dualistic" at least in the sense that his sleeping self is radically dissociated from his waking self. Each morning and each night, he crosses and recrosses a threshold, thereby changing his identity.

To an extent, therefore, mystery and mystification seem inevitable. Every man has his "secret," an awe too deep for the boldness and shrewdness of rational verbalization. There is the "trembling veil" of sleep, which he cannot draw without risk, usually being content, sometime before midnight,

---

* Since the transcendence of conflicts is here contrived by purely *symbolic* mergers, the actual conflicts may remain. And in "untranscendental moments," they may again make their pressure felt. Hence, the poet may require a *repetition* of purificatory rituals (by the use of *new* materials, since the old materials, by becoming public property, commercially negotiable, take on an element of alienation for their creator).

The speculation incidentally suggests the possibility that the receiving of financial pay for the production of rituals also contributes to the cancellation of their psychological effectiveness for the creator of them. The ritual cancels the sense of guilt—but the pay cancels the penitential value of the ritual. It is somewhat as though a devout Catholic were to ask payment from his church for a "good rousing confession." We should note how capitalism here leads to the proliferation of secular-artistic rituals by both the monetary cancellation of the ritual's effectiveness and by the monetary inducement to ritualize, provided by the genius of the market. There is a steady demand for sinfulness, with a corresponding selection of experts, specialists, equipped to supply it with esthetic commodities.

to curl himself up like an embryo, and abandon himself to that vague area of experience which, in the filing systems of day, we must put in a folder marked "Miscellaneous." Even Freud, so enterprising in the "debunking" of "repressions," has testified in a recent autobiographical statement that he reached a beyond-which-not, a point at which he could not bring himself to further disclosures.

Is it possible that much of the guilt sense, stimulating men in both religious and secular frames to "justify" themselves by the paying of social tribute, and thereby giving a groundwork for sociality in "original sin" (as cancelled by the "socialization of losses")—is it possible that this feeling can derive in part from symbolic crimes committed in sleep? Not in the dreams that we remember on awaking (for the dreams made accessible to consciousness may be either exonerated by ritual or cancelled by the "debunking" of rational enlightenment). But in the dreams that are forgotten, the dreams we dream without awaking sufficiently for conscious memory to give us a grip upon them. They are as truly a part of our "experience" as any offense committed in conscious awareness—but insofar as we commit such symbolic crimes without consciously remembering them, the experience is stored up as crime without expiation. We have much evidence that scientists, inventors, poets have worked out crucial problems in their sleep. May not criminal transgressions also occur? In fact, may not even some of the *socially* accepted formulae be criminal, as judged by the moral perspectives of the irrational or non-rational valuations prevailing in sleep? Such a possibility would explain the frequent tendency, on the part of innovators, to belittle their innovations, to be genuinely *humble* at accomplishments that might seem to justify great pride.

The "introspective," who seem to be extending the

frame of "cosmos" further into the areas of "chaos,"* to
that extent "integrating" the two (the "conscious" experience as "cosmos," the "unconscious" as "chaos") are often
bad sleepers, perhaps because even in their wakefulness they

* Chaos and cosmos. Recall the lines in a poem by Wallace Stevens:

> I placed a jar in Tennessee,
> And round it was, upon a hill.
> It made the slovenly wilderness
> Surround that hill.

The symmetrical "cosmos" of the well-formed jar, in other words, did
not confine its organization to itself. From it there radiated lines of
meaning that incidentally organized the disordered "chaos" of the
"slovenly wilderness." We have noted that the Greek city-state was
considered, by the Greeks, as a tiny cosmos bobbing on the barbarian
waters of chaos. Their theory of creation was analogous, cosmos being
a little bit of order corralled amidst surrounding disorder. We may also
note that the Greek emphasis upon the rational, the verbalized, maintained the same pattern, in contrast with the unconscious, unverbalized,
"visceral."

I. A. Richards has suggested that, by the ordering of the conscious,
we may sympathetically, by a kind of homoeopathic magic, establish
order in the unconscious. In other words, one must let not the sun go
down upon his wrath. Stevens' imagist poem, whether implicitly so
intended or not, seems to be making assertions in keeping with these
considerations. Perhaps he is meaning what Voltaire meant when he asked
us to cultivate our gardens, or what is meant by the saying that "charity
begins at home." By organizing a little "cosmos" one incidentally organizes "chaos."

But:

To say as much is not to forget the Marxist lesson: that "chaos" may
invade the "cosmic" garden, and even deprive us of it.

On the other hand:

Marxists are wrong in ridiculing the "change of heart" theory of
social betterment. The individual, to work co-operatively for the transcendence of capitalist conflicts, must "cultivate his garden," contrive
a private "change of heart," begin his charity at home, organize a little
jar of cosmos, to fit him for the public enterprise of endowing socialism

never wholly abandon their sleeping personality. Thus, that troubled sleeper, Coleridge, ordered "chaos" within the criteria of "cosmos" even to such an extent that his resulting product was publicly negotiable, and he could bring it to market. The terror that runs through his poems also gives evidence that he was close to the "trembling veil" of the "secret" (his particular core of mystery and mystification).†

Poe's cult of death may indicate a similar sensitivity, since sleep is a dying. Dostoievsky's mystic sense of duality, heightened by the hypnotic functions of epilepsy, is in the

---

with its appropriate "bureaucratic body." His "virtue" will not arise automatically, as with Adam Smith's theory of a mechanical Providence. He must "earn" it, by an "individual act of will." The doctrine of "grace" lurks behind the Marxian vocabulary of secular determinism, since the individual as such can transcend the morality of his class (people always rightly pointing to Marx himself, a "bourgeois renegade," as an example of this). Also, in identifying himself with a proletariat that is to redeem the world by a blood sacrifice, he may even be said to have rounded out his morphology along the usual lines of guilt and tragic expiation.

(If you want a less pious way of stating the matter, note simply that capitalism developed by providing maximum resources for the expression of criticism. And criticism may transcend itself by becoming self-criticism. "Dialectically," the critical resources developed by capitalism can finally be turned, by a kind of "economic introspection," against capitalism itself.)

† It is customary to think of crime and horror stories as merely providing an opportunity for poet and audience to vent criminal or sadistic impulses by the comparatively harmless route of symbolism. But this explanation, right as far as it goes, seems too mechanically over-simplified as an account of the full process. It suggests that people are little more than heated boilers needing to "let off steam."

Horror stories serve to *debunk* the sense of mystery and awe, by embodying it in shapes that we know to be "just fiction." They do in their way what Democritus did in his, by reducing fear to manageable proportions.

same mode. And in the prelude to the first of his Joseph novels, where he delves so profoundly into the mysteries of sleep, death, and rebirth, Mann asks himself: "Why do I turn pale, why does my heart beat high—not only since I set out, but even since the first command to do so—and not only with eagerness but still more with physical fear?" (The "esthetic" cult of crime, as exemplified in Gide's typical heroes, arises when a symbolic offense is "exonerated," not by expiatory cancellations, but by a wilful, "revolutionary" assertion that the crime is "right.")

To sum up: For various reasons, one has many disparate moods and attitudes. These may be called sub-identities, subpersonalities, "voices." And the poet seeks to build the symbolic superstructures that put them together into a comprehensive "super-personality." Even in the "best possible of worlds," then, there will be many factors stimulating men to the construction of symbolic mergers. Even if you remove the class issue in its acuter forms, you still have a disparate world that must be ritualistically integrated. And artist, philosopher, moralist, publicist, educator, politician, sociologist, or psychologist are all "idealistic" in the sense that they must give great attention to superstructural adjustments.*

The natural tendency of symbolic enterprise is towards integration (which explains the conscientious resistance, in bourgeois states, to the doctrine of class struggle). And in-

* In a shift from one mood to another, there is no "conflict," there is simply "change." But if a mood has broadened to the extent of becoming an *attitude*, and if that attitude has attained full *rationalization*, the shift to another attitude, requiring a different rationalization, does involve "conflict." Insofar as we do not "travel light," we thus assemble much intellectual baggage, and the attempt to reshape this to new exigencies may require considerable enterprise. Otherwise, a man either leaves himself in pieces or "freezes" at a simpler stage of development.

sofar as individuals or groups are not a "perfect fit" for the emphases required by a specific bureaucratic mode, the natural tendency is to seek symbolic ways of "taking up the slack" (as the thinker or poet in a socialist state would try to *bridge* any conflict between manual and intellectual workers, or between urban and rural workers; he would attempt, in other words, to obscure rather than clarify such demarcations).

The lure of Fascist nationalism resides precisely in the fact that it involves the resumption of this tendency without concern for the Marxist "interregnum," which thwarts the integrative prayer by showing that it is uttered in verbal denial of an actually disintegrative situation. Hating the *situation* that Marx describes, the Fascist "solves" the problem by hating *Marx* for describing it.

Ambiguities of Symbolism

We might illustrate the issues by analyzing a recent critical battle in Russia. Recall the attacks suddenly directed against Shostakovich's opera, *Lady Macbeth of Mzensk.* Shostakovich had enjoyed especial favor. But sometime after the appearance of this opera, those in high places manifested their disfavor. The result was a sudden "climbing on the bandwagon," as all critics hastened to compete in condemnation of the work. Such shifts are necessarily intensified in Russia, since ideological "correctness" attains most definitely its equivalent in monetary reward.

Where literature is frankly a function of the state (in contrast with the bourgeois pluralistic or "disintegrative" theory whereby everything is in a separate bin), those whose ideas are officially "right" tend to take office at the expense of those encumbered by an unfavored "line." A kind of "non-parliamentary election" takes place, the Ins changing places with the Outs. Such processes occur in any society, but perhaps they are made most obvious in an"integrative" state. The equivalent, in a bourgeois state, is found, in covert form, in the disproportionate royalty checks of a writer with "a good weather eye" and of a writer less agile at "jumping with the cat."

We are not here attempting, however, to gauge the sincerity of the critics involved. The sincerity of a writer, as *writer*, is a subtle matter. Dryden, for instance, inaugurated his career by a laudation of Cromwell, when the Puritans were in authority. With the shift of authority at the Restoration, he shifted to Anglican monarchism. And on the accession of James II in 1685 he again revamped his politics and his religion, forming himself henceforth by the coordinates of Roman Catholic authority. Each change brought him material rewards in pensions and honors, though his personal reversals, that matched the reversals of the state, provided much ammunition for the polemic criticism of his competitors—and he did adhere to his third policy, at the expense of material rewards. But even had he shifted once more, we should probably have to consider his work substantially "sincere," as we noted the consistent modes of assertion maintained throughout his literary career. Since we don't have to worry about defending him (don't have to care if our apology looks ironical) let us note that he remained faithful throughout to the "heroic couplet," and to the "craft morality" implicit in it. We can say as much, or as little, and pass on—for we are here concerned with another aspect of the matter.

Partially, the attack of the Soviet critics was made against Shostakovich's *music*, which was inventive and discordant in ways that the popular taste had not followed. To this extent, he was not entitled to qualify as an official repre-

sentative of the popular taste. (Here again we may introduce questions. A musician is a *specialist*, for instance—and
his specialized devotion to the morality of his craft would
seem necessarily to carry him beyond the responses of those
who had not similarly specialized. The musician is at least
justified in specializing as much as a dentist does. But the
dentist, however extreme his specialization, can "communicate" with his layman patient by stopping the toothache;
whereas the artist, specializing in the medium of communication itself, may develop his trade to the point where he
does not communicate to the musical layman.)

We got only garbled reports of the episode in the press,
which is not noted for its clarification of subtle esthetic issues. But on the basis of what we did get, we should hold
that this "problem of the specialist in a society of specialists" was slighted, at the expense of critical clarification.
This concern also is an *obiter dictum*, however. What we
want mainly to discuss, for its bearing on the symbolic
superstructure, is the *plot* of the opera.

This plot deals with a kind of Russian Emma Bovary, who
lived around 1860, and committed moral infractions as the
result of boredom and a "petty bourgeois" hankering after
luxury. Now, let us suppose that there will always be Emma
Bovarys with us. A given social structure may produce more
of them, it may stimulate the maximum proliferation of
such traits—but such potentialities, in less "efficient" form,
are present in people at any period of history. If one can
believe this, if one can believe that luxuriant and self-indul-
gent fantasy is never completely "transcended," but is only
comparatively so, when social emphases make on the whole
for healthier expressions; or if one can imagine that there
will always arise some artists or non-artists whose situation
invites them even to a modicum of ribaldry (as in the heav-

ings of the orchestra during the seduction episode), one should radically disagree with the interpretation that Soviet critics seem to have placed upon the contents of Shostakovich's plot.

For what could be "politically more appropriate," we might say, than the symbols by which Shostakovich gave vent to luxurious and ribald tendencies? He expressed them, for people living in a "proletarian" state here and now—yet he attributed them to a "petty bourgeois" goose living in 1860. By this strategy of symbolism, it would seem to us, he accommodated his art as nearly as possible to the tactics required by the situation. He brought forth, and by the course of his plot symbolically punished, any luxurious traits that may "survive"—yet he did so by keeping the "proletarian" system of meanings intact.* He even, at the end, contrived a very appropriate piece of "transcendence," as we see on a gloomy winter evening the departure of this Bovary and her kind for imprisonment in Siberia; and when the ferry moves

* Can there be a distinction drawn between "factional" and "universal" tragedy?

In universal tragedy, the stylistically dignified scapegoat represents everyman. In his offence, he takes upon himself the guilt of all—and *his* punishment is *mankind's* chastening. We identify ourselves with his weakness (we feel "pity"), but we dissociate ourselves from his punishment (we feel "terror"). The *dissociation*, however, coexists with the *association*. We are not onlookers, but participants.

The "factional" scapegoat, on the other hand, is closer to the strategy of satire. We may see its subtler forms revealed in its lowest form, the psychology of war, where each camp "projects" its sadism upon the other camp. Each camp, in other words, takes out its vengefulness by attributing "atrocities" to the enemy alone. Similarly, the "propagandist" poet can both commit an offence and disclaim it by imagining it with engrossment while attributing it, as an act, to the characters of the opposition.

The distinction throws some light upon the relationship between "practical action" and "tragic catharsis." Since "universal" tragedy

into the shadows, to a dirge-like song sung by the criminals, the funereal tone suggests imposingly the crossing of the Styx. Thus had the "evil" been given life, and killed. To our way of thinking, this illustrates the way in which the symbolic manipulations of art supply the vents for "anti-social" impulses, taking up the slack, by tragic ambiguity, between

---

accuses all men in the lump and absolves them in the lump, it cancels to zero. There is no "unfinished business" still to be done beyond the confines of the ritual. The experience is complete and final. Hence, it calls for "contemplation."

The "factional" tragedy, on the other hand, attributes the evil, not to *all* men, but to *some* (the other faction). Hence, since one's offence has been transferred to the shoulders of the other faction, the "cleansing" leaves one with a "program of action" *beyond* the ritual. That is, in some way he must act to weaken the other faction, the vessel charged with his own temptations.

We can illustrate the distinction by comparing and contrasting two short tragic pieces by Thomas Mann, "Death in Venice" and "Mario and the Magician." The earlier work is "universal" in its use of the tragic scapegoat—the latter is dissociative in the "factional" sense. In "Death in Venice," both author and reader are asked to "identify" themselves with Aschenbach in his erotic criminality, which is punished by death. There is no "spectator" here; there are only "participants."

But in "Mario and the Magician," a dissociation has taken place. Reader and author are *spectators* of the offence, as we identify ourselves with the narrator, who sits among the audience with his wife and children, observing the performer Cippola commit the offence, take the guilt upon himself (as he explicitly says that he is doing), and be punished.

Mann, you will recall, has long been concerned with certain *dubious* ingredients in art, even while devoting his whole life to artistic production. In earlier days, he wholly took upon himself the "responsibility" for these dubious traits, feeling obliged to identify himself with even the reprehensible aspects of his craft. The new political perspective, however, suggests now a change in strategy. For "Mario and the Magician" is explicitly an admonition against Fascism. By reason of the factional emphasis, he can now dissociate himself from the reprehensible aspects of art. He, in the audience, is *one kind* of artist—and Cippola, on the stage,

189

the given society's norms and the individual's necessarily imperfect fit with these norms.†

---

is *another kind* of artist, a grotesque intensification of the *unregenerate* ingredients in art.

By reason of this dissociation, Cippola can be made to offend much more bluntly than Aschenbach (whose criminality, though punished, does not go beyond a conflict of conscience, a purely subjective abandonment of scruples). Cippola, on the other hand, employs his art to make one boy stick out his tongue (the phallus?—since much is said in the story about the ambiguity of meaning) and to make another boy kiss him (under the hypnotic impression that he is kissing his *sweetheart*). As this scapegoat lies dead, the narrator says that the ending had not only horrified him, but *gave freedom*. And perhaps we may link the effects of this ritual, in requiring an act *beyond* the story (since the evil was now "Fascist") with Mann's final ability, after much hesitancy, to abandon his ironic vacillation (henceforth ceasing to waver between factions and taking a stand with one faction against another).

The crucifixion of Christ might, by our distinction, be considered as a *universal* tragedy made *factional* by the processes of bureaucratization. That is, Christ died for *all*—but insofar as all were not *believers*, the tragedy called for "action" with respect to the *non-believers*. Thus, the Jews that crucified him ceased to represent all mankind, becoming instead a faction of mankind. In primitive tribes, all were implicated in the guilt that went with the strength-giving killing and eating of the totem animal. Perhaps we may note the emergence of the "factional" scapegoat when, instead, he is ritualistically loaded with the burdens of collective sin and driven off. Here a strongly dissociative ingredient may be noted. The "homoeopathic" ambiguity moves towards the "allopathic" (counterpart as "replica" becomes counterpart as "opposite").

† It should be added, however, in defense of Shostakovich's critics, that "tragic ambiguity" may also be "prophetic." It may not merely express-and-kill; it may also serve as the strategic way of *recommending* a trend which will later attain its "bureaucratic embodiment." But we

GENERAL NATURE OF RITUAL

The Tracking Down of Symbols

A study of symbolism is annoying, we must admit, because it requires us continually to be "off the subject." If a writer speaks of life on a mountain, for instance, we start with the impertinent question, "What is he talking about?" We automatically assume that he is not talking about life on a mountain (not talking *only* about that). Or if he gives us a long chapter on the sewers of Paris, we ask: "Why that?" —and no matter how realistic his account of the locale may be, we must devote our time to a non-realistic interpretation of his chapter.

We get cues as to his "non-realistic" or "symbolic" meaning in two ways. By examining the internal organization, noting what follows what, we disclose the content of a symbol in disclosing its *function*. The trend of the whole plot, for instance, may show us that the mountain, or the sewer, symbolizes a *transition*, a crucial point in a ritual of rebirth by which the author is able to "transcend" some previous

---

question whether a purely "sanitary" theory of art is sufficient to explain the esthetic function. We question whether an art that fully abided by the criteria of "sanitation" would in the end be a satisfactory solution. Since it would deprive anti-social trends of *all* expression, it would not supply "catharsis" by providing for their symbolic release and punishment. It would try to put "sales arguments" (or simple "glorification") in place of "pity-and-terror." We question whether such sanitation is possible, particularly in view of the fact that Malraux has characterized the communist frame as "tragic." And we suspect that the Soviet critics will eventually salute, in other works, the same symbolic procedures that they have rejected in this one, though the means chosen by the particular artist may contrive to embody these procedures in ways that either escape the detection of the "sanitary" or commend themselves to his "criminality" by hitting upon luckier tactics.

conflict. We can check such disclosures by "metaphorical analysis," as we note the tenor of the imagery which the author employs.

Consider various attitudes that have prevailed towards the "problem of the symbol." The simplest is the naive rationalism of the allegory, where the artist programmatically makes a concrete symbol deputize for an abstraction. We get this in the early morality play, and in a work like Spenser's *Faerie Queene,* where the characters in the narrative signify truth, temperance, deceit, pride, etc. The type roles in Ben Jonson's comedy of humors have something of this allegorical feature. It is even present in the "realism" of sophisticated Restoration comedy, where moral attributes are linked with social status in such roles as "Sir Fopling Flutter," "Colonel Bully," "Sir John Brute," "Squire Sullen," "Scrub" (a servant), and "Gibbet" (a highwayman).

Symbolism (as a formal school) with its contemporary offshoot, Surrealism, is mainly concerned with the subjective overtones of objects, putting together the symbols for them with reference to a criterion of order that "transcends" the order prevailing in everyday experience. (Thus, in the paintings of Chirico, we find oddities of perspective and chiaroscuro, horses, and statues, all assembled together, not by the tests of everyday experience, but presumably because they all share, for the painter, the same emotional overtones.)

Imagism is a halfway stage between realism and surrealism. The imagist (sometimes adopting the word "objectivist" as a new trade name for his product) devotes great attention to the "photographic" attributes of the object— yet the object is singled out for attention precisely because the poet feels that it is "more than" its literal self. He may not specifically attempt to locate the symbolic overtones.

He may not even be sure just what these "unseen existences" are (particularly if he lacks a thoroughly rounded frame of interpretation such as Whitman possessed in his vision of democracy). But as he deals with the object, he intensifies his realistic account precisely because he feels loose associations hovering about the edges of his focus. He feels the imminence and immanence of what I. A. Richards has called "free imagery."

Joyce's later puns are an attempt to reshape words in accordance with the symbolic overtones, or "free imagery," that hover about their edges. *Ulysses* utilizes allegory for the mechanical organization of the plot. That is, there is an ingredient of naive rationalism in his scheme of parallels whereby he locates modern equivalents for the events in the *Odyssey*. But his enterprise carries him far beyond allegory, into the halfway ground of imagism, and finally to surrealism.

The strategy of imagism suggests the reason why, however desirable pure realism may be, the "statistical approach" of criticism necessarily carries us beyond it. The world contains an infinity of objects. The artist's engrossment involves a selection from among them. As soon as you look for the pattern underlying his selectivity, and the pattern whereby he proceeds from one kind of event to another, his "social attributes" (as "member of a class") are found to "transcend" his "realistic individuality." The poet's selectivity is like the selectivity of a man with a tic. He squints or jerks when some words are spoken, otherwise not. You disclose the "symbolic organization" of his tic when you have found the class of words that provokes it. Similarly, the poet's selectivity is tic-like—and the discovery of its organization is *per se* the discovery of its symbolic aspect.

Again: the mere fact that a realist must put adjectives or verbs with his nouns categorically involves him in the symbolism of non-realistic punning. A poet calls object A "severe," let us say. Or he says that it is "shot through with something" (he often does, so often that he shouldn't). He also calls Object Q "severe," or finds it "shot through with." Object A might be a book, and Object Q might be a landscape. They may, "realistically," have nothing to do with each other. Or in any event, they are not realistically *interchangeable*. But insofar as both are "severe" or "shot through with," they do possess an interchangeable quality. Each may be the "symbolic overtone" or "free imagery" of the other.

And this symbolic or non-realistic kinship, whereby an author contrives his selectivity and his plot's development from-what-to-what, may often be revealed in the associative clusters of his symbolism. If he writes, *with engrossment*, about landscape, for instance, you may soon find him either mentioning books, or describing his landscape in metaphors that apply to books. Thus when the issue of the gold standard was rife in the press a few years ago, we found joy in noting how Senator Carter Glass, who led in the establishment of the Federal Reserve, and whose moral co-ordinates are apparently interwoven with the symbolism of money, would begin with a discussion of the gold standard, and within three paragraphs was on the subject of God.

As we have previously noted, discontinuities in procedure (such as the shift from verse to prose in *Murder in the Cathedral*) are particularly valuable as "leads" for the critic who would track down the meaning of symbols. Since we consider this method essential to analytic exegesis, we shall offer a further example of it:

It is a commonplace, for instance, to note the preoccupation with death in the poetry of A. E. Housman. Suppose that we wanted to locate the "symbolic overtones" of this. We find a cue in a recent biography of Housman, by A. S. F. Gow, as reviewed in *The New York Times*. The reviewer quotes a passage by Housman giving his opinion of a work by two scholars. Among other things, Housman writes:

"Indeed, I imagine that Mr. Buechler, when he first perused Mr. Sudhaus's edition of the Aetna must have felt something like Sin when she gave birth to Death."

Such gratuitous, or somewhat irrelevant metaphors we consider particularly revealing. For they break through, or intrude upon, the subject matter at hand. And we believe that this power to intrude, to force themselves into expression, is supplied by constants of preoccupation broader than the subject of the moment.

Thus, the passage would induce us to look for evidence of a sense of sin, as an important ingredient in the poet's preoccupation with death. And by "metaphorical analysis" we should proceed to examine the specific associations (the "clusters of imagery") in his poems themselves, to learn whether our hypothesis could be corroborated by the evidence of internal organization.

Frankly, we have not gone through Housman's poems to learn whether such evidence is strong. The "lead" may, when you track it down, turn out to be a false lead. In which case, it should be abandoned. We are playing fair with the reader by purposely showing an hypothesis that we have left untested. The noting of discontinuities merely puts one on the track of something. It is a rough-and-ready way of sizing up a poetic organization in advance. It ceases to be tenuous and dubious only when we have backed it with the internal evidence supplied by the clusters of imagery.

Since writing this conjecture, we have come upon a wholly relevant passage by R. P. Blackmur, in *The Southern Review*. Here Blackmur says of Housman that he was "a desperately solemn purveyor of a single adolescent emotion. He wrote, as he said, when he felt ill, and he wrote, as if by consequence, almost entirely of death, and almost entirely of one sort of death, the blotting death which has no relation to life. The advantage of this sort of death is that, if you apply it, it cancels the obligations and conditions that lead to the desire for it. It is a very practical sort of death, and very popular with the adolescent sensibility of our age; it is both your alternative and your revenge, and being complete does not seem to suggest any weakling desire for escape." It seems to be precisely the kind of obliteration one would ask for if immortality meant for him the possibility of punishment. Such death would be the perfect antidote for a sense of sin uncancelled.*

Synthesis and Analysis

A book in itself is a symbolic act of synthesis. The writer of the book is in a personal situation involving a myriad different factors. His own particular combination is unique —and the book that has engrossed him is the summing-up of this unique combination. But though his situation is unique, it is in many ways *like* the situation of other people. Hence, their modes of summing-up will manifest patterns that correspond with his.

---

* In general, this entire third section, on the nature of ritual, is weakened by its emergent or incipient treatment of matters that we developed in later books. See, for instance, the fifteen variations on death as motive: "Thanatopsis for Critics; a Brief Thesaurus of Deaths and Dyings" (*Essays in Criticism*, October 1952—and to be republished in the forthcoming volume, *A Symbolic of Motives*).

However, the very fact that the work of art is a symbolic act of synthesis makes difficulties for those who would break it down by conceptual analysis. We could state the matter another way by noting how the critic becomes involved in a theory of "multiple causation." The same phenomenon can be "explained" by different factors, which are not mutually exclusive. We have "explained" the death or suffering at the end of a tragedy, for instance, by noting the symbolic expiation for the symbolic committing of crime. And in another work we have noted how tragedy may also *recommend* an impulse, by giving it maximum dignity. (The writer "proves" it to be dignified by showing us human beings who are willing to die for it.) But we might offer also a purely "formal" explanation of the matter, in this wise:

An author's work is presumably deeply personal. And there is a strong reluctance to part with the truly personal (except when one gives it to another whom he loves sufficiently to identify with himself). Note in Frazer, for instance, the savage's fear of letting others come into possession of that essentially personal property, his name. And the work of art is but a complex way of *giving* one's name to the public. Frazer likewise notes the savage's fear lest other portions of the person, such as hair or the clippings of fingernails, come into foreign possession. Note also the primitive resistance to commerce (since most primitive commodities, made by handicraft, have the maximum percentage of personal projection). Conversely, we find in the high development of trade, the maximum of impersonal or non-personal goods (quantity-production, which applied as much to Greek and Roman factories, driven by slave power, as it does to the modern factory driven mechanically).

Thus, there is in the artist a kind of "parting with," or symbolic "dying," when the "implicitly imaginative" attains its "explicit bureaucratization" in public materials. This sense of dying may contribute to a preference for funereal endings—the poet feeling particularly solemn as he gets towards the end of his work. We may note it also in the tendency, often expressed by artists, to fear that they may die before a given piece of work is done. In a symbolic sense, they are dying, hence no wonder their apprehension.*

A symbol may transcendentally fuse an author's attitude towards his parents, his friends, his State, his political party, his métier, his memories of childhood, his hopes for the future, etc. If you try to consider these various components analytically, there is no "logical order" by which to progress. You should talk about them all at once. You are really engaging yourself to make a dictionary without having the organizational convenience of the alphabet.

Symbolic analysis cannot attain the "lawyer's brief" mode of organization. If you are on the subject of "New York City," for instance, what comes next? You might

---

* We might note how this "symbolic dying," that goes with the delivery of the imaginative "mystery" in bureaucratic embodiment, stimulates the artist's tendency to evolve by "stages" or "phases," as he must "leave his old self" behind, a development he frequently hastens by making each work itself a ritual of death and rebirth (change of identity). It may also account for his comparative instability in social relationships. Goethe, for instance, tended to round out each new phase of his career by reshaping all the ingredients of his life correspondingly. Hence, his shifting allegiances to different women, each successive woman functioning as the completion of his new phase in the sexual sphere. And we may note in Edmund Wilson's novel of Bohemia, *I Thought of Daisy*, his references to the heroine's sense of having died so often (as she did, in her succession of attachments to different lovers, who each embodied a different "world" or "personality" for her).

This may be the factor that Rank is on the track of, when he talks of a "death impulse" in the artist. We should call it, not a "death *impulse*" but a *death* (matched, incidentally, by a *birth*). The saint who exhorted

reasonably go from "New York City" to "traffic regulation." Or you might go from "New York City" to "agrarianism." Or you might go from "New York City" to "the three great centers of abstraction, New York, Washington, and Hollywood, the respective co-ordinating centers of finance, politics, and popular drama." There is no "logical progression," like a Q.E.D., through points, 2, 3, 4, etc. Since the work of art is a synthesis, summing up a myriad of social and personal factors at once, an analysis of it necessarily radiates in all directions at once.

Further, the synthetic symbol can be divided into conceptual components *ad infinitum.* Such possibility of infinite conceptualization seems to have made a deep impression upon Thomas Mann—for each time he hits upon a new critical distinction, he is astounded to find that it had already been exemplified in the symbolism of his novels. Great as he is (and perhaps he is our greatest contemporary novelist) he may here be attributing to himself a mere "pseudo-

---

us to "live a dying life" was apparently obeyed only too often, with a difference, in the artistic and social antics of nineteenth-century romanticism. One can envisage, on paper at least, a writer so thorough in his secular development by cruciferous stations, that each new emphasis of personality induced him to embody it by its own peculiar locale, its own special circle of associates, its own kind of material prosperity or indigence, its own authority symbol, etc. We can conceive the possibility on paper, though actually, in this "imperfect world" such "chemical purity" of the esthetic is out of the question.

For the writer is always relatively stabilized by the gravitational pull of bureaucratic factors accumulated from past stages. The binding relationships that accrue from his permanent role as citizen protect him against absolute discontinuity. For this reason, the chemical purity we have conceived *in abstracto* is but remotely approximated, except in those who live by overly romantic criteria. And this deviation from the "ideal" is felt, not as a shortcoming, but as a benefit.

greatness." He is interpreting as a special gift of his novels something that is the automatic by-product of criticism's conceptualizing resources. Every act is a miracle, a "synthesis" that can be reduced to an infinity of components.

Tests of Selectivity

The critic's tests, whereby he gets his own pattern of selectivity, choosing to stress some distinctions and to neglect other possible distinctions, is the pragmatic test of use. Facing a myriad possibile distinctions, he should focus on those that he considers important for social reasons. Roughly, in the present state of the world we should group these about the "revolutionary" emphasis, involved in the treatment of art with primary reference to symbols of authority, their acceptance and rejection. The critic thus becomes propagandist and craftsman simultaneously; he serves a didactic purpose in that he constantly reaffirms, in varying subject matter, the necessary tactics of transition; and he gives proper attention to the formal organization of poetry in that such an approach reveals the basic strategy of poetic symbolism (ritual, "secular prayer," dramatic change of identity, etc.).

To borrow from our terminology of history, applying a "macrocosmic" metaphor for "microcosmic" purposes, we should say that a writer, in "bureaucratizing" his "imaginative," tends to become involved in a secondary level of interests arising from the need of adjusting the bureaucratic parts to one another. The "imaginative" was his situation in life, with the direct bearing that it had upon his attitudes and formulations. By the medium of his symbols, he "bureaucratizes" this. And he approaches the "alienation" of "art for art's sake" insofar as his concern with the internal adjustments of the bureaucratic medium causes him to deflect his interest from the original imaginative stimulus. His problems of craft "transcend" his problems as layman.

Such alienation applies particularly to the imitators, the academicians, who simply inherit the bureaucratic order of the inventors and use it without "earning" it.

We may consider another variant (this time with relation to the internal adjustments of the poet rather than the critic):

A given material order of production and distribution gives rise to a corresponding set of *manners*. (In other words, insofar as the productive pattern attains fixity, it engenders fixed habits, typical occupations, stock situations, and moral evaluations in keeping. These are all summed up, in human material, as manners.) The equivalent of these manners in poetry is *style*. Style is the ritualistic projection or completion of manners (as when the need of "push" and "drive" in selling attains its stylistic counterpart in the breezy hero). As the productive order changes, manners must adapt themselves accordingly. (We have already noted how long it took to reshape feudalistic manners for the needs of capitalism.) But by the time the need for this reshaping of manners has risen, a whole tradition of "good style" has evolved and been "bureaucratized" (its embodiment giving new writers the "cues" that induce them to perpetuate its standards). Writers suffer impoverishments of "alienation" insofar as they attempt to retain and cultivate these purely traditional values of style, "projecting" from one literary heir to the next, while the productive order that gave rise to them has been radically altered, and a corresponding code of new manners has "slid out from in under" the traditional style. (This tendency towards stylistic lag is further enforced by the fact that the traditional style becomes the insignia of privilege, which even an indigent author can own vicariously by taking possession of the insignia.)

A writer must watch that the real needs of his internal development (such as is necessary for the proper adjustment of his symbols to one another) do not function for the reader like a "bureaucratic alienation." Of course, readers vary in their ability to feel, beneath a work's internal adjustments, the work's general bearing upon vital situations outside the work. A reader trained in philosophy may find the subtle solution of a given problem relevant not merely to the work, but to life, while readers not so trained do not even feel it as a problem.

We believe that such matters as "authority symbols," "identification," "acceptance and rejection," "rituals of purification and rebirth," "transcendence upward" and "transcendence downward," "character-building by secular prayer," "the collective poems of socio-economic organization," "bureaucratization of the imaginative," "alienation" and "repossession" are at the very basis of both esthetic and moralistic strategy. We would inspect them in the symbolic acts of art, because of our belief that art is the dial on which fundamental psychological processes of *all* living are recorded. The "poetry exchange" is to human living as a whole what the stock exchange is to production and distribution under capitalism. A slight fluctuation in carloadings may register, on the stock exchange, as a big fluctuation in the price of securities. And similarly, the tenuous fluctuations of impulse that apply in practical life may show as wide fluctuations in the "poetry market."

We know a man, of considerable learning and critical acumen, who under certain conditions becomes pig-headed to a fantastic degree, making pugnacious assertions that are beyond all reason. Noting such conduct on his part, we have assumed that these particular conditions must have another meaning for him than their purely "rational" meaning. He is presumably meeting new people, not on their merits, but on the basis of some likeness they suggest to people he met in the past. In some way, such furtive analogies are "conditioning his responses" in a way that the mere ideological issues under consideration could not account for. They are "driving him into a corner," forcing him for the time into sectarian compensations, as he meets a new situation in terms of old quarrels that are irrelevant. It is not hard to imagine situations in which such automatic bellicosity could cause him unnecessary disadvantages, as were it to make him disaffect a person who was in a position to benefit him and might have benefited him if his resources had been properly expressed, without this trammelling. Were this man, by critical conceptualization, to locate the particular set of conditions that thus negatively incite him, he would be equipped to "discount" them. And this, to our mind, is the social function that a psychology of art should perform, as it sought to locate, on the recordings of the "poetry exchange," the processes of social commerce operating in life as a whole.

Analytic "Radiations"

We have already offered our reasons why the attempt to discuss the symbolic acts of art or life involves us in a kind of pursuit that radiates in many ways at once. Since the symbol is synthetic, any attempt to break it into its component parts is somewhat fictive. And if you center upon any chosen component long enough, your concept must necessarily become blurred again, as the other components upon which it impinges come crowding in. We have frequently, for instance, referred to the symbol of the mountain. Taking a "cue" from Baudelaire's sonnet on the "giantess," we have suggested that, implicit in the realistic meanings of a mountain, there may be "symbolic overtones" of the "mother." A period of seven years spent on the mountain, as recounted in Thomas Mann's *Magic Mountain*, may thus symbolize the "regression" of rebirth. Here Mann very explicitly depicts a character in transition—and at the end, his disastrous "resocialization" prepares him for the regimentation of military obedience after his return to the "flatlands."

However, an adult's symbolic return to the mother also involves "incest awe," which may take expression in the symbolic castration of the snow scene (with its connotations of frigidity) where Castorp "dies" and comes to life again. After the punishment, as thus symbolized, he has "transcended" his earlier existence—it is the "peripety," the "dramatic change of identity," that inaugurates the beginning of his new career. (The whole ritual was presumably needed by Mann to prepare himself, a pacifistic liberal, for enlistment in the polemic battles for Germany against the allies; it is the novelistic counterpart of the symbolic warfare in his *Betrachtungen eines Unpolitischen*, where he mobilizes his ideas for work in the intellectual trenches. The ritual of rebirth in his Joseph novels is presumably designed to fit him for participation in a broader concept of collectivity than was symbolized in the nationalistic acceptance terminating *The Magic Mountain*.)

Such considerations may thereupon "radiate" to the symbol of the *Magnetic Mountain*, as employed by a contemporary English poet ritualistically "resocializing" himself with relation to communistic co-ordinates. As we note also the presence of homosexual imagery in this poet, we may ask ourselves whether the new communist society, to which the poet is drawn as to a magnetic mountain, may here again be a symbolic response to the attraction of the mother (the earlier non-political level attaining a new political refurbishment).

When we get to "The Magnetic Cactus," which attracts in its adjective but in its nouns repells, and even pricks, here again, to find out "what is going on," we might "radiate" in many directions. We might note the expiatory castration motif lurking in the connotations of *infertility* surrounding the cactus as a growth in the desert. Or we might shift to another contemporary work containing homosexual imagery, Glenway Wescott's *Apple of the Eye.* The first section gives us the portrait of "Bad Han," who is probably a kind of "male mother." She is a woman, to be sure, but with the gruffest of masculine attributes. And eventually she seduces her lover by aggressive acts of possession. (Her function, or destiny, might be foretold punningly in the magic of her name, as Desdemona's death by strangulation is foretold tonally in a proper name that sounds like "death" and "moan." "Bad Han" might be "Joycean" for "bad hand," her name symbolizing her role as one who physically and literally "takes" her lover.)

The reader need not have followed these random "radiations" too closely. They are presented merely as a sample of the problem in organizing an analytic dictionary of the "symbolic merger." We could just as well have taken countless other zigzag paths. For instance, we could have compared Mann's use of the mountain symbol in Castorp's ritual of rebirth, with his use of the pit symbol for the same purpose in his Joseph novels. In the latter books, Joseph when being reborn in the pit, "regresses" even to the infant level, as Mann tells us that he cannot speak, and befouls himself.

The difference between the two symbols might be the

difference between rebirth by symbolic castration (the "purity" of sterilization) and rebirth by a variant of the "sewers of Paris" route, the "acceptance" of filth. And we might advance to a contrast between Pasteur and Dostoievsky, thus:

Would it not be legitimate to look for a symbolic ingredient behind Pasteur's concern with the technique of medical sterilization (to the bureaucratization of which his methods and rationalization added so notable an advance, *fertile* in its cues for the further perfection of *sterilizing* devices)? At least, the extraordinary motion picture, *The Life of Louis Pasteur*, that imposingly dramatized his conflicts with the academic authorities of medicine, unwittingly stressed such an ingredient, in the scenes concerned with doctors who spread puerperal fever by touching parturient women with unclean hands. And his exceptional pugnacity (as disclosed in his actual life rather than in the drama) seems to have been more than a mere reaction against opposition. It seems to have been a *bid* for opposition.

In any event, we might note that the bureaucratization of sterile cleanliness caught the human fancy at the time when the desire for birth control was gaining favor. The technical interdependence of the two movements may be matched by a psychological interdependence. We should note also that the methodology of birth control has spread principally from Protestant countries, which were usually the cleanest. A Dutch kitchen is a *Puritan* kitchen; the scouring is partially a ritual, a "symbolic" cleansing. This purely material expression of ritualistic purification may derive in part from the dropping of the confessional from Protestant religious practices. Catholic countries could be materially dirtier without a sense of contamination, because the sense of the unclean was periodically mitigated by purificatory rituals (admission and remission of sin, sin *cancelled* by penance). Others have noted the vast literature of *secular* confessions that developed in Protestant countries, following the lead of the Genevan Rousseau, who forestalled the Catholic method by proclaiming the innate goodness of man.

True, there is Augustine, the father of the line. But much of Augustine's life was lived in the active assertion of heresy —hence he had to counter the pattern by an active assertion of orthodoxy. He "confessed" in order to symbolize an important change in his life, a radical shift in his allegiance to the symbols of authority. The "secular confession" of the typical Protestant whose religion has grown tenuous is of a different order. It "confesses" *persistence* in one's ways rather than their *abandonment*. The quality of the "peccavi" is dubious, being rather a strategic kind of boast.

If you question our interpretation of Pasteur, note at least the contrasting symbolism in Dostoievsky as revealed in the biography by Avrahm Yarmolinsky. When considering Dostoievsky's early tendencies to reverie, as one who walks through life "with averted eyes, dreading every new situation, fearful of having to meet the world on its own terms," he observes that Dostoievsky dated his career as a realist from a "sudden illumination."

"The episode that he thought marked this crucial point in his development occurred in his early manhood . . . On a bitter January evening as he was hurrying home, he halted on the river-front to watch the sunset sky: The smoke was building an ethereal city above the snow-locked streets and the glittering river, and the real city looked as insubstantial as a dream. It was one of those moments when the world sets the senses vibrating so exquisitely that they seemed to be keyed to a truth beyond their grasp. Ambiguous though his report of the experience is, the implication seems to be clear: he was startled into a perception of the mysterious, the fantastic, quality of reality itself. From that wintry sunset on the Neva—he called the moment a vision—he dated the beginning of his 'existence': his birth as a writer."

This moment of "transcendence" recalls the similar exaltation of Whitman, during his trip on the ferry from Brooklyn (his "crossing of the Styx" as symbolized in the fact that he casts the poem as a testament, to be consulted by readers after his death). It recalls also the peculiar hush of Wordsworth's sonnet, "On Westminster Bridge," where he seems almost to greet the sleeping city as a city of the dead. We may note also the snow theme, as introduced in Mann. After this episode Dostoievsky was able to consider the realistic details of a world which he has elsewhere called a "*cloaque.*" Henceforth abjuring reverie, he could bring himself to confront "damp, filthy, ill-smelling stairways leading to rooms with grimy green walls which exude a putrid odor." By this rebirth he was equipped to "accept" the "sewer"—though Yarmolinsky is quite right in discussing, in the same chapter as this account of his transcendental change of identity, Dostoievsky's "interest in the theme of *The Double*—an interest that was to remain with him to the last." It was his variant of Whitman's "unseen existences."

We shall drop our "sampling" for the moment. It is meant to be suggestive rather than exhaustive. And we shall close the chapter with a schematization, a kind of "progress report," that charts some of the significant interrelationships so far touched upon.

GENERAL NATURE OF RITUAL

Main Components of Ritual

The organization of a work can be considered with relation to a "key" symbol of authority. The work is a ritual whereby the poet takes inventory with reference to the acceptance or rejection of this authority.

If he symbolizes flat rejection, there will usually be, more or less clearly limned, the outlines of a counter-authority, as many nineteenth-century poets rejected the "practical" frame of authority, putting an ideal "esthetic" frame in its place.

If the ingredient of acceptance is uppermost, the poet tends to cancel the misfit between himself and the frame by "tragic ambiguity," whereby he both expresses his "criminality" and exorcises it through symbolic punishment.

Authority symbols of the mature adult involve such intellectualistic or philosophic concepts as church, state, society, political party, craft. They are largely "forensic." But in treating them with *engrossment* (as the organized selectivity of his work requires) he is induced to integrate them with the deepest responses of his experience. These are found in the "pre-political" period of childhood. They deal with rudiments (tables, chairs, attic, cellar, food, excretion, animals), with peculiarities of sense (different qualities of voice, the sound of rain and wind, the soft thud of wet snow against the window pane, phenomena of heat and cold, etc.), with "formative" events (accidents, illnesses, Christmas, excursions, dreams), and with intimate relationships (parents and other relatives, nurses, teachers, priests, doctors, policemen, etc., incipient manifestations of the authoritarian relationships).

"Symbolic regression" takes place in that the poet, in the thoroughness of his sincerity, necessarily draws upon the pre-forensic, pre-political ("autistic") level of informative experience, even when symbolizing his concern with purely forensic matter. A concern with a purely social symbol of authority, when the poet organizes a work with relation to it, will be found to contain vestiges of meanings derived from his family patterns of experience (for instance, his King or his God or his philosophy may be much like one of his parents, in the "quality" he attaches to the symbol).

This bearing of the forensic upon the autistic introduces such ingredients as symbolic parricide (when rejection is uppermost) and incest-awe, with symbolic castration (when acceptance is uppermost). And since the ritual of "transcendence," whereby he adjusts himself to his adult responsibilities as he sees them, involves a "dramatic change of identity," symbolic regression takes place in that he symbolizes rebirth.

The change of identity (whereby he is at once the same man and a new man) gives him a greater complexity of co-ordinates. He "sees around the corner." He is "prophetic," endowed with "perspective." We need not here concern ourselves with the accuracy of his perspective; we need only note its existence. It makes him either "wiser" or "more foolish" than he was—in any case, it forms the basis upon which the ramifications of his work are based. Thus, in Mann's novels, Joseph is not equipped to be a "prophet" until he has been reborn in the pit.

Rebirth is a process of socialization, since it is a ritual whereby the poet fits himself to accept necessities suggested to him by the problems of the forensic. It will also, as regression, involve concern with the "womb-heaven" of the embryo, and with the "first revolution" that took place when the embryo developed to the point where its "shelter" became "confinement." Hence, when you examine this ritual, you find such symbols as the "pit," a symbolic return-to, and return-from the womb.

This involves "incest-awe," since the adult can return to the mother, not as a sexually inexperienced infant, but as a lover. It involves homosexuality (actual or symbolic) since it involves an affront to the bipolar relationships of mother and father, and since a shift in allegiance to the symbols of authority equals the symbolic slaying of a parent. It involves castration symbolism, connotations of the "neuter," by way of punishment for the symbolic offense. The "neuter" may also take on connotations of the "androgynous," because of the change in identity effected by the ritual. (The profoundest way of symbolizing a change in identity is in the symbolic change of sex. Might even Wagner illustrate this symbolic change of sex when, in *Tristan*, the final statement of the new love-corporation is in the soliloquy of a woman?)

Oedipus, when learning of his offense, *blinded* himself. Often one will find the change of identity symbolized by references to blindness, or at least by an intensified reference to phenomena of vision. Mann tells us that when Joseph was cast into the pit, he was suffering from a wound that blinded him in one eye. The monstrous Cyclops (the opposite of the Greek rational idea) had but one eye.

The eyes are the "remotest" of the senses. They lack the immediacy that goes with experiences of taste or contact. They have been called a protrusion of the brain. We used to "grasp" ideas, but tend more and more to "see" them. The writing of scientists and philosophers is addressed to "visual reading." It is hardly more than a protracted kind of *graph*. And since the perspectives of adult orientation

211

are largely ideational (made of "forensic" matter), shifts in perspective tend to be symbolized by imagery referring to behavior of the eye.

Vision, compared with touch, has a quality of "alienation." And similarly, philosophic ideas (abstractions) have a quality of alienation. Thus, there is an ingredient of homelessness involved in the vast public superstructure of symbolism whereby we regulate the traffic of material and social intercourse. Poets are ever at work trying to "repossess" this territory.

On the other hand, once it has arisen, it becomes a reality of its own. One can become so much at home in it that one can devote all his talents to the manipulation of its bureaucratic possibilities. Thus, the international banker may in time become almost oblivious to the underlying realities of living, as he devotes his whole time to the manipulation of the superstructural symbols. And doubtless he mitigates his desiccation somewhat by covertly making his profession his "mother" or his "home." His occupation becomes a "vessel" holding many more connotations than are disclosed by its public label.

This may be a tolerable solution for him. It prevents the full ravages of alienation. It is the "comes after" for his own "goes before." But it does not similarly provide fullness for those who are recruited, by financial compulsions, to keep his books and file his papers. They must struggle in other ways to "repossess" their world, to regain it from the regions of "alienation." And they do so by recourse to shifts in allegiance to the symbols of authority. As their "boss" he is their "father," to whom they owe fidelity, and to whom they want to manifest fidelity. But insofar as they hope to repossess their world by ways analogous to his, they have thoughts of replacing him. In this they are "treacherous."

Hence again the stimulus to the ritual involving acceptance and rejection, with the various conflicts we have epitomized.

The forensic material accumulated from the past and by present co-operative practices provides also the "virtues" of alienation, as well as its "vices." By consulting these rich archives, we are enabled somewhat to "see ourselves as others see us." Here are the rudiments of "human freedom." We are forensically equipped to observe our own symptoms, primarily because of the instruments provided by speech.

Hence, we get to *language*. We get to the "methodology of the pun," as thinkers learn how to *plan* reorganization of the linguistic categories. This is managed essentially by metaphor, as we, by discounting, transfer a word from its literal setting into a figurative setting. From this we advance to the "dead metaphors" and "mixed metaphors" of abstract thought. Atop abstraction we erect further abstractions, as holding companies are erected atop operating companies. And they are marvelous short-cuts. They are shorthand, like higher mathematics. They can define a complexity quickly and easily—and without them we could at best vaguely sense a particular complexity. But they may carry us far from the immediacies of the senses and of childhood— hence, the poet strives to repossess them.

A new idea is a new invention. As such, like an invention it is full for its inventor, it is "earned" by him, since it is the "comes after" for his own "goes before." Others must earn it anew. Insofar as they don't, they fall into the dessications of psittacism (academicism): alienation is under way.

Poetry, criticism, poetry. One is born a poet; one acquires the social equipment of criticism; one becomes a poet-and-critic insofar as one "earns" the critical document by the pressure of his own experience.

As poet-plus-critic, one both acts and observes his act.

By this faculty of observation, he matures his acts with relation to other people.

As poet he is "synthetic." He puts things together by symbolic mergers. As critic he is "analytical." He can speculatively reassemble in a new way what has been taken apart. This is his "perspective," matured as far as possible by adjustment to the documents left by other people's perspectives. His "action" is his "passion" insofar as he can do no more. This is his "burden," and he makes the best of it. Beyond this he is resigned, humbled, mystified.

Looking at art, the critical documents, others, himself, he develops the tempered form of hypochondriasis that is called "diagnosis." He wins in defeat by "charging it off to experience." And we all, as poets-and-critics working together, win somewhat by developing poetic symbols and critical formulations that enable us to size up the important factors of reality (particularly by recourse to the comic critique of social relationships) and to adopt workable attitudes toward them.

The resources of critical analysis, whereby we may observe ourselves, have become very rich, particularly since the time when rationality attained such powerful bureaucratic embodiment in the methods of science (technology) and the methodology of science (philosophy). Since we have amassed the documents, it would be "cultural vandalism" not to use them. Hence, the "moral obligation" to do as much as can be done with the resources of analysis now open to us.

Had the world, for some fabulous reason, quieted down after the age of Elizabeth, we should probably now be doing nothing other than to find the critical-conceptual equivalents of the strategy involved in Shakespeare's metaphors. We should be verbalizing the processes involved in his synthetic acts. Our "Asiatic quietude" would take this form. As it is, the pressure of new necessities makes it impossible for us to pursue this "humane" task alone. However, these new necessities are such that they require the maximum of such analytic effort. For technology itself has produced an analytic world—hence, no other instrument but analysis can confront it with the necessary precision. This analysis on the other hand, is *integrative* insofar as it gives substance to a synthesizing *attitude*.

We grant that, up to this point, we have been attempting the analytic substantiation of a synthesizing attitude by writing a dictionary-without-alphabetical-sequence. We shall now turn from our preparatory "smattering" method to an alphabetically arranged series of little essays on a few dozen of the terms we consider pivotal. Our dictionary is meant to serve simultaneously as recapitulation and further development.

CHAPTER TWO

DICTIONARY OF PIVOTAL TERMS

Alienation

A TERM borrowed from Marx, who borrowed it from
Hegel, who borrowed it from Diderot.* We use it to
designate that state of affairs wherein a man no longer
"owns" his world because, for one reason or another, it seems
basically unreasonable. Alienation has both spiritual and
material aspects. The "proletarian" is materially alienated,
if he is deprived of the "goods" which his society has decreed
as "normal." He is "spiritually" alienated insofar as this
deprivation leads him to distrust the rationale of purposes
by which he is deprived.

He "repossesses the world" somewhat by forming allegiance to a new rationale of purpose (though this involves all
the "ills of interregnum" we have discussed with reference
to the symbols of authority). Even many who still receive
material benefits from the ailing structure likewise become
aliens, in that they have lost their belief in the society's
reasonableness. Thus, materially rewarded but spiritually
alienated nobles were friendly to the Encyclopedists, who
offered them a new rationale of purpose. And materially
rewarded but spiritually alienated members of the bour-
goisie may be in varying degrees prone to the Marxist
critique of capitalism.

The growing resistance to education on the part of those
who are particularly conscious of their "stake in" the pre-

* Its full genealogy would apparently carry it back to the church,
which named as "alienation" the transfer of property from church
hands. A good synonym for our purposes is "estrangement."

216

vailing property relationships stems from their very correct awareness of the fact that knowledge accelerates the process of spiritual alienation among their own class. Their own children threaten to become "dispossessed" of their belief in the "reasonableness" of the capitalist order, and in this way they poignantly dispossess the fathers (who are denied their "rights" to their children's allegiance). Such disastrous "deflations" can be "cushioned" psychologically (insofar as they can or should be cushioned at all) only by a terminology that makes the discussion of the issue itself "reasonable."

The bourgeois ideals of "freedom" were built upon the "right" to alienate the serfs' "property in" the use of communal lands. By fighting for the alienation of property, the rising merchants pried lands from those whose unwritten title to their use had survived via the feudal sanction-by-custom. The growth of alienation also greatly increased the proportion of *mobility* in society, which must be matched by a conceptual mobility of a sort not possible in rigid ideologies.

As a motto for our notes on alienation we might borrow a text from an author who wrote when the new criteria were gaining implementation through the social order. Our lines are from *As You Like It*. Rosalind, the friend of Celia, has been forced to depart, at the command of Celia's father, a noble. Celia decides to flee also, though her flight will cost her her feudal inheritance. And to conceal her real identity under a false identity, she chooses another name:

Rosalind: But what will you be called?
Celia: Something that hath a reference to my state:
    No longer Celia, but Aliena.

A compensatory increase in sensuality generally accompanies a loss of faith in the reasonableness of a society's purposes. People try to combat alienation by *immediacy*, such as the senses alone provide. Ages of strong social fervor are somewhat Puritanical (as for instance contemporary Russia) because the logic of the social framework can engross them.

In particular, the vastly non-sensual world of technology, accountancy, and abstraction necessary to operate the modern industrial plant would seem to make for compensatory sensuality, whenever for any reason extreme social fervor abates. Such fervor may abate under industrial socialism in proportion as the productive plant nears completion. It abates under capitalism long prior to such completion, owing to cynical loss of faith in capitalism's reasonableness. Thus, since capitalist morality is integrated with the structure of money, periods of inflation are always strongly sensual. And erotic literature acts then as a kind of "informal casuistry," taking up the slack by sensual "prayers" that are often as remote and abstract in their way as the counter-abstractions of technology and finance.

Compensatory immediacy, by the imagery of sensualism, usually begins with the paradoxical formula: "Our *page* is lascivious, but our *life* is pure." But since attitudes are incipient acts, in time the paradoxical ingredient is efficiently filtered out of this formula, life and page becoming identical. The paradox is the period of transition. But when others build upon it, carrying on the development where the paradoxist left off, their own "comes after" must be of a different order. The *consistently sensual* (in both imagery and life) is the "comes after" that matches a *paradoxically sensual* "goes before."

When pure sensuality in turn has become the "goes before," one must advance to sadism as the adequate "comes after." But usually, when alienation has advanced to the stage where sadism is felt necessary as the means of restoring immediacy, there are also many "rationales" of hatred to add other sadistic invitations.

"Running amuck" is the response to the alienations suffered by a primitive people under the imperialist domination of a more "civilized" people who possess the insignia and instruments of authority. The power of the invader has destroyed the people's faith in their traditional frame, while property relations and social proscriptions prevent them from making peace with the new frame.

Alienation creeps into literature in this wise: A given productive pattern leads to the crystallization of a corresponding pattern of manners. These manners are in turn projected into literary tradition as style. And new men arise to form themselves in keeping with these norms of style. However, even as they do so, the rise of new material causes the productive pattern to be altered. Hence, it "slides out from in under" the stylistic tradition by which the writers are still forming themselves.

The matter of "insignia" also operates here. In the feudal period, for instance, the "reasonableness" of the society's purposes was headed in the insignia of the nobles, insignia which the serfs could own vicariously. Nor were the underlings, in the heyday of the structure, psychologically cheated in their enjoyment of such vicarious ownership. Eventually, however, the rise of new productive methods changed the nature of these insignia. They did not merely exemplify the "logical culmination" of the whole society's purposes, the focus of its "reasonableness." Rather, they were vessels of an *antithetical* privilege, representing owners *in contrast with* the dispossessed. The insignia thus became, as Veblen would say, "invidious." Hence, a writer in taking possession of them was stylistically laying claim to preferment. And insofar as the productive pattern that gave life to the stylistic procedures was crumbling, he was investing in a property that became more and more restricted and unreal. We believe that Shakespeare, whose investment in courtly diction was considerable, can be analyzed as a writer who felt, in the course of his production, the ways in which new modes of production and ownership (matched by new manners and style) were arising to endanger his stylistic property, a threatened alienation which he countered by shifting his holdings (mainly through the devices of "tragic ambiguity").*

Being Driven into a Corner

Children, in their moral thoroughness, tend to feel themselves either "good" or "bad." Let them do some slight deed on the plus side, and they possess a sense of "absolute virtue." Let them do some slight deed on the minus side, and they

---

* Does not the present controversy about the Supreme Court hinge, in its psychological aspects, about a matter of alienation?

We have noted, for instance, the part that a sense of a structure's *reasonableness* plays in giving people a sense of ownership (in that they can *identify themselves* with the insignia in which that reasonableness is vested). We have also noted the *truncated* nature of the democratic state, in that the appointment of puppets for carrying on the political business of the state militates against the full expression of the father-symbol as the head of authority. (So strong is this requirement that even in a Communist play, *Let Freedom Ring*, we find an old man left, at the end of the play, to serve as the "vessel" of the proletarian movement, even though the young agitator has been killed. This "patriarch," standing stolidly at the coffin of the younger man as the curtain falls, turns "defeatism" into "sanction.")

We should also note the lure (with respect to tests of "reasonableness") behind the Townsend Plan, which proposes in effect that old age be *rewarded* (in contrast with competitive tests requiring that men of advanced years be scrapped like obsolete machinery). There is latent here

feel themselves to be the very essence of villainy. They do not "discount." They supply no "graded series."

Theologians did supply a "graded series" of sins, with a corresponding graded series of penances. They invented a kind of celestial book-keeping to regularize spiritual commerce. Like incipient Benthams, they erected a structure of theological legality that found the "exact quantitative equivalent" for every offense (whereat they could decide in quantitative terms the balance due in penance). This was the first "moral arithmetic," awaiting its completion at the Renaissance in the secularizing of its heavenly accountancy.

As a salvation device it was extremely efficient. It supplied the necessary graded series whereby all shades of grey could be introduced between the intolerable opposites, the white of absolute goodness and the black of absolute wickedness. The invention was obviously of benefit in mitigating the schizoid tendencies that we note particularly in the

---

the "reasonableness" of gerontocracy, the "council of elders" informing the "logic" of life in most primitive tribes. Even a young man can "identify himself" with such a course of events, since it gives a logic to the inevitable biologic curve of his own development. It makes old age a promise rather than a threat.

Now, we suggest that in our democracy, the Supreme Court comes closest to possessing the attributes of patriarchalism (as in British democracy the same "magical" role is vested in the monarch).

And this strong psychological resistance exists, to be "cashed in on" by financial interests who find the present structure of the Court helpful to their maintenance of the *status quo*, threatened by the legislative and executive branches of the government (the less "patriarchal" branches, by reason of their closer subjection to the democratic delegation of authority to puppets). Because of the appeal in such symbolic factors, among the agrarian elements in particular there is resistance to the President's proposals (a resistance strengthened by the stronger sense of

antithesis-thinking of the nineteenth century, the "either-or" of Byronism. But in proportion as the easing of conscience became so thoroughly implemented by the theologians' accountancy, there was a tendency to produce indulgences on a quantity basis, with corresponding deterioration in quality. And in time the complete rationality of this legal structure was "cashed in on," in the most literal sense of the term.

Further, although anyone might purchase exoneration so long as he allowed the church's teaching *as a whole* to remain intact, a question at any point put him outside the pale of this graded series. If he did not recant, he was forced, so far as the church's standards were concerned, again to rate himself like the wayward child as "absolutely" bad.

This is what we mean by "being driven into a corner." We refer to such situations as become "amplifying devices," requiring the man who would reject a little to reject a great deal. For when a priesthood has built a structure that bears

---

family relationships in agrarian communities, and leading to sympathy with the Court as "fathers" despite the long history of adverse decisions which the Court has meted out to them since the days of populism).

Hence, attacks upon the dignity of the Court are secret threats of alienation, as they attack whatever insignia of "reasonableness" our ailing economic structure is still felt to possess. The Court is a "vessel," a "psychological investment" in which even the victims of its decisions share, being "stockholders" by identification with its insignia. And scrupulous people, prone to such naive but profound responses, can agree to the President's proposals only insofar as their anguish or their impatience makes them willing to adopt somewhat the role of "symbolic parricides." Such a role is more natural to the proletariat, which has veered towards other symbolizations of the patriarch (such as Marx, Lenin, Stalin or, in the maternal aspect, figures like Clara Zetkin and Mother Bloor—or, at present, that phenomenal vessel of "non-delegated authority," John L. Lewis).

upon every important aspect of a man's social relations, they thereby make it hard for him to question the structure at any one point. Each item involves all the others. And before he is through, he is forced to reject all sorts of ingredients that he might, originally, have left unquestioned.

He can avoid the issue sometimes by astute "casuistic stretching" of his own. He can rephrase his position so that it makes a fairly satisfactory fit with the demands of the orthodox.

If, however, there is some marked conflict of material interests also involved in his ideological innovation, the likelihood of reclamation is greatly lessened. In such instances, the orthodoxy excommunicates him. And since the orthodoxy "owns" all the recognized avenues of approach to sociality, if the excommunicated would avoid the corner of negativism, he must recruit a group who steal the insignia of the orthodox. To this extent, his group is "saved by logomachy," since it still builds its character by using the prayers of the orthodox. But there is also the possibility that the whole group will be "driven into a corner," at least during the "interregnum" between the formulation of their doctrine and its eventual enshrinement as the new basis of orthodoxy.

Occasionally, when one makes a statement, his auditor will reprove him by observing that some Nazi ideologist has made a similar statement. No account is taken of the difference in the statement's function, due to the difference of *context* in which it is used.

This kind of "refutation" exemplifies to the fullest the process of "being driven into a corner" whereby one despoils himself of an idea's serviceability simply because his opponent has misused it. And when hearing objections of such a sort, we have sometimes been fervently grateful that no Nazi ideologist happens to have grown rhapsodic in praise of the multiplication table. Presumably, if he had, the thoroughgoing anti-Nazi would feel it necessary to condemn arithmetic.

Bridging Device

The symbolic structure whereby one "transcends" a conflict in one way or another. Thus, the philosophic framework of Aquinas bridged the distinction between serfs and nobles by a theory that located and justified the status quo. Authority was grounded in custom. The distinction in status was established by custom. And this customary order was established by God in punishment for the fall of man (whereby government, property, and slavery were made inevitable by natural law). The bourgeoisie "transcended" a distinction in status by conceiving of all men in terms of bourgeois man. The Marxist proposes to recognize the conflict, which he "transcends" by a philosophy of history that is a "bridge" into a "classless society" of the future.

All "symbolic mergers" can be called "bridging devices," as they cannot be explained with reference to their face value alone, but are a "way across" to many other ingredients (as when one man says "liberty" and means the right to retain his capitalist holdings, and another by the same word means socialism). There are also explicitly conceptual bridging devices whereby one may use an opponent's statement by "discounting." When objects are not in a line, and you would have them in a line without moving them, you may put them into a line by shifting your angle of vision.

Thus recently we saw an irritating example of such strategy. A man had written a book to show the corruption of newspaper advertising. The reviewer in a newspaper praised it highly. And he "bridged" the discordancy by his moral: "These facts show you conclusively that you should only believe the commercial advertising published in this newspaper."

Bureaucratization of the Imaginative

This formula is a "perspective by incongruity" for naming a basic process of history. Perhaps it merely names the process of dying. "Bureaucratizaton" is an unwieldy word, perhaps even an onomatopoeia, since it sounds as bungling as the situation it would characterize. "Imaginative" suggests pliancy, liquidity, the vernal. And with it we couple the incongruously bulky and almost unpronounceable.

Gide has said somewhere that he distrusts the carrying-out of one possibility because it necessarily restricts other possibilities. Call the possibilities "imaginative." And call the carrying-out of *one* possibility the *bureaucratization* of the imaginative. An imaginative possibility (usually at the start Utopian) is bureaucratized when it is embodied in the realities of a social texture, in all the complexity of language and habits, in the property relationships, the methods of government, production and distribution, and in the development of rituals that re-enforce the same emphasis.

It follows that, in this "imperfect world," no imaginative possibility can ever attain complete bureaucratization. Even capitalism, as Sombart has pointed out, has not attained its "ideal" perfection. Capitalism would not be ideally perfect until we had a monetary equivalent for everything, until every last bit of material exchange among friends were done for profit, until every casual greeting were given at a price (and that price as high as the traffic would bear).

In bureaucratizing a possibility, we necessarily come upon the necessity of compromise, since human beings are not a perfect fit for *any* historic texture. A given order must, in stressing certain emphases, neglect others. A bureaucratic order approaches the stage of alienation in proportion as its "unintended by-products" become a stronger factor than the original purpose. The heightening percentage of alienation corresponds with an intensification of class struggle because, at the point where the accumulation of unintended by-products is becoming impressive and oppressive, there will be a class of people who have a very real "stake in" the retention of the ailing bureaucratization. From this you get a further alienation—as the dispossessed are robbed even of their spiritual possession, their "right" to be obedient to the reigning symbols of authority.

Obedience to the reigning symbols of authority is in itself natural and wholesome. The need to reject them is painful and bewildering. The dispossessed struggle hard and long to remain loyal—but by the nature of the case, the bureaucratic order tends simply to "move in on" such patience and obedience. Eventually, sectarian divergence becomes organized (as thinkers manipulate the complex forensic structure, to give it a particular emphasis in one direction). But those in possession of the authoritative symbols tend to drive the opposition into a corner, by owning the priests (publicists, educators) who will rebuke the opposition for its disobedience to the reigning symbols. The opposition abandons some of the symbolic ingredients and makes itself "ready to take over" other symbolic ingredients.

Insofar as it can unite in a new collectivity, progressively affirming its own title to the orthodoxy, tendencies toward the negativistic, satanistic, sectarian, disintegrative, and "splintering" fall away. But insofar as its own imaginative possibility requires embodiment in bureaucratic fixities, its necessary divergences from Utopia become apparent.

Many persons who scorn the very name of Utopia become wounded as the "imperfect world" of bureaucratic compromise is revealed. They are simply Utopians-scorning-the-name-of-Utopian. At times, the doctrine of *Zweck im Recht* is required to understand a policy. By this doctrine, we are advised to "discount" the face value of a statement by noting what "interests" it protects. The principle of the discount advises us to note that many advocates of socialism, for instance, can gain asylum for their views by interlarding their appeal with attacks upon Russia. Thereby they can advocate an unpopular philosophy by "sharing" with their audience the usual capitalist aversions. They need not be hampered by the realistic problems involved in the "bureaucratization of the imaginative." Or in explicitly condemning Utopianism, they can conceal from both their auditors and themselves the underlying Utopian pattern of their thought.

We concede the close relationship between this concept (bureaucratization of the imaginative) and Spengler's culture-civilization dichotomy. But we should hold that every individual man, at any period in history, must develop his own mature "civilization" out of his own childhood "culture." Again, Spengler's use of the formula vows him to an overly mystical notion of historic change. And it asks us to think of culture and civilization as historic absolutes, with one reigning at one time and the other reigning at another, a schematization that makes for a false philosophy of purpose. Yet undeniably the accumulated by-products leading to "alienation" are greater in some periods than in others. And our concept might offer a method of conversion whereby Spengler's formula could be sufficiently "discounted" to make it useful for a comic critique of social relationships.

In the modern laboratory, the procedure of *invention* itself (the very essence of the imaginative) has been bureaucratized. Since the time of the Renaissance, the West has been accumulating and perfecting a *methodology* of invention, so that improvements can now be coached by routine. Science, knowledge, is the bureaucratization of wisdom.

We could state the principle of the laboratory in this proposition: "Every machine contains a cow-path. That is: there are embodied somewhere in its parts the variants of a process that remains simply because the originators of the machine embodied this process in their invention. It has been retained, not because it has been criticized, evaluated, and judged to be the best possible process, but simply because no one ever thought of questioning it. And it wasn't questioned because it was never even formulated, never given explicit verbalization. If the original inventor used a variant of reciprocating motion in one process of his machine, for instance, improvements may have been designed that simply introduced new variants of reciprocating motion. Once you *name* this, by the "efficiency" of abstractions, you are equipped to ask yourself whether the basic process might be altered: could you change from a reciprocating motion to a *rotary* motion, and would the change be more efficient by reason of its advance from the *cradle* to the *wheel*? Maybe it would, maybe it wouldn't; in any case, you have a "cue," a "lead," for criticism and experiment. As it stands, the process is a "cow path," in pious obedience to its secret grounding in the authority of custom.

Our formula, "perspective by incongruity," is a parallel "methodology of invention" in the purely conceptual sphere. It "bureaucratizes" the "mass production" of perspectives. It "democratizes" a resource once confined to a choice few of our most "royal" thinkers. *It makes perspectives cheap and easy.*

Must there follow the usual deterioration in quality? Unquestionably. But "deterioration" from one standpoint is "improvement" from another standpoint. The deterioration that would go with the democratization of planned incongruity should be matched, we hold, by a corresponding improvement in the quality of popular sophistication, since it would liquidate belief in the absolute truth of concepts by reminding us that the mixed dead metaphors of abstract thought are metaphors nonetheless.

It should *make one at home* in the complexities of relativism, whereas one now tends to be *bewildered* by relativism. And relativism cannot be eliminated by the simple legislative decrees of secular prayer (as when one tries to exorcize it by verbally denying its presence). We must erect new co-ordinates *atop* it, not *beneath* it. For this reason we hold that a popular understanding of the rational pun, as made bureaucratically available by a "methodology of the pun," should be a *social* improvement. The issue will be discussed more fully in our remarks on "perspective by incongruity."

Casuistic Stretching

By casuistic stretching, one introduces new principles while theoretically remaining faithful to old principles. Thus, we saw the church permitting the growth of investment in a system of law that explicitly forbade investment. The legalists "took up the slack" by casuistic stretching, the "secular prayer" of "legal fictions."

The devices for ostensibly retaining allegiance to an "original principle" by casuistic stretching eventually lead to demoralization, which can only be stopped by a new start.

The term, for our purposes, certainly need not be confined to law. It could apply, for instance, to the strategies of "tragic ambiguity" whereby a new trend is given its first expression in the role of a reprobate. The court fool, in plays at least, introduced serious views casuistically in profiting by his "professional immunity." And if there never were court fools so philosophic as those portrayed by dramatists, the dramatist doubtless felt sympathy with the role because the dramatist himself, as entertainer to the tyrannic public, was often forced into analogous casuistries.

All "metaphorical extension" is an aspect of casuistic stretching. Our proposed methodology to "coach" the transference of words from one category of associations to another, is casuistic. In this technical sense, it is casuistic to speak of the "head" of a "corporation" or the "network" of a "broadcasting" system. Since language owes its very existence to casuistry, casuistic stretching is beyond all possibility of "control by elimination." The best that can be done is to make its workings apparent by making casuistry *absolute* and *constant*. In Shakespeare, casuistry was absolute and constant. He could make new "metaphorical extensions" at random. He could leap across the categories of association as readily as walking. The mortmain of dead metaphors ("abstractions") that has gripped us since his time has rigidified this original liquidity. All sorts of "academicisms" have arisen, even among those who belong to no formal academy. We propose by the casuistry of "planned incongruity" to follow in the conceptual vocabulary the lesson that Shakespeare taught us with his.

The nature of our language, for instance, leads us to be shocked at the idea of putting opposites together. And our reliance upon *phonetic* writing, instead of *ideographic* writing, re-enforces this tendency. To illustrate: Suppose we had an ideographic writing. Suppose that, in this script, the sign for "unlawful" was the *gallows*. And suppose that the sign for "lawful" was the *halo*. If, then, we wanted to invent a sign for "law," we might simply put the signs for "lawful" and "unlawful" together, getting *gallows-halo*. (The Egyptian hieroglyphs seem to have done precisely this, as does the story of Christ's crucifixion between two criminals.) Such ideograms would be in themselves reminders that a concept like "law" automatically "contains opposites." But since our *phonetic* notation does not reveal such matters, we must wait for an adventuresome philosopher to discover by years of military thought that "everything is its other."

Or, if we had a sign for "good" and a sign for "bad," we might put them together quite simply to get our sign for "morality." But when you start with "morality," in our phonetic form of notation, you go on developing by *grammar*. Instead of starting with morality as "good-bad," you start with it as a sound. And you can put another sound, "a" privative, in front of it—whereat you begin worrying, not with "good-bad," but with "morality and amorality."

Our language is somewhat haphazard. Sometimes we have the words for the opposites, without the "higher" abstraction that would unite them. Sometimes we have the "higher" abstraction, and believe so thoroughly in its pristine unity that we don't even seek for the antitheses subsumed in it.

A truly liquid attitude towards speech would be ready, at all times, to employ "casuistry" at points where these lacunae are felt. We believe that the result, in the end, would be a firmer kind of certainty, though it lacked the deceptive comforts of ideological rigidity.

The reader may legitimately ask why, after the many deceptions we have attributed to casuistic stretching, we should nonetheless want to say something in its favor. First, we believe that dissociative trends can be arrested only by a return to integrative thought (the over-simplification of which is manifested in adherence to a "party line"). And this over-simplification must be corrected in turn by *latitudinarianism*, which is another word for casuistic stretching. But also:

The process of casuistic stretching must itself be subjected continually to *conscious* attention. Its own resources (for simply providing a "higher level" of deception, a new unction) must be transcended by the explicit conversion of a method into a methodology. The difference between casuistry as a method and casuistry as a methodology is the difference between mystification and clarification, between the concealing of a strategy (*ars celare artem*) and the description of a strategy (criticism as explanation).

Our remarks on "Control" will indicate why we feel that one must seek to enunciate a methodology of casuistry rather than to eliminate casuistry. The latter choice would be preferable if it were possible. But since the world is too complex for such simplifications, one can only hope to "take up the slack" by increased awareness.

Clusters

Significance gained by noting what subjects cluster about other subjects (what images *b, c, d* the poet introduces whenever he talks with engrossment of subject *a*). Excellent examples are provided by Caroline Spurgeon's charting of Shakespeare's imagery.

Were we to have a survey of the hills and valleys of the

mind, to match our government's geological surveys, it would be done by the charting of clusters, which have a momentous effect upon history. For instance, a certain man may be a great popular idol. But this does not necessarily mean that his popularity belongs in the cluster that could make him a good candidate for president. It may be in a cluster that absolutely forbids his election as president.

The humorist, Will Rogers, was a popular idol, but in an anti-presidential cluster. This situation was paradoxically apparent when, at a political convention during the pre-liminary balloting for presidential nomination, one bloc of delegates came forward with Will Rogers as their candidate. The move was meant as an hilarious indication that they had not yet made up their minds as to whom they would support. It said, in effect, "We like Will Rogers, and we don't like the way in which the balloting is going, and we'll show our liking for him and our uncertainties about a presidential candidate by this gesture. We can propose him without fear of our joke's being misunderstood because he is not in the presidential cluster."

By charting clusters, we get our cues as to the important ingredients subsumed in "symbolic mergers." We reveal, beneath an author's "official front," the level at which a lie is impossible. If a man's virtuous characters are dull, and his wicked characters are done vigorously, his *art* has voted for the wicked ones, regardless of his "official front." If a man talks dully of *glory*, but brilliantly employs the imagery of *desolation*, his *true subject* is desolation.

The charting of clusters will eventually reveal how thor-oughly the syntheses of poetry manage to eschew the "law of excluded middle" dear to argumentative thought. The symbol, as "vessel," may quite easily unite logical opposites. The same symbol may contain meanings of parents, child, wife, career, promise, and fear. It may contain both sexual gratification and castration, both retreat and aggression. Perhaps it is not complete as a "vessel" until it has secretly performed this merger of opposites by "transcendence."

Communion

In society, as a going concern, the network of co-operative practices is matched by a network of communicative symbols. "Communion" involves the interdependence of people through their common stake in both co-operative and symbolic networks. The artist specializes in the manipulation of the symbolic structure. He tends generally to communicate by reaffirming the norms of the co-operative structure. (And when discrediting one of the norms, he usually does so by affirming another of the norms: he pits one of his society's values against another of its values, so that even in an attitude of "rejection," he is not wholly "outside" the values of his society. Thus, in *An Enemy of the People*, Ibsen first prejudices us in favor of Dr. Stockman, who is to advocate the virtues of *isolation*, by dramatizing his *hospitality*.)

However, the problem becomes subtler. A given productive order necessarily requires over-emphases. It requires the hypertrophy of some human preferences and the frustration of others. Hence, in even a productive order as "nearly perfect" as we might imagine in "this imperfect world," there would be some amount of resistance or "deviation." The productive order would thus tend to establish not only a common set of norms, but also a common set of deviations from those norms. And an artist may "communicate" by symbolizing some latent deviation that the society shares in common. He may first do so by "tragic ambiguity," both giving vent to the deviation and symbolically punishing it. Or he may introduce it in "disarming" guise, as Empson shows when tracing how revolutionary values are first attributed to rogues, idlers, children, rustics, and fools. A writer like Cummings, we might say, deals almost completely in this "deviational" area, "communicating" not by re-enforcing the norms required for co-operation, but by sharing in our resistance to co-operative norms.

Malinowski has a term, "phatic communion," to designate the exchange of words not for explicit informative purposes, but as an easy way of establishing a bond. Stereotyped greetings, comments on the weather, polite inquiries about health, are examples. A subtler variant would be gossip, where people malign an absent friend, not so much because of a vindictive attitude towards the absent, but as an easy way of making allies for the moment. By setting up a "common enemy," they establish a temporary league. They are merely embodying, in a trivial way, what the Allies in the last war embodied when they shelved their differences for a time in their common cause against the Central Powers.

Socratic irony is perhaps the most ingenious possible development of phatic communion. The asking of questions is obviously a masterly shortcut for the establishment of "phatic communion." The young girl, with little to talk about, soon discovers how easy it is to establish communion by asking the young man about his plans. So Socrates, by asking questions, was apparently doing the most *social* of acts. But Socrates was an ironist. He did not merely ask questions. He *kept on* asking questions. He persisted. He *insisted.* And by driving on and on, piling one question atop another, he subtly converted the business of phatic communion into an extremely annoying occupation. In fact, people felt like killing him. In fact, they did kill him.

Another complex twist, whereby the *appearances* of communion actually *function* as exclusion, might be called "Christian vengeance." Thus: A man enters a room, lays something on the table, and goes out. That is all you saw. The performance was purely "neutral." But Mr. A was also present, and Mr. A is an adept at Christian charity. He is so charitable that he begins *forgiving* the man for the way in which he entered the room and laid the object on the table. He explains the poor fellow's mistakes with sympathetic understanding. And by the time he has finished with this efficient example of charity, he has indirectly contrived to *pile up many accusations* against the fellow. As the church "moved in on" such delicate resources (in so many profound variants that people could not possibly gauge what was going on) the mass production of negativism was inevitable.

Control

To control a bad situation, you seek either to eradicate the evil or to channelize the evil. Elimination vs. the "lightning rod principle," whereby one protects against lightning not by outlawing lightning but by drawing it into a channel where it does no damage. Naive liberal apologetics was too often of the elimination sort. In the end, it was at a disadvantage (which it rectified by simply howling down the opposition). Pamphleteering. When liberals began to think, not of eliminating war, but of finding "the moral equivalent for war," liberalism was nearing the state of maturity.

Cues

If you call a man a hero or a bastard, and mean it, it is unnecessary for us to seek, by tricks of exegesis, the "moral weighting" of your term. Your attitude is made obvious, since your private use of the word corresponds to its public connotations. On the other hand, you may use many words which seem neutral, but in actuality possess hidden weighting.

A man organizes an essay. He necessarily chooses certain pivotal verbalizations about which he hinges his discussion. He chooses these particular verbalizations because they *appeal* to him. Some other terms might be substituted in their place, so far as the pure logic of the case is concerned. But he makes a selection in accordance with subtle, personal tests of "propriety." Though the words are, on their surface, neutral, they fit together into an organic interdependent whole precisely because of their common stake in some unifying attitude of his. We may get cues prompting us to discern the underlying emotional connotations of words that even the user may consider merely "scientific" or "neutral." By locating these, we get glimpses of a subtler organization than is apparent when we take the words at their face value.

In this book, for instance, we have said much about the "comic frame." We have advocated, under the name of "comedy," a procedure that might just as well have been advocated under the name of "humanism." Presumably we selected "comedy" because, for one reason or another, the word "sounded better" to us. And when the author selects one word rather than another because it "sounds better" to him, his choice is guided by "overtones" that may not apply to his auditor at all.

The syllables of one's own name (or one's mere initials, if one is strongly "initial-minded") may subtly influence one's preferences for certain words or one's aversion to them. We have omitted from this edition some personal speculating on this point. While we still believe that it is correct "in principle," we also feel that it is far too tenuous.

We have also omitted similar speculations based on Sir

Richard Paget's book, *Human Speech*, attributing the origin of speech sounds to "gestures" of the tongue, throat, and mouth. However, the omissions should not be taken to imply any loss of faith in his theory, which still seems wholly convincing, particularly since it seems the perfect physiological counterpart to a "Dramatistic" theory of language. But our discussion here lacked the distinction between *philology* and *poetics* which we consider essential for our purposes (as explained in *Philosophy of Literary Form*, pp. 12-17). However, reverting to the magic of names, and having in mind the possibility that one might like to carve his personal name in the tree of language, we might at least retain the suggestion that "Maybe in our use of "*bureaucratization*" we would 'burke' the issue," though not, let us hope, in the stifling manner of Burke of Edinburgh, who, in the interests of science and money, committed the criminal acts that transformed the noun into a verb, a verb of such meaning as might dyslogistically name much of the thinking of Edmund Burke. However, we might note a special reason for discussing in this book the possible basic significance of *m* and *p* as "tonal gestures." For the "contact *m*" (of *mamma* and the sacred syllable *oom*) would be the phonetic reduction of "acceptance"; and the *p* (of *puke* and *spew*) would similarly enact the basic tonal dance of "rejection."

A purely logistical vocabulary, constructed of conventional signs almost totally lacking in tonal values, might seem to avoid such punning. But we doubt whether it really would succeed in doing so. Our confirmed belief in the impossibility of "control by elimination" would lead us to suspect that the same procedure was going on, at a subtler level. Everywhere in our society we see the mere *displacement* of symptoms rather than their *elimination*. The growth of complexity permits us to shunt them obscurely from one point to another (as with the coupon clipper, who need not himself be personally cruel; he can be kindness itself, while the organization behind his coupons performs the cruelty function). And so we tend to believe that a logistical vocabulary would merely conceal our puns more deeply, making them still more inaccessible to "discounting." The resultant puns might have to do with relationships of shape rather than sound.

The whole matter, incidentally, might suggest the need of a more charitable attitude towards the atrocious puns in Shakespeare. It is customary to dismiss them as mere "concessions to the populace." The crude members of his audience had to have their clowning. So Shakespeare simply "tithed," his apologists tell us in effect. He gave the vulgus just enough atrocious jingles to make them endure his subtler imaginative enterprises. We doubt this. Had he not sometimes "punned atrociously" in his blunt jingles, he could not have "punned subtly" in his most delicate metaphorical leaps. The blunt tonal pun and the subtle metaphorical pun are merely opposite ends of a single "graded series." His specialization in such matters required him to run the whole gamut. We may even say that, had he not sometimes punned atrociously, he would by the same token have had to drop some of his most vigorous characters from his plays. We do not mean literally that the vigor of their lines depended upon jingles. Their best lines are most often the ones in which there are no jingles. We mean that, by beginning with puns, he could *refine* them as he proceeded; but had he begun by legislating against them, he would have had nothing to refine.

One also, as we have indicated in other sections of the book, derives cues by noting discontinuities (important breaks in logic, subject matter, style, etc.). And one gets cues by noting the quality of the imagery that emerges at strategic points (as at beginnings or endings). One may also get cues by noting a *curve* of imagery (as a radical shift in imagery from one part of a work to another, or from one stage in a writer's career to another, would indicate a process of "conversion" or "rebirth"). Thus, an examination of the different contexts in which Shakespeare uses the words "ambition" and "ambitious" might reveal important changes in his attitude towards them, as it moved from its feudal to its bourgeois setting (as this "salvation device" became "democratized"). Complete shifts probably do not occur. There is a continuous identity persisting along with a change of identity. Even the "twice born" retain much of what they were (when the warrior Saul became a Christian, he was a "militant" Christian, even though he did change the first letter of his name).

Jacques' speech on the seven stages of man, in *As You Like It*, lays out for everyone (who completes the full cycle from birth to death by old age) a sequence of seven identities. He says, in effect, that even were there no such historical confusions as "class struggle" to perplex us, the mere glandular changes of the body would force us to act several different roles, varyingly at odds with one another:

> All the world's a stage,
> And all the men and women merely players;
> They have their exits and their entrances;
> And one man in his time plays many parts,
> His acts being seven ages.

He then proceeds to detail briefly these "situations," or

"motives," arising from the sojourn of the personality in its different "glandular environments": "the infant, mewling and puking in the nurse's arms"; the "whining schoolboy" (insufficiency of the "plaint"); "the lover, sighing like a furnace" (under "Imagery," we discuss the stove as sexual symbol); the "soldier, full of strange oaths" (the scurrility of war, when arising incongruously from a vocabulary of peace?); the "justice, in fair round belly" . . . "full of wise saws and modern instances" (the matured "forensic"?); the sixth stage, in "lean and slipper'd pantaloon" . . . "a world too wide for his shrunk shank"; and finally "second childishness" . . . "sans teeth, sans eyes, sans taste, sans everything."

Shakespeare does not here discuss the further issue: How much of one's past identity must be forgotten, how much remoulded, as he moves from one role to the next? The rituals of rebirth in art dredge this problem. Precisely what is omitted from *Jacques'* statement, the strategy of transition, forms the essence of *Shakespeare's* work. *His own* drama is the sequence of his plays. And in our closing remarks on "Imagery" we discuss the kind of "cues" one should note in charting this.

In his keen and scrupulous analysis of E. E. Cummings, in *The Double Agent*, R. P. Blackmur makes a point that we can very profitably borrow for our purposes. Cummings, he observes, has a stock of words that are frequently introduced without imagistic relevance, though the words themselves are the names of images. Their meaning is *purely* symbolic or abstract, despite their *apparent* concreteness.

Suppose, for instance, a poet used the word "flower" in all contexts involving associations with an enjoyed mistress. Hence, if the thought of an enjoyed mistress is associated with dainty shoes, or dainty conversation, or sojourn by the seashore, etc., then when discussing shoes, conversation, or sojourn by the sea, he might metaphorically refer to flowers or attributes of flowers. Or if there is a certain kind of rainfall associated in quality with the quality of an enjoyed mistress, we might read of an umbrella opening its petals, or perhaps the descent of the rain would be

petal-drops—flowerfalling

(which would mean, translated into "symbolistics": "To me raindrops are falling like the petals of a flower—and I think so, not because they particularly *look* like that, but because this is such a rain as makes me think of an enjoyed mistress").

In this hypothetical instance, there is some fair amount of purely imagistic, or descriptive relevance. But we may imagine a further step. The poet might be thinking of such a house as he would like to make love in—and so might say

your house—this brightly flower

—whereat the obedient reader might, in all good faith, try to persuade himself that he "saw" the house, imagining perhaps that the poet was referring obliquely to bright awnings. But as a matter of fact, the word in that context referred to no image. It signalized an *attitude*. It said: "This is a house towards which I have such *attitude* as is symbolized by my word 'flower' and its associates—don't try to figure out why the house looks like a flower, because I had no such thought in mind—I used the word here, not because it names an *image*, but because it names an *attitude*. Call it my 'flower' attitude. Or, if you will, say it is one of the *characters* that I keep intact in my lyrics, as though these

242

lyrics were a novel, and I were keeping one character as distinct from another as Scrooge is from Tiny Tim." By disclosing the occasions on which Cummings departs from the imagistic (descriptive) nature of a word, to use it purely as a symbolic (attitudinizing) function, Blackmur has exemplified with extraordinary imaginativeness one way of getting a "cue" from the perception of a discontinuity.

It is possible that a philosophy loses as much in translation as a poem does. The attempt to situate the value of philosophic verbalizations in their purely *conceptual* function, looking upon all else as mere "deception," may derive in part from the fact that we have studied the sources of philosophy, in Plato and Aristotle, without an intimate response to Greek. Thus we tend to get the mere *externality* of their verbalizations, somewhat as modern artists grasped only the externalities of African sculpture. The word "imitation," for instance, is *not* the "exact" translation of "mimesis," since the tonalities of the latter place it so much more fully in the "food and mother" category. Thus, "imitation" as a concept could not "sum up the full range of meanings" contained in the puns of "mimesis." For in pronouncing the two "m's," with approval, the Greek philosopher did not merely *conceptualize*, but also *acted*. His word, we might say, would be more like a *dance* than like a *concept*. And the dance contrived in effect to sanction an artistic process as "adult breast-feeding." "Imitation," on the other hand, is not half a meal.*

* See a very serviceable study by Richard McKeon, "Literary Criticism and the Concept of Imitation in Antiquity," charting the variety of contexts in which Plato employs the word. Looking through the lot, one is prompted to ask himself, "What is the organizing motive behind so many disparate usages?" And applying Paget's mode of thought, we

Discounting

Making allowance for the fact that "things are not as they seem." The methods whereby, as one looks at one thing, one reads something else into it. If a friend tells us something about ourselves, we discount the observation otherwise than we should if an enemy had made the same observation. The term is basic to an understanding of "what is going on." By proper discounting, *everything* becomes usable.

For instance, we have talked about the limitations of the caricature, or polemic. If one knows how to discount such forms, making due allowance for the ways in which necessities of emphasis drive one into a corner, realizing that a sentence cannot be designed to say everything at once (recalling that a man, writing on the run, as we all do, cannot supply all the modifiers) one can properly discount, and so properly use. If a man says "yes," you cannot conclude that he is a "yea-sayer," until you know the question he is answering. Often you cannot take a sentence at face value (you do not "understand its meaning" until you know the biographical or historic context subsumed by the speaker when he spoke it).

Sidney Hook has done valuable work analyzing the apparently "contradictory" statements of Marx by such "discounting." John Dewey did an excellent piece of discounting in his remarks on Aristotle's notions of "imitation." You

---

should say that the philosopher, in naming so many different manifestations by the same name, is organizing the complexity of experience by a *unifying attitude*, and that this attitude, as an "act," is rounded out mimetically, choreographically; by the choice of a "food-mother-grip" mode of verbalization. He is doing tonally what Benjamin Paul Blood (a picturesque writer quite sensitive to such matters) was doing when he selected, as the essential word of poets, "*memory*."

here learn that Aristotle did not mean "holding the mirror up to nature." He meant that a poet "imitates" when he reproduces the cultural norms of his group. If he made such a character as never was, Polyphemus for instance, he would be "imitating" insofar as the character faithfully embodied a typical pattern of attitudes prevailing in his culture. The pragmatic method is especially useful in admonishing us to discount. It does not take a doctrine at face value, but gets the meaning by observing how the doctrine behaved when released into a social texture. *Zweck im Recht* discounts—in fact, like Bentham, it even over-discounts.

By such "discounting" we can understand the true meaning behind Marx's formula, "dialectical materialism." In strict theory, the statement that there is "a constant *interaction* between *spiritual* and *material* factors" would provide no grounds for taking materialism as the starting point, the "essence" of the pair. There is no "starting point" for an "interaction," since the word by definition begins with both phases at once. Thus, it would be literally nonsense to say "This is both A and B, but it is only A." Formally, it means: "dualistic monism," which can't be. The choice of *materialism* as the essence is not "logical," but "sociological." The word is a slogan, a comprehensive bit of shorthand. The church had also recognized the interaction of spiritual and material factors. But the church's way of handling this recognition had been "moved in on." And since the church had taken "spirit" as the essence of the pair, Marx stressed the antithesis. Marx was seeking to restore the same insight in a way that could afford a new start. Thus, we do not get the full meaning of his philosophic statement until we "discount" it by considering its behavior in a social historical texture.

Those over-scrupulous philosophers who would discuss

such terms by formalistic co-ordinates alone, are bound to impoverish themselves by discovering that all thought is nonsense. The naive take philosophic symbols at their face value—and the logical positivists are simply the naive turned upside down. Neither extreme knows how to "discount." The naive rate the symbol at 100; the logistically sophisticate rate it at zero. Zero is not a discount—it is a massacre. And since we are "all in the same boat," the massacre becomes a self-massacre, and the "logical positivist" becomes the least positive of men.

"Earning"..One's World

There is no state of leisure. Every inheritance must be earned anew (otherwise, you get alienation and demoralization). Imbeciles who parrot the teachings of science without imagination are trying to take what they have not earned, and the result is discouraging. One tries to "bureaucratize" his own life—and even if he succeeds in part, the process is not alienation *for him*. It is the "comes after" that matches his own "goes before." It is the proper logical completion of his life (the imaginative being the seed, and the bureaucratization the fruit; they are two stages in the development of himself as an "entelechy"). But we hand on to others some measure of our own bureaucratization. And we thereby "dispossess" them by this inheritance, unless they find their own positive ways of "earning it anew." Bureaucratization equals sterility and death, except insofar as men make it the "goes before" for a new "comes after" of their own.

The remarkable insight bureaucratized in *money* (a shorthand-by-abstraction, whereby one can trade in the *symbols* of exchange and "state the relative value" of all commodities in a unified vocabulary, a quantitative Esperanto) has contributed the maximum "efficiency" to the notion of "earning one's world." Since morality is basically rooted in the framework of production and distribution (deriving its "gravitational pull" from these firm material aspects of sociality) capitalist morality is dependent upon the stability of the monetary structure at the same time that capitalist necessities continually threaten to destroy the stability of the monetary structure. Hence, "earning" tends to become a purely quantitative notion.

The relationship between "earning" and "alienation" thus tends to be simplified as a flat distinction between "employment" and "unemployment." But "employment" and "unemployment" are not absolute opposites; they are aspects of a single graded series wherein one is always more-or-less employed and more-or-less unemployed. Those whose unemployment goes by the more favorable name of "leisure" usually "earn" their world by the rigors of neurosis, as do those whose work does not sufficiently engage their capacities. Often the gangster is "more fully employed" than the honest trifler.

The opportunities for employment, in the wider sense, are best when the co-ordinates of the society seem most reasonable to its members. At such a time one can perform even a menial task with satisfaction, since he locates it by reference to the social purposes as a whole. He "identifies" his minor role with relation to the aims of the collectivity. And he "takes up the slack" between his capacities and his opportunities by the bridging devices of symbolism, that fit him as an individual to his corporate identity. Thus affirmation and resignation, action and passion, become one. It is obvious that insofar as society itself is torn asunder, the possibilities of such symbolic ambivalence are proportionately lessened.

Efficiency

Endangers proper preservation of proportions. If one invents a new breakfast food, he may efficiently delight our palates by leaving out some ingredient necessary for the total economy of the body. And someone else must efficiently over-specialize in dietetics to discover that the missing ingredient must be put back. All emphases, arising out of biological or historical necessities, are efficient in this way. The apologetics of liberalism was more efficient than was the thinking of the church, in that it overstressed the element of liberty and strategically ignored the element of obligation (and the church was closer to the truth in stressing the fact that rights and obligations are obverse and reverse of the same coin). On the other hand, the economic situation itself had been efficient in giving rise to an over-emphasis (a class had moved in on the opportunities provided by the religious frame, with drastic demoralization, pugnacity, and frustration as a by-product). Hence, the efficient over-emphasis of the situation itself required a counter-over-emphasis on the part of the liberators. A man cannot say everything at once. Thus, his statements are necessarily "efficient" in our sense; they throw strong light upon something, and in the process cast other things into shadow. We try to rectify this false efficiency by the counter-efficiency of "discounting."

The grotesque anchorites of the Dark Ages were typical of "efficiency." Having decided that the "essence" of religion was ascetic, they shaped their routines of living in strict accordance with a *rationale* of asceticism. They could thus be more "efficiently" ascetic than they would have been without this rationale. Theories of "pure beauty" stimulated a similar "efficient" search in esthetic movements of the nineteenth century. Art was supposed to contain an element of "beauty," present in varying degrees of density or diffusion. All that one should do, apparently, was find a way of straining off this "beauty," and then construct a work of this element alone. Hence, the search for "pure form"—beauty "in the abstract."

The attempts to get "religion" or "beauty" in pure isolation, rather than as a function of "practical impurity," are variants of the fertile lead suggested in *Alice in Wonderland*; the smiling cat vanishes, leaving only her smile. It was "pure" smile, the most "efficient" smile possible. And that's all you need ever do, to isolate one quality, making it the whole of life. Just get the smile without the cat. Or start with the cat, make it smile, and then take away the cat— and if you have performed the experiment properly, you are left in possession of an unadulterated smile, the *smiliness* of smile, an "efficient," abstract essence.

Sombart has charted the ways in which the development of money proved "efficient" in rationalizing human purpose. War is another extreme example of such "efficiency." In war, the whole life of a nation is organized for the purpose of winning the war. All issues are simplified in accordance with this test. Had one previously been *debating* the values of free speech? The needs of war efficiently settle the matter—even such a typical liberal as Woodrow Wilson agrees to the imprisonment of "conscientious objectors." The efficiency of war is also present in the efficiency of polemics, the lawyer's brief. The polemicist, or caricaturist, adopts a simple criterion for stressing certain considerations and omitting others. As a consequence, his tactics can assist us to understand the world only insofar as we know how to discount them by considering the *interests* behind his caricature. We understand the true proportions of a situation not on the basis of the work itself, but by making allowances for the planned disproportion.

At one time, news was transmitted very "inefficiently" by bards, who shaped their statement by all sorts of subtle tests (*saying* only what could be *sung*, for instance). This imaginative procedure has now been bureaucratized with the most astonishing efficiency—and as a by-product there have arisen wholly new criteria of purpose and procedure. These have become "the norm," so that our "bards" now shape their work by the tests of "headline thinking," literature becoming a mere offshoot of journalism plus the one-man enterprise. Journalism itself is a kind of haphazard philosophy, developed out of an organized method for assembling a literary product with maximum speed. We can discern the distortions of a yellow journal, but we can only speculate gropingly, on paper, as to the ways in which *all* journalistic efficiency becomes distortion methodized.

"Efficiency," to borrow a trope from the stock exchange, is excellent for those who approach social problems with the mentality of the "in and out" trader. It is far less valuable for those interested in a "long-pull investment." Otherwise stated: It violates "ecological balance," stressing some one ingredient rather than maintaining all ingredients by the subtler requirements of "symbiosis."

Let us close with a parable:

On a table there are many objects. Imagine one artist after another painting them, from different angles, in different lights, etc. Then imagine an artist who discovered a *flea* on the table. He might conceivably "revolutionize" the subject. He might so paint the scene as to emphasize the *new* discovery, the flea. Leaving in vagueness all the other objects upon which the other artists had been focusing their attention, he might bring out the little flea with startling singleness. He would tell us a "new thing" about the scene.

If he lived long enough, under sufficiently stabilizing conditions, he might in time lose his excitement about the flea. He might rectify his bad proportions, again giving proper consideration to the other objects on the table. He might in time very nearly restore the scene to the kind of emphases it had before he discovered the flea.

But other factors intervene. For instance, there is the factor of the market. His way of starring the flea may have market value; his innovation may be more salable precisely because it attracts attention like the flash of a traffic signal (a flashing light is more noticeable for advertising or animadversion than a steady one). With this "pragmatic test" to guide him, he "bureaucratizes" his discovery. He applies his method *mutatis mutandis* to other subjects, with "scientific efficiency." Perhaps he even puts in fleas where there were none (as the bureaucratization of "headline thinking" now makes it possible for the novelist to picture a universal rottenness with maximum "efficiency"; confronting a spectacle of human relationships that has much wholesomeness, he can "transcendentally" see it as wholly corrupt).*

In his case, we may not arrive at "emptiness." The incitement that led to his original stressing of the flea may carry

---

* We sometimes wonder whether our journals, even our better journals, have done anything other than to "bureaucratize" the Poe story, by bringing the communicative resources of the whole world to bear upon an isolated theme.

We refer among other things to the ideal of horror, whereby the author "sells" his masterpiece in competition with his competitors, by contriving to make the issue even more calamitous than they do. We once did ghosting work on a drug book—and our employer soon taught us that the "best" preparation for a proposal to control drugs was a picture of the world being destroyed by drugs. Find the threat of drugs everywhere—and you have established the "crying need" for the proposed legislation.

him over. He may once have been very badly treated by a flea, and would never forget it. Or he may, humble fellow, "identify" himself with the flea (and so with "extensions" of the flea-principle to other lowly forms of life).

But suppose a Flea School of Art develops. It starts without this intimacy. It approaches the whole subject *from without*. It picks up the *mannerism*, without the *drive*. By this stage, the "imaginative" has become thoroughly "bureaucratized." "Efficiency" of this sort explains why Jones always at some point warns his friends against Jonesism.

Essence

An act has either co-operative or competitive features. You select one or the other as the "essence." Thus the euphemistic may say, for instance, that the act is done "for the glory of God." The debunkers (in the Nietzschean line of thought) may select the militaristic ingredient as its essence; or in the Bentham line, may say that the act is done for "gravy," self-interest, self-aggrandizement. A "comic" term for the essence of motivation accepts neither—it expects an act to be moral, and it expects the actor to "cash in on" his moral assets, in one way or another. It is not unduly

------

This is the way in which the "esthetic of the Poe story" has come to dominate the news, tending to make *all* journals yellow journals.

Allied with this, is the piecemeal character of news. Everything must be in a separate bin. Each article must have one simple theme, treated independently of everything else in the universe. Find out something about the tariff that you can tell your friends in a sentence. Expand it by adroit variations into an article. And you are the ideal reporter— whereupon, in the course of a lifetime, many handsome trees have been chopped down, as you learn how to say, very swiftly in several hundred words, something that can be said quite slowly in one short paragraph.

exalted, hence not exposed to cynical disillusionment. It seeks to "size things up" in a way that makes one shrewd, but not in a vocabulary that would make co-operation impossible if the implications of the vocabulary were logically carried out. It takes for granted people's readiness to exploit whatever insignia they may possess.

"Essence" is an aspect of "efficiency." The "propagandist" writer of "proletarian" fiction, for instance, believes that the "class struggle" is the "essence" of the contemporary situation. Accordingly, he writes stories about strikes and lock-outs, that stress the "class struggle" with great "efficiency." The critic who so lives that his encounter with such experience is secondary, resents this essence as "schematization," "over-simplification," and "sentimentality." His situation enables him to adopt a somewhat Olympian attitude towards this particular efficiency.

But such critics' discussion of art often seems to be based upon an implicit "perfect world" system of judgments. In a perfect world, art would be devoid of "efficiency." The writer would be a perfectly balanced sub-whole in a perfectly balanced super-whole. He would be the microcosm that matched the macrocosm. He would define his identity by membership in one single all-inclusive corporation.

One could find no quarrel with this criterion, if it were *explicitly* offered as an "ideal" norm. Critics are expected, by the rules of the game, to be explicit. And the explicit adoption of a "perfect world" criterion would abide by the rules. The difficulty enters when they discuss the manifestations of an "imperfect world" without stating that they are testing by perfect-world ideals.

Were they explicit, they would not find it enough to "condemn" efficiency. They would rather, like Aquinas, temper their own notions of absolute, all-inclusive essence by a distinction between "essence" and "existence." Aquinas was a realist. He knew that if you adopted a perfect-world criterion of essence, you must modify it with imperfect-world considerations of the "existential." One may take wholeness as the "essence" of art, for instance; but he should proceed to add that, since any one man's *existence* necessarily leads to an over-stressing of certain ingredients and an under-stressing of others, society as a going concern here on earth always leads to some measure of "efficiency" (the destruction of complete "ecological balance").

To justify their position, they should state precisely what is the one super-corporation of which all men are members. And they should show that there are no other corporations legitimately claiming rival allegiances. They must explicitly discuss and refute the manifestations of "pluralism," resulting from the fact that a man may be at one and the same time "a member of several corporations whose identities are not wholly in agreement with one another."

Forensic

Material supplied by the forum, the market place. The materials of law, parliamentary procedure, traffic regulation, scientific-causal relationships evolved by complex and sophisticated commerce (of both the material and spiritual sorts). In primitive societies, the forensic is at a minimum, but not wholly absent. Its basis is to be found in the council of elders, who seek to evolve an explicit verbalization and rationalization of the tribal acts, attitudes, and policies. Insofar as it grows rich, it becomes more capable of sectarian stressing (on the part of "specialists" who emphasize and logically extend one or another of its ingredients).

The child necessarily develops without much awareness

of this forensic material. He is concerned with his immediate relatives and playmates, his toys and animals, material objects like food, chairs, tables, trees, cellar, and attic. Even if you explicitly tell him of the complex situations involved in our broad social relationships, he does not grasp their relevance. He can, it is true, be taught a set of terms. But they remain essentially *alien*, since he has not yet *earned* them by his own experience.

Often, when he becomes mature enough really to grasp something of their true significance, he is overwhelmed. This is particularly the case when he has been trained by a smattering of religious co-ordinates, with which the sophistications of the forensic lore can make a bad fit. But any naive heroism, even of a purely secular sort, prepares him for the same disillusionment, as he gradually becomes mature enough to size up the ways in which people cash in on their moral assets, and as he discerns the same behavior in himself.

Hence, the onslaught of the forensic must always come somewhat as a shock. In our own case, the shock was paralleled by a purely physical phenomenon. Your correspondent was near-sighted. As a result, the world was composed of soft, blurred edges. Just at the time when he was making his first "cynicizing" acquaintance with the sophisticated lore of the forensic (as embodied in the vast comic literature developed since the rise of capitalism) he was sent to an oculist. As he emerged, with glasses, he came suddenly into a world of harsh outlines. He had not been immunized to the sight by small homoeopathic doses. It "hit" him. He saw the lines and blotches on peoples' faces, and the discomfiture was *alienating*. We submit that this same process prevails, in subtler ways, when one first begins really to understand the documents of the forensic.

There is a natural tendency to rejection (the "negation"

of the childhood "thesis"). The "debunker," no matter how mature his writing may be on the surface, remains at this stage. "Transcendence" does not occur until he "negates the negation." This process whereby he puts the pre-forensic and the forensic together, has also been called the state "beyond good and evil," or "beyond the opposites."

"Good Life"

A project for "getting along with people" necessarily subsumes a concept of "the good life." So let us formulate it briefly:

Maximum of physicality. Insofar as people outrage the necessities of the physical economic plant, they become soulful in grotesque ways. Many psychologists are making a dubious living by selling cures to people who think that cures can be bought, whereas these people might have earned a cure, or earned immunity from the state of affairs wherein they needed a cure, by adequate physical expression. The more that is done by the pressing of a button (or its equivalent, the hiring of help) the greater will be the quantity production of poetasters (the neuroses of the psychologically unemployed, the over-sedentary leisured, are bad poems). We must, unfortunately, resort to the semi-decadence of "sports," insofar as technological "advance" does us all out of adequately physical jobs and casts us for the dignified role of filing clerks (engaged in keeping the books that our machines require to keep themselves at work). There will be no better day until or unless a society at home in comedy will have been established long enough for its citizens to lose their reverence for these exploitive playthings.

There is an over-emphasis upon "things of the mind," due

partly to snobbism (the insignia of mental work ranking higher than the insignia of physical work)—and you know many Communists who talk glibly of the proletariat while not even walking to the office, such purely verbal admiration of physicality doing the work once done for the sedentary by Wild West fiction. This higher rating upon "things of the mind" is also a secular variant of the earlier religious duality between "mind" and "body." (The body was "vile" and the mind was "pure"—and eventually vile body would attain the spirituality of pure mind. People now seem to hope that such "transcendence" shall be done here on earth, by machinery.)

If the metaphors by which the neurologists explain the functioning of the brain are correct, we have another reason for holding to the justice of a physical emphasis. Presumably there are two kinds of neural fibre, some leading outward towards physical action, and others leading across to one another, developing the internal activity of association. These associational fibres, it seems, are growing thicker, in proportion as purely mental activity takes the place of physical activity. The "ideal" of such development would obviously be close to that of Valéry (the creator of "Mr. Head"), who finds that the "complete philosophical method" would make expression in overt act a pure irrelevance. Such method would be developed in its internal perfection, concerned with associational adjustments alone, and would have the symmetry of a "closed circle."

The importance of Marx's materialistic emphasis is precisely the fact that it admonishes us against this "onanistic" ideal. The pressure *comes from without* the circle—and the circle *leads to an act* outside itself.

The Greeks realized the necessity of physical correctives, in their tendency to keep physical and mental gymnastics in adjoining bins. The "ideal Greek symposium" admitted the athlete along with the philosopher. And that wise biological conservative, Aristotle, founded a school of anti-sedentary philosophers, who gave their views *while walking* (the peripatetics). The difficulty in general was that, although both physical and mental athletes were represented in the ideal philosophical symposium, they tended to come as specialists, each representing one aspect of the duality. Thinkers tended to "take up the slack" between ideal and reality by their "healthy mind in a healthy body" formula —but too often, it seems, the mere *statement* was considered enough.

Maximum opportunity for expression of the sentiments. Distrust of the passions. The passions are "ambitious." They are stimulated to the maximum by the "creative psychiatry" of capitalism. In an ideal society, a man would not go to a doctor when he *lacked* ambition—he would consult a doctor to help him *cure* ambition. In the paradoxes of capitalism, inordinate ambition has become the norm; the man who loses it simply "drops out the bottom." And he loses it as soon as he ceases to want all sorts of idiotic baubles that keep millions frantically at work.

"Things of the mind" enter in this way. Conceptual and imaginative symbolism is required to favor the play of .the sentiments. And it is required to "take up the slack" (to bridge inevitable conflicts, and to name the important socio-economic relationships with sufficient accuracy for the adequate handling of them).

Construction, to channelize the militaristic by "transcendence" into the co-operative. (The constructive, the creative, the co-operative being the "moral equivalent of war.")

Patient study of the "Documents of Error." To avoid

"cultural vandalism" there must be constant exposure to the *total archives* accumulated by civilization (since nothing less can give us the admonitory evidence of the ways in which people's exaltations malfunction as liabilities). Not "parochial" in attitude, however. Not with the self-congratulatory notion that everybody was a fool before November 14, 18—, etc. Our stupidities are ever born anew. Even the most accurate, astute, and comprehensive of sciences would not be foolproof.

Above all, criticism should seek to clarify the ways in which any structure develops self-defeating emphases ("inner contradictions"). It should watch for "unintended by-products"—and should seek to avoid being driven into a corner in its attempt to signalize them.

Stress always upon the knowledge of limitations. In other words, an ability to carry out the proposition, essentially *Spinozistic*, that "freedom is the knowledge of necessity."

Distrust hypertrophy of art *on paper*. More of the artistic should be expressed in vital social relationships. Otherwise, it becomes "efficient" in the compensatory, antithetical sense. So completely do we now accept capitalist standards that we test everything as a *commodity for sale*. Hence we feel that "a mere artist at living" has "wasted his talents." Rather let him "release" his artistry through a total social texture. Let it take more "ecological" forms, though its "use value" as a commodity is thereby lessened.

To be sure, we do not thereby dispose of the whole issue. There is also the artist's desire to immortalize the transitory. He wants to see a "good thing" made permanently available, as Plato made the statements of Socrates permanently available. Plato "implemented" the conversations of Socrates for purpose of transmission. He was the instrument for "broadcasting over a history-wide network." One must salute the pious tendency to immortalize the transitory. One need simply note an important distinction in quality between this act and the act of a man who gets art on paper at the sacrifice of art in living.

"Heads I Win, Tails You Lose"

A device whereby, if things turn out one way, your system accounts for them—and if they turn out the opposite way, your system also accounts for them. When we first came upon this formula, we thought we had found a way of discrediting an argument. If a philosopher outlined a system, and we were able to locate its variant of the "heads I win, tails you lose" device, we thought that we had exposed a fatal fallacy. But as we grew older, we began to ask ourselves whether there is any other possible way of thinking. And we now absolutely doubt that there is. Hence, we should propose to control the matter not by elimination, but by channelization. That is, we merely ask that the thinker *co-operate with us* in the attempt to track down his variant of the "heads I win, tails you lose" strategy. It will necessarily be implicit in his work. And we merely ask him, as a philosopher whose proper game is Cards-face-up-on-the-table, to help us find it, that we may thereby be assisted in "discounting" it properly.

The whole matter is related to the scholastic distinction between "essence" and "existence." A thing has many aspects, good, bad, indifferent. You "transcend" this confusion when, by secular prayer, you "vote" that *one* of these aspects is the *essence* of the lot. For instance, you may vote that the essence of man is "the way in which he is like a god"; or you may vote that his essence is "the way in which he is like an animal." When you have, by an "act of will" (a "moral" choice) completed your balloting, the attributes that do not confirm your choice of "essence" are labeled "accidents."

Thus, in our discussion of principles and policies: the constant principle is the "essence" of motivation, and the shifting policies, often directly contrary to one another, are the "accidental" variants. If you decree by secular prayer that man is "essentially" a warrior (as did Nietzsche) you may then proceed, by casuistic stretching, to discern the warlike ingredient present even in love. If on the contrary you legislated to the effect that man is essentially a communicant, you could discern the co-operative ingredient present "essentially" even in war. Capitalism is "essentially" competitive (on this point, both opponents and proponents agree). But despite this essence, we note the presence of many non-competitive ingredients (there are many examples of true "partnership" in the competitive struggle).

"Heads I win, tails you lose" is a technical equivalent of the formula named moralistically "opportunism." Thus you get the "opportunism" of Whitman who, by his doctrine of "unseen existences," could welcome an event in spirit ("in principle") where the same event, in its raw existential attributes, might have wounded him. That is, the "essence" of a real estate boom was in its "unseen existence"; and this unseen existence was not speculation for profit, but the zeal and zest of collectively building up a continent; when beholding men *building capitalism*, he could "transcendentally" welcome their existential act by a vote that they were *building socialism*, as, to an extent, they actually were. (Addendum, 1955: In either case, they would be *building sociality*.)

"Perspective by incongruity" is a "heads I win, tails you lose" device—and we hereby lay our cards on the table by saying so. For example, take the excellent "planned incongruity" in Palme-Dutt's intellectual pun (his definition of Fascism as "the organization of decay"). By the pliancy of this term, you can't lose.* You name the militaristic ingredients of the Nazis by italicizing one of the words: the organization of *decay*. You name the co-operative ingredients by italicizing the other: the *organization* of decay. Decay is the "essential," organization the "accidental."

We select this formula for exposure because we ourselves would wholeheartedly vote for it. Philosophers, in helping us to play Cards-face-up-on-the-table, should look for two other manifestations of the "heads I win, tails you lose" formula in their work. They should seek to discover the "master metaphor" they are employing as the cue for the organizing of their work. Thus: "man is herein to be considered a god, an ape, a machine," etc.—and I shall tell you what can be said of him by the use of this metaphor. Or, further, I shall try to help you in discovering just where I mix my metaphors and subtly shift from one to another. I started by saying that I would consider man as a machine, for instance, but at this strategic point you will note that I "opportunistically shift and begin discussing him as a hero (that is, a god)."

One must say why he feels called upon to choose the metaphor he does choose. We choose the "man as communicant" metaphor, for instance, because we feel that it brings out the emphases needed for handling present necessities.

* When the banished Duke in *As You Like It* says his speech about the theme, "Sweet are the uses of adversity," he is carrying out a "perspective by incongruity" for "heads I win, tails you lose" purposes. While banished, he seeks the "rewards" of banishment—and when his ducal properties are restored to him at the end of the play, he is ready to resume the rewards of dukedom.

We modify it with the dead, mixed metaphor "bureaucratization of the imaginative" because we think that people thereby are kept from being too sensitively exposed to disillusionment as they are affronted by the "let down" that necessarily occurs when when a tender imaginative-Utopian possibility is implemented by being given its practical embodiment in "this imperfect world."

Identity, Identification

All the issues with which we have been concerned come to a head in the problem of identity. Bourgeois naturalism in its most naive manifestation made a blunt distinction between "individual" and "environment," hence leading automatically to the notion that an individual's "identity" is something private, peculiar to himself. And when bourgeois psychologists began to discover the falsity of this notion, they still believed in it so thoroughly that they considered all collective aspects of identity under the head of pathology and illusion. That is: they discovered accurately enough that identity is *not* individual, that a man "identifies himself" with all sorts of manifestations beyond himself, and they set about trying to "cure" him of this tendency.

It can't be "cured," for the simple reason that it is *normal*. One may, by analytic debunking, assist him in breaking loose from some particular identification that is disastrous (the normal tendency of the Germans, for instance, to identfy themselves with Hitler had disastrous implications, since Hitler in turn was identified with malign economic relationships). But the mere removal of an identification is not enough. The man who dies in battle, as the result of a faulty identification, is better off than a man who can identify himself with no corporate trend at all. And whatever he might *think* he was doing, the psychoanalyst "cures" his patient of a faulty identification only insofar as he smuggles in *an alternative identification.* (Often, for instance, the patient identifies himself with "the corporate body of psychoanalytic science.")

As Hellenism drew to a close, and the disorders of the state made it impossible for the earnest man to identify himself with the emperor (as the Stoics had done) many of the "enlightened" were enfeebled by the attempt to avoid all identification whatever. And in thus attempting to reject any corporate identity, they automatically despoiled themselves (with inanition, emptying, boredom, alienation as the result). Christian evangelism met the situation actively by introducing a new concept of corporate identity. And because of this important social asset, it prevailed. Similarly, the corruption in Russia, involving both Czar and Church, frustrated the needs of corporate identity, until you got as substitute the Marxist doctrine of the "proletarian corporation."

The so-called "I" is merely a unique combination of partially conflicting "corporate we's." (See Harold Laski's writings on social "pluralism.") Sometimes these various corporate identities work fairly well together. At other times they conflict, with disturbing moral consequences.

Thus, in America, it is *natural* for a man to identify himself with the business corporation he serves. This is his birthright, and insofar as he is denied it, he is impoverished, alienated. But insofar as business becomes a "corrupt sovereign," his only salvation is to *make himself* an identity in an alternative corporation. The struggle to establish this alternative corporation is called the struggle for the "one big union." Hence, the drive for "industrial unionism," for parties of "farmers and workers," etc.

Loyalty to the financial corporation is necessarily impaired insofar as the obligations are of a one-way sort. Complete corporate identity must be of a two-way sort. The overlord requires fealty of the underling—and in exchange he guarantees certain protection to the underling. By various insurance systems, the big financial corporations are attempting to establish this two-way system. Hence their resistance to *federal* insurance projects, which turn the worker towards an identification with his *government* instead of his *company*. Such issues illustrate the reasons for the partial struggle between "business" and "government" that goes on *despite* the willingness of political parties to do all they can in league with business. Their allegiance cannot be complete (however much they might desire to make it so) because businesses themselves are in conflict with one another. Hence there is no such thing as "one business corporation" with which the political party can identify itself on all points. Insofar as "industry" neither *will* nor *can* do all that would be necessary to establish a full two-way relationship between owners and workers, the confused shufflings of identity must go on.

We should also include the corporate identity of family, since property rights in the feudal structure were rigorously fixed by its co-ordinates. In *King Richard the Second*, we note how Bolingbroke, who took an oath of banishment under his corporate identity as Hereford, can violate the oath with good conscience by returning under his corporate identity as Lancaster:

> As I was banish'd, I was banish'd Hereford;
> But as I come, I come for Lancaster.

By this "prayerful" device (by attributing a different

"essence" to himself as individual) he could avoid the magical strictures placed upon him, as an individual, by the king. The use suggests analogies with the contemporary conveniences afforded by the modern concept of financially corporate identity (where the individual, by *reincorporation,* can "transcend" the limits put upon him in a previous corporate role).

There is a clear recognition of "corporate identity" in the "editorial we." The editor selects and rejects manuscripts, and writes comments, with vague reference to his membership in an *institution.* (He also, of course, quickly learns to "cash in on" the privileges of such an identity, as he rejects your manuscript with a frank admission that "the editors" could not agree on it, without adding that he may have deputized for the lot.) A variant is the "we" of business correspondence, where the writer of the letter pronounces his *corporate* role without so much as a thought on the matter.

The simplest instance of conflicting corporate identities is to be found in the old stories showing the hero "torn between love and duty." "Duty" is a shorthand way of indicating identification with some larger corporate unit (church, nation, party). "Love" is shorthand for membership in "the smallest corporation," a partnership of two. Alienation (culminating in divorce) characterizes the partnership insofar as it *not* a "collective enterprise," but is the "war of the sexes" celebrated by nineteenth-century novelists (a war in which "rivals" may unite for a time against the "common foe" of loneliness).

To sum up: Identification is not in itself abnormal; nor can it be "scientifically" eradicated. One's participation in a collective, social role cannot be obtained in any other way. In fact, "identification" is hardly other than a name for the *function of sociality.* At other times, people use the word to mean *"bad* identification" (such as occurs when one identifies himself with the reigning symbols of authority while these symbols of authority are in turn identified with covertly anti-social processes).

One may note, however, the subtle ways in which identification serves as braggadocio. By it, the modest man can indulge in the most outrageous "corporate boasting." He identifies himself with some corporate unit (church, guild, company, lodge, party, team, college, city, nation, etc.) — and by profuse praise of this unit he praises himself. For he "owns shares" in the corporate unit—and by "rigging the market" for the value of the stock as a whole, he runs up the value of his personal holdings. We see the process in its simplest form, when the music-lover clamorously admires a particular composer, and so "shares vicariously" in the composer's attainments. Such identification will be observable even among mistreated clerks of rival business concerns, as the sales girls of one department store are somewhat contemptuous of the goods offered by the department store across the street (an attitude that the heads of the business are prompt to "cash in on" by putting "company loyalty" against "interference from outside agitators and union organizers").

The function of "vicarious boasting" leads into the matter of "epic heroism" and "euphemistic" vocabularies of motives. When heroes have been shaped by legend, with irrelevant or incongruous details of their lives obliterated, and only the most "divine" attributes stressed, the individual's "covert boasting" (by identification with the hero) need not lead to megalomania. In fact, it should tend rather to make for humility. For the legendary hero is, by definition, a *superman.* He is the founder of a line. He possesses characteristics which his followers can *possess only in attenuated form.* The truly religious man, for instance, had no ambition to "be as good as Christ." His vicarious share in Christ's perfection was precisely the factor that freed him of such ambition. He wanted to be as near like his hero as possible within his human limitations.

Heroism loses this property of humility as soon as the "divine" emphasis gives way to a secular emphasis. The secular hero is, by definition, a hero whom one can emulate, and even surpass. Hence, insofar as the ideal of heroism becomes secularized, we hold that a corresponding shift to comedy must take place. The individual hero is replaced by a collective body (and one has a property in this body insofar as he participates in the use and strengthening of its traditions). Thus, in proportion as the church lost its Byzantine aloofness, it gravitated towards the "comic" in the stress it laid upon a *body of thought* matched by a *collective organization*. When the proposals were first brought forward for translating the Bible into the vernaculars, whereby "each man could read it and interpret it for himself," the churchmen were scandalized. They held that no one man is qualified to interpret a text, that interpretation must be corrected by a group. If, for the moment, we consider only so much of the case, the churchmen were right. (What we are omitting, of course, is the way in which people had "moved in on" this collective body of interpretation, hence requiring reinterpretation for the ends of a "new start." And since those who advocated reinterpretation necessarily had to be somewhat individualistic as a way of introducing their wedge, they were "driven into a corner" by upholding a principle manifestly dubious.)

Identity involves "change of identity" insofar as any given structure of society calls forth conflicts among our "corporate we's." From this necessity you get, in art, the various ritualizations of rebirth. Change of identity is a way of "seeing around the corner." For since the twice born begins as one man and becomes another, he is at once a continuum and a duality. Such changes of identity occur in everyone. They become acute when a person has been particularly scrupulous in forming himself about one set of co-ordinates, so scrupulous that the shift to new co-ordinates requires a violent wrenching of his earlier categories.*

From this shift of co-ordinates (intense in some, more subtle in others) he derives his "perspective." In a sense, all perspectives are "perspectives by incongruity." For they are obtained by "seeing from two angles at once" (quite as the stereopticon camera gives the sense of depth by putting two different focuses upon a subject and remerging them,

* We saw a letter from a man who referred to his wife and himself as being, for the time, "mummies," "dead to social life." A child had recently been born into this previously childless "corporate unit," with corresponding need of reidentification on the part of the parents (a change all the greater on his part, perhaps, because his past symbolism had shown strong traces of "secular monasticism"). Also: "my book was finished to the last semi-color. in the fall, just at the time —————— was born." It was a work on which he had been engaged for several years— hence its completion likewise required of him some large measure of reidentification. No wonder he "had hardly ventured out, had seen nobody, read little, thought hardly at all."

Also we read in *The New York Times* of December 29, 1936, the news of a new "calculus of individuals," put forward by H. S. Leonard and H. N. Goodman, of Harvard:

"The practical applications of the new formulae are not particularly valuable at the present time, the philosophers said, but further applications may be possible. By using these new symbols and equations devised by the Harvard men, logicians will be able to describe relationships among several individuals or objects by creating a fictitious 'whole' out of some of them, they explained.

"Thus, they said, John, James and Arthur may be lodge members.

whereas the one-eyed camera sees flat). The change gives one a sense of direction; hence he "prophesies." Thomas Mann has symbolized the process most "efficiently" in his Joseph novels, as we get:

> Stage one: Joseph's self-satisfied mooniness and moodiness
> Stage two: The transition, his being cast into the pit
> Stage three: The new social sense of identity, and the ability to "prophesy."

It is obvious that if such prophecy is not shaped with reference to the collective body of criticism, it is exposed to the risks of the heroic-made-secular. Mann himself, by his strict adherence to the forensic materials, is an excellent example of a man who has avoided the temptations of the individually vatic. And in keeping, he is concerned with a subtle notion of legendary identity, suggesting that the individual gauges his role by analogy with roles already given the advantage of complete "group criticism" (for in the shaping of the Biblical characters by legendary processes of revision, all irrelevant features are removed by the simple

---

Instead of describing mathematically the relationships between John and James and between John and Arthur, the method of Drs. Leonard and Goodman allows the philosophers and mathematicians to express the relationship between John and Arthur and James by considering Arthur and James as a single unit. . . .

"By allowing the mathematicians to lump the two women in a man's life, or the two men in a woman's life, together as a unit, the new philosophical concepts may be able to express the 'eternal triangle' as a sum of this or that, Dr. Leonard added."

Are not these logicians considering, in their vocabulary, the same paradoxes of identity that we are considering in ours?

process of *forgetting*; a role defined by legend is the ultimate of "auscultation, creation, and revision").

Roughly, we may say that a man "identifies" the logic of a human purpose with the following *points d'appui*: God, nature, community (lodge, guild, race, etc.), utility (capitalism, and naive pragmatism), history. At times he has tried another, *the self*, with the inevitable punishments visited upon the narcissistic.*

Or we might divide up the field in this way:

Totemistic identification. Individual relation to tribe. Magical ways in which obedience is given or exacted in small primitive communities. Manipulated by variants of the medicine man.

The carrying of the "family" perspective into the treatment of a vast corporate, latently political organization, as

---

* What we call identity with the self is often merely vagueness of identity. Vagueness of identity is often symbolized by travel (sometimes actual mobility, sometimes the consumption of travel books). We refer particularly to the kind of traveler who lives in transit, among aliens. The anthropologist, living as observer among primitive peoples, usually adopts a very definite identity in his relations with them. While, as "member of his academic corporation," he retains the role of spectator, the people he is studying often make calls upon his authority, and in this way he may gradually come to integrate his science with their customs (a process made all the easier by the admiration and sympathy they may arouse in him).

One who experiences difficulty in remembering the names of close acquaintances when introducing them might console himself somewhat by noting that such sudden forgetfulness indicates sensitiveness to the subtleties of identity. At the moment of introduction, he alters his relationship to each of the introduced, seeing them as strangers (in keeping with the nature of the situation). And so closely are names associated with identities, that in thus changing his attitude towards the personal identities of the persons he is introducing, he loses his grip upon their names.

in Catholic-feudal thought. Non-intimate relations were handled as though they were intimate relations. Manipulated by priests.

The parliamentary. The turn to delegated authority. Abandonment of the attempt to handle "forensic" relationships on a purely "family" basis. Usually managed by retention of many intimate relationships, however. Manipulated by the politician.

Transitional. Based primarily on concept of historic purpose (whereas the strictly bourgeois-parliamentary had been rationalized by co-ordinates of "profit" or "utility"). Concerned with clarification of conflicts underlying the so-called "co-operation" of the bourgeois forum. Would coach shift in allegiance to the symbols of authority. Propagandist ("informal adult educator").

Universalizing opportunities to be plumbed by establishment of new co-operative frame, once the economic maladjustments underlying the social order are removed. Coordinated by "planners." Ideal: comic self-consciousness. "Neo-catholicizing." Ideological homogeneity, to be corrected by a *methodology* of latitudinarianism.

In Russia, the lack of synchronization between revolution there and elsewhere has brought up problems extrinsic to the political pattern *per se*. The rabid rearming of Germany, for instance, has imposed upon Russia as drastic a contradiction as any to be found in capitalism. For it requires the allocation of enormous manpower and the squandering of vast material resources in purely unproductive ways—that is, the training and equipping of the army. As judged by the standards of peace (the proper tests for judging a socialist economy) this vast expenditure for the military is precisely the same as the "unearned increment" given to the coupon-clippers of the capitalist economy. Insofar as the army must train for battle, and millions must devote their efforts to its equipment, constructive enterprise is strangled. And since Russia would have no other choice but to let herself be overrun by Hitler, she must continue to build up her military (which *functions* as a rentier class, as the "idle rich," so far as peacetime criteria of production are concerned).

Nor is this difficulty lacking in "spiritual" counterparts. The euphemisms of the "secular heroic" are an integral aspect of military action (and the preparation for military action). Where an army is so necessary, it must be exceptionally *dignified*. Instead of "planners," who are deputies (subject to comic co-ordinates) you get magical-heroic vessels of authority ("superior" to the comic).

There arises another contradiction: Members of a co-operative enterprise founded along sufficiently rational lines to make for peace must identify themselves with a corporate unit devoted to war. Such paradoxes must inevitably distort the logic of a truly socialist development. We ask only that those who gloat over such distortions pause long enough to suggest how matters could be handled otherwise. The methods of adjustment in a going concern composed of 160,000,-000 people cannot be as subtly pliant as the methods of adjustment operating between a couple of private individuals. And even when you get things down to that scale, you find considerable unwieldiness.

Imagery

We have previously mentioned our delight in Caroline Spurgeon's study of *Shakespeare's Imagery*. To be sure, Mr. M. D. Zabel, whose opinions on matters affecting poetry we respect, has expressed his reservations concerning this book. He finds the analysis of imagery somewhat slovenly. We are inclined to be more charitable on this score, however, because we doubt whether the analysis of imagery can ever attain scientific precision. It serves better to point in the general direction of something than for acute microscopic divisions.

On an earlier occasion we had hit upon something like the project Miss Spurgeon has developed with such provocative results. At the height of the depression, we came forward with the proposal that, in cases where a concordance of a poet's work had been made, one might chart the overtones of the poet's imagery by looking for the quality common to all his uses of a word. (*Counter-Statement*, Hermes Edition, p. 159.) Our project, however, had been penurious. We proposed simply to exploit research already done by using concordances already made. Miss Spurgeon started anew, charting each play, image by image. For it is in such usage, as she very aptly says, that a writer "gives himself away."*

Even had we exploited our own proposal to the fullest, we could not have got the astounding results that Miss Spurgeon gets by hers. Her method can disclose statistically how

---

* We have been wondering what this manner of critique may lead to, if poets, and even philosophers, come to feel its justice. If a thinker advocates a perspective, for instance, and advocates it as the method of the "advocatus diaboli," does he not thereby reveal "satanic" ingredients in his perspective? Or when a philosopher, at the exhilaration of ending a long book, says that the man who adopts his way of thinking is the "true sovereign," is he revealing some yearning for dictatorial mastery as the "essence" of his motives?

"Watch your metaphors" could come to mean, for the writer of the future, what "Watch your step" has meant for crowds in the subway. Or, otherwise stated: the checking of one's imagery is the nearest ap-

DICTIONARY OF PIVOTAL TERMS

Shakespeare frequently organized a play about a key or pivotal metaphor, which he repeated in variants (like a musical "theme with variations") throughout the play. She discovered, for instance, that *Romeo and Juliet* is organized about images of light; *Hamlet,* the ulcer or tumor; *King Lear,* bodily torture; *Timon of Athens,* dogs; etc. We could then see how *Antony and Cleopatra* derived some of its majesty from imagery of the world, as embodied in the imperialist Roman vision of the *orbis terrarum.* And she was able to contrast the everyday imagery of Shakespeare with the somewhat celestial and bookish imagery of Marlowe.

There is even some ground to suspect that Shakespeare may have been partially conscious of such choices. He got his plot for *Coriolanus* from North's translation of Plutarch—and in both, the emphasis is laid upon analogies referring to the *body.* It was, however, a political play, and thinkers of all sorts tend naturally to rely upon such analogies when discussing the "body politic." Hence, we shall not press the possibility that Shakespeare's choice of a master image may have sometimes been deliberate (a "method" clarified by a "methodology").

---

proach, in matters of method, to the quantitative checking of temperature, weight, and blood pressure in physiological matters.

It is even possible that a new kind of "corrective hypocrisy" could emerge, as the writer, deciding that certain spheres of imagery were "healthier" than others (or morally superior) deliberately *coached himself* to cultivate them, until they became the spontaneous grammar of his expression. (Addendum, 1955. "New Kind? See Boileau: *"Que votre âme et vos moeurs, peintes dans vos ouvrages, /N'offrent de vous que de nobles images."* And recall Yeats, about sleeping on boards to harden his style.)

Then what? Might such choice then serve as "character-building by secular prayer"? Might the mimetics of the "right" imagery serve to

Perhaps we were so enthusiastic about Miss Spurgeon's book because it seemed so "usable." One cannot read it without having possibilities suggest themselves at every point. It lays out a whole new world for study. She notes, for instance, that when Shakespeare would picture war or hell, he relies upon the imagery of noise and stench. Whereupon, each time we return to this clamorous, stench-laden city, we ask ourselves: "Well, which is it? War or hell?"

At another point, she notes his imagery concerning stillness. Her study establishes clearly the fact that Shakespeare had always the notion of a haven. Stillness was associated in his mind with peace and harmony. And when we read this, we suddenly recalled a story by Poe we had once read, a minor story the title of which we have forgotten. It was constructed in accordance with a simple dualistic pattern. The first half of the story depicts a lonely and anonymous figure (the vaguely limned "poetic traveler" so recurrent in nineteenth-century work). He is moving through a landscape in turmoil. A heavy wind is blowing; trees are bend-

---

remake him, quite as the deliberate adoption of upright posture, sturdy stride, and firm handshake can work, by "incantation," to make a man more vigorous? Or as Pascal sought to arrive at belief (and did in a measure succeed) through the use of holy water?

In any case, there is unquestionably the correspondence between the objective and subjective whereby the selection of appropriate objective gestures can *lead into* desired subjective states, as Eastern mystics enter the state of calm by the practice of calm breathing. And if the objective details of horror in a story by Poe can induce in the reader the sense of horror, why could not a poet eventually "make himself over" (or at least try to) in accordance with the suggestiveness of imagery *deliberately* specialized in?

We could also foresee a tendency to *decree* the adoption of imagery too much at odds with the exigencies of one's day (as were one to perfect a mimetics of calm breathing while, all about him, the world was panting

ing and heaving; for several pages we are given variants on the theme of troubled motion. The protagonist, of vague identity, grows impatient. He cries out his command that all this turmoil cease. And of a sudden, his command is obeyed. Complete stillness prevails. There follow several paragraphs of variations on the theme of total stillness. And at the end, the poet rushes away in horror.

Here, we thought, the distinction between Shakespeare's imagery and Poe's reveals a momentous difference. Poe had no haven. Movement and stillness, both, had connotations of the forbidding. So he vacillated between drunkeness and collapse. In drunkenness, he heard the roar of his own blood in his ears. And he presumably sought it because stillness was to him equally unthinkable. Stillness was *immobility*—and the pressure of his unhappiness demanded above all that he be mobile, hoping to get in death alone the haven that Shakespeare, for all his turbulence, seems to have preserved behind his experiences here-and-now.

---

with fear and rage). Yet does not our delight in the mimetics of irresponsibility practiced by our comedians derive in large part precisely from the fact that they *have* perfected a mode of prayer in blunt opposition to the gravity of world events?

We believe that some of Shakespeare's fright, in confronting the rising philosophy of "power-knowledge," derived from its threats to his investment in prayer (his secularized inheritance from religion). Words threatened to become "words, words, words." Style would be "mere style." To question an equipment he had developed so thoroughly was to dissolve his identity. Richard the Second, we believe, is his first version of the role perfected in Hamlet. In Richard he dignifies his stylistic problems by transferring them to the problems of a king (whose every attempt at coercing events by prayer is promptly countered by an adverse turn in the objective situation). It is also worthy of note that Richard becomes the true king only as he approaches the deposition (thereby revealing Shakespeare's basic affinity with the churchly "prosperity of poverty," threatened by the incoming bourgeois morality of acquisition).

Another disclosure that stimulated us was Miss Spurgeon's statement that *Cymbeline* was constructed about two poles of imagery, one drawn from country life, the other from "the theme of buying and selling, value and exchange, every kind of payment, debts, bills, and wages." And when discussing the other two great romances of his closing period, *The Tempest* and *Winter's Tale*, she notes that the first is constructed about the imagery of sound, "from the clashing discords of the opening to the serene harmony of the close." *Winter's Tale*, she concedes, is more tenuous—but she offers good grounds for holding that the imagery here, though subtler, more "ideal," is organized about the sense of undulant, interacting natural law. She writes:

"And above all, it is perfectly and exquisitely in keeping with this central imaginative idea, that Florizel, in the height of his emotion and adoration of the beauty and wild natural grace of Perdita, should see the poetry of the motion of her young body as a part of the ordered and rhythmic flow of nature herself in the movement of the tides, and would have her stay for ever part of that larger movement, so that he cries in ecstasy,

> when you do dance, I wish you
> A wave o' the sea, that you might ever do
> Nothing but that.

We could do nothing better than to write glosses on the possibilities brought up by Miss Spurgeon's remarks on these three plays. And for this purpose, we would establish the "curve" of Shakespeare's writings, with relation to the curve of historical processes operating in his day.

Shakespeare's earlier plays were predominantly feudal in their co-ordinates. This we see clearly in the feudal nature of the conflict in *Romeo and Juliet*. Feudalism was constructed about the metaphors of the family, and this play involved a quarrel between families. The ideals of grace and elegance embodied in his early plays were integrally linked with *courtly* standards. You get here the euphuistic element of Lyly, the high manners of Sydney's pastoral, plays constructed about moral and esthetic values like those given ideologically in Castiglione's book *The Courtier*.

Gradually, the influx of new co-ordinates begins to make itself felt. They appear in the grotesque crime of Macbeth. They take another grotesque manifestation in Falstaff. Perhaps we may note their incipient expression as early as Mercutio, who dies as the victim of his "individual enterprise."

The period of the tragedies marks, in one form or another, the period of crisis. Shakespeare's growing sensitiveness to the new standards is going to the roots of his imagination. As a profound poet, he feels the change profoundly. So we get the confusion of Lear (who loses his feudal property of kingship) and Othello (who loses his "property in" courtly love).* And in *Hamlet*, the whole problem of relativity becomes so intense that it nearly submerges Shakespeare as a craftsman. His play becomes confessional and essayistic. It makes statements not merely because of their function in the play, but because Shakespeare *as a man* had to say them.

A playwright deals in moral *certainties*. If an audience

---

* In discussing Walter Huston's interpretation of Othello, Joseph Wood Krutch makes a comment wholly serviceable to our purposes when he stresses as a "central motif" of the play "the fact that in Desdemona Othello has 'garnered up his heart'." That is, she is "the symbol of his faith in life," and "much more than merely herself." The "loss of her" is the "loss of everything else which losing her implies." Hence, Shakespeare's knowledge of the deeper areas of unemployment, in the brief and poignant formula: "Othello's occupation's gone."

holds to certain standards, the playwright provokes it, stimulates it, exercises its sympathies and antipathies, by constructing characters that *act out* these standards. But in *Hamlet*, which dwells upon the regions of *uncertainty*, Shakespeare is threatened with loss of his essential identity, his identity as playwright. His exposure to the rise of new standards threatens to deprive him of his "property in" the craft of writing itself. His doubts bring up the possibility of "psychological unemployment"—and for a man *whose every faculty had been employed*, whose method of communion, justification, appeal, "secular prayer," had engaged his fullest resources, this threatened loss of property and identity was awesome.

Shakespeare met the crisis and surmounted it. He says as much in the very title of *The Tempest*, for the tempest ends as the play begins. The play is the aftermath of the tempest. The tempest was the period of the tragedies. And this delicate comedy is the Mozartian harmony that follows its subsidence. The curve is also symbolized by the direction taken in its imagery of sound, "from the clashing discords of the opening to the serene harmony of the close."*

We might also note another possible symbolization in this play. At the end, the magician Prospero releases the uncouth Caliban. He is set free, because he has been purged. We may note that in the release of such characters, the playwright is releasing his stock in trade. He needs such figures, in unregenerate guise, to operate his plays. Presumably therefore he is making ready to abandon his profession, though he does so with connotations greatly different from the prospect contained at the time of *Hamlet. Then* he was threatened

* The histories are Shakespeare's variant of the didactic, propagandistic. They manipulate the shift from feudalistic to nationalistic thought.

with psychological unemployment. But *now* he has completed a task. He has worked his way through a crisis and surmounted it.

The other two romances fit the same pattern. In *Cymbeline* he symbolizes two triumphs. First, by interweaving country imagery with the new imagery of trade, he "integrates" for himself the feudal and mercantile worlds. He does in his way what Henry Ford has done in his, when he integrates childhood on a farm with maturity in a factory by evolving plans to "grow Ford cars on the farm." And he tests the depth with which he has accepted the new coordinates by interweaving the imagery of trade into the texture of his play.*

Winter's Tale in its title attests to connotations of subsidence. And the author's dramatic philosophy is rounded out by his somewhat pantheistic sense of "universal undulation" in which all spiritual and bodily movements are subtly merged.

One cannot long discuss imagery, the reader may have noted, without sliding into symbolism. The poet's images are organized with relation to one another by reason of their

---

* At this point, the reader may legitimately ask: How does this observation gee with the present writer's proposal to retain the commercialist vocabulary, for exegetic purposes, at this late date? Frankly, we like it somewhat for its "quaintness." For although it is still full upon us, because of our tendency to discount it in theory it has already begun to take on somewhat the "pathos of distance." Perhaps we would "embalm" it stylistically, as a changing Hellas liked the archaisms of Homer. (Addendum, 1955: "!")

Furthermore, we feel that any sophisticated society, erected above the complexities of industrialism, must necessarily carry over much from the commercial symbolism of exchange. It would be "cultural vandalism" for one to throw away the contributions that bourgeois thought has made to our understanding of the "human comedy."

symbolic kinships. We shift from the image of an object to its symbolism as soon as we consider it, not in itself alone, but as a function in a texture of relationships. And so we may frankly turn now from imagery to an out-and-out discussion of symbolism.

If a man climbs a mountain, not through any interest in mountain climbing, but purely because he wants to get somewhere, and the easiest way to get there is by crossing the mountain, we need not look for symbolism. But if we begin to discuss why he wanted to get there, we do get into matters of symbolism. For his conceptions of purpose involve a texture of human relationships; his purposes are "social"; as such, they are not something-in-and-by-itself, but a function of many relationships; which is to say that they are symbolical. For eventually, you arrive at an act which a man does because he is interested in doing it exactly as he does do it—and that act is a "symbolic" act. It is related to his "identity."

We once read a book, *Plutarch Lied*, describing the plans of the French military *prior* to the opening of hostilities in 1914. These plans were "Utopian," and highly *symbolic*. The war academy had laid out a campaign that looked very much like Valéry's respect for the rules of sonnet-writing. The genius of the French Academy was present in these war plans. The whole system of tactics was developed as though war were a game with fixed rules, like tennis or chess, and each side would abide by these rules. (This assumption was not explicitly stated. Had it been so stated, it would have been questioned. It was implicit, surviving as a "cow path" from the early days of chivalry, when combats were organized by rule.)

When hostilities began, the French Military Academy began to put its symbolic strategy into operation. It moved a unit in preparation for a flanking attack against the Germans. And it left behind another unit to prevent a flanking attack against its own formations. The Germans did likewise. So the process continued, until the two armies had moved across northern France, all the way to the sea. And in place of strategic manoeuvres like the flying wedges of football, you got the "formless" unrolling of two military ribbons. The "realities" of the situation itself imposed new necessities. The Utopian symbolism of the war plans was changed by the demands laid upon those engaged in the practical task of bureaucratizing them, fitting their "perfection" to the real necessities of "this imperfect world." In place of feudal manoeuvring, you got two opposing trenches—and the unintended "war of attrition" was on (though the costly taking and retaking of "salients" continued, as a "cowpath").

The lesson to be drawn from this book for our purposes is that even war plans, *prior* to their testing, show symbolical ingredients.

It has been said, for instance, that the American Army is working on plans for an army of one-man fighting units, each unit equipped with car and munitions. If this information is wrong, it *shouldn't* be. For such a military plan would seem to be "symbolically perfect." One could hardly imagine a more accurate way of symbolizing our gift for putting individualism, industrialization, and regimentation together in one piece. (Addendum, 1955: Consider notable symbolic difference in Japanese one-man suicide planes of Second World War.)

Indeed, this possibility has led us to speculate on the symbolic ingredient in the new Russian strategy: its squadrons of parachute jumpers who are trained for the dropping of a force *behind* the lines of the enemy. When a practical test arises, we may or may not find that this strategy is a good one. But whether the recalcitrance of a real situation proves it correct or false, the possibility remains that the strategy itself was suggested by a strange caricature of Marxist philosophy. Communists believe that, if a war against Russia takes place, they must try to *fight behind the lines of the enemy.*

The strategists symbolize this attitude in their war plans, which embody totally different connotations. They do not exemplify "fighting behind the lines" in the true Marxist sense at all. They are a distortion of Marxism. But the paradoxes of a "national Communist war" are inherent in the paradoxes of another real situation: the fact that Communism *could not* be established throughout the world simultaneously. This was the recalcitrance that the "realities" of life introduced into the "ideal symbolism" of Marx's historical morphology (necessarily written before the test).

In sum: even something as practical as a war plan may be examined for its symbolic ingredients (which may require great transforming when the full tests of bureaucratization in worldly materials are met).

One more instance of symbolism. We were impressed when, following the trial and execution of the "old Bolsheviks," the press carried reports of a "joke" on the part of Stalin. Stalin is not a typically jocular man—hence, in accordance with our thesis that a break in continuity is revealing, we examined this "discontinuous" jocularity for its possible ingredient of symbolism. A story had gained currency in Russia that Stalin himself was dead. Finally, he issued a statement, signed with his own hand, "confirming" this rumor. Was there not something significant in this departure from his customary role? Could it not be said that, when these old associates of his were found inimical to him and were executed, a portion of his "identity" really *had* died? And did he not symbolize this partial death, within himself, by "jocularly" confirming the rumor?

However, even readers who are willing to agree with us in general may resent it that we have nowhere, in this book, offered a complete schematization of symbolic ingredients. Our basic principle is our contention that all symbolism can be treated as the ritualistic naming and changing of identity (whereby a man fits himself for a role in accordance with established co-ordinates or for a change of role in accordance with new co-ordinates which necessity has forced upon him). The nearest to a schematic statement that we might come is this:

In general, these rituals of change or "purification" center about three kinds of imagery: purification by ice, by fire, or by decay. "Ice" tends to emphasize castration and frigidity. (Severe mountains, winter, Arctic exploration, death of the individual or the world by cold. We should thus note the difference between Eliza's *crossing atop the ice* with her child in *Uncle Tom's Cabin* and the opening of Odets' play, *Paradise Lost,* another story of "redemption," where the leading character complains that he lies drowned beneath ice.) Purification by fire, "trial by fire," probably suggests "incest-awe." (As in some mystics' dream of "the sun death," where one is both welcomed into the sun and consumed by it. The sun was originally a female, the goddess of fertility as preserved in the German "Frau Sonne." The feminine character of fire is preserved in Wagner's opera depicting Siegfried's rescue of his bride across a circle of fire. You may find such connotations preserved in the stories of Erskine Caldwell, where imagery of fire, mother, and earth is merged.) Redemption by decay is symbolized in all variants of the sprouting seed, which arises in green newness out of filth and rot. Often it seems to gravitate towards connotations of the homosexual (as in the novels of André Gide). We may also note the two symbols of perspective, the mountain and the pit (sometimes merged in symbols of bridges, crossing, travel, flying). The mountain contains incestuous ingredients (the mountain as the mother, with frigidity as symbolic punishment for the offense). So also does the pit (ambivalence of womb and "cloaque," the latter aspect tending to draw in also ingredients of "purification by decay").

We happen to have noted a passage in Nathan and Charles Reznikoff's "Early History of a Sewing-Machine Operator" that comes nearest to being a perfect text for epitomizing purposes. First we shall quote it entire, and then follow its separate stages analytically:

"When I came into the house, she [my chum's mother] said, 'Come, sit near the stove and warm yourself.' Her husband looked at me sideways, out of his angry eyes, and went on chanting the psalms—not sorrowfully as my father and others did. When my chum's father came to the verse, 'I lift mine eyes to the hills whence comes my help,' he lifted his eyes, but saw the barrels of whiskey he had for sale."

"When I came into the house, she said, 'Come, sit near the stove and warm yourself'." This would equal: "I identified myself with my chum closely enough to think of entering his community. When I changed my identity by entering his community (the house) the mother-symbol of that community said to me, 'Come near me (in my associated form, the warm stove) and feel prosperous'."

"Her husband looked at me sideways, out of his angry eyes, and went on chanting the psalms—not sorrowfully as my father and others did." This would equal: "The father-symbol that belonged to this new identity did not like the mother-symbol's offer that I should share her. This was symbolic incest. He meanwhile was proclaiming *his* identity in turn, with respect to membership in a still *wider* community, the religious community. But his words of affection were belied by his manner. He was a *bad* member of his community. He alienates me in my attempt at identification."

"When my chum's father came to the verse, 'I lift mine eyes to the hills whence comes my help,' he lifted his eyes, but saw the barrels of whiskey he had for sale." This would equal: "When the father-symbol of my new identity was proclaiming in turn his identity, and came to the verse, 'I look guiltily and beseechingly at the mystery of *my* mother, whence comes my prosperity,' he looked not *beseechingly*, but with *brutal boldness*. And no wonder: for he had made of her a whore. Her belly is accordingly caricatured as a barrel—and he offers it for sale. It very properly contains a purely material kind of spirituality, to be derived from *alcohol*. And in selling it, by a purely *quantitative* test of profit, he arrived at the monetary caricature of religion."*

In sum, the child suggests that, after considering the evidence, he has no intention of carrying his identification with his chum to the extent of identification with his chum's

---

* The disputes between Marxists and Freudians often arise from the ambivalence of parental symbols, which have both political and pre-political radiations.

Louis Aragon's *Bells of Basel*, for instance, tells us that "there are only two kinds of women." The first, the erotic and promiscuous, is associated with decadent capitalism. And at the close of the novel, he finds the alternative kind, what we might call the "Communist mother," in the figure of the aging Clara Zetkin. (Between the beginning and the end there was a transition, during which a formerly promiscuous woman lives chastely on becoming imbued with political purpose.) It is interesting that there is a decided break in the continuity of the novel, noted by

"community." We may note, incidentally, three stages in the connotations of "community." In *The Apple of the Eye*, Glenway Wescott seems to symbolize the *individualist* community, when the hero is taught by the mother that "Your body is a temple." Others widen the notion from body to house, thereby stressing intimate connotations of community. Thus, we think of Cummings' *The Enormous Room*, or James Daly's likening of communism to a house in *One Season Shattered*. In *The Narrow House*, Evelynn Scott finds the house dimensions untenable, but she still tries to think by such co-ordinates. Others tend to think of the community after the analogy of "the city." This city, upon closer examination, may turn out to have overtones of "the city of the dead." To an extent, this ingredient seems inevitable, insofar as the individual must "die," with relation to autistic and intimate frames, to fit himself for identification with the more "abstract" frame of "the city" (as extended to either religious or historical notions of community).

We have not organized our material in strict accordance with the psychoanalytic emphasis upon "perversions" because such an approach, if pursued exclusively, would frustrate our purposes. We are trying to note the presence of symbolic acts only insofar as it bears upon *social action*, as

---

the critics and even by the author himself, at the moment when the figure of Clara Zetkin enters. The previous narrative frame is abandoned, and the author steps forth in his own right, as a person *outside* the fiction. We attribute this to the fact that Aragon learned his trade in the traditions of decadence. For several hundred pages the subject-matter was a perfect fit. But at the mention of Clara Zetkin he must abandon his method. The new "political" identity steps forward to replace the older "esthetic" identity. In place of the whore, there is the mother. And the accents change accordingly.

related to symbols of authority. We believe that the co-ordinates of individual psychology invariably place a wrong emphasis upon symbolic acts. Individualistic co-ordinates are too non-social, whereas the basis of cure is socialization.

There is a momentous qualitative difference, for instance, between an individual "death impulse" and a death impulse completely socialized. The first may take expression in suicide, whereas the logical expression of the latter is an intense desire to live, to be useful, and to maintain a continuity of physical or spiritual progeny in one form or another. Individual psychologists will admit as much in a sentence; but they usually proceed to deny it in their practices, for they are usually hired by people who wish to save themselves as "individuals," not as "socialists." By their co-ordinates, sublimation or "transcendence" becomes something equivalent to a benign *illusion*—for once you define identity in purely individualistic terms, "corporate identity" becomes a slip in rationality, a *self*-deception. Hence, one must simply congratulate himself upon his "enlightenment," while yearning to be "fooled," and "envying" the "naive" who adopt corporate identifications spontaneously.

To be sure, there *is* the individual. Each man is a unique combination of experiences, a unique set of situations, a unique aggregate of mutually re-enforcing and conflicting "corporate we's." But he must build his symbolic bridges between his own unique combination and the social pattern with relation to the social pattern, instead of treating his uniqueness as the realm of an uncrowned king. He forms and implements his individual role by utilizing the bureaucratic body of his society. In doing so, he must "die" and be "reborn" in quite the same way that a pure, Utopian war plan could be said to die and be reborn, as it encounters the recalcitrance of objective factors. If a psychologist were to note in such necessary revisions *merely* a "death impulse," or a masochistic repression of sadism, or some such, his very insight might be more misleading than no insight at all. For he has located an event by too restricted a set of co-ordinates (somewhat as though one were to see Mr. A plunging into a house on fire, and were promptly to explain his act as a "death impulse," through not knowing that Mr. A was trying to rescue something in the house very necessary to his welfare). It is only by interweaving social co-ordinates *at every point* into the discussion of individual psychology that such faulty emphases (worse than no emphasis at all) can be rectified. And such interweaving is most decidedly *not* done by the statement of a simple antithesis between "individual" and "society" (like the nineteenth century's flat distinctions between "organism" and "environment").*

Individual psychology pays too little attention to the matter of communion. It does not follow out the therapeutic leads contained in its clinical variants of "original sin." One must "pool his liabilities," by the "socialization of losses" (burlesqued in the practices of finance). And the mimetics of such socialization cannot be confined to matters of the confessional—they must also be bureaucratically completed in the practical sphere.

* We may note also the individual psychologist's great preference for taking *brutal* co-ordinates as the frame for locating psychological events. One might very reasonably discuss the brutality of prison guards, from the reverse perspective, as the "suppression of kindness." One might note how the bureaucratic necessities of their trade finally organize harshness, and how their resistance to these necessities ends by making them still more harsh. But the current psychologist would tend, rather, to take brutality as the "norm," conversely considering kindness or tenderness as the mere "suppression of brutality." The brutal guard becomes "truer to himself" than the kindly, who have merely found benign but twisted ways of "suppressing" their birthright. If you *must* choose either one

DICTIONARY OF PIVOTAL TERMS

Legality

Ideally, we begin with custom. And get to law as the efficient codification of custom. The abstract resources of law are implicit in speech. For abstractions are dead metaphors. You build abstractions atop the abstractions by mixed dead metaphors. And thinkers can even coach the language, deliberately inventing new abstractions, after the analogy of usages already established. Here is a resource to be "cashed in on." Men cash in on it when the authority of customs threatens to wane (owing to the encroachment of new material in one form or another). Law then becomes a form of "secular prayer." (It usually begins in theological law, which comes closest to magical sanctions. However, as Bentham made clear, "the court" draws on the same psychological sanctions as "the church," when *individual* judges are felt to act in their *corporate* identity alone.

The attempt to pray by legislative fiat is particularly stimulated by distinctions in occupational and property relationships ("class struggle"), as those who command the loyalty of the legislators encourage them to "take up the slack," between what is desired and what is got, by legal exhortations. Hence we see the inducements to casuistic stretching, by the introduction of legal fictions and judicial "interpretations" that further serve to bridge the gap between principle and reality. (Such forms of "secular prayer" by legislation are themselves *real* enough, when they are further backed by the bureaucratization of constabulary resources.)

---

extreme or the other as the "essence," either defining brutality as suppressed kindness or kindness as suppressed brutality, why select the more ominous as the essence of your one-way series? In such preferences our psychologists seem to be contributing their modest share to the rising cult of brutality (that accompanies the rising angers of alienation).

Inherent in law there is naturalism (as the accumulation of forensic material makes for a body of knowledge concerning "causal" relationships that can be applied by analogy to the charting of natural phenomena). And as law becomes more highly bureaucratized, more "efficient," being seized casuistically for the protection of special interests, it moves out of the field of magical sanctions and into the field of traffic regulation (where the efficient backing is solely the threat of force or fine).

Law also provides the proper culture for heresy, sect, and schism, as it provides a bureaucratic body of thought so complex that groups can stress one aspect and neglect other aspects (thereupon either being reclaimed after the analogy of the monastic orders, or being outlawed as heresy until the time when they are strong enough to form the new orthodoxy).

Legality, in all its forms, makes for the "efficiency" of rational isolation, as distinct from "ecological balance." Thus, it would be a matter of "legality," in our extended usage of the term, if the Pharaoh took up the slack, between Egypt's productivity and the faulty distribution of its fruits, by employing the excess labor supply for a "spiritual investment" in the construction of a pyramid (as Rockefeller might similarly take up the slack by the construction of Radio City). A pyramid, however, did not endanger similar investments (in other pyramids) in the way that one real estate project might endanger other holders of real estate.

The "bottle neck" in the Pharaoh's spiritual investment (which was "collective" in the sense that, given the established co-ordinates, *all* the people "had a stake" in the ritualistic immortalizing of their king) would arise in another way. Whereas the state of productivity might be able to spare *three* men out of ten for economically unproductive labor on the pyramid, the efficiencies of legality could enable the Pharaoh to requisition *five* men out of ten for this work. (We select arbitrary percentages.) The corresponding loss of necessary productivity, arising from the faulty allocation of two men's services, would then have to be distributed ("socialized") as a lowered standard of living for the people as a whole. The factor of "legality" may thus be discerned today in the growing proportion of sales force to productive force, the "spirituality" of the salesmen's occupation thus removing them from the productive economy quite as work on the pyramids did. The legalities of technology in turn have served to take up the slack, by the efficient increases in productivity.

Lexicological

Leibniz has suggested that philosophy is in reality a sequence of definitions. Conventions of the law court have stimulated thinkers to present their systems as "arguments." As a matter of fact, they are merely a *set of interrelated terms.* And one's real job is to disclose and discuss their interrelationship, thereupon testing their relevance by applying them to the interpretation of events. The reader, observing the attempt, judges for himself whether they really apply. The writer seeks to avoid subjectivity by reading the documents of other men (documents which were organized by terms having similar functions). He looks for tests of "convertibility" (the ways whereby other men's terms can be shown to have co-operated in the formulation of his own). And he gets further co-operative guidance from the kind of resistance or acceptance that his terms encounter.

A writer may "exploit" a set of terms in the lawyer's-brief manner. He may advocate a "cause" as the barrister pleads a "case." But insofar as he is concerned with the "definition of terms" *per se*, he is denied this procedure (the "polemic" procedure of logical cogency, that is, "compulsion"). His main emphasis is lexicological, and he "reaches conclusions" merely as a by-product of definition (that is, a "decision" on a particular issue of controversy is itself offered as one more way of defining his term).

Our terms should meet another test of "convertibility" besides that of their "collective origin." They should apply to three different "spheres" of action. They should apply to intimate relations (processes of development in different stages of the individual's development, in personal contacts). They should apply to public relations (as exemplified in the processes of past and contemporary history). And they should apply to the processes of engrossment whereby works of art are organized.

When we discuss "bureaucratization," for instance, one is invited to note the ways in which he bureaucratizes his own life, the ways in which society becomes bureaucratized, and the ways in which the externalizations and objectivizations of art or invention become a "bureaucratic" body. We are not completely "efficient" in seeking at every point to chart this tripartite convertibility with schematic precision. Frankly, we were not sufficiently aware of our procedure until we neared the end of the book (that is, we did not verbalize our implicit method into an explicit methodology). It is probably better so, since an over-exactitude of schematization, maintained throughout, would have wearied writer and reader both.*

* When specifically discussing relations between art and society, we might speak of a "visceral" or "mimetic" level (the body as actor), an "intimate" level (personal relationships) and an "abstract" level (the conceptual material that becomes a "vessel" of our attitudes, hence involving mimetic and personal organization).

DICTIONARY OF PIVOTAL TERMS

[Incidentally, when we decided to write this dictionary as a way of rounding out our book, we hit upon a "cue." On many occasions, readers have complained at our preference for quotation marks. Occasionally, it was admitted, the marks were justified by the fact that we were using a word in a somewhat metaphorical sense. But on many other occasions, we seemed to be using a word in its usual connotations. This objection has, in the past, seemed so unanswerable that we dropped many of our quotation marks (though always grudgingly).

But as soon as we began work on this dictionary we understood what these quotation marks had meant. We understood their "magic" (if we may apply the word to something that the reader will probably consider the very opposite of magic). For we found that, were our dictionary to be complete, we should simply go through the text and define every word we had put in quotation marks. In other words, these quotation marks that have been cluttering our pages with increasing insistence for several years, were simply the "incipient manifestation" of our dictionary.

However, when considering the prospect of defining all the terms we had put in quotation marks, whether used in their ordinary connotations or transferred to new settings by "metaphorical extension," we quickly confronted the law of diminishing returns. So we have made a selection of the terms we considered vital.]

It is our belief, or at least our hope, that a definition of terms as here contrived frees one from the ideals of the "perpetual motion machine" embodied in the attempt to relate meanings by the symbols of "mathematical logic." Our terms are not "neutral," but "moral." And our "extensions" are designed merely to match the extent to which moral issues are themselves made complex in this "imperfect world" of overlapping confusions. And we believe that the tripartite test of convertibility, plus the element of collective convertibility contained in our borrowings from other men, will serve to attain maximum relevance.

Another corrective of convertibility, we believe, is provided by borrowings from "folk criticism." By "folk criticism" we mean those remarkaby "efficient" shortcuts, equal in their "abstract shorthand" to any scientific term imaginable, which our people have developed or borrowed, and passed around, to name the situation, processes, and strategies that strike them as typical and recurrent. Such terms stem particularly from the vocabularies of politics, business, sports, and crime. We have in mind such curt critical formulations as are contained in namings like: "steamroller," "gang up on," "sales drive," "come out the little end of the horn," "build-up," to select at random. In the future we propose to pay still more attention to this lore—for if education and printing have done great damage to the *imaginative* aspect of popular expression, they have made for a great fertility of "folk *criticism*." And we suspect that the highly alembicated vocabularies of science, particularly social sciehce, are often developed, whether the terminologist knows it or not, by following the "leads" he got from this folk vocabulary in his childhood.

To be sure, when one speculates in the changeable values of this lore, he may be tempted to ignore the tests of "long-pull investment," seeking merely for the "quick turnover" of the "in-and-out trader." He may "invest in" stocks that he himself knows to be unsound, if only he feels that he can "unload them at a profit" in a week, when some piece of news will "break" that "favorably affects them market-wise." Hence, we cannot take them without discrimination. The mortality rate among these "fly by night" issues is high.

We must not choose them, therefore, for their mere picturesqueness, or for their ability to suggest the homey. These
qualities are so ephemeral as to be febrile. We must choose
them for their *accuracy*. Eventually, of course, the whole
structure of material relationships that gives them meaning will "slide out from in under" them. To this extent,
their values perish. Insofar as the material structure becomes
altered, the meanings of its symbols are altered. But insofar
as the new structure retains aspects analogous to the old
structure, the meanings of the old symbols remain intact.

Is there not also, somewhere between "pure" permanence
and "pure" change, a nostalgic attitude of appreciation
towards that which we feel to be *fast receding*? May we
enjoy the terminology on the financial page of our news-
papers almost as we might enjoy the style of Emmanuel
Kant? For is there not a great affinity between them, as regards the grotesque words they choose to name the springs
of human action? Are not both vocabularies the "fossils and
dinosaurs of poetry," exhibits in a Museum of Unnatural
History? And is not Kant's "cameral" language by far the
more pliant of the two?

In a general way, our project for a "tripartite" vocabulary takes the following forms: We extend the religious vocabulary of motives into the naming of practical and esthetic
processes—we extend the capitalist vocabulary of motives
into the naming of religious and esthetic processes—and we
extend the esthetic vocabulary of motives into the naming
of religious and practical processes.

Otherwise stated: the religious best illustrates the intimate (the "family" metaphor); the capitalist best illustrates the historical ("abstract," "impersonal," factors of
past and contemporary history); the esthetic best illustrates
the social elements involved in the engrossment of indivi-

dual creativeness. The interweaving of all three vocabularies stresses the "integrative" nature of all acts. "Integrative" is the "good" word for a lexicological method that the reader who preferred a "bad" word could call "eclectic."

Neo-Malthusian Principle

Designates not the proliferation of *people* to their physical limits, but the proliferation of *habits* to their physical limits. A given situation offers a related set of *possible* laxities (which could also be analyzed from another angle as *necessary* laxities). By the workings of the neo-Malthusian principle, for instance, the combination of capitalism and technology both *permitted* a great proliferation of private-enterprise habits and *demanded* this proliferation. And the proliferation continues to the breaking point. Thus, though the number of a given population remained stable, you could still get the neo-Malthusian proliferation of certain habits, which at first apply to only a small portion of the group, and would eventually recruit the lot.

The Technocrats have shown an astute application of this principle in their concept of the "bottle neck." By the "bottle neck" they refer to the fact that a vessel, no matter how large, cannot pour at a greater speed than is permitted by the size of the mouth. Thus, whereas naive students of "America's capacity to produce" get their figures by adding up the maximum possible productive capacity of all its farms and factories, the Technocrats were more "tragic." They pointed out, for instance, that the maximum use of this total productivity was impossible, since physical necessities would require one to *allocate* the raw materials. One industry could not receive all the iron it was capable of using except by preventing some other industry from receiving all that it was capable of using. And, as a corollary of this, only a fixed proportion of the population could be employed in production at all. Many would necessarily be subtracted from the productive plant, since their assistance would be required for distribution, servicing, accountancy, amusement, education, political co-ordination, and the like. In this reservation, the Technocrats were more "ecologically minded" than the naively "efficient" adders to a grand total.

The neo-Malthusian principle is simply another way of stating the admonition that every structure has its "bottle neck." Our term is an extension of the same notion beyond economics, to the fields of individual and social psychology. It warns us, for instance, to look for even subtler forms of limitation. You have read articles celebrating the avoidance of "wastage" that chemical advance has introduced into farming. They tell you, for instance, how at one time as much as ninety per cent of a farmer's corn was "wasted," whereas now, as the result of chemical progress, the whole crop can be utilized. By astute chemical transformations, corn can become the most paradoxical of things. But as you read a little further, being a bit more Socratically insistent in your questions, you make an important discovery. You find that the "efficient" exploitation of corn has ("at the present stage of chemistry's progress") been accomplished by a wastage of chemicals. The process of transforming the corn led in turn to many chemical by-products, and thinkers are now busily at work looking for ways in which these by-products can be utilized. Otherwise, you merely avoid a corn-wastage by getting a chemical-wastage.

You can avoid this chemical wastage, in turn, by finding all sorts of new uses for it. In part, these new uses merely do other industries out of a job. If you find a cheap way of making window glass out of corn, for instance, you compete with those who have been making window glass out of sand.

You avoid this competition in part by the invention of "new needs." You invent a new gadget. With astounding "efficiency," you put hundreds of men seriously to work turning out an automatic back-scratcher for people riding in automobiles. Or you make a device for telling you what time it is without taking your watch out of your pocket or turning your head to look at the clock.

This "new need" might, by an extreme act of charity, be said to have utilized the chemical wastage. But here too, alas! you get a bottle neck. In a capitalist country, it can only be sold by competing with other "old needs" or "new needs" for the customer's dollar. If the customer's dollar goes to buy the total possible output of New Need A, that involves a tragic wastage in the productivity of a plant devoted to the satisfying of the craving for New Need B. And even in a socialist economy (if we can imagine one that persisted in operating on such a principle), this same bottle neck would apply.

There is the further fact that "inefficient farming" can be a quite "efficient" way of living (as regards the subtler tests of "ecological balance") whereas a man's intensive devotion to the "efficient" production of gadgets can be an "inefficient" way of living. Subtract the need of getting a wage (which would apply in any economy) and it comes closest to a human status that we should call *humiliation*.

How long, the admonitions of the neo-Malthusian principle admonish us to ask, can such a concept of "progress" continue to engross mankind? Where do we reach the absolute breaking point, the degree of alienation beyond-which-not? How long before even those who are most wholeheartedly enrolled in the School of Human Wastage in Disguise (a school that shunts the issue along from one point to another, and relies solely upon the complexities of the structure itself to prevent us from realizing as much) cease to feel the reasonableness of their society's purposes? (Addendum 1955: The recent "advances" in the manufacture of plastics have greatly added to the exhausting of the soil, through "efficiency" in the production of crops that are turned to purely industrial uses.)

As a given bureaucratization nears its "Malthusian limits," you find a growing dissociation between "rights" and "obligations." The ambivalence wherein risks and rewards are interchangeable is destroyed (though a "priesthood" may still attempt to maintain the myth by casuistic stretching). As *ambivalence* gives way to *dissociation*, you tend to find one class enjoying rights-without-obligations, and another class suffering obligations-without-rights.

Another important manifestation of the principle may be characterized by the relations between mobility and immobility. An abstract concept of relationships *allows* a considerable measure of mobility. That is, the organized network of communication (both material and spiritual) makes possible a large amount of transmigration within the network. In sum, one can move from New York to California without changing his "identity" with relation to the abstractions of nationality. Or one may go to the heart of China without changing his identity with relation to the abstractions of business (if he goes to manage an oil company). And in the middle ages, despite the small size of feudal units, one could travel across a great variety of local customs without losing his "universal identity" as a Catholic.

Mobility of this sort is made possible by the growth of abstractions. And these abstractions eventually lead to the maximum codification of *law*. Impersonal, legal relationships come to replace personal relationships. (One may illustrate the difference by distinguishing between the "personal right" of a man to hold a property in something because "he has always held this property" or because "his father held it," and the "right" of a man to hold it because he "legally" purchased it. The second kind of "right" obviously makes for greater mobility. And the greater mobility of property means a corresponding opportunity for "alienation" of property.) Further, as rights shift away from the personality of custom towards the impersonality of law, you get a corresponding trend towards the parliamentary (which is the equivalent of impersonal legality in the sphere of polity).

Insofar as a given structure exploits its mobile opportunities to the fullest, it begins to *demand* mobility. Hence, migration becomes an *economic necessity*. As the mediaeval structure began to disintegrate, migrations increased from *pressure*. For a time surplus labor was exported by pilgrimages and crusades. Later there was the exodus of dispossessed yeomen from the farming areas to the rising industrial towns. And eventually you get the mass export of population to America. In America to-day, you get the great forced migrations during harvest season in the southwest; the forced migrations of the lumbermen; the shift of labor from country to city, from city to country, and from city to city, in accordance with the shifting "stagnant pools of unemployment."

If such extreme mobility arises from "alienation" in one form or another, it also tends to increase alienation. Such impersonality of relationships is precisely the right "culture" in which the crooked politician may breed, for instance: his tiny personal band controls the impersonal body quite as a few "insiders" get control of an industrial corporation.

As the psychological and economic pressure towards extreme mobility increases, many attempts are made to *immobilize*. In the middle ages, for instance, the church gradually accumulated wealth, which it held in mortmain. Monasticism, as an economic phenomenon, was a kind of "immobile migration," whereby the individual could escape economic pressure. He simply abandoned the ailing "secular" economy, with its increasing trends toward private enterprise, and transferred his identity to the monastic-collectivist economy. It is as though a dozen of our largest millionaires were to erect a special polity out of their investments, and individuals were to "save their souls" by going to live in this polity. (In a less clearly demarcated way, the sums left by the wealthy to endow large charitable and educational institutions establish something like this *imperium in imperio* to-day. They are somewhat "otherworldly," as one outside their protection will often observe when he reads some "findings" of their "priesthoods.")

Or an arbitrary attempt may be made to immobilize prices, as the steel trust contrived to do despite the great deflation of farm prices during the last depression. On the surface, this may seem a less drastic forcing of immobilization (upon a structure *demanding* mobility) than occurred in the decrees of the Roman emperors (when they decreed a fixity of both occupation and residence). But finance itself is more "spiritual" now than it was in those days, so that its ways of doing the same thing can be correspondingly spiritualized.

Since people invariably tend to meet the growing pressure by recourse to secular prayers of the most extremely casuistical sort, confusions multiply. The church, for instance, permitted the alienated a choice between two kinds of decadence. For not only was the emergent bourgeois morality "decadent," as judged by the church's standards, but the church itself was decadent, as judged by its *own* standards.

We note an analogous situation to-day. The priesthood of capitalism warns us against the decadence of socialism. And at the same time, the documents of corruption and crime paraded in its own press proclaim the decadence of the established order. So, if you believe the teachings of the casuistic stretchers, your only choice is between an old decadence and a new one (*both states,* we repeat, *being "decadence" in accordance with the moral standards of capitalism itself*). Faulty praying (the proliferation of criminal statutes) under such circumstances is necessarily backed by *force.* The use of force leads in turn to the hiring of *spies.* And by the cruel operation of the neo-Malthusian principle in the purely psychological field, in time those who hire spies must come to feel that they are being spied upon. The contribution to demoralization is obvious.

Another interesting variant may be noted in closing. In business polities, the *conflicts* among business interests are handled by *politicians.* Every discord in Congress faithfully reflects a corresponding discord among the business interests whom the legislators represent. Businessmen promptly "moved in on" this opportunity, by despising, in the wrangles of the politicians, the reflection of the policies they as businessmen demand. So that they can admire the *cause* in themselves while despising the *symptom* in their henchmen.

This handy salvation device is further assisted by the fact that businessmen compete with one another by trying to *praise their own commodity* more persuasively than their rivals, whereas politicians compete by *slandering the opposition*. When you add it all up, you get a grand total of absolute praise for business and a grand total of absolute slander for politics. Hence the considerable resentment on the part of "industry" when a temporary dissociation between business and politics has occurred, so that congressmen begin investigating "industry" and finance, instead of sticking to their "proper" task of investigating one another.

Culturally, the best state of affairs seems to be one in which there is a large reserve of immobility, leavened by a small percentage of the mobile and adventurous. In the ideal state of affairs, the resources of mobility have not been stretched to their Malthusian limits, and such stretching is not necessary. A little mobility goes a long way. In fact, if a few people are mobile enough, they may even add a valuable contribution to immobility (as a small and mobile group of artists may add exactly the right percentage of ferment to a much less mobile public). At one time the adventurer, be he a philosopher like Abélard or a traveler like Marco Polo, could venture forth, confident that there was always remaining behind him a fixed network of custom; if matters got too difficult, he could return, and be "reclaimed." Now the situation is reversed. It is the *people* who are forgetting their proverbs, and it is the *adventurers* who are preserving such lore. It is the *people* who are unstable, and the *artist* and *thinker* who are trying to stabilize things.

In an ideal social structure, the maximum amount of contentment is provided by the *practical* order. And whatever discontent is left over and above this, is stilled with the aid of symbolism. But to-day, when so little contentment is provided by the practical order, symbolism is called upon to perform a much more drastic function. It cannot be merely the *completion* of a social structure: it must seek to *make* one.

Opportunism

Casuistic stretching, without a sufficiently broad rationale and sufficiently sophisticated methodology to make it positive. It has its back to the wall. A low form of "secular prayer" whereby a sect has been forced to "sell out" its sectarian principles, and snatches at the most quickly available rationalization as a pretext. The term applies also to an individual, when he verbalizes in a way that, he knows in his heart, is but a stop-gap. A shift in *policy*, not matched by a broadening in *perspective*.

Opportunism is the verbal denial of a fact on occasions when one cannot "transcend" it by adopting a more complex rationale through which he can safely and comfortably admit the fact.

A calls B an opportunist when he means "I don't like what B is doing." Technically, everyone should be an opportunist, in the sense that he should change his policies in response to changes of situation. But this pliancy is realistic, rather than demoralizing, only insofar as one's verbalizations become correspondingly mature. The demoralized opportunist trades in "Now it can be told." When he is at *d*, the truth can be told about *a*, *b*, and *c*. When he is at *g*, the truth can be told about *d*, *e*, and *f*. Desiderandum for elimination of demoralized brand: sufficient honesty and sufficient verbal enterprise, to be able to "tell all" about *g* while one is at *g*.

The charge of opportunism centers in the distinction between a principle and a policy. A principle is eternal—a policy is its embodiment in a unique situation that never recurs in all its particularities (or even in all its important particularities). The politician seeks to justify his change from policy A to policy B by showing that both of them embody the same unvarying principle (once you have "discounted" the apparent difference by taking up the slack with circumstances-alter-cases considerations). His oppo- nents call him an "opportunist" as a shorthand way of say- ing that they do not accept the validity of the intermediate steps he has offered in the rationalization of his shift. Thus, the charge of opportunism has exceptional opportunities to proliferate in an ideological texture stressing historicism, "time-mindedness," "time-serving," as the politician neces- sarily does.

Once we heard a Trotskyite and a Stalinist arguing about the justice of the "united front." The Trotskyite said, "If the principle was wrong two years ago, it is wrong now. Stalinists were against the principle two years ago. Now they are for it. Such shiftiness is unprincipled opportunism. They must admit either that they were wrong then or that they are wrong now." The Trotskyite's statement of the case was fallacious. The "united front" is not a principle, but a policy. It is the most natural thing in the world for a policy to be correct for one situation and incorrect for another. And the *shift* in policy could be motivated by a *continuity* of principle. The "united front" might or might not be the proper formula for the specific situation, but the Trotskyite's argument was irrelevant as a discussion of such propriety or impropriety. Marxism, with its political, his- toricist emphasis, is essentially "time-minded." The Trot- skyite in this instance was not being time-minded. His argu- ment, in this instance, was no answer to the Stalinist, who could simply justify a shift in policy by the "dialectical" observation that circumstances alter cases.

Incidentally, the example shows that "casuistic stretch- ing" is indigenous to historicism. It is as easy as breathing.

Every situation in history is unique, requires its own particular gauging or sizing-up of the factors that shall be considered pivotal in the situation. The "scientists" of history have brought us unintentionally to the realization that the gauging of the "right historical moment" is a matter of *taste*. Thus, every situation calls for a policy that is a "casuistic stretching" of the principle. To sum up: implicit in both historicism and politics there is the technical problem of opportunism—and the detection of this technical problem is given a moralistic twist (leading to the charge of opportunism in the censorious sense) when a speaker would employ a shorthand version of secular prayer for recruiting allies against an opponent.

Perspective by Incongruity

A method for gauging situations by verbal "atom cracking." That is, a word belongs by custom to a certain category—and by rational planning you wrench it loose and metaphorically apply it to a different category.

Our contemporary orthodox economists, hired by business to provide the scholastic rationalization of its procedures, might best be defined by incongruity, as we carried over a term from semi-feudal Germany: they are our "cameralists," bureaucrats who were "introspectively" concerned solely with the "internal adjustments" of the bureaucratic order. And as we are warned against the spread of "bureaucracy" in Russia, or in our own government, we are encouraged to forget that if one were to transplant a typical American business from the United States to Russia, leaving all its managerial and co-ordinating processes intact, its functionaries now dignified as examples of "private enterprise" could automatically, in the new setting, be stigmatized as "bureaucrats." One would thus be using a "perspective by incongruity" if he named the business man's own associates as "bureaucrats." (We intentionally use an instance that is dissolving, to lend weight to our contention that "perspectives by incongruity" do not belong to a cult of virtuosity, but bring us nearest to the simple truth.)

Perspective by incongruity, or "planned incongruity," is a methodology of the pun. "Pun" is here itself metaphorically extended. Literally, a pun links by tonal association words hitherto unlinked. "Perspective by incongruity" carries on the same kind of enterprise in linking hitherto unlinked words by rational criteria instead of tonal criteria. It is "impious" as regards our linguistic categories established by custom.

The metaphorical extension of perspective by incongruity involves casuistic stretching, since it interprets new situations by removing words from their "constitutional" setting. It is not "demoralizing," however, since it is done by the "transcendence" of a new start. It is not negative smuggling, but positive cards-face-up-on-the-table. It is designed to "remoralize" by accurately naming a situation already demoralized by inaccuracy.

Such pliancy is the basis of the "casuistic stretching" in Shakespeare's metaphors. Recall, for instance, the lines from *Romeo and Juliet*:

> For nought so vile that on the earth doth live
> But to the earth some special good doth give,
> Nor aught so good but strain'd from that fair use
> Revolts from true birth, stumbling on abuse:
> Virtue itself turns vice, being misapplied,
> And vice sometimes by action dignified.

Carry out the "policy" of Friar Laurence's speech, and you have a "plan" for putting incongruities together. You get, for instance.. Act V, Scenc II of *Antony and Cleopatra*, where Cleopatra exposes her flesh to the sting of the asp, and says:

> Peace, peace!
> Dost thou not see my baby at my breast,
> That sucks the nurse asleep?

The "whimsical Barrie" contrived to expand a "perspective by incongruity" into a whole play. He wrote a play in which he tried his hand at one of Empson's "pastoral" revolutions. A group of upper-class people were marooned on a desert island—and their butler, who alone among them is equal to the situation, becomes their "ruler." If we remember correctly, however, the play has a happy ending: in the last scene you are back in England—the party has been rescued—everything is as was—and the butler has returned to his proper role.

In his book on recent movements in painting (cited elsewhere in these pages) James Johnson Sweeney tells us that at one period the artists were attempting to introduce a variety of perspectives, seeing the same objects from many sides at once. And after they had made such purely disintegrative attempts at analysis for a time, they began to search for a master perspective that would establish a new unity atop the shifts. Was not this concern akin to Einstein's method, whereby he gets shifting frames of reference, but co-ordinates their relativity with reference to the speed of light as a constant?

Perspective in painting arose with the rise of individualism. It depicts nature by stressing the *point of view* of the observer. And precisely at the terminus of individualism, we find some artists who would return to two-dimensional painting (abolishing perspective) and others who would stress a multiplicity of perspectives. (Often the same artist exemplifies both of these tendencies at different stages in his development.)

In a sense, incongruity is the law of the universe; if not the mystic's universe, then the real and multiple universe of daily life. Driving our definition to the fullest, we could say that a table is incongruous with a chair. Our term refers, however, to a relationship less purely technical. The incongruities we speak of are moral or esthetic. Our experience with tables and chairs, for instance, makes their togetherness congruous. Hence, to get incongruity in our moral, esthetic sense of the term, the artist would have to go outside this combination. The chair might be upside down, for instance. Or, we could imagine a table and two chairs: on one chair there might be a bloated, profiteering type such as Grosz draws—and opposite him, as his female guest, a long-lashed manikin dressed as they are in the window displays. Table, chairs, and diners are congruous, since experience has made them so. But table, chairs, living diner, and a dining lady manikin are incongruous. The result is a perspective with interpretative ingredients. The picture, by its planned incongruity, would say, in effect, that Grosz's profiteer is typically himself when entertaining the simulacrum of a woman.

In sum, we contend that "perspective by incongruity" makes for a *dramatic* vocabulary, with weighting and counter-weighting, in contrast with the liberal ideal of *neutral* naming in the characterization of processes. Simplest example: a concept like "the democratization of salvation devices" might be named, in typical "liberal," simply as "diffusion." But we hold that such a vocabulary is mimetically truncated. Its "improvisational" feature is weak. It is

less of an "act," quite as "the diffusion of investment" is less
of an act than "the democratization of investment, with
attendant deterioration of quality, as it spread with casuistic stretching, to the point of demoralization, whereat it was
remoralized by Calvin's changing of the rules."

The neutral idea prompts one to forget that terms are
characters, that an essay is an *attenuated play*. The essayist's
terms serve to organize a set of interrelated emphases, quite
as Othello, Iago, and Desdemona are inter-related emphases.
There are "hero" and "villain" terms, with subsidiary terms
distributed about these two poles like iron filings in a magnetic field, and tracing somewhat of a "graded series" between them. Emphases cannot "contradict" one another, so
far as the "total plot" is concerned, any more than Iago's
function in the play can be said to contradict Othello's.

The element of dramatic *personality* in essayistic *ideas*
cannot be intelligently discerned until we recognize that
names (for either dramatic characters or essayistic concepts) are shorthand designations for certain fields and
methods of action. Perhaps Samuel Butler was both *on* the
track and *off* it when he said that "Men and women exist
only as the organs and tools of the ideas that dominate them"
(on the track, insofar as he recognized the integral relationship between people and ideas, but off it insofar as, under
the stimulus of idealism, he took the ideas as causally prior).

In line with such thinking, we cannot say enough in praise
of the concept, "the socialization of losses," as a pun for
liquidating the false rigidity of concepts and for inducing
quick convertibility from moralistic to economic categories. The operation of this salvation device in the investment
field has its counterpart in the "curative" doctrine of
"original sin" whereby a man "socializes" his personal loss
by holding that *all* men are guilty. It suggests, for instance,

the ingredient of *twisted tragedy* behind Swift's satire, whereby he uses such thinking, not to *lift himself up*, but to *pull all mankind down* (the author himself being caught in the general deflation). "I have ever hated all nations, professions, and communities; and all my love is towards individuals. . . . But principally I hate and detest that animal called man, although I heartily love John, Peter, Thomas, and so forth."

In men as different as Malraux and Whitehead, we see the essentially religious attempt to *socialize* one's loneliness, though Whitehead stresses purely idealistic strategies in the accomplishment of this, whereas Malraux seeks the corrective "dialectically" in collective action, in accordance with Marx's formula for the socialization of losses, to the effect that "I am not alone as a victim; I am in a *class* of victims." Swift, being essentially religious, was essentially tragic; but over-individualistic emphases turned the tragic scapegoat into a satiric scapegoat, thereby turning a device for solace into a device for indictment. Lack of religiosity is a convenience; but religion gone wrong is a major disaster.

Recently we heard a speech that ran somewhat as follows: It was confessional in tone, an intimate talk by a writer addressing writers. The speaker first humbled himself: "I am a bad critic. There is too much that I still have to learn. I should not write a word for five years. I should simply study and practice. In sum, I am a bad critic." Whereupon he went on, to "socialize" this loss, by adding, "In fact, we are *all* bad critics."

Hence, the more we look about us, the greater becomes our belief that the "planned incongruity" in the concept of the "socialization of losses" gets us pretty close to the heart of things. The formula seems basic for purposes of "putting things together," by establishing modes of convertibility between economic, religious, and esthetic vocabularies. But we have not as yet been able to locate the author of the term. So far his contribution to the architecture of thought remains like that of some anonymous mason who contributed an especially accomplished bit of stonework to a mediaeval cathedral.

Problem of Evil

Every policy is a policy of lesser evil. Thus the religious Augustine and the atheistic Jefferson unite when the first explains government as a punishment for the fall of man, and the second calls it a necessary evil. For, in our terms, government necessarily means bureaucratization; and bureaucratization eventually produces a preponderance of unwanted by-products.

The problem of evil is met by transcendence—the process of secular prayer whereby a man sees an intermingling of good and evil factors, and "votes" to select either the good ones or the evil ones as the "essence" of the lot. And a choice between policies is not a choice between one that is a "lesser evil" policy and another that is not. It is a choice between two lesser-evil policies, with one of them having more of a lesser evil than the other.

Repossess the World

As the imaginative becomes bureaucratized, the bureaucratic body brings up new problems of its own. Thus, the bureaucratic complexities of modern business bring forth the need of complex filing systems. The persons who must devote all their genius to such incidental by-products (the filing systems) are, to that extent, threatened with "inanition" or "alienation." They are robbed of the world, since their efforts are expended in so cramped a territory.

And they must struggle to repossess the world. Usually, when such a state of affairs becomes aggravated, you will find strong material for "class struggle," as the development of the bureaucratic body will have led to a class actually or apparently enjoying the fruits of the given bureaucratic order and another class of relatively alienated or dispossessed. Their struggle to repossess will involve all the tactical issues concerned with shifts regarding allegiance to the symbols of authority.

A rationale of history is the first step whereby the dispossessed repossess the world. By organizing their interests and their characters about a purpose as located by the rationale, they enjoy a large measure of repossession (a spiritual property that "no one can take from them") even though they are still suffering under the weight of the bureaucratic body oppressing their society. Maximum alienation prevails when the oppressed suffer oppression without a rationale that locates the cause of the disturbance and the policies making for its removal. By a rationale of history, on the other hand, they own a "myth" to take up the slack between what is desired and what is got.

Such a myth, incidentally, may also operate on other occasions to promote the ends of resignation. Imagine a man running the same elevator the same number of hours under three different economies: capitalist, Fascist, communist. Though the material processes were the same in all instances, the act would be a different act, in accordance with the change in rationale, the logic of collective purpose by which this individual act is located. This important difference can make a man willing to undertake without protest a dismal kind of work, if only its ultimate relationship to a rationale of history is genuinely believed by him. The resources for casuistic stretching are obvious (as men might conceivably be asked to infuse with the spirit of the rationale kinds of job which were too thoroughly drudgery). To this extent, we move towards "alienation."

Money is *per se* an alienating device, leading to impersonality and individualism (rationalizing effort by purely quantitative tests of reward, and inducing an "abstract" attitude towards the commodities produced). By this very fact, it has well served to stimulate capitalist action in making drudgery tolerable (by introducing purely quantitative tests of satisfaction) and then making available the purchase of amusements and distractions (built up in antithesis to the drudgery). Its power of alienation thus makes it wholly adequate to a system based on alienation.

The soundest reward for a service (in either practical activities or art) is an improvement in one's human relations. Money enables us to buy only a fraction of this improvement, and even often militates against it (as when an employer can by wages make his employees *function* as loyal, regardless of their attitudes).

This breach between attitude and function can be traced through many aspects of capitalist disorder. A young novelist, for instance, quarrels with his neighbors. The quarrel was started in part, let us say, by their subservience to questionable standards. It was aggravated because the novelist was himself stimulated by the same standards. In many ways his ambitions for rewards and public esteem were frustrated. He leaves. He comes to the great abstract city of New York, itself built upon complex money relationships. From this haven, he "retaliates" against his neighbors. He writes a work that excoriates them (it is written for the consumption of his new allies). The home town is scandalized. But also to an extent it is impressed. It boasts of its vicarious share in the local talent that gained recognition in New

York. And the novelist, from his new abstract haven, sends back such "impersonal" communications as might belong to a nation-wide radio hook-up, so far as concerns the subtleties of intimate social relationships. His work is "efficient," "uncompromising," "relentless." He has settled a score—and, strengthened by the insignia of success, may even make terms as a victor, and be welcomed home.

Yet, has he not merely attained individual salvation at the expense of the collectivity? For has his work not contributed more to the *blunting* of human relationships than to their *refinement*? By "cashing in on" the resources of mobility and abstraction, he has not had to remain among his group. Hence he has not had to release his message slowly, strategically, with the maturity of gradations, placations, concern for sensitivities. Whatever his work's "forcefulness," imaginative richness is made almost impossible. It is an aspect of *reporting* (with the genius of headlines in mind), lacking the pliancy that would go with the fear of embarrassment (such embarrassment, that is, as would arise if his product were an integral part of his life in his community—so that an insult on the page would be the same as an insult to a man's face). It has the bluntness of efficiency, and it repossesses by vengeance, by antithesis, rather than by the subtler modifications of one's social role.

Rituals of Rebirth

Particularly in periods extremely transitional in emphasis, art will be found to depict changes of identity. In more stable eras, however, the same process underlies artistic ritual, since the maturing of the individual exposes him to "climacteric stages" of one sort or another. If there were no important historical change taking place in society, the mere changing of one's glandular system would involve him in "new situations." And each change of "situation," in this purely physical sense, would require a reorganization of the mind with relation to the public, forensic structure. Similarly, a man must be "reborn" in order to fit himself for genuine partnership with a woman—and if this partnership is ended, he must again be "reborn" in order to take new problems of identity into account. Hence, even in a stable structure, problems of rebirth (of dramatic change in identity) will be found to vitalize the symbolic structures of art.

The symbolic regressions, involved in rebirth, are kept *public, collective* inasmuch as the artist is required, for purposes of communication, to retain his contact with the forensic texture. Hence, there seems to be a very important difference between the symbolic regressions of the mature artist and the neurotic regressions of the private individual who allows himself to become divorced from the forensic texture. Symbolic regression becomes dangerous insofar as the artist permits his medium to depart too far from the forensic texture (otherwise stated: insofar as he overstresses "self-expression" and understresses "communication"). Some measure of departure is necessary (particularly in times requiring shifts in purpose and authority, when the communicative medium itself becomes involved in the general confusion). But fortunately, the destruction of a forensic texture is always far from absolute—the difference between stable and unstable forensic textures is merely relative— hence, there is no need, other than the author's private ambitions, for a complete regression to autistic thought.

Our great admiration for Mann, our conviction that he is the greatest of contemporary novelists, derives from the fact that he has exposed himself most profoundly to the risks of symbolic regression while managing to retain a powerful grip upon the forensic texture. Gide is another writer who has accomplished much in this risky kind of activity. Joyce's mighty enterprise induced him, for purposes of "scientific efficiency," largely to abandon the stabilizing resources of the forensic. Thus, other writers may derive much stimulation from his *manner*, but they cannot without great risk imitate his *method*. Most contemporary writers who proclaim their admiration of Joyce seem to be attracted only by the *superficial* aspects of his innovations. A genuine admiration for his *method* (the kind of admiration that is attested by a profound attempt to develop along the same lines) would probably lead a writer into great discomfiture.*

Salvation Device

Every once in a while, some salvation device or other becomes organized, with accumulative efficiency. Such devices are by no means confined to the magic of the priests, though in eras when religion is authoritative, they tend to take priestly forms. Business enterprise is a salvation device, as is talk about the weather. Any conscious or unconscious, adequate or inadequate way of saving one's soul, saving one's hide, or saving one's face is a salvation device.

These devices usually start from the top, and spread

* While specifically on the subject of "rebirth," we should like to call attention to an article by Harold Rosenberg, "Character Change in the Drama" (*The Symposium*, July 1932) that anticipates some of our own elucubrations on the matter. We should also refer the reader to Maud Bodkin's *Archetypal Patterns in Poetry*, a study of literary symbolism that we did not encounter until this work was already in type. Many of our speculations could have been made much more explicit had we had the advantage of this fertile volume.

downwards ("democratization"). Thus, the feudal lords originally had much greater access to the "salvation device" of borrowing at interest, than did the people at large. Gradually it spread in scope, through Protestantism; its democratization became complete with capitalism. As a salvation device spreads, it manifests a deterioration in quality (notice, for instance, the much "higher quality" of the government assistance afforded big financial interests through such agencies as the R.F.C., as compared with the poor quality of assistance distributed to the small proprietor and the unemployed). It becomes linked with the demoralization of casuistic stretching, and with conflicts involved in bureaucratization.

There is no reason to believe that, given any form of socialism, the processes of bureaucratization, involving the unforeseen and unforseeable recalcitrances of "this imperfect world," will avoid "unintended by-products." A set of abstract co-ordinates for locating the processes of history must prepare us to discern and discount these by-products. Otherwise stated: Marx carried his analysis of historical processes *up to* the establishment of Communism. But why should not one extend his "leads" into the abstract formulation of Communist history also? One's justification for doing so in a non-Communist society arises from a concern with the "graded series." Quite as there are collective elements in capitalism, there will be capitalist elements in Communism. Hence, the justification for an "extension" of Marxist sociology to consider also the *continuities* preserved despite a *discontinuity*.

Sect

Composed of those who, faced with the danger of being "driven into a corner," counter by forming a new collectivity. Their co-operation gives them a new positive campaign base, from which they may sally forth to steal the recognized symbols of authority from their opponents. A sect is always threatened with defensive, negativistic, "splintering" tendencies so long as the ingredient of rejection is uppermost.

Troeltsch has pointed out the part that the spread of literacy has played in sectarianism. Sectarianism is "colony thinking." It attains full expression when a group of the like-minded develops a material co-operative enterprise that translates their Utopian vision into its bureaucratic organizational equivalents. The spread of literacy, however, led to a subtler kind of colony, usually lacking material body: the "colonies of the mind." By his preferences in reading, one "recruits his band," who may be scattered across all the earth and through all periods of history.

The nineteenth century was particularly prolific in sectarian colonies, of both material and spiritual sorts. There were colonies of special scientific disciplines. And here and there a lonely man, off by himself, shaped his identity by membership in one or another of such vaguely corporate units.

Secular Prayer—or, extended: Character-building by Secular Prayer

Secular prayer is usually called "word magic" by those who think that they can propose contrivances for its elimination. We have always been impressed with the feeling that these contrivances themselves are examples of prayer, albeit in disguise.

Secular prayer would not, by our notion, be confined to words. Any mimetic act is prayer. Even "psychogenic illness" may be a prayer, since it is the "substantiation of an attitude" in a bodily act.* All mimetic procedures, in the dance, the plastic or graphic arts, music, and verbalization are aspects of "prayer" in our technical sense of the term. And they have a great deal to do with the building of character. In fact, the man who does not "pray" cannot build his character.

Secular prayer, as a "moral act," is the *coaching of an attitude* by the use of mimetic and verbal language. Naturalistically, the necessity is explained by Piaget, who noted how children, at an early age, play by muttering commands to themselves: "Now you must do this—now you must do that." Also, the children decree by *naming the essence* of their play objects, assigning names that violate realistic identity: thus, picking up a block of wood, the child decrees by legislative fiat: "This is a train"—or "This is a house." The child "transcends" the material reality by "discounting." Like Whitman, it sees "unseen existences" in the object— and this is its prayer.

An adult may do the same in adult ways when, looking at the welter of the world, he "sees" the class struggle there. You can't *see* the class struggle. It is an *interpre-*

* The two-way relationship between the mental and the physical, in other words, can lead from the physical to the mental as well as from the mental to the physical. The mimetics of agitation may lead to a state of agitation, or a state of agitation may lead to the mimetics of agitation. Hence, such a state of mind as guilt or fear may induce its corresponding visceral expression (in glandular and nervous actions), or *v.v.* Applying such considerations to the matter of "psychogenic illness," we should say that the mental sufferer is an actor—and in the process of enacting his role as sufferer, he adopts the mimetic expression (including visceral, glandular responses) in keeping with his attitude. Thus, if his mental role leads him towards "regression," he may "round out his act, in the mimetic sphere," by developing such a "regressive" illness as asthma (if we assume, for the moment, the correctness of the psychoanalytic hypothesis that

tation of events. The events themselves are confined to such matters as the possession of railroad securities by one man and the unemployment of another. Upon this legislative act (the enunciation of class struggle as a basic factor in capitalism) he erects other "prayers." He may be a petty bourgeois for instance; but he *decrees* that he shall be recruited among the proletariat. (The lure of Fascism for the middle class resides in the fact that a worker in an office would rather pray by decreeing that he owns the insignia of the management than by decreeing that he owns the insignia of the underlings—particularly since many of the underlings prefer the same kind of identification.)

Thus, we differ from those who would eradicate "word magic": we hold that it is not eradicable, and that there is no need for eradicating it. One must simply eradicate the wrong kinds and coach the right kinds. One does so by the "secular prayers" of his propaganda, his interpretation of property relations and his exhortations as to how he and others should act on the basis of these property relations.

---

some forms of asthma symbolize an attempt to re-establish the conditions of the womb, the respiratory disorders being a mimetic response to the fact that the embryo in the womb does not breathe, an hypothesis that seems applicable at least to such a rememberer of things past as Marcel Proust, whose cork-lined chamber was a kind of objective womb, constructed with the aid of modern scientific progress).

Linking such an hypothesis to our speculations on "homoeopathic" strategies of cure, we might consider a possible attempt to cure mental illness by a kind of "inverted Christian Science." That is, whereas such projects of "auto-suggestion" attempt to arrest physical ills by a "transcendent" change in attitude (whereupon the body, as an actor, is invited to change its mimetic expression accordingly, shifting from physical illness to physical health as the "artistic counterpart" of the change in attitude), might we speculate on a paradoxical attempt to arrest *mental* disorders by deliberate infection with the corresponding *physical* disorder?

And his prayers can be extremely accurate, just as they can be extremely inaccurate. People usually reserve the words "magic" or "prayer" for the inaccurate ones alone. Such usage may be of some service for hasty pamphleteering purposes, but in the end serves to obscure rather than clarify our ideas as to "what is going on."

The forensic material of the law offers excellent opportunities for secular prayer. The jocular proposal that Congress pass a law against bad weather is regularly carried out with great seriousness. Such parliamentary and dictatorial praying is also generally backed by the most drastic material reality, since the prayer is implemented by the constabulary resources. The percentage of constabulary resources provides you with a quick rule of thumb for sizing up the relative accuracy of secular prayer. In proportion as the constabulary proliferates, you have *per se* evidence that the modes of secular prayer are unsuited to the full realities of the situation. To "discount" the growth of the constabulary

---

Might the psychopathologist, in other words, seek to arrest the full ravages of mental regression by finding material means of *giving his patient asthma*, in cases where his regression had been, for some reason or other, "frustrated in its attempts to acquire its appropriate mimetic counterpart"? In other words, might a little of the *physical* disease be introduced as homoeopathic inoculation against the full ravages of the *mental* disease?

Something of this sort seems to be going on, in the experiments with the arresting of dementia praecox by injections of insulin. Is it not possible that the *physically* engendered fear imparted to the patient by the injection serves as immunization against the ravages of his subtler and vaguer *mental* fears? He *burns out fear*, somewhat as a man might get over social shyness by going through some bigger ordeal, like an earthquake. Recall also our remarks on the function of horror stories in *debunking* horror, by reducing the vague mental state to the manageable proportions of an objective fiction. Might not a similar process operate if, by inoculation with a *physical* illness, the focus of disturbance would

(usually stated in its reverse aspect, the "increase of crime") we should take the proliferation of constabulary functions as *per se* evidence that our countrymen are praying their heads off and backing their prayers by a considerable outlay in money (relying upon the use or threat of force to "take up the slack" between the prayer and the reality).

The essence of prayer is *petition*. Its simple reverse, we might say its grotesque *caricature*, is denunciation, invective, excommunication, ostracism, the pronouncing of anathema. It is *polemic*. Such prayer-upside-down has been used profusely by both clerical and secular antagonists. (In fact, might we not discern the original genius of French political invective in Pascal's vituperative championship of the Jansenists against the Jesuits?)

Prayer "transcends" a given conflict (involving a yes and no) when it adopts a "higher" point of view from which the

---

shift from vague and unwieldy mental terrors to their psychologically *more negotiable* material equivalents?

Thus, instead of the "allopathic antidote," we should get the "graded series" of "homoeopathic infection" (the "tragic" strategy of "knocking on wood," in systematically welcoming a little disaster as immunization against greater disaster).

Our objection to most psychotherapy, as now conducted, is that it is accomplished, insofar as it is accomplished at all, by the systematization of triviality. Its dissociative modes of treatment, in being non-moral, are immoral; its lack of social co-ordinates makes it function anti-socially. There is a need to broaden its individualistic, isolated co-ordinates to embody attitudes that fit into a larger social texture. In short, there must be a remoralization of therapeusis.

One may glimpse the difference in such a speculation as the following: Suppose that one scientifically debunks a pious terror. Consider the difference between thus "dissolving" its mystery (saying, in effect, "There is no mystery") and the *completion* of the homoeopathic attitude, which would say in effect: "There is a mystery; but we reduce it to manageable proportions because you cannot tolerate it in its fullness."

opponents are found to merge. Thus, if one heard two men heatedly arguing whether money should yield two per cent or three per cent, he might "transcend" them both by saying that money should not yield anything. But it is obvious that his "transcendence" would but form the basis of another conflict, with petitions and invectives of its own.

One of the most irritating variants of secular prayer is to be noted in Pareto. Pareto speaks fervently of the need for a "strictly scientific" sociology, a sociology possessing the objectivity and precision of mathematics. He disposes of other sociologies by showing that they lack this objectivity and precision. And thereby he can pray himself and his disciples into thinking that *his* sociology *does* possess mathematical objectivity and precision.

Another convenience of prayer, that people are quick to move in on, may be illustrated in this wise: A puts forward a very difficult theory. You cannot grasp it, but there is a salvation device ready to hand. You "transcend" the confusing issue by a "sentimental" vote upon the "essence" of the difficult theory. That is, if you are in Germany, you call it democratic or Jewish, in Russia bourgeois or Fascist, in America Fascist or communist; if you are a churchman, you locate its essence in sacrilege, etc. Thereby you don't merely attack; you symbolically enlist a whole society on your side; your selection of "essence" is *per se* the pitting of a whole historic movement against the doctrine. The *"Zweck im Recht"* doctrine would warn us that this extreme kind of prayer is used particularly when there is some conflict in material interests underlying the ideological issue.

"Secular prayer" involves "character building" in that one shapes his attitudes, the logic of his life, by the co-ordinates he chooses, and one shapes his actions with reference to the judgments that follow from the co-ordinates.

Cassirer has called attention to the verbal scrupulosity of Socrates. He notes how Socrates could not feel *moral* until he had found the exact names for all the relationships and interrelationships he considered significant. Socrates, by our formula, was intensely engrossed in a project of "character-building by secular prayer," as he struggled like the great writers of Greek tragedy to integrate the new lore of the forensic with the traditions of epic heroism surviving from the primitive period of Greece. The sophistication of the Sophists was the simple negation of the earlier pieties— and Socrates tried to "transcend" it by "negating the negation." He did not want to be forensic-versus-primitive, but primitive-plus-forensic. This drive for a "higher synthesis" he named by shorthand as his "demon." The *act of definition* in his conversation (his dialectic as "drama") is paralleled in a play like Ibsen's *Enemy of the People*, which is a five-act redefinition of the word "enemy." In fact, as you watch Ibsen's play, you watch the slow emergence of its title, which does not come into full expression, in the words of the characters, until the dramatist has prepared you by the action to accept *his* meaning.

Some contemporary critics, when noting the manifestations of "secular prayer" in the field of the didactic ("propaganda," moral education) tend to excoriate its results as a "literature of the will." And often they may win us by smuggling into their word "will" the connotations of "willfulness." Such deterioration, we admit, was present in many typical nineteenth-century philosophies — but one must not adopt the polemic, pamphleteering attitude so quickly, unless he is more interested in winning an argument than in understanding a process. In such cases, he himself prays on too simple a level.

ATTITUDES TOWARD HISTORY

Stealing Back and Forth of Symbols

The divine right of kings was first invoked by secular interests combating the authority of the theocrats. It held that God appointed the king, rather than the church authorities, to represent the secular interests of "the people." Later, when the church made peace with established monarchs, identifying its interests with the interests of the secular authorities, the church adopted the doctrine as its own. And subsequently the bourgeoisie repudiated the doctrine, in repudiating both monarch and state. It did so in the name of "rights," as the doctrine had originally been promulgated in the name of "rights." Among these "rights" was "freedom." And Marx in turn stole this bourgeois symbol for the proletariat. The stealing back and forth of symbols is the approved method whereby the Outs avoid "being driven into a corner."

Symbolic Mergers

There is a hidden "discounting" in transcendence—but this factor is hard to see behind our verbalizing. The man who says, for instance, that "everything is material," may be found to subsume all sorts of reservations. And the man who says "everything is spiritual" may subsume other reservations. The scandal arises when the idealist approaches the materialist's sentence with the meanings it would have for the idealist if he (the idealist) were to affirm the materialist's sentence. Under the symbol of "atheism," one man may subsume precisely the social attitudes that another man subsumes under the symbol of "God."

"Metaphorical analysis" is required, to get a close glimpse of the secret ways in which a symbol integrates. If a man uses the symbol "atheism," for instance, and is found to express his thoughts, at strategic points, in imagery having the *connotations* of diabolism, we may take it that the symbol is *not* the verbal equivalent for the believer's symbol "God." On the other hand, we may subject the God symbol to analysis, and make disclosures that would horrify the owner of the symbol. We may find that by "God" he means something quite spiteful.

A symbol is a vessel of much more content than is disclosed by its "face value" as a label. Words may contain attitudes much more complex and subtle than could possibly be indicated in the efficient simplifications of a "practical" dictionary. And so with all "symbolic mergers." Thus, once a man has integrated his whole life about his business (interweaving it with a full texture of social relationships and personal transcendences) you will be far from knowing what is going on if you try to analyze his motives as merely the "desire for monetary profit." His business has become a "vessel," it is "charismatic."

Symbols of Authority

Admittedly a vague term. Better designed for pointing-in-the-direction-of-something than for clear demarcation of that-in-the-direction-of-which-we-would-point. It puts together in the lump our attitude toward rulers, courts, parliaments, laws, educators, constabulary, and the moral slogans linked with such. Fundamentally connected with property relations. And even the dispossessed tends to feel that he "has a stake in" the authoritative structure that dispossesses him; for the influence exerted upon the policies of education by the authoritative structure encourages the dispossessed to feel that his only hope of repossession lies in his allegiance to the structure that has dispossessed him.

The authoritative property relations, let us say, either rob a man of a job or shunt him into a wretched and poor-paying job. If he would get a job or better the job he has, he must win the good favor of those in authority. He may even know that this solution will not work for everybody—but he has at least a "spiritual" stake in the reigning structure of authority so long as he dares hope that he at least may finally get himself a berth in one niche or another of the ailing structure. He is further stimulated to such an attitude by the fact that obedience to the structure of authority is *natural*. An ideal world would be one in which one's allegiance to the reigning social criteria (headed in symbols of authority) could be paid without disaster. One would shape his mind as an individual with reference to the shape of the total collective pattern. Insofar as he cannot do this, to that extent he is "dispossessed," even if he enjoys material wealth.

One "owns" his social structure insofar as one can subscribe to it by wholeheartedly feeling the reasonableness of its arrangements, and by being spared the need of segregational attitudes. Insofar as such allegiance is frustrated, both the materially and the spiritually dispossessed must suffer. We may not be in the mood to pity the losses of those who are not dispossessed materially; but it would be poor gauging for a critic not to take them into account when considering historical processes. Such spiritual dispossession explains why so many men with a material "stake in" feudalism could take a sympathetic interest in the revolutionary writings of the French Encyclopedists. It even explains why Marx, when given a fairly sufficient income from Engels' cotton mills, could nonetheless persist as a "renegade." An over-stressing of material possession alone may lead one to alienate men who may be his allies in the gigantic task of engineering a shift in allegiance to the symbols of authority. In fact, the peripheral class (of those spiritually alienated but still materially rewarded) can contribute insight of a sort to which the wholly dispossessed are blinded. To the wholly dispossessed, the matter may look *too simple*, thereby inducing them to make an over-simplified drawing of alignments. And in such over-simplification, they not only organize themselves; they also by antithesis organize the enemy—forcing into the enemy camp many who might otherwise have been with them. The issue is aggravated by the negativisitic processes we have discussed elsewhere, in connection with the problem of authority and its rejection.

Our own program, as literary critic, is to integrate technical criticism with social criticism (propaganda, the didactic) by taking the allegiance to the symbol of authority as our subject. We take this as our starting point, and "radiate" from it. Since the symbols of authority are radically linked with property relationships, this point of departure automatically involves us in socio-economic criticism. Since works of art, as "equipment for living," are formed with authoritative structures as their basis of reference, we also move automatically into the field of technical criticism (the "tactics" of writers).

The followers of John Dewey's educational theories make a distinction between "education as a function of society" and "society as a function of education." To restate our own position with reference to this terminology, we should say that a society is normal when education can be a function of society. That is, the principles and directives of the society are operating smoothly, and education prepares the minds of the young by equipping them to maintain these same principles and directives. We are "alienated," "dispossessed" insofar as this order must be reversed, as the followers of Dewey would reverse them. To say that "society" should be a function of "education" is to say, in effect, that the principles and directives of the prevailing society are radically askew (that the society has been despoiled of its reasonableness) and that education must serve to remake it accordingly.

This amounts to saying that educators must to some degree turn against the reigning symbols of authority, aiming to put another rationale of authority in their place. But on the other hand, Dewey as a philosopher realized the risks involved in the attitude of rejection. He knew that one is "at home" in the world when he can "accept" it. So Dewey advocated an educational theory that sought to alter the modes of authority, while distrusting the explicit formulation of class struggle. The contradiction, as we have said, probably arises from his realization of the ways in which, when the explicit theory of class struggle is released into the texture of naive society at large, it induces all sort of excessive responses (as per our paragraphs on "Being Driven Into a Corner").

A fundamental revolution takes place when men shift from magical notions of authority (authority sanctioned by custom, as with king or parents) to the forensic concept of delegated authority (stemming, we might say, from the "democratization of peerage"). But though the comic critique of deputies ("puppets" as social functions) has its valid place in a sophisticated society, we dare not chart events by too great reliance upon the metaphor of deputization.

Words are not puppets. They have more than mere "delegated power." They also command -- and a theory that seeks to consider them after the analogy of puppets alone must leave important questions unanswered.

DICTIONARY OF PIVOTAL TERMS

Put it this way:

If a man wishes to lift something, and picks up a lever for that purpose, it is not enough that he simply "delegate powers" to the lever. The lever has its own properties as well. Its "character" is not identical with this delegated function. In fact, the metal may be too weak to perform the delegated function at all. Or the lever may be too heavy. Thus, in effect, the lever would *refuse* to perform its puppet-function.

Similarly, words are public properties, and the individual "has a stake in" their public ownership. He cannot merely "delegate" powers to them. It would be as true (or as over-simplifyingly false) to say that they delegate their powers to him. He uses them, and they use him.

Particularly in the case of a great poet, the insufficiency of the parliamentary metaphor becomes apparent. Insofar as the poet is "born, not made," he obeys "authority established by custom." Both he as "ruler" and his words as "subjects" must obey "natural law." In the mediaeval fiction, the class of serfs and the class of nobles each "obeyed" after its fashion. A similar arrangement applies to the functions of speech—and the parliamentary metaphor obscures these functions.

The "voting" of poetry is essentially *non-parliamentary*. Otherwise, a poet might conceivably "vote" to write a great and noble epic in praise of the latest advance in commercialized medicine, the Lux-Lax tablets, that "can make you regular, as easy as turning on the light." A noble epic, to glorify your emancipation, through Lux-Lax, from the bondage of physical exercise. Be as sluggish as a bump on a log—sit and dope all you please—glut to your heart's content—and all is well if you merely become a good customer of Lux-Lax. You are freed for absolute devotion to your business. And a poet would write a great epic in praise of this miraculous product (particularly as its promoters are prepared to offer him a handsome price for his services, plus five per cent on the movie rights).

This sweeping epic *cannot* be written. Many would be only too glad to write it, "for a consideration." But they can't. And they can't, precisely because the authority of words cannot be delegated.

It is precisely because the authority of words cannot be delegated, we might add, that one must watch the "poetry exchange" to learn what is really going on in the world. The usual "parliamentary" method of gauging is as follows: One wants to foretell the course of history. One wants to know "the trend." So one draws up a simple questionnaire, on a post card. It reads:

$$
\text{I think America needs} \left\{ \begin{array}{l} \text{fascism} \\ \text{communism} \\ \text{private enterprise} \\ \text{religious revival} \\ \text{primitivism} \end{array} \right.
$$

One gets up a sample mailing list. And when the addressees have sent in their answers, checked off and dropped in the nearest mail box, one tabulates the returns. If the list was not "selective," if it represented an "accurate cross section of the population" (if, in a word, it was "scientific"), by a matter of simple arithmetic you can learn the "attitude of the public" on this important issue. And you size up the "trend of history" accordingly.

As a matter of fact, the expression of the vote (if by "voting" you mean this empty, passive, random process) tells you *nothing.* The future is really disclosed *by finding out what people can sing about.**

What values can enlist the most vigorous and original craftsmen? And what values, on the other hand, can merely enlist the public relations counsel? It is in such *qualitative* tests, requiring the active enlistment of a man's full faculties, giving *full psychological employment,* that you find the materials for prophecy. You find history foretold in the areas where people cannot possibly "sell out" or make decisions at random (decisions such as you get when the voter asks himself, "Shall I vote for A or B?"). You find the course of Germany foretold, for instance, in the fact that

---

* A qualification is needed here. The scientific vocabulary is a kind of "withholding" with the idea of *future* action in mind. Like financial investment, it is induced to forego immediate rewards by the promise of subsequent rewards. It *stoops* to conquer. Precisely by reason of such "spiritualization" (its divorce from strictly mimetic assertion) it has enabled us to make so many powerful assertions on a "higher" level (as the almost zero mimetic content of mathematical symbols enables us to construct so mighty an assertion as a trans-Atlantic liner). Such visions of promise give it vigor "vicariously," as with the earnest boy who studies while others play, and eventually becomes a great corporation lawyer, and so can *assert* in business, while those who *asserted* too much on the "lower level" of childhood games can later afford no games at all. Or their sons can carry the golf clubs whereby the earlier adept at withholding now asserts himself mimetically on the green. Similarly, primitive tribes who retained too closely the mimetic level of assertion were at the mercy of Western nations who enjoyed, in the spiritualities of finance and laboratories, returns on their investment in "organized doubt," so that the primitives' mode of assertion in communal dances protected them not at all against the Western empire-builders who had decided to regiment them in tin or copper mines. The "ecological balance" of close mind-body correlations is a poor match for the spirituality and fanaticism of capitalist "efficiency," once the rewards of withholding have been given body in property relationships, scientific invention, and constabulary resources.

Germany's best writers cannot delegate their powers to the service of Hitler. The government commands—and there have been some who would willingly carry out the command—but the commands of "natural law" (translate: "historical necessity") rule otherwise. The words of the poet are not puppets, but acts. They are a function of him, and he is a function of them. They are a function of society, and he is a function of society.

The parliamentary metaphor, of "delegated power," does not encompass enough to give us the proper "cues" for an analysis of speech. Insofar as speech is haphazard (as in the hastiness of news) perhaps its words can be largely "delegated." But insofar as it involves engrossment, as in poetry, its nature is "authoritarian."*

Transcendence

When approached from a certain point of view, A and B are "opposites." We mean by "transcendence" the adoption of another point of view from which they cease to be opposites. This is, at present, the nearest approach we can make to the process by verbal means. As a matter of fact, such verbalizations completely slight an all-important qualitative ingredient (what even the articulate French might be willing to call a *je ne sais quoi*) that makes all the

---

* Perhaps we fail to realize how far the parliamentary metaphor has intruded into areas where it does not belong. The "scientific" student of esthetics, for instance, wants to find an "ideal proportion." He makes about ten different designs, illustrating different proportions, and asks people in "many walks of life" to name the one they prefer. And he expects to attain valuable knowledge from this mere "passive vote" on the subject of proportion. The most valuable service performed by such quantitative efficiency resides in its power to help him feel his triviality as earnestness.

difference between a true transcendence and the empty acquisition of the verbal paraphernalia.

Thus, an act might be debunkingly motivated, in efficient popular shorthand, as "sour grapes." The comic frame (halfway between the extremes of "hagiography" and "iconoclasm") should say "sour grapes plus." But one might be an unregenerate debunker, yet "take up the slack" verbally by *saying* "sour grapes plus," while his attitude was still chemically pure "sour grapes." Such simple "secular prayer" might *eventually* "redeem" him, preparing the way for "transcendence" to the comic frame. But the verbalization would not *per se* signalize the change in quality.

Primitive peoples recognize the process of transcendence in their initiation rites whereby, at different periods in the life of the individual, he is symbolically endowed with a new identity, as he enters some new corporate grouping within the tribe. The church tries to coach a similar process by its rites of communion. One discerns it behind even the crudest of hazing ceremonies, that seek to impress, by picturesqueness, terror, or wound, the sense of a new identification (a new way of defining the individual's identity with relation to a corporate identity). Purely secular, scientific investigators like Jean Piaget are concerned with it in their studies of the ways whereby the child changes from "autistic" to "socialized" thinking (or, as we might say, attempts to integrate the forensic with the pre-forensic).

Our terms "transcendence downward" and "transcendence upward" are also at best bungling approximates. If one says that a human act is done "for the greater glory of God," his euphemism is the simplest possible example of "transcendence upward." (Heretics may drive the "logic" to its extreme conclusion by deducing the theory that such "spirituality" requires as its corollary the deliberate degradation of the flesh.) "Debunking," the doctrine that a human act "is done purely for gravy," is the simplest example of "transcendence downwards." (Such naive materialism is the heretical over-doing of "dialectical materialism.")

One may "transcendentally" organize his interpretation of human motives by the following broad emphases: a human act is done for God, for an ideal (humanity, culture, justice, truth), for a corporate grouping (political or otherwise), for oneself. Historical-collectivistic emphases generally play about an intermingling of *ideal* and *corporate grouping*.

CONCLUSION

MIGHT we, for envoi, put the main points together briefly:

In names, there are implicit the act and the command. (Piaget shows us the child picking up a block and saying: "This is a boat." The child next moves the block, commanding itself: "Now, make the boat go across the ocean." In time, name and command become inextricably intermingled, the command being *implicit* in the name.) To name various manifestations by the same name, is to organize a strategy with reference to these manifestations.

Such acts, on the rudimentary biological or mimetic level, occur when the poet, feeling (let us say) agitation, gives us agitated sound and rhythm; or feeling calmness, he slips into liquid tonalities.

Such verbal choreography is the material basis of linguistic action. One embodies the act in manipulating the "superstructure" of values arising from "the original economic plant," the human body. (Thus the body, as an "economic enterprise," may on occasion prepare itself by the increased secretion of adrenalin, which induces an increase in muscular tension, and may in turn be correlated, in the "superstructure" of emotions, as fear or rage. Or the body, as predacious, may require *acts* of grasping—and these acts have their counterparts in *attitudes* of grasping—hence, if one in the act of grasping tends to compress the lips, the poet may *dance* the act of grasping when, in expressing some attitude of contact, he alliterates with the letter "m"—or he may "dance rejection" in another situation by the selection of words featuring the letter "p," etc.)

339

But:

This rudimentary field of action becomes buried beneath many kinds of social accretion. The "original economic plants," for instance, are unit "operating companies" held together corporately by the "holding company" of a *social* economy. The social economies are bound together by co-operative acts and corresponding linguistic counters. These words "transcend" the purely mimetic level. The word "Fascism," for instance, takes on meaning purely by reason of its social significance. It becomes a "vessel." And in its use by an advocate there is an "act" different from its use by an opponent.

As the result of social accretions, language in time becomes preponderantly constructed of such "transcendental" words. The abstractions of scientific or philosophic description are too complex for mimetic assertion. They are "tonally opportunistic," since there is no rudimentary choreographic act related to their pronunciation. Yet there is a "program of action" implicit in their use, as with the promise of a "return on the investment," the "rewards for postponed consumption," implicit in the "power-knowledge" that derives from mathematical symbols. The language of abstraction being full of words that "act" only thus derivatively, the poet "reclaims" these areas, as far as possible, by using them in tonal and rhythmic contexts that give them something of a mimetic content (as were the enemy of Fascism to use the word in a context having the imagery and tonalities of anger).

The "mimetic" level becomes interwoven first with the "intimate" level, in the "pre-political" or "pre-forensic" ("familiar") experiences of childhood. This "familiar" level may become so authoritative, since it necessarily is the first form in which we encounter the world at large, that its informative cues will always figure in our incorporation of later materials.

This level is "transcended" in turn by the "abstractions" of the adult, the many "bridging devices" he learns to employ in organizing his attitudes with relation to "forensic" materials.

The complex intermingling of these three levels (the mimetic, the intimate, and the abstract) is named in the lump "character-building by secular prayer." Hence, since one's names are shaped at every point by tests of conduct, the accuracy or scope of naming becomes a "moral" act. Hence, the need of a vocabulary as pliant as the situation it would encompass. Hence, the need of "planned incongruity" to "remoralize, by accurate naming, a situation already demoralized." One gets a vocabulary as pliant as the situation is complex, by "casuistic stretching," by tests of "convertibility" that, considering abstract concepts as mere metaphors, "liquidate" their categorical rigidity.

The individual, by reason of his "property in" the public grammar, the "collective" property of speech, becomes concerned with processes of socialization. These needs of socialization are implicit in the nature of human relations, the productive and distributive patterns and their corresponding concepts of right and obligation. And they are implicit in the nature of the language that gets its shape by reference to such economic foundations.

That is: the mind, being formed by language, is formed by a *public grammar*. And this public grammar involves at every turn material factors. It coaches the realm of "values" that takes form, as a "superstructure," to match the material "substructure."

The "social" aspect of language is "reason." Reason is a complex technique for "checking" one's assertions by public reference. And insofar as one forms his mind by encompassing such linguistic equipment, he learns to use this technique of checking "spontaneously," with varying degrees of accuracy and scope. (It is formed, in other words, as a way of "thinking backwards"—and he learns to "think forwards" with it.)

Hence, implicit in both language and reason (logos, word) there is a *social* basis of reference affecting the individual.

Linked with this is the need to feel the "reasonableness" of one's society, the reasonableness of its aims and methods. This reasonabless comes to a focus in symbols of authority, which combine simultaneously materialistic and evaluative matters of "property"—as they are tied with modes of ownership and norms of conduct ("manners," and "style"). And one "owns the reasonableness of a structure vicariously" insofar as he can feel that he has a "property in" the structure's insignia. In this sense, even the feudal serf "owned" the insignia of the nobles, to the extent that he could believe in their conduct, with its corresponding ethical and esthetic norms, as the "logical culmination" of feudal ways. Insignia obviously cease to represent a "logical culmination," representing instead "antithetical" privilege, insofar as emphases of the "class struggle" come to the fore. At such a time writers may "boast symbolically," may "own privilege vicariously," by continuing to develop their style in accordance with the insignia (ethical and esthetic norms) of a privileged class.

"Alienation" enters insofar as a belief in a structure's reasonableness is impaired. We get material or spiritual alienation, or both.

Here arise all the tactics, either accurate or excessive, involving a "shift in allegiance to the symbols of authority."

CONCLUSION

Hence we get to the problems of sect and schism, of the "stealing back and forth of symbols," of "being driven into a corner," as all the forensic equipment is seized and manipulated by "legalists" (formal or informal) to redirect concepts of social purpose (with attendant concepts of property) in line with the tests of "reason." The strategies of comedy, tragedy, satire, burlesque, and the like are formed by the relationship between the writer's private situation and the general situation. One can also note the macroscopic counterpart of such literary forms in the *collective* strategies (the broader aspects of emphasis or perspective) prevailing at different periods in history. (The necessities of history are the "villain" that makes the total drama go.)

The emphases of historical context call forth corresponding "legal" emphases (sometimes "efficient" in over-emphasis), which become "vessels," with experiential or attitudinizing content much different from that disclosed by their mere "labels." And, similarly, any aspect of experience may become an organizing vessel (one's family or one's job, for instance, may be a fulcrum about which all other aspects of one's life are made to fall into place). The subtlety and complexity of such "vessels" is beyond the powers of verbalization, though we may find cues for "discounting" their hidden content to a degree. And in the bungling and unwieldy processes of history, this *"Bundschuh"* aspect of symbols (making them not merely the counters or scientific labels they disclose as their face value, but "vessels" with unchartable emotional implications) becomes tied with "character-building by secular prayer," involving in the end attitudes towards the reigning symbols of authority, hence attitudes towards the economic arrangements with which they are openly or deviously identified, hence programs for social and political alignment.

From this we get to the issue of "corporate identity," involving in turn "rituals of rebirth." And a concern with such rituals leads to a concern with the use of the tragic scapegoat in symbolic purification. This obliges us in turn to note the ambiguous relationship between tragedy and crime, involving distinctions between "homoeopathic" and "allopathic" attitudes towards danger, anguish, death (whence our critique of overly simple "sanitation" theories of art and conduct).

When confronting the total situation, as critic, we are led to our slogans concerning "comedy." And even were one to abandon all the specific formulae we have offered for the charting of human relationships, we might still plead for this much: Perhaps the most important thing is not our formulae, or any other formulae, as it is the *attitude* to which *any* formulae give substance. The important thing is to continue the search for a vocabulary that, as Gide might say, could provide humility without humiliation.

A comic vocabulary should be framed with this as its ideal. But a comic vocabulary of motives, we admit, cannot be attained insofar as people are at war, or living under the threat of war. Militarism makes naturally for the extremes of heroic euphemism, with corresponding dislocations of gauging. Yet even in war itself, much that happens falls within the category of peace. The peaceful routine of production, distribution, and administration must continue, even during the efficiencies of military destruction. And to the extent that war is not a mere act of physical risk, but draws upon the organization of peace, the area of comedy is kept intact.

AFTERWORD TO SECOND EDITION

PERHAPS the major change in attitude, between the author's point of view when this book was first published and his point of view now, involves the matter of political symmetry. Political symmetry does not seem nearly so appealing to him now as it did then. In fact, a degree of looseness in the interrelationships among governmental bodies (be they "political" governments or purely "business" dynasties) seems to offer better opportunity for individual freedom to find a place among the interstices. "Feudal" unity seems preferable to the "monolithic" sort within States—and international union seems best when it is of a loosely federated sort.

By the same token, in the discussion of collectivism there was perhaps a tendency to assume too clear a distinction between outright socialization and the roundabout kind, the "socialization of losses." Symbolic manipulations are so intrinsic to all monetary systems and their corresponding modes of accountancy, it is likely that such resources will be stretched to their Malthusian limits.

When we originally wrote this book, we were more moved than we suspected by the outcry then being raised against the few billions of added public debt that President F. D. Roosevelt's administration began by incurring in behalf of economically useful government spending. Since then, we have lived to see hundreds of billions added to the public debt, and usually with the sanction of the very persons who were previously so distressed, though a preponderant percentage of these later sums was expended not for economically useful things but for war-goods.

It would be impossible to decide whether such collective expenditures are to be classed as outright socialization or as making for the roundabout variety, the socialization of losses. And cutting across the distinction, we can compromise by merely taking it for granted that, insofar as purely symbolic resources (of financial manipulation) are available, such resources will be exploited, and even unto their Malthusian limits. How could we expect otherwise of governmental policy-makers? For they are human; that is, they are symbol-using animals. And such manipulations of money and credit are essentially operations with the symbols of accountancy.

However, we should note the different form which such operations have taken, as contrasted with the heyday of foreign investment in the twenties, when there was a great boom in the floating of foreign loans. The market crash in 1929, we may recall, resulted largely from the dawning realization that these loans were bad debts which the international bankers had unloaded at a profit on the United States investment public. And thereafter much government spending under Roosevelt was required, to take up the slack caused by the general loss of confidence in the foreign investment field.

At first glance, one might think that this activity in foreign investment had never recovered, whereas to a large extent it has but taken a different form; and actually in *function*, throughout the years when the floating of foreign issues by private international bankers was apparently at a minimum, the circle of people involved as investors in uncollectible foreign loans has not only not decreased but has instead increased enormously. In fact, the process of foreign investment has now been democratized to the point where every citizen of our nation is in function a foreign investor, regardless of whether he knows he is, or wants to be. Nay more, whereas in the old days a bad foreign debt could run but a relatively few years before its weakness was disclosed by an inability on the part of the foreign debtor to meet the interest charges, the interest charges are now paid regularly. For if the federal Government advances vast uncollectible sums to areas abroad, and meets these charges by selling Government bonds on which the people as a whole pay the interest charges, then the people as a whole are investors in this debt, plus the fact that they themselves, out of taxes, meet the interest charges, which are paid to the smaller group who are the holders of the bonds.

Inasmuch as, the monetary system being what it is, such devices do keep our usual business in operation, they assist generally in the production and distribution of goods. Hence it would obviously be hard to say just what kind of "socialization" this is. But in any case, clearly, it is a glorious instance of man's birthright: his skill at the manipulation of symbols (the symbols of money and credit).

Our stress upon the "bureaucratizations" of politics, business, and industry (technology) led us into one major neglect. Above and beyond the course of governmental organizations, or beneath them, or prior to them (almost as a "pre-historic" heritage), there is the motive of human goodwill as such (and thus, of ill will!), human sociality in its most general use. And that is not discussed, though it figures implicitly as an ingredient in our plea for the "comic." But if the reader considers this book in connection with its earlier companion volume, *Permanence and Change*, he will find the slighted element considered amply.

Indeed, our concern in the earlier book is with the motive of communication—and "communication" is the most generalized statement of the principle of "love." (In the

"Curriculum Criticum," added at the end of the new Hermes edition of *Counter-Statement*, there is a discussion of the relation between *P & C* and *ATH*.)

As a "radiation" from this thought, it might also be worth remarking on the relation that "attitudes" bear to "persons" or "characters." Insofar as a person acts "in character," then we might say (in accordance with what in *A Grammar of Motives* we call the agent-act ratio) that the person is the *principle* of his action. His character, we might say, is a set of "congealed policies"; it is infolded principles of conduct that unfold themselves in his dealings with temporal situations. "Attitudes," in their nature as incipient acts, likewise have this "fixed" quality, summing things up like a lyric. Thus one can understand how the realistic study of "attitudes" might lead into a more idealistic, "novelistic" study of "character" (or, in sociology, "personality types") when one thinks, say, of such obvious personal strategies as in the case of the "good nigger," who charms his white "superiors" by his "childlike simplicity," and thereby gets himself a certain degree of patronage and protection, and genuine affection, too. Here is the direction one should take, when looking upon *personalities* as strategic developments in the encompassing of social situations. (See on "situations" and "strategies" in our *Philosophy of Literary Form*.)

One final matter of emphasis should be noted. In later books, the problem which is here discussed in terms of bureaucratic order is treated in terms of the "socio-political pyramid," with its corresponding "hierarchal psychosis." This motive bears an important relation to tragedy. Thus it might even be said to call for a "tragic" frame of interpretation rather than for a "comic" perspective. But as the issue looks from the comic point of view, however "tragic" tragedy may be in itself, the critical analysis of "tragic" motives is in essence "comic." Much of our material on this subject is still to be published in our projected volume, *A Symbolic of Motives*. But there is much on the "hierarchal psychosis" in *A Rhetoric of Motives*—and it is discussed in an article on "organizational behavior" that is reprinted as an appendix to the new Hermes edition of *Permanence and Change*.

This man but wants to till his acre. That man but wants to ply his craft. A third would, at a profit, help the two exchange their wares. Whereby there arises a vast set of interrelationships among the many locally motivated agents. Priests, judges, administrators, tax collectors, educators, purveyors of information, and the like all come to take part in this collective effort, as it grows complicated in its bureaucratizations, with some pyramidal notions of Up and Down, however fluctuant the norms of preference may be.

The network of interrelationships attains great profusion and abstractness (despite the concreteness of every person's particular spot in the general muddle). Conditions thus allow for (and call for) the over-all unifications of *empire*, whereby hitherto alien areas (once out of bounds but related loosely by commerce) are brought within the same realm of rule. And thereby arises the need for offices still farther removed from the basic humble acts of work and trade, with their comparatively simple and direct kinds of gratification and vexation.

And to fit the rarer motives of these more supervisory offices, odd kinds of mentality must be developed, with the aid of the poetic imagination, too (and the poet, to educate his king, may school himself to think governmental thoughts, in corresponding imagery, thus making finally for engrossment in grandeurs and glamors that are a mockery of his own reality, except insofar as he may be rewarded by "royalties"). And all this adds up to the unending burdens of The Scramble, the glories of "man's divine discontent," less honorifically known as the "rat race." Until even children begin by training themselves in similar thinking.

"I am King of the Ashpile!" shouted the boy who, by pushing and pulling, had scrambled to the top, and stood there holding off all other contestants who were lower down the cindery slope but struggling vigorously to mount and displace him. "I am King of the Ashpile!" he shouted exultantly. And he shouted in a hurry, too. For already the others were attacking him from all sides—and he knew it would be at most but a matter of minutes until one of the others shoved him from his perch—then up would rise a new rival, in turn soon to be ousted from his place of eminence. And the contestants could all expect to get, for their efforts: scuffed shoes, torn clothes, and skin rubbed raw by grinding in the ashes.

"I am King of the Ashpile!" the boy shouted, as both boast and challenge, thus succinctly symbolizing the comic principle of tragedy.

P. S. 1959.

In a final reading, some spots I admit to being content with, others greatly vex me. Despite my complaints against "nineteenth-century antithesis-thinking," I often failed to see the full implications of my own stress upon the principle known as the "socialization of losses," which cuts across any flat distinction between "capitalism" and "socialism." And the closely analogous ways in which thermo-nuclear power was developed in U.S.A. and U.S.S.R. suggest that Big Technology *cum* accountancy overrides the current political fictions.

THE SEVEN OFFICES

I

THERE IS NO END to possible theories of motivation, with their corresponding ways of defining and classifying motives. Our hero can do what he does because he is of some particular religion, race, nationality, social class, historical tradition, occupation, personality type, glandular makeup, or has been psychologically wounded in one or another of the ways specified by the various competing experts. If we say that he did as he did because of the situation in which he was placed, there can be endless variation in our terms for what he did; and the situation in which he did it can be interpreted in terms of varying scope, ranging from a view of his act as done against a background of one or many gods more or less actively concerned with his conduct, or against a purely secular background of "nature" ("environment" variously interpreted); or we may place his act with reference to the most minutely particular of circumstances, as when explaining exactly why Mr. Q., Republican, retired, Yale graduate, wearing glasses, and just having quarreled with his wife, turned his car exactly as he did in the particular combination of factors that made up one particular traffic accident. In view of such a motivational jungle, a good basic proposition to have in mind when contemplating the study of motives would be: Anybody can do anything for any reason.

Thus there is a sense in which this essay, which would propose one more terminology of motives, is like focussing upon one leaf in a jungle and proclaiming exultantly, "This is *the* leaf. This is *it*!" But first, by way of apologetic introduction, let us explain our motivational simplification by explaining how we got to it.

Recently, teaching a course in the theory of language (trade name for the course: "Language as Symbolic Action"), I used as text a book on philosophies of education: *Philosophies and Education,* edited by Nelson B. Henry, University of Chicago Press. Students and teacher alike were struck by the pragmatic fact that, despite the great differences of outlook among the various *philosophies* we considered, when the authors got to the subject of the *pedagogical methods* that they thought implicit in their philosophic position, they all seemed to wind up by recommending much the same procedure: teaching by means of the guided critical discussion (a schoolroom variant of the procedure used by Plato in his Socratic dialogues). All the philosophies gravitated around this same educational method, though each approached it from a different point of view. (Thus in effect each philosophy "grounded" the *method* in different sets of *principles*).

The situation suggested a happy analogy with the situation in the United Nations (where, by the nature of the case, delegates with a considerable range of motivational backgrounds agree on a kind of procedural charter common to the lot). And whereas some people are inclined to think that no true peace can prevail in the world until or unless all the world unites in a common set of ultimate beliefs, does not the machinery of the United Nations suggest that nations might sufficiently agree on methods while still greatly differing as to the routes by which they approach these methods? They might all congregate in the same clearing, though they come to it by many different paths through the jungle.

Here would be a good instance of the liberal ideal: a sufficiently peaceful world of many varied motivational centres, each with its own unique character, but all brought together, somewhat like an assortment of portraits in a portrait gallery.

But would this mere conglomeration be enough? Whatever the differences, there must be some notable elements common to the lot; otherwise, agreement even on methods of procedure would be impossible. What, then, of the necessary elements in common? How chart *these*?

II

First, obviously, there would be the *generically human* element. Whatever else this world forum is, it is a congregation of word-using (symbol-using) animals, assembled from many regions, and relying above all upon the attribute that most sharply distinguishes this species of animal: *Talk*. Just as the philosophies of education, all being systems of talk, gravitated towards a procedure best adapted to a mixture of freedom and authority in Talk (the "guided critical discussion" of the Socratic dialogue), so this body accepts, above all, principles of order imposed upon it by the genius of Talk.

But we can't stop there. Talk is too universal a human motive. For our scheme of motives, for guiding our notion of what we call the "Seven Offices," we need something less highly generalized, yet without descending to such extreme localization of motives as we get when asking exactly why one particular person does one particular thing on one particular occasion.

To be sure, since man is the typical Talking Animal, a major concern of education should be the question: "What does it mean to be a talking animal? What are the advantages, *and the possible risks*, of this particular resourcefulness? To what extent does language free us, and to what extent enslave us, even divorce us from our 'home' in nature?" Education should devote major attention to this problem, unquestionably. Yet there are notable respects in which such a concern is too general, as regards the *administrative* attitude suggested in our title, the "Seven Offices." Talk is too "grand" a motive.

Still with the example of the United Nations in mind, and asking what more specifically might be the end of education, we might next ask ourselves: With what other specifically human faculty, what other distinguishing aptitude, is the speechifying faculty radically interwoven? And the answer is: the tool-using faculty (or, above all, the tool-making faculty — for there is a sense in which many animals can be said to use rudimentary tools, but you have moved into the realm of the exclusively human animal when you get to the more involute stage where things are used as tools for the making of tools for the using and making of tools, and so on). A Detroit factory would have a fantastic time indeed trying to get itself planned, built, and managed without the technical terminologies needed for assembling its equipment and materials, for indicating their proper use, and for keeping the necessary records (since the accountant and the file clerk are as indispensable to a factory as the machinist).

The very ungainliness of the technical words which technology has added to our vocabulary helps us to realize how closely the developments of technology are tied to such resources of conceptualization and naming as go with the ability to use and invent words. So, for our next step, combining thoughts of verbalization in the United Nations with thoughts of the tie-up between man as tool-maker (*homo faber*) and man as verbalizer (*homo sapiens*), we come to this proposition: The ideal question for education *today* (as distinct from education "always") would be: "How adapt man to the needs of world-wide empire progressively made necessary by the conditions of technology?"

III

At this step, an aside is in order. Note, first, that in going from "tool-using" or "tool-making" to "technology," we have gone from the "universal" or "generic" to the "global." (That is, we are somewhere in between a "grand" view of motives and the *particularized* view). We use the term "world empire" with relation to technology because technology's vast and ever-changing variety of requirements means in effect that areas hitherto widely separated in place and cultural affinity are *integrally* brought together. If a factory in New Jersey establishes some connection whereby it uses, for one of its processes, raw material produced in a remote area of Africa, then to that extent a portion of Africa and a portion of New Jersey are joined in "technological empire." Each area is in effect "annexed" to the other, within the conditions of this transaction.

"Empire," as so conceived, is *not* identical with "absolute rule." We do not imply that one central governmental authority is needed for such shifting kinds of "technological annexation." *On the contrary.* Our term, "technological empire," as so conceived, involves simply the notion that technology establishes, however waveringly, the conditions of world order. And the United Nations would seem to be the institution that comes nearest, as regards man's generic verbalizing trait, to a liberal solution of the problem—though one might grant that in world order there is always at least the *temptation* to round things out by a corresponding centrality of authority, a temptation that should itself be a subject for warnings on the part of educators concerned with teaching man how to discount such urgent forms of hierarchal imagining and ambition as are especially stimulated by "imperial" situations.

We are now ready to begin.

IV

On considering the "global scene" from the standpoint of technology, our next problem was: How best categorize, or classify, the motivational field *from this point of view?* A notable element in technology itself gives us the cue: the element of *use*. Thus, in what may be a modified brand of post-utilitarianism, we shall approach our subject from the standpoint of use, however broadly we may interpret the term (a broadening indicated by our term, "offices"). But there is another matter to be considered. Ideally, for our over-all motivational chart of "offices," we should adopt as many terms as are necessary, but no more than are sufficient.

Along the lines of early Roman concerns with the motives of world order (though the Roman notion of the *orbis terrarum* was more ideal than actual) we take it that the desired terminology of motives should have a strongly *Neo-Stoic* cast. And thus, combining the Stoic idea of service with the technological idea of use, we shall guide our choice of over-all terminology by asking, "What do people do for one another?" Once this matter were decided, the next consideration would be: "What kinds of motives help or hinder such (ideally) 'fraternal' services?"

Of the seven "offices" that we thus tentatively propose (in line with the principle that we should have just enough terms and no more), the terms we would propose are not related to one another in a fixed or absolute order of relative worth. That is, they can be evaluated variously, depending upon the point of view from which they are approached. So we must be content with merely listing them, in somewhat arbitrary order, and then we shall comment on them briefly. The basic offices (their number still tentative) that people perform in their relations to one another, are: Govern, serve (provide for materially), defend, teach, entertain, cure, pontificate (minister in terms of a "beyond").[1]

V

As regards these seven over-all categories for an "official" terminology of motives, or rather, "duties": whereas they are intended to exhaust the field, they are not mutually exclusive. Any particular act may fall on the bias across their divisions, quite as the divisions themselves do not logically exclude one another. Thus, when Cicero said that the first office of an orator is to teach an audience, the second to please it, and the third to move or "bend" it, his second office would obviously fall under our head of "entertain," his third would fall under "govern." And, ironically, he notes that the orator should lay the *apparent* stress upon the *first* office (of teaching) whereas the oration is actually designed for the *third* office (of swaying). But let's consider the terms one by one, in the order we have arbitrarily assigned to them.

In this scheme, entries under "govern" would first of all comprise rulers: emperors, kings, tyrants, dictators, presidents, and the like. Here would belong secondarily managers (managements), labor leaders, ward bosses, moderators, chairmen. The term would also be broad enough to include legislatures and judiciary, since they are functions of government. (Possibly the old Stoic identification between "reason" and "rule" led us to place the term "govern" at the top of our list, since we hope that the proposed scheme of offices will seem reasonable.)

[1] One step in our progression has been omitted here. Just before deciding upon the seven offices, we had begun listing at random various purposes for which an ideal educational system might be designed. At this stage we considered such items as: education for business enterprise, for free inquiry, for particular skills, for political fanaticism, for slavery, for bureaucracy, for divine worship.

Insofar as we restrict the meaning of "serve" to the idea of "providing for materially," then obviously the first entries under this head are agriculture, industry, transportation, and the correspondingly necessary clerical work (a vast item in technology, a still much vaster item in technology under capitalism, since under capitalism we should also include under this same head those bringers of glad tidings that are usually called advertising agents or sales promoters—or should they, perhaps, be classed under "teaching," insofar as they "educate" the public to yearn for things?). In any case, when one is considering the relation in our society between the categories of "govern" and "serve" ("serve" in the sense of "providing for materially"), it is good to remember a distinction Thurman Arnold once proposed, when he spoke not only of political government but of "business government." He noted that, so far as sheer *functions* are concerned, a financial dynasty can govern (even while being outside our rules for the political electing of representatives, as the general public cannot vote on the directorship of a corporation, though that corporation can in effect levy *taxes* upon the community, under the guise of the *prices* charged for goods and services). In this sense, business and finance covertly *govern* while they overtly *serve* (a power of the treasury that they further exercise, of course, in their ability to grant or withhold funds for advertising). Labor unions can also exercise a measure of government, insofar as they can affect business policies and methods of production.

Under "defend" would fall primarily the military and police, and secondarily the system of "intelligence" that helps carry out defensive tasks as they are conceived to be (a conception usually narrowed by the distinctive nature of the occupation itself). Insofar as a nation's policies are guided by considerations of "security," the office of *defense* permeates the principle of *governance* ("setting the tone" for them, or even actually "taking over"). The susceptibility to such overlapping is indicated in the sheer etymological kinship among the words: police, policy, polity, and politics. Traffic regulation, essentially a function of *service*, is usually performed by police because of need for authority in enforcement (hence, again, the road back to the office of governing).

Under "teach," besides the obvious main function of formal education, would fall in general the institutionalized purveying of information (as with journalism). We have already discussed the ambiguities of advertising in this regard. Speculations in "pure theory" would seem best classifiable under this head; and here would fall those rare but necessary moments in which some few members of a society pause to examine critically the very assumptions or presuppositions on which that society is based (as speculative methods are offered, in the interests of discovery, for systematically questioning principles that are otherwise taken for granted). Teaching has an implied function of government insofar as it inculcates values and attitudes that lead to corresponding modes of conduct. Recall that Plato would have rounded out the symmetry by having the philosopher a king.

In primitive societies, there is one sense in which the office of "entertainment" is very limited, being confined to such functionaries as the tribal bard (and later, the court fool). But in another sense, entertainment is implicit in all group rituals (such as ceremonial dances), though they may be rationalized in terms of utility, along lines indicated in the theory of "homeopathic magic." In our society, where entertainment (including professional sports) has become a major industry, there is the maximum split between activity of the performer and passivity of the observer, as the observer, with many cheap and even free entertainments to choose among, can develop an "amuse me, or off with your head" attitude once possible only to a fabulous jaded Oriental monarch.

News, in its role as the purveying of information, would fall under the head of "teaching." But in its role as "drama" it is a form of entertainment, with stories of persons who actually undergo the sufferings and hardships we should otherwise not dare to be entertained by except in fictions. The news gives us a kind of Roman circus in which we behold not merely imaginary victims but real ones. The attitude is made still more apparent in the case of documentary films and news photos assembled and distributed by organizations that regularly comb the entire globe, to keep the reader entertained by a daily authentic recital of other people's miseries. (Or should we, along the lines of some remarks in Aristotle on tragedy, say simply that such things have the appeal of the "marvelous"?) News is an adjunct of *government* insofar as, by selectivity, timing, and emphasis (by placing and headlines) it forms people's view of "reality" and thus influences their judgment as to what would be the proper or reasonable policy in a given situation. Insofar as news thus misrepresents, it is an adjunct of misgovernment.

Entertainment shares with teaching the possible indirect kind of governance that comes with the shaping and intensifying of such attitudes as have their corresponding role in practical conduct. It is in this sense that we might subscribe to Shelley's final sentence in his *Defence of Poetry*: "Poets are the unacknowledged legislators of the world." The symmetry is impaired somewhat by the fact that people often make quite a dissociation between the aesthetic self and the practical self, admiring in fiction kinds of action and character that are quite alien to them as citizens. On the other hand, even governments are eager to identify themselves with entertainment, as is indicated by the tradition whereby the President tosses out the first ball at the opening of the baseball season in Washington. Often our political contests make more sense when judged as entertainment than as the citizen's rational choice between governmental policies. And the nature of our advertising mediums strongly associates business with entertainment. However, ideas of entertainment vary with different social climates; and presumably in early New England there was a time when the public got its strongest entertainment from a morbid engrossment with trials for witchcraft, quite as with public executions, either witnessed or read about.

Material medicine and hygiene are primary entries under "Cure," with mental therapy and prophylaxis taking on an ever-increasing importance. Under "Cure" would also be included the *care* of those suffering infirmity (in sickness, infancy, or age). The overlap between cure and entertainment was explicitly considered as early as Aristotle's Poetics, with its reference to the kind of emotional cleansing (purgation, "catharsis") that could result from the sympathetic witnessing of a tragedy. And one can see how "Cure" overlaps upon our last office, "Pontificate," when one recalls how the doctor cultivates his "bedside manner," or the psychologist his air of long-suffering omniscience, as aids to the curative effect deriving, or thought to derive, from his role as a person of higher authority. (Such behavior impinges upon the dramatizing methods of priestcraft.) As evidence of the way in which "Cure" can impinge upon "Govern," think how successfully the officials in control of the American Medical Association have used their positions to block certain social policies in the name of certain business policies.

Though our terms for the first six offices suggested themselves spontaneously, we had trouble deciding upon the term "Pontificate" for the "last" function. But at least one can see why, whatever the arbitrariness of the order among the others, we should keep this one for the end. At first we thought of calling it the office of "Consoling." There is a point beyond which no one can "Cure" us—and for such inevitable sorrows of separation, suffering,. death, the only office left is that of Solace, insofar as possible. There is a "qualitative break," the passing of a "critical point," when the doctor lays down his duty and the "man of God" (with funeral artist as sub-officiator) takes over. Hence, the distinction between "Cure" and "Console."

But when considering the highly verbal nature of the theological doctrines by which all religious creeds and priestly functions are guided, we felt impelled to think of this last office as essentially *terministic*. Whether or not you believe in a "beyond," this office treats man *in terms of* a "beyond." And such treatment is "pontification" in the sense that it "builds a bridge" between two terministically differentiated realms, by viewing the "temporal" *in terms of* the "eternal" (or the "natural" *in terms of* the "supernatural").

"Console" has the momentary advantage of placing stress upon the "peace of mind" that is now so popularly asssociated with religious faith (in case, with understandable humanitarian weakness, one is not capable of vividly imagining the lot of those poor devils who are condemned by a loving God to the agonizing tortures of eternal hell). But "Pontificate" has the advantage of leading more directly into other major duties that are clearly connected with a priesthood, most notably the function of *solemnizing,* or *formalizing* (as with officiation at a wedding, or at the coronation of a monarch). Here, obviously, a contribution of the priestly role is in the modes of *dignification* in terms of which the occasion is *interpreted,* and thereby *"sanctioned."* And this dignification essentially involves the interpretation of a temporal or natural event in terms of an ultimate eternal or supernatural ground (a "beyond"). So all told, "bridge-building" seems the best term for this office.

When we recall that the Roman emperor, by reason of his double role as both pagan deity and head of the secular order, was given the title of *pontifex maximus,* we likewise glimpse the route whereby the priestly office can lead to theocracy. And it is obvious how both the promissory and admonitory aspects of the priestly office can mesh with the machinery of secular government, insofar as the priestly doctrines may induce a believer to police himself. The old Greek word from which we get our term, "therapy," indicates a susceptibility to the overlap of offices, as it applies to employment as a servant or attendant, (free employment, as distinct from that of a slave), to divine worship, to fostering or nurturing, and to medical treatment or nursing. In her *Prolegomena to the Study of Greek Religion,* Jane Harrison brings out the word's priestly connotations, when she proposes such a range of meanings as "service," "the induction, the fostering of good influence," "tendance, ministration, fostering care, worship, all in one." The word also could be applied to (inferior) military service, to paying court (hence flattering), and to *providing for* in general (a usage that would bring it within the orbit of our second office).

Insofar as priestcraft is the spreader of doctrine, it overlaps upon the category of Teaching, though such teaching involves the addition of a terministic dimension that, while it is all-important to this office, may be slighted or even ignored in the purely secular office of teaching. Secondarily, metaphysics would likewise "pontificate," though usually in a somewhat hesitant, or even shamefaced manner, as it seeks to think of man not just empirically, but in terms of hypothetical "ultimates" that seem to the metaphysician implied in the nature of human reason. Farther afield, there are vestiges of pontification in mediatory roles generally, whether performed by a priesthood or by secular agents. The technical kinship between religious and temporal mediation is indicated in the traditionally close connection between secular law and supernatural "sanctions."

So much, then, for a general review of our terms for the offices which we perform in the course of our dealings with one another. If these seven terms are well chosen, all human "offices" can be made to fit under these heads, without unreasonable strain. Such would be a Neo-Stoically "official" approach to the problem of human motivation.

But when we get this far, there are some related matters crowding in for consideration—so we turn to those.[2]

---

[2] Aristotle's *Politics* is built primarily around his list of political systems (Royalty, Aristocracy, "Polity," and their corresponding perversions: Tyranny, Oligarchy, and Democracy, while he opts for "polity," a compromise between Democracy and Oligarchy, with leanings towards the Democratic side). But at two points he offers lists of what he considers the "necessary parts" of a State. The earlier list (IV, iii, 9-15; 1290b 21-1291b 14) contains eight "parts": (1) farmers, (2) craftsmen, (3) traders, (4) manual laborers, (5) warriors, (6) councillors and judges for litigation, (7) the rich, and (8) public servants.

His first four classes would fall primarily under our second category: "serve (provide for materially)," as would his seventh. His fifth would be our third ("Defend"). His sixth would probably fit best under our heading of "Govern," and similarly with his eighth (in their administrative role they are perhaps the beginnings of what we would now call a "civil service" or "government bureaucracy"). Aristotle also notes that these various offices may be performed by the same person. Indeed, in what looks to me like a solemn academic wisecrack, he notes that all men incline to think themselves capable of carrying on most offices, except that they cannot be both rich and poor (hence the stress he lays upon wealth as the main mark of class distinction).

Our last four categories ("Teach," "Entertain," "Cure," "Pontificate") are omitted. However, in his later and shorter list of occupations, "parts" or *erga* (VII, vii 4-5; 1328b 4-1328b 24) he adds the

VI

Note that whereas these seven offices, or "duties," have a motivational slant, they are names for *acts* rather than for the *motives* that lead to acts. One man might govern simply because he felt that he "ought" to; another might govern through a near-mad desire to impose his will upon his subjects; a third would compensate for a secret sense of personal insecurity—and so on. A similar range of possibilities confronts us when we ask about the motives figuring in any of the other offices.

---

priestly function. According to this list, the State's indispensable needs are: (1) food; (2) handicrafts; (3) arms; (4) money; (5—or as he puts it, "fifth and first") religious service; (6—"most necessary of all") machinery for dealing with questions of citizens' rights and interests. Here, by condensing, he has covered more ground under fewer heads. But "Teach," "Entertain," and "Cure" are still omitted.

Perhaps such modern institutions as publicly supported hospitals and "socialized" or semi-socialized medicine now sharpen our notion of "Cure" as a "civic" function. Also, of course, whereas Aristotle was thinking of the "necessary" offices of a *city* specifically, our list is more broadly conceived (in terms of what people do for one another *socially*). And perhaps our long familiarity with compulsory education (including "propaganda" and indoctrination") sharpens our awareness of "Teaching" as a basic "office." But it is surprising that he has omitted "Entertainment" as a function of his city, in view of what he has written on the "catharsis" supplied by music and poetry, and in view of the fact that the Athenian stage was a civic institution.

However, the occupations that are omitted from these two lists are duly considered in the *Politics* as a whole, as they were also in Plato's *Republic* (about book II of which Aristotle's discussion in connection with his first list gives a somewhat misleading idea). There Socrates gradually builds up a State by beginnig with a minimum of indispensable social functions for dealing with man's sheerly bodily needs. Drawing an analogy between the person and the State, Aristotle holds that Plato's view of primary functions stresses the *soma* at the expense of the *psyche*. Hence, according to Aristotle, even more important than considerations of material utility would be such spiritual parts as the judicial, the deliberative, and the military.

In brief, to each of the offices people bring such traits of personality as may make one person rather than another the best fit for a given ministry in some particular situation. Also, the seven offices require reciprocals: a certain kind of ruler would be best suited to a certain kind of subjects; a certain kind of entertainer needs a certain kind of audience; the psychologist who cures Mr. A may not himself have the kind of incipient morbidity that best equips him to cure Mr. B— and so on.

Behind our Neo-Stoic view of human offices, there lies the muddled area of personal motives that usually have their start in *familial* situations. And while such situations reflect the over-all *public* situations of which they are a part, they are experienced by the child primarily in *personal* terms. Thus, at first, all these seven offices are felt to be performed exclusively and variously by persons within the immediate family or close to it (like the family doctor). Gradually persons *from outside* (from "beyond"?) are differentiated as to office (the workman who comes to repair some mechanism and makes mysterious motions; the policeman whose function as "defender" is usually thought of, rather, as that of *punisher;* the circus clown, whose simplified face is a kind of face-in-general, as indeed is the face of Great Man barely glimpsed while his limousine whisks past in silence after the motorcycle escort had bubblingly prepared the way; the robes of the man of the cloth—and so on). Here we are back among the whole jungle of human motives that is lying about us however we may reduce our terms for the basic kinds of office.

In this regard, think again of Cicero's tract On Duties (*De Officiis*), which he wrote when deprived of office by the death of the Republic. In his discussion of stately offices, Cicero was mainly concerned with the *virtues* that best fitted a man for the responsibilities of citizenship. Thus, he devotes the major portion of his book to discussing the "four sources of upright living" from which "all duties flow." These are: prudence, justice, high-mindedness, and self-control (while he secondarily considers the motives that lead to the perversion of these virtues). Few would deny that, if these traits of character were in the saddle, all would always be well with the State — particularly since Cicero takes great pains to "prove" (to his own satisfaction, at least) that true expediency is also to be equated with these four virtues, whereas we might otherwise think of expediency as running counter to them.

The build-up is of a sort that attains its culmination in such "strength" as a sculptor would seek to convey by an equestrian statue in a public park. For they are the kinds of traits that, rightly or wrongly, the general public associates with the historical figures whom it clamors to acclaim as its leaders.

Typical modern theories of motivation, along the lines of Pope's formula, "As the twig is bent, so is the tree inclined," would favor a quite different direction, when speculating on the derivation of man's fitness for office. They would look for the future architect in the child playing with his blocks; or for the future policeman in the young deliquent who was given the task of keeping other delinquents in line; or for the world ruler in a morbid child, physically weak, deformed, undersized, or otherwise clearly with a bad mark—and so on.

Yes, in the alembics of history, alchemic transformations of that sort will most likely figure, too. Christianity will have done much for theories of motivation, if it but leaves us with the suggestion that, when looking for the handsome prince, we should first of all look for the ugly duckling. Or is this a lesson learned from paganism, too? In any case, note its design in the principle of the Beatitudes.

Cicero would incline to skip the paradoxical possibilities—

yet they were all about him, beginning with this very book of his, on civic virtues. For it was written to his no-good son, who doubtless knew, as perhaps only his wife knew better, that there was something radically questionable about the old man's oratorical tributes to the equestrian virtues, however true it might also be that the State could prosper only if the virtues he extolled were somehow in the saddle. In any case, about a year after writing his tract On Duties the great Cicero˙was slain, and by assassins apparently hired by the avenging figure (Mark Antony) to whom our sweet Shakespeare assigns a stately role in the tragedy of *Julius Cæsar*.

VII

How round things out? Quite as an "official" theory of motives subsumes a purely "personal" realm (generally associated with the "familial" experiences that have their roots in the purely *natural* "services" involved in the generation of offspring, and that most impress themselves upon the human animal in the period of emergence from infancy into the early years of childhood), so this "personal" realm in turn shades off into a realm of "pre-history" that requires its own kind of "pontification," if we are to build speculative bridges between the human person and the purely "cellular" organism out of which, according to Darwinian thinking, it has evolved.

Here all is a jungle, literally. And the best we can do would be to propose a fanciful, quasi-scientific myth, designed simply to "give the idea" of what might be said to lie behind the animality of man, the political, word-using, tool-making animal. How might the offices of the human community be erected atop the purely "natural" community of the human organism, considered as an animal that somehow retains within itself the motivational traces of its development from "simpler" and "lower" biologic forms?

First, we might imagine an original faint distinction between pleasurable and painful impressions, beginning perhaps in the distinction between a metabolic process that proceeded without interference and one that was in some way impeded or disturbed. Possibly, at this stage, the condition of "awareness" would be greater when the process was disturbed than when it proceeded without interference. That is, "pain" might be "prior" to pleasure," or stronger, in the sense that the organism would be more aware when something was wrong than when everything was right.

For instance, after a meal, one is more aware of his digestive processes if he gets indigestion than if everything proceeds smoothly; in fact, the "natural" response to a state of digestive euphoria would be for the happily digesting organism to fall asleep. However, one might argue that such "sleep" applies only to the "higher" centers of consciousness, and that each of the cells involved in the digestive process may be profoundly gratified, and humbly glowing with its own kind of pleasure, the perfection of the digestive process itself being sufficient evidence that the cells are as vigorously "awake" as the vibrant insect life of a swamp.

In any case, whether one thinks of pain or pleasure as primary here, or thinks of them as, from the very start, equally implicating each other, our notion is: The general "feeling tone" that adds up to either pleasure or pain would begin with this preponderantly internal functioning, though its internality would be of a sort that enabled it to have a close reciprocal relation with its placenta-like environment (a relation that our body probably comes nearest to enjoying when rested, sufficiently fed, sexually appeased, free of danger, without ailments, and near water, on a balmy day.[3]

[3] To round things out we might add: And just having received word of a legacy.

Such rudimentary *pleasure* would also presumably be indistinguishable from the kind of satisfaction that was later to get the name of "love" for an object deemed "good."

Perhaps the esssential difference between "pleasure" and "love" is suggested by Stendhal's definition of beauty as a "promise of happiness." That is, pleasure is a state that *just is,* whereas love involves the element of *desire,* a sense of union with something with which one is identified but from which one is divided. Insofar as the organism could be estranged from its pleasurable circumstances, its metabolistic process would give rise to a *need,* a need for some element now experienced as more or less *external* to it (as with a desire for more food or shade or warmth than were at that moment actually available).

By the time biological differentation had developed to the point where there were vertebrate animals preying upon one another and competing with one another sexually, the promissory factor would make readily for complicated situations whereby the immediately painful can have its kind of pleasure, if the present pain is a sign of future pleasure. Or insofar as rage equips for combat, competitive "love" contains the rudiments of "hate." Or again, as with parental care of offspring, the kind of natural "office" that we would associate with "love" points toward the "hate" category as regards the parent's tendencies to protect its offspring by ferocity.

If love leads via fight to anger or hate, pain leads more simply to fear. Aristotle makes much of the point that anger and fear are mutually exclusive, but fear can become pleasurable, because pain can. (Thus Huysmans in *A Rebours* depicts one perverse route whereby fear, in becoming pleasurable, serves his hero as an aphrosdisiac. Nor should we forget the kind of fear associated with the "tragic pleasure.") Further, while the perfect behavioristic counterpart of anger is attack and the perfect behavioristic counterpart of fear is flight, in some species there is also an intermediate state, a kind of sheer immobilization, that happens to serve as a protection insofar as immobility is a way of escaping detection. It has been suggested that this condition is the biologic origin of catatonia, which can also be induced by self-defeating situations, as when conditions are so arranged that a movement which would "naturally" make for the obtaining of food serves rather to push the food beyond reach.

But the talk of "catatonia" might serve well as the step from speechless organisms to the language-using species. For language is itself a kind of midway stage, the sheerly verbal blow and the sheerly verbal flight falling short of these acts physically. With our words for things, in the poet's images of the philosopher's ideas, we somehow half-possess the entities they name. Words are a mediatory realm, that joins us with wordless nature while at the same time standing between us and wordless nature.

Once words are added (with the word-using faculty that a more honorific terminology would call "reason") the purely biological nature of pleasure, pain, love, hate, fear is quite transcended, since all are perceived through the coloration that the inveterate human involvement with words imparts to them. And the same is true of all sheerly bodily sensations, which are likewise affected by the new order of motivation made possible (and inevitable!) once this extra odd dimension is added to man's natural animality. From that point on, no matter what man's motives might be in their nature as sheerly animal, they take on a wholly new aspect, as defined by the resources and embarrassments of symbolism.

You could state the matter bluntly thus: Pleasure and pain can no longer be exactly what they would be to us sheerly as animals, and similarly with love and hate (or fear), once we approach problems of "acceptance" and "rejection" through the genius of that specifically linguistic pair, "Yes" and "No" (to which we should add the strategic midway stage of "Maybe").With the negative, "conscience" is born (as attested in the Biblical formula, "Thou shalt not...," conscience being the power to say no to the self, deep within the self, or equally deeply it may say no to the thou-shalt-not's of others).

And the same would be true of our sensations generally (with their range from mere neutral "recording" to the extremes of pleasure and pain), and of imagery generally, (with its range from mere neutral attention to the extremes of love, hate, fear): all this variety of bodily and mental awareness would be colored by the "conscience" (the genius of that exclusively linguistic marvel, the Negative).

And the "positives" of "conscience," as translated into terms of social behavior, are the Seven Offices, involving the many ways in which these offices can become perverted.

The ultimate perversion (or more accurately, the point at which we find it hardest to make sure just where the good office ends and its perversion takes over) comes from the fact that the various offices are made possible only by the regularities of *order*; and the more closely you scrutinize the conditions required by order, the surer you are to discover that order is impossible without *hierarchy* (a ladder of authority that extends from "lower" to "higher," while its *official functions* tend towards a corresponding set of *social ratings*).

Call this design "hierarchy" when you are feeling friendly towards it. When you are feeling unfriendly, call it the "hierarchal psychosis" — or, more simply, The Scramble; or still more simply, the Rat Race, which is what the conditions of empire add up to, in their drearier manifestations.

In sum, then, problem-wise (as seen from the standpoint of the Seven Offices):

374

(1) The over-all aim of secular education would be to discover just what it means to be a symbol-using animal. (Such would be the "grand" aim of education.)

(2) The basic educational problem at this stage of history would be: How best adapt the symbol-using animal to the conditions of world empire that are being forced upon us by the irresistible "progress" of technology? (Such would be the "global" aim of education.)

(3) Finally beginning with either of these propositions: to locate the typical source of individual anxiety, in not more than three moves we should get to Neo-Stoic contemplation of the "Hierarchal Psychosis" (or Rat Race), that is a reflex of the need for a pyramidal or ladder-like order in human "offices."

ATTITUDES TOWARD HISTORY:
IN RETROSPECTIVE PROSPECT

IN THE "CURRICULUM CRITICUM" added to the Hermes
Publications reprinting of *Counter-Statement*, I comment on
the fact that this companion volume to *Permanence and Change*,
Attitudes Toward History, is not just a sequel, but in one respect
an early revision of the first. *Permanence and Change* was originally planned as tripartite in design, loosely paralleling in its
way what was later called by many sociologists a "paradigm,"
the term that would be proposed by Thomas S. Kuhn in *The
Structure of Scientific Revolutions*. I thought of *P&C* as having
a beginning, middle, and end, related to one another as orientation, disorientation, and reorientation. Yet on reconsidering it
recently, I came to realize that the principle of "perspective by
incongruity" featured in the middle section had not been resolved,
but at the end was still going strong. Thus the so-called reorientation of the third stage could be more accurately characterized as
a continuation of the *destabilizing* developments that marked the
innovative developments of stage two. The situation was further
complicated by the fact that the style of perspectival incongruous-
ness could be viewed as ranging all the way from new precisions,
"breakthroughs," to sheer laxities, playfully manipulated "conceits."

Though I did not think of it at the time, the five-part "curve of
[Western] history" that *Attitudes Toward History* builds around
reveals an awareness of the shift whereby I was to see *P&C* not
as a beginning-middle-end structure, but as a confrontation of
permanent technologic change. For the curve ends on a stage
called "emergent," a "collectivism" so problematical that, on the
very page (160) where I list the five stages, I turn to the likelihood that such collectivism may enter " 'by the back door,' as

377

signalized in that highly ironic term of modern economists, the 'socialization of losses,' " itself a shrewd "perspective by incongruity"—and it has become so "naturalized" that any other kind of "socialization" grows hard to conceive of.

The principle of "analogical extension" featured in *P&C* gets a variant in *ATH* under the name of "casuistic stretching." Whereas, with regard to the first book, once the purely terministic matter of perspective by incongruity in general was introduced, and it was there to stay under *many* guises, *Attitudes Toward History* features *one* such figure, "the *bureaucratization* of the imaginative." But in that term's way of going from "bureaucracy" as the name for a specific kind of social or economic *group* to "bureaucratization" as a broadly generalized name for a structural *process*, there is the added "attitudinal" dimension that Lincoln Steffens provided for the term "organize," as per the anecdote herewith on page viii of the introduction to an earlier edition of this text. Also, insofar as the "bureaucratizations" connected with the innovations of Technology make for new emergencies, the term proclaimed the *open-endedness* of the "emergent" as the "last" stage in a historical development and in that respect introduced a parallel of the unfinishedness I subsequently spotted as lurking in the earlier book's would-be tripartite design (where a supposed new *order* could be more accurately characterized as a modified continuation of the cultural *instability* that marked the second stage).

Attitudinally considered, the situation now seems to line up thus: The human animal's specific prowess in the ways of symbolicity makes for two kinds of perspective. One encompasses the vast complex of social relationships, properties, authorities that centers in the principle of *personality*. The other starts from the kinds of transformations in the conditions of living (departures from a primitive state of nature) due to the technological development of *instruments*. The two perspectives (one *doctrinally* culminating in myths of the Supernatural, the other driving toward fulfillment in a *technologically* ever-"emergent" realm of Counter-Nature) are variously at odds.

Nietzsche's self-proclaimed *Perspektivismus* (with its almost persecutional, and hence to that extent self-persecuted, devotion to a "transvaluation of all values") is at the very center of these radically divergent eschatologies, involving a corresponding clash of nomenclature which shows up as a series of exercises in a kind of *stylistic* virtuosity that could be called "perspectives by incongruity." Hence it is as open-ended as are the possibilities of further "bureaucratizations" in the realms of both instrumental innovations and the corresponding adjustments in the realm of personal relationships. In all, Nietzsche's tangle of attitudinal transformations involves a "will to [technological, instrumental, manmade] power" that abandons the perspective of the (traditional, personalistically) Supernatural; but even when so doing, it rounds things out by introducing a new personal principle in the name of the Superman; and his doctrine of Eternal Recurrence provides the mythic fiction that gives his dialectical maneuvers the pomp of a Wagnerian opera.

I am not without troubles here. For while building about Nietzsche as the representative figure, I am in the paradoxical position of at the same time noting wherein his statue of the Superman is in one sense a misfit for the very situation that he so radically confronts, while in another sense for that very reason it fits the case all the more.

Attitudinally, as I have said, the two perspectives (the *personalistic* and the *instrumental*) are quite at odds. To the extent that Technology succeeds in perfecting instruments of precision designed for the study of the body's behavior as an electrochemical mechanism, scrupulously discriminating among the physiological processes that match corresponding stages of expression and communication in the realm of "symbolicity," to that extent the very documentation of the parallels between those two orders will accentuate our awareness of their difference. On one side would be the inborn susceptibilities of the individual as a *person*, on the other that same individual as a sheer *biological organism* the behavior of which is to be defined only insofar as Technology invents adequate devices for the laboratory or clinical analysis of such discriminations, its "dissecting" in terms of graphs, meter-readings, "scintillations," and the like.

If we called an audience's sympathetic personal response to the unfolding of a drama "esthetic," we could call the use of mechanical "sensors" to detect concomitant bodily responses (such as changes in blood pressure, temperature, respiration, heartbeat) "anesthetic." Conceivably a contrivance might be designed to distinguish thus "anesthetically" between the bodily behavior of a person weeping in wretchedness at the actual loss of someone dearly loved and the bodily behavior of a person in an audience sympathetically weeping at a fiction, a dramatic imitation of such a loss (an experience which, Aristotle tells us, affords the audience "tragic pleasure"). The correlation between the personal and instrumental realms seems to allow for two opposite approaches. "Esthetically," by the resources of symbolic action, the drama can induce in the audience the attitudes which the body responds to by behaving accordingly. Or "anesthetically,"* drugs

---

* I have left these traces of my attempt to settle on a word to distinguish the *personal* kinds of discriminations that an audience might evince when responding to a drama from the purely instrumental kinds of discriminations that the "sensors" of an air-conditioning apparatus are designed for. Their discriminations have to do with the temperature and the contents of the atmosphere in a theater, without any reference at all to the contents of the drama to which the audience is responding. I tried "anesthetic," "unesthetic," "nonesthetic," but the objection to all three is that, although the "sensors" are totally unaware of the story to which the audience is responding by bodily effects such as changes of respiration, they *are* discriminating *after their fashion*—and those adjectives lack such connotations.

Aristotle's expression "tragic pleasure" gave me the cue I needed. Quite as with the titles applied to two of his texts, the *Physics* and the *Metaphysics*, so the discriminations of the *personally esthetic* could (by the introduction

can produce in the body the kind of physiological behavior that manifests itself in corresponding attitudes. And the concept of "psychogenic illness" suggests the likelihood that a sufferer's mode of attitudinizing is being psychologically paralleled.

Interwoven with all this is the Story that in *Attitudes Toward History* is called "the bureaucratization of the imaginative." The term is applied to many kinds of confused developments, some quite locally personal in the range of their attitudinizing. But constantly recurring are the Stories whereby the instrumentalist genius of Technology (interwoven with capitalist aspects of the case) is equated with the kind of unfoldings and corresponding human relationships that I subsumed in the attitudinal perspective of my wanly comic term "bureaucratization."

Going along with the general notion that the influence of modern Technology began to show up in an urgently crucial, critical way toward the end of the eighteenth century, I have proposed to "privilege" Nietzsche's attitudinizings as the most thorough sample ("model" even!) of a response to the "transvalua-

---

of a mild neologism) be paired with the *instrumentally "metesthetic."* The contents of the drama are in the realm of symbolic action. The contents of the atmosphere (which the sensors of the air-conditioning equipment are "metesthetically" gauging) are in the realm of nonsymbolic motion. The members of the audience are "composite" creatures, symbolically reenacting the "fable" of the play while their bodies, as physiological organisms in the realm of nonsymbolic motion, behave in ways that alter the purely physical conditions of the theater. The vibrations of sight and sound that the audience interprets as an "imitation" of humans in action are in themselves as insensitive to the contents (the discriminations) of the drama that is unfolding as the "sensors" are, at the other end of the process. Only the audience, as Bodies That Learn Language, brings these two realms together. *ATH* talks of "transcendence upwards" and "transcendence downwards." Perhaps my term "metesthetic" has belatedly added a mode of "transcendence sideways," as with discriminatory meter-readings that might represent various kinds of outcries, but with no more personal feeling than the vibrations in the air that made them audible.

tions" ("new attitudes") associated with the increasing pace of technologic "fulfillment" in what I'd now want to call manmade "Counter-Nature." And I'd include the moodiness of the style in which Nietzsche re-personalized the transpersonal genius of technological instruments (a twist probably implicit from the start in the fact that the innovations and developments of Technology are human products).

All organisms have "attitudes" in the sense that they "want" (are *in need of* getting) from their environment certain ingredients without the ingestion of which they cannot survive. Such conditions constitute their necessary "attitudes" ("perspectives," with corresponding tropisms toward and away from). But their "built-in" perspectives are wordless, hence sans Story, and to that extent not quite like ours, which involve modes of acceptance and rejection wholly local to our kind of organism.

Among our perspectives, countlessly more than a "twice-told tale," is "the bureaucratization of the imaginative," which I have referred to as a "Story." In temporarily summing up, let's ask how the cultural issue looks if, with regard to Nietzsche's "radical" formula "transvaluation of all values," we substitute the term "attitudes" as a synonym for "values." Note first that all human attitudes have an overall double provenience. By the very nature of language, an essential form of duplication arises. And it will be with us, as a determining influence upon our destiny, as long as we continue to be the kind of creature we now are. I refer to a kind of duplication that arose when our primeval ancestors, by learning language, no longer experienced a sensation solely as a sensation. For instance, when they touched something that *felt hot*, their newfound ways with language enabled them to *duplicate* the *sensory* experience in "transcendent" terms of a *nonsensory* medium such that our aforesaid primeval ancestors could say, *"That feels hot."*

And precisely at that time here on Earth the realm of *Story* entered the world. The taste of an orange *is a sensation*. The words "the taste of an orange" *tell a story.* And the story they tell is such that it must be a somewhat different story, depending on whether the hearer has or has not tasted an orange. Once such words have arisen as terms for *sensations,* their use can be extended *attitudinally* to encompass such steps as the one from "That feels warm" to "He, or she, is warm-hearted."

Bentham called such analogical extensions "fictions," while observing that in such fields as psychology and ethics there could be no discussion at all if the whole nomenclature couldn't be traced back etymologically to an origin in wholly "physicalist" terms. (In this connection, see among many places, my article "(Nonsymbolic) Motion/(Symbolic) Action" [*Critical Inquiry,* Summer 1978].) Also, whatever is going on with regard to the "meaning" of any words as communications *not reducible* to "physicalist" terms (as Bentham would by no means reduce them), we should keep in mind that the words as such could not be shaped by the speaker and sent through the air for the hearer or put on the page for the reader without a complicated "infinite manifold"* of *wordless* physiological motions by which the message *in* the bodies and *between* the bodies of speaker (or writer) and hearer (or reader) could come to fruition as a *sentence* (which is *its form, its kind* of "purpose").

By this resource, which adds narration to speechless nature, there arose in time Stories of the Supernatural, of astrology, astronomy, alchemy, chemistry, geology, biology, geography, history, myths and rituals, ideologies and routines, etc., beginning with gossip and the news (all animals, even inanimate things, have purely physical modes of communication, but only human

* Max Weber's term for the fact that each situation is unique in its countless details, not just those in the realm of wordless motion. And with regard to my notion that we can learn language at all only because we can apply the same words to situations that *can't be identical* but *are analogous,* T. S. Eliot formulated the matter to perfection, but I know not where: "Each case is unique, but similar to others."

animals can gossip, tell one another Stories—and long before Nietzsche, humans were noting how "naturally" speech becomes lie).

When referring to speech (in comparison with other humanly developed mediums of expression and communication such as painting, sculpture, and music)—and in this connection calling it "the medium that can 'most comprehensively' discuss itself, all other mediums, and the realm of nonsymbolic motion (as per the terminologies of geology, biology, archaeology, etc.)"—I thought we might linger on the term thus: "The situation allows for a cosmic pun, as we try to comprehend (in the sense of 'understand') the vast speechless infinitude which comprehends us (in the sense of 'including' us, being all about us)." And reminding myself, as often, what a fantastic difference there is between immediately experiencing a sensation (as when something *feels hot*) and using words that *tell about* the sensation ("That feels hot"), a sensation that in its immediate bodily self is wordless, not in the realm of Story, I would propose these lines to "polarize" the issue:

> that Undefinable *Definiendum*
> the Infinite Wordless Universe
> with the Countless
> Universes of Discourse
>
> that Story can make of it . . .

The Story of Evolution tells us how, quite as there was a time when the geological and biological processes of Earth went on wholly devoid of human Story, so the conditions that at present "comprehend" the human animal will eliminate the creatures whose Stories seek to "comprehend" them, hence things will again proceed sans Story.

In the meantime, the storytelling words designed to duplicate the wordless aspects of our environment greatly expand the range of *attitudes* by which we relate to one another in keeping with the clutter of concordant and discordant *interests socially rife among us.* No matter how impersonal a high percentage of such conditioning factors may be, the Old Adam in us is such that, close up, they all turn out to be variants of the pronomial, each after its fashion as *personal* as Martin Buber's "I-Thou Relation." When so looked back upon, all of my "pivotal terms" show up as personally attitudinal as pronouns. And even terrorists who smash into things with little claim to exactitude are addressing some Power *personally*, that is, attitudinally.

The primary duplication whereby our words about the wordless aspects of our environment help us find our way about overlaps the related but not identical duality of personal repute and instrumental power with its "vaulting ambition." And here, for their attitudinal aspect, I would adapt some lines from my poem ("Tossing on Floodtides of Sinkership") anent "the Traffic War ... each driver going somewhere, the whole thing nowhere, ... our mechanic boastfulness ... a quick easy magnifying of the self" via a variant of what Marx called the "fetishism of commodities" when we so identify ourselves with a "massive technologic demon," a car that, "since cars, like guns, / are medicine for the ailing ego," allows us by such a twist a pronominal "unacknowledged leap / from *This is mine* / to *By God, this is ME!*"—for where there's a willfulness there's a waywardness, and we're on the subject of the "will to power."

I may be overstating the case when I impute so direct a relation between Nietzsche's concept of the "will to power" and the exponential curve of technological "progress" during the past two centuries that is in keeping with Henry Adams's "law of the acceleration of history." For I have no trouble seeing even Blake as a harbinger of attitudes intrinsically associated with the increasing pace of technological innovation and its corresponding manmade realm of Counter-Nature. And I can do so all the more readily because in both cases I lay great stress upon complicating factors that even *reinforce* the personal moodiness of their presentations, giving their responses to the sheerly *instrumentalist* nature of technological power an attitudinal twist quite irrelevant to Technology's "computerological" bureaucratizings recently "surfacing."

The incongruous disproportion between the powers of our modern instruments and the many minuscule details of accountancy involved in their "programming" and control is paralleled by a kind of physiological grotesqueness that is in the offing, as a bathetic opposite to the pathos of the heroic stance that Nietzsche identifies himself with. But before risking my next exhibit on the subject of attitudes, I would offer these considerations in my behalf:

Besides (1) recognizing the heroic, after (2) offering an apothegmatic tribute to the duplication of the "comprehensive" wordless Universe in terms of would-be comprehending Story, reduced to five lines that are as near to the solemnly statuesque as these observations "attitude-wise" enabled me to make them, I (3) fell to haggling on the subject of how, the resources intrinsic to Technology being what they are, there is a "natural" invitation for the owner or driver of a powerful contrivance to feel personally powerful. In some not very glamorous lines of mine I would refer to a further conceivable dimension (4), this one in the grotesque sign of *Gulliver's Travels* and other such schematically incongruous perspectives by Swift, in this case a kind of "double vision." They run:

The Body Beautiful

a conglomerate of pipes, girders,
filters, drains, conduits,
gas chambers, sewage, cesspools—
the whole
slick with primeval slime

stuffed with a meatlike substance
generally deemed inedible
and a-swarm with micro-organisms
as a warm
stagnant
fetid
swamp . . .

True, this gargoyle, this grotesque straining at the edges of
the perspectival, is in effect a "sophistication of a higher order." A
sophistication of the first order might, for instance, but designate
the measurements and movements of the body beautiful in terms
of whatever criteria we agree upon when choosing for Miss
America this particular contestant rather than one of the others.
A sophistication of the second order might be a bit sportive, in
considering the candidates' comparative investment-value to promoters who were interested in financial advantages to be gained
by backing one candidate rather than another. The above lines
are to *ATH's* "comic" frame of "acceptance" somewhat as, in *The
Iliad*, Thersites is to the heroics of the Trojan War (except, alas!
that the author can't disavow this gargoyle as thoroughly as
Homer did Thersites).

The verses have as their title a traditional usage, a cliché, that
is in the dimension of the *humanistic*. The title is Step One of
the poem (anti-poem?) proper, the opening lines of which
abruptly introduce a perspective by incongruity designed to
anatomize the *body* of the beauty, rather than speaking of such
"poetic" features as eyes, lips, hair; and the expressions chosen to
this end have a grotesque twist whereby the internality behind
the appearance (the superficies) of the body's beauty (Latin
would say the body's *species*, a good word for the "specious" as
thus good to look upon) is reduced to "intimate" (privy) terms
for the digestive system. Then there is the further twist whereby
the terms for these *organic, biological* processes are of *techno-*

logically instrumental cast (referring to such hardware as plumbing fixtures, with their relation to septic systems and the like).

When the details associated with such functioning eventuate in "cesspools," conditions are set for the transitional Step Three of the fifth line (hinting about the indeterminate words "the whole," which serve as a kind of subtitle for what follows). True, that word for such "cisterns at the termination of a drain, to collect sediments or superfluous matter" was in common use long before the extended development of modern hygienic "facilities" for the disposal of waste (notable technological contributions to the manmade expansion of Counter-Nature). Thus, said vocable introduces "bacteriological" connotations that are one with the very essence of *Nature*: the human body inherits a cellular way of life from times before there were such things as human bodies for cells to inhabit or to compose by collectively inhabiting, thereby to become the physiological dwelling-places for human tenants that are identified as individual citizens and taxpayers, each differentiated from the others by a unique combination of partly consistent, partly conflicting attitudes, "personal equations" as shaped by the resourcefulness of symbolicity.

(Think of me as a would-be propounder of a "comic" frame. And how could I, when here rounding things out, decently have omitted this Aristophanic aspect of our subject?)

But why should I maneuver myself into such unnecessary trouble? A matter of principle is involved. These pages are on the subject of "attitudes." And as I mention in my afterword to *Permanence and Change*, with regard to Bentham's three "appellatives" (the "neutral," "dyslogistic," and "eulogistic") I have opted for a mode of attitudinal exercising that is more like a debate with oneself than is the case with Bentham's Utilitarian "felicific calculus." The grotesque bathos of the "B*d* B***t*f*l" is as proper to our ponderings on the "human condition" as Nietzsche's scheme for displacing *Menschheit* with *Übermensch*. And his idealizations of *Krieg, Kraft, Stärke, Macht* don't need exceptionally close inspection of the imagery surrounding them to reveal traces of the puerile.

For instance, I offer this translation of a passage in a copy of *Will to Power* that I happen to have: "A worthy little lad [*ein kleiner tüchtiger Bursch*] will glance at you ironically if you ask him, 'Do you want to be a good boy?' But his eyes will open wide if you ask him, 'What if you could grow stronger than the other boys?' "

But here turns up a problem. Quite as I have confessed to kinds of modern biological conceits somewhat on the slope of Aristophanic comedy, so on the side I always note, without knowing exactly why in some cases, any expressions that suggest survivals from the infantile. And surely the observation seems relevant in the case of a half-mad genius who is identifying himself with the grandeur of a "Superman." I take it that the words I have quoted implicitly identify the musculature of his aphoristically bellicose style with motivational vestiges of the infantile. And I assume that Freud would interpret the figure as a "preconscious" acknowledgment of such a complex.

Incidentally, when writing my new comments on Nietzsche in the *P&C* volume, I reread my early (German) copy of his *Will to Power*, a book I hadn't looked at for nearly half a century. And I was astounded to hear quite often in it the accents of the "declamations" that comprise the eighteen chapters of my novel (anti-novel?) *Towards a Better Life*, depicting a cantankerous character who in the first chapter avowed, "I would speak as a gargoyle would speak which, in times of storm, spouted forth words," then gradually built himself up to a total falling-apart, the last chapter being but fragments, the last of which is: "Not only not responding, but even refraining from soliloquy—for if we tell no one, the grave burden accumulates within us. Henceforth silence, that the torrent may be heard in all its fulness."

Whereat, speaking in behalf of the shrewd reader, have I not implicitly labeled the aphoristic element in my book "vestigially

infantile"? *Touché*! However, there is at least room for a qualification of this sort: What if the underlying story of the crack-up
figures a *rebirth*? What kind of "neo-infantile" affinity would
that be? There are hints of that sort among the final fragmentary
"jottings," too. For instance: "The sword of discovery goes before the couch of laughter. One sneers by the modifying of a
snarl; one smiles by the modifying of a sneer. You should have
lived twice, and smiled the second time." Looking back (in retro-
spective prospect) on that book, I now, long outside it, see it as
precisely that, namely, a ritualistic transformation of the author
from the vestiges of the "autistic" in childhood, through the
ambiguous moody ordeals of adolescence, to what (for better or
worse) became the attempt at a "comic frame of acceptance" that
this book plumps for. In my later speculations on us humans as
"Bodies That Learn Language," I have inclined to think that
ejaculatory styles (as with Nietzsche's successive challenges)
have the quality of *interjections*, which are nearest to our mode of
utterance as sheer animals, and thus in that respect are like the
infantile in the immediate expression of an attitude (though of
course the *verbal* aspect of such expressions is not at all reducible
to such a rudimentary motivational dimension).

And for a mellow variation on the childhood theme, consider
Wordsworth's "Ode on Intimations of Immortality," which eu-
logistically associates his mature literary selfhood with vestiges
of the infantile, in keeping with the "revaluations" implicit in
the refusal to distinguish between the adjectives "childish" and
"childlike" when he is in principle platonistically "recollecting"
in words the primal *state of wordlessness*, a pious attitude that
can't even be exactly called a contradiction in terms.

Also (and despite my "Devotional Lines Anent the Primor-
dial Descent of Sewage," I can't wholly resent those readers who
would resent my saying so) there is an increasing range and
precision of observations made possible by the new contrivances
in the "metesthetic" realm of wholly technological "sensors"

(stupid dials which know not what they do for us via their ways of being set up to record discernments never available in all human and pre-human history here on earth prior to the "progress" of modern Technology in expanding the manmade realm of Counter-Nature). Innovations of that sort can reveal to us, toward our closer anatomizing of the body's privy physiological functions, further glimpses into an Ultimate Undefinable *Definiendum* both from away back and in countless interactions now. Thereby one can in theory even glimpse possibilities such that the burlesqueable Story of what goes on in the bodily dwelling-place tenanted by the Miss America of Some Particular Year is to be seen as a complex of wonders capable of being made manifest by the instruments of laboratory and clinic, even to the end of our quite solemn edification.

Actually, in my autobiographical narrative "The Anæsthetic Revelation of Herone Liddell"* I did some "attitudinizing" of that sort. The narrative deals with "post-operational symptoms" which it labels "perspectival" (the corresponding "revelation" being the author's variation on the standard theme of a patient's experiential response to the "partial distortion of drugs"). But, although the experience "had been primarily a matter of unaccustomed chemicals," the recounting of it happens to have dealt with these issues in a way that combines clinical details (totally *infra dig.*) with meditations that have somewhat the quality of my lines anent the "Undefinable *Definiendum*, the Universe," and the "Countless Universes of Discourse" that "STORY can make of it." Let's patiently spell it out, in the cause of attitude, the strategic focus of which term is still to be definitively made clear.

*This piece was first published in *The Kenyon Review* (Autumn 1957) when its founder, John Crowe Ransom, was its editor. The reader will come to realize that I bring up this first because Ransom's poetry is so outright and winsomely "gallant." The character's name is pronounced "Herŏn Liddĕll," an ironically twisted way of saying "little hero."

Being in the hospital to be operated on, "Herone was impressed first of all by the extreme *physicality* of his condition." These developments begin with such invasions of privacy as when "lying with distended bowels, a loathesome tube inserted through one nostril into his stomach, he tried to wince ('in that most bodily house, where there was no place to wince to')." During the weeks immediately following H. Liddell's "revelation" and including a period of recovery in the South—the time covered by the narrative—I kept thinking of a remark that my friend William Carlos Williams had made to me in a moment when, as often, his duality as poet and physician spoke as one. Given the localizing of the augury in the groin and of the postoperational pains in the bowel, along with my share of the not unusual modern tendency to wonder in what respects such mythic figures as the Worm Ouroboros might be classed under the head of "natural science," it is quite understandable why, in response to his suggestion, I kept remembering: "First, there would be the sheer physicality of life, the human organism as one more species of alimentary canal with accessories . . . digestive tract with trimmings."

But Our Hero by no means interprets human motives in terms of reduction to such sheerly physiological origin. Already his author (as would be later attested in *A Grammar of Motives*) had learned (perhaps a lot from George Santayana) how substantially the realms of symbolicity (Essence, Spirit, Truth) transform the realm of nonsymbolic motion we are grounded in. Whereat, within conditions of the valetudinarian narrative, "haunted by ecology" but now in the warm South and "watching young Keats die," Our Hero feels himself growing stronger even while wincing at the "progressive" revelations in the wretchedly gallant letters that that poor prisoner of fate and of Fanny Brawne wrote to her. And with great stress on the reality of a purely *symbolic* sort that really exists because it so exists for us, the text risks saying such things thus:

Here would be the realm of "gallantry," of purely ideal gestur-
ing, the realm where, for instance, a masculine alimentary canal
pays a deft compliment to a feminine alimentary canal, using to
this end all the resources of symbolistic finesse necessary for acting
"as if" these were not *au fond* animal organisms dredged up from
the seabottom.

That "as if" (a Kantian twist that Kant would probably quite
disown) is surrounded (qualified) in various ways, primarily by
observations all on the same slope as the "stylistics of gallantry,"
like on the occasion when "the sea was as mellow as an over-ripe
cantaloupe," which was his "ideal of culture," or with his avowal
that "even a trivial tune, floating at night across waters, seems a
bit fate-laden."
So much for samplings among the moodinesses of attitudinizing, though I do wish I had been able to suggest, by sheer bits, the
poignant role of Keats's letters in contributing to Liddell's con-
valescence through its contrast with their imminent deathiness
under the meanest of conditions, the separation from his beloved
Fanny. I had intended, long before this, to be on the subject of
C. Wright Mills's book, *The Sociological Imagination,* and soon
thereafter be done. But before that I should refer to the "genera-
tively grammatical" role of a medieval hexameter with regard
to "attitudes."
As early as my first book of literary criticism, *Counter-Statement,* I had run across this hexameter; but I quoted it without
realizing at all the implications it would have for me when, about
fifteen years later, I hit upon the notion of turning those inter-
rogatives into the categories of my "Dramatistic Pentad." Thus,
quis quid ubi quibus auxiliis cur quo modo quando (who, what,
where, by what means, why, how, when) became agent, act, scene
(in space), agency, purpose, attitude, scene (in time). But even
then (in my *Grammar of Motives*) the term "attitude" for *quo
modo* did not quite come clear. If it had, my Pentad would have

been a Hexad from the start. However, under "Act" the book had a chapter entitled " 'Incipient' and 'Delayed' Action," where "attitude" is discussed (including a notable ambiguity), particularly with relation to I. A. Richards, George Herbert Mead, and Alfred Korzybski, while a book by Houston Peterson, *The Lonely Debate*, suggested a way of distinguishing between the "dramatic arrest" of a Shakespearean soliloquy and the "lyric attitude" of a poem such as Wordsworth's sonnet "Composed upon Westminster Bridge." There I forgot my earlier investment in the term.

But, whereas the *quo modo* of the medieval formula was originally treated as but a figurative variation on the theme of "agency" ("he did the job with hammer and saw, with alacrity"), in time the strategic role of the term began to become apparent. For it designates the point of *personal mediation* between the realms of nonsymbolic motion and symbolic action. Its "how" refers to the role of the human individual as a physiological organism, with corresponding centrality of the nervous system, ATTI-TUDINIZING in the light of experience as marked by the powers of symbolicity (both in themselves and in the realm of the Counter-Nature that has developed as the results, intended and unintended, of those powers). Hence our notions of "reality" amount to a tendentious though unstable complex of "personal equations" that are *implicit* in such a simultaneously unique and socially infused "orientation."

At this point, cutting in from another angle, we find three dimensions in the kind of terms that our kind of animal "behaves" by: equations, implications, transformations. The force of terms as "equations" is analogous to the "creativity" of magic (as God said, "Let there be"—and by His words, there was). Whatever "universe of discourse" a given nomenclature centers on, as a way of demarcating some situation, process, or relationship (or by a shortcut, "thing") from the "Universe in general" (with countless possibilities of demarcation and corresponding attention), any such nomenclature sometimes explicitly, more often implicitly, says *what equals what*. In my *Rhetoric of Motives* I have discussed the twists and turns of this matter in connection with Remy de Gourmont's (to me eye-opening) essay "The Dissociation of Ideas." But at that time I didn't approach his shrewd analysis in terms of the whole equation-implication-transformation line-up.

Any term can have the property of an "equation," quite as Pavlov conditioned dogs to salivate at the sound of a bell (or, more specifically with regard to the human animal, recall the proverbial advice never to mention rope in the house of a man who was hanged). Bentham's "censorial appellatives" are ideal outright examples.

Obviously, by the same token, all "equations" have "implications."* Trade, for instance, may be treated as a subdivision of justice," while both trade and justice could be seen to impinge upon a principle of "sacrifice," inasmuch as, in any kind of barter, one "sacrifices" something "in behalf of" something else. In my *Rhetoric of Religion*, beginning with the polar terms "order" and "disorder" (which imply each other), I propose a whole "Cycle of Terms Implied in the Idea of 'Order.' " Such equations and implications can "just be," in "timeless" interrelationships. But when one introduces a time dimension, terministic conditions are thereby set for "transformations," as with a Story about a change from Order to Disorder, or vice versa. Transformations are most grandly embodied in overall dialectical structures of theological cast. Consider the Christian Eschatology, the Story of an infinity in which the Chosen and the Reprobates continue (a supernatural principle of personality that is said to prevail eternally after the vast Universe that comprises the ground of our existence here and now has ceased to be). But whereas that supernatural design is said to last forever, the Marxist Eschatology charts an unfolding in the realm of Counter-Nature such that the pro-

---

*In *ATH* this relationship is considered in terms of "analytic radiations."

gressive stages of class conflict terminate in the inevitable disso-
lution of all classes as so defined (the dialectic thus in effect
abolishing itself). Correspondingly, the analytic resources of
transformation are such that the overall dialectic of Greek tragedy
could be "heuristically" viewed as a solemn stylistic magnification of the sacrificial principle manifested in even the humblest
of commercial transactions. The dialectic of Aristophanic comedy
would reflect matters of "just price" in ways obviously closer to
the marketplace.

Much in the design of *ATH*'s comic frame would be at home
with such bargaining, such haggling even. But also, with the
"radiating" of the book's "pivotal terms" around that incongruous perspective the "bureaucratization of the imaginative," the
dialectic of the design introduced a principle of wider "eschatological" implications than had been apparent at the time. Indeed,
to the extent that the processes of bureaucratization are synonymous with the curve of exponentially developing Counter-Nature, the formula even suggests that the earthly *end* of human
history is manifest *already*, in our predicaments *now*—and particularly by reason of the fact that Technology can be neither
criticized nor controlled nor corrected without recourse to still
more Technology. The *opportunities* to produce further and
further "generations" of contrivances are indistinguishable from
the *compulsions* to do so. Accordingly, implicit in the concept
(or, some philosophers would say, the idea) of bureaucratization
thus expanded are the outlines of a Destiny predestined by instruments (often devilishly ingenious) of our own making.

The issue as modified by my later speculations comes to a
focus in what I would call "double provenience." There is, for
instance, the psychoanalytic concept the "return of the repressed," according to which the repression that gets expressed by
a devious route is caused by problems of the personality. But there
is also a purely technical kind of repression, due to the kind of
attention that is needed if one is to use language at all. For the

process of *attending to* one matter involves *ruling out* the claims of other matters to one's attention. But whether it be the sheerly *technical* nature of attention or a *psychological* factor that causes the repression, the elements repressed can become manifested roundabout.

In the last analysis, that kind of repression probably ties in with one's purely "personal" quandaries, as I have noted and professionally confessed to in my own case. See, for instance, comments on my "Atlantis" sonnet (*Language as Symbolic Action*, pp. 229–230), where that "island of Antiquity" is equated with "inland music." That would be the poem's "let there be," its "creative" fiat ("and there was" being the corresponding development of this "magical decree," its "dialectic," in tracking down the *implications* of that initial *equation*). But these implications were not deliberately intended, being "repressed" because I was actually attempting to "dignify"a bodily process not "normally" or "properly" so identified. (In his *Psychology of the Unconscious*, Jung systematically discusses cases where "the anal region is very closely connected with veneration," as per "the traditional faeces of the Great Mogul," and "An Oriental tale . . . of Christian knights, who anointed themselves with the excrement of the pope and cardinals in order to make themselves formidable." Or one can spot the same association as revealed in the style of an Aristophanes by the jocular folk reference to the toilet seat as a "throne.") This grotesque dimension of the poem would mark the "return of the repressed." I contrast it with a "rationally vituperative" item, "Newspaper Editor's Prayer," punning on the idea of "yellow" journalism (printed matter, "By the rules of hygiene / To use once and throw away").

But though I can detect traces of "repression" in the personal sense with regard to these books, there was a quite different "return of the repressed" for me to be nearly overwhelmed by, a purely "logological" kind, rooted in the fact that both *P&C* and *ATH* had involved me in considerable improvising. For I did not work from a complete outline already decided on in advance. Rather, in the course of writing, each step arose out of suggestions that I had found to be implicit in the previous step. And since there had always been more than one implication or radiation for me to settle on, there is a sense in which other possibilities were being "repressed."

In going back over the material, perhaps in part as a result of intervening experience, I found a bewildering clutter of considerations to do with things I had not said at each of these spots, but wanted to add now. Besides, many of my "memories" were not out of the past, but involved ways in which the ideas, and even images, had been transformed since—and thus I was also "remembering" these later developments, until I was trying to write everything all over again, in an attempt to get it more definitively "placed."

In the prospective retrospect of *P&C* I confess to coping with the tangled avalanche of a roaring furnace that I was (in principle) being snowed under by. (I should have got "fall-out" in there somehow.) But about that time there was a transit strike in New York. And the newsmen gave me the word I needed so that I would at least have an adequate name for my vexations: "gridlock." Yet even that was wrong in one respect. For whereas "gridlock" meant the kind of traffic jam in which the cars could not go forward, backward, or sideways, I had to invent the word "counter-gridlock," since I was going every which way. After slapping down eight or ten pages along one line, I'd find myself trailing off. So I'd have to abandon that route and try some other, with the same damnably irritating outcome.

Then I centered on the subject of "double vision" that I associated with my concept of "perspective by incongruity." That's when I began to realize that *P&C* was not the tripartite form I had taken it to be (beginning/middle/end . . . orientation/disorientation/reorientation). The principle of transition that I had let in by tying it to my way of operating with the term "bureau-cratization" was there to stay.

And precisely then, at a time when I was focusing on the concept of "double vision" and as I began seeing the design of my whole project changing, the twist of vision became actual. On the road to go shopping, I saw two cars coming whereas I knew it was only one, looking double. I could see close up without the doubling, but the farther off things were, the wider apart the two images became. What was this? Cancer of the brain, perhaps. I was driven to a hospital, where I consulted an expert neurologist, who soaked me for more than the government would allow me to write off as expenses. I got enough X-rays to give me cancer if I were likely to be around much longer. Yet so far, no diagnosis; nothing but plans for further and costlier examinations.

I have had several occasions to learn that, if we get involved enough in the using of words, the words in turn begin using us. "Inspiration" is an *honorific* word (thus dangerously deceptive) for a process of self-hypnosis that can result from over-susceptibility to whatever terms one happens to be engrossed with. So I diagnosed the situation thus: When speculating on the resources of the term "double vision" at the same time that I was shifting my perspective on my own books on perspective, I began seeing double. So I worked tentatively on the assumption that I was subjecting myself to the magic of some obvious "let there be" equations. I clearly "solved" the dizzifying formal problem thus brought to the fore when the Nietzschean theme of "transvaluation" in the middle section of *P&C* introduced what the Trotskyites might call a variation on their theme of perpetual revolution. My recovery followed forthwith—and you can't imagine what a truly sybaritic delight it was, to look down the road and see just one car coming. It was so gratifying that often, when I heard a car go by, I'd rush out and look down the road, to watch *just that one* disappearing around the turn.

When letting Nietzsche into the middle section of *P&C* and tying the concept of perspective by incongruity in with his theme of "transvaluation," I had not confined my double vision to a reseeing of that one book. The key concept of *ATH*, the bureaucratization of the imaginative, was a perspective by incongruity. But also I wondered just how the term "bureaucracy" itself had fared. Consulting *The International Encyclopedia of the Social Sciences*, I noted a reference to Max Weber's definition in keeping with his concept of "ideal types." Administrators fulfill their role as bureaucrats to the extent that they succeed "in achieving the exclusion of love, hatred, and every purely personal, especially irrational and incalculable, feeling from the execution of official tasks," instrumentalist specifications that only a computer could comply with perfectly. Though the bibliography of the article (by Reinhard Bendix) lists eighty-six entries, the term "bureaucratization" shows up in only one of the titles. But the first subhead is "Bureaucratization of Government," and Bendix discusses many processes of bureaucratization in that strictly sociological sense, which "naturally" excludes such a "universalization" of the term as *ATH* subjected it to "automatically" (by equational decree) in the formula "bureaucratization of the imaginative." But just as the article nears its end, it expands from talk of bureaucratization in such a strict sense to the subject of "organizational behavior" in general, its last sentence thereby being, "These perspectives suggest the possibility of linking the study of bureaucracy . . . and the study of organizational behavior, to the benefit of both." That wouldn't go far toward the usage in *ATH* whereby not only a *routine* but even an outright *ritual* could be classed under the head of "bureaucratization." But it does open the door at least a little in the direction of my usage. Actually, when the book was first published, the term "bureaucracy" was a red-hot rhetorical weapon, as used by the Trotskyites in their attacks against the Stalinists, through application of the term "bureaucracy" exclusively to the Stalinist dictatorship. And one stalwart word-warrior had at me on the grounds that my widened use of the term "bureaucratization" was designed purely to weaken Trotsky's charge against the "Stalinist bureaucracy," whereas I took it for granted that not only was *every government* a mode of bureaucratization, but every business, church, conference, ball game, picnic, and ordered set of words on a page. Then I began to view the counter-natural innovations of Technology in the aggregate as a vast "creatively" destabilizing clutter, a bureaucratization of ingenious imaginings that takes on truly eschatological dimensions, powerful, pervasive, wasteful, pollutant, and challenging its human inventors to somehow round out the technical developments by developing a political bureaucratization competent to control them.

Let's turn now for some tributes to C. Wright Mills's turbulent text *The Sociological Imagination*, with its doubtless high-blood-pressure rage against "Grand Theory," "Abstracted Empiricism," and "The Bureaucratic Ethos." I can but touch upon some of its major aspects here, and in hardly more than a headline manner, beginning with the fact that Mills's book had much to do with the original pandemonium that took over after I had started the afterwords to *P&C* and *ATH*. But though Mills's appendix "On Intellectual Craftsmanship" welcomes me specifically with reference to my kinds of "perspective by incongruity" in *P&C*, the discussion of it fits in *ATH* because of the many comments on "bureaucracy" and "bureaucratization." Yet there is a tangle because Mills begins with an attack upon Talcott Parsons as an exponent of "Grand Theory"—and though all would agree that Parsons's style is far from *gracile*, when writing these pages I deviated into many counter-gridlock spurts in defense of Parsons. My months at the Center for Advanced Study in the Behavioral Sciences (1957–58) had happened to coincide with one of the times when Parsons was there. So I had had an opportunity to see him operating at various conferences. His analytic competence was quite impressive. On the occasion of discussions on the verge of becoming formless, he might suddenly bring things into line by noting exactly how many positions were represented, characterizing each, and proceeding from there.

There can be a considerable lift in such impromptu performances, despite their susceptibility to what Mills quotes my friend Malcolm Cowley as calling "socspeak." Since I feel close to both Parsons and Mills (though in different respects), Mills's excoriations of analytic "Grand Theory" would seem to replace unmercifully my both/and with an either/or. And since styles swing back and forth in all academic universes of discourse, with oscillations accentuated by the market for the publication of textbooks, "it stands to reason" that Parsons, recently deceased, is in some quarters on the Out Slope; to what extent In or Out is later to be discovered. In the meantime, as a debt to both him and myself, my traffic between him and Mills was in a state of gridlock only now letting loose.

My obligations are these: (1) I must be loyal to Parsons; (2) I must plead in behalf of his analytic method even if an opponent objected to his particular way of practicing it; (3) I must go on from there, in the light of my particular dialectical investments with their corresponding visions, "to the end of Logological Timelessness." Whereat I quote this footnote of Parsons's on page 970 of the compendium *Theories of Society* (co-edited by him with E. Shils, K. D. Naegle, and J. R. Pitts), a passage that attests both to our overlap of interests and to my self-serving reason for attesting to such overlap:

> A classic analysis of the structure and implications of meaningful order in the present sense is given by Kenneth Burke, "On the First Three Chapters of Genesis," *Daedalus*, Summer 1958.

This is the basis of the analysis I developed more thoroughly in my book *The Rhetoric of Religion*. I applied the position somewhat controversially to a controversy in *The Journal of*

Social Issues (October 1962) involving two essays, "The Image of Man" by Isidor Chein and "Personality and Career of Satan" by Henry A. Murray. The controversy started with a flyleaf by Richard E. Carney, inserted in a later issue. As with the battle between Homoousians and Homoiousians, this controversy got down to a sheerly visible distinction between "man" and "Man." Carney was emphatically for "man," insisting on the natural continuity between humans and other animals; Chein just as emphatically for "Man."

I first sided with Chein, as against Carney's insistence that the difference between humans and other animals is but a matter of *degree*. I have to contend that our modes of symbolic action (such as "verbal behavior") are different in *kind* from the behavior of other animals. But next, I had to depart from Chein, whose zest in praising the "Active" nature of "Man" could profit greatly by a prerequisite course in the fourth part of Spinoza's *Ethics*, the section "Of Human Bondage." There were other differences, owing to the fact that my analysis treats the "Creation" and the "Fall" as interwoven, whereas the "division of labor" implicit in the fact that the subject of one article was "Man," the other "Satan," obscured this irony. (The issue is discussed on pages 58–60 of my *Language as Symbolic Action* and more fully in the essay "Order, Action, and Victimage" [in *The Concept of Order*, edited by Paul G. Kuntz, published for Grinnell College by the University of Washington Press, 1968].) I not only confess, I profess the likelihood that the analytic method employed in my discussion of that issue is on the slope of what Mills might have excoriated in the name of "Grand Theory," yet I must admit that the prowess of his attack, in reducing elaborate analytic intricacies to a few quite simple and direct commonsense summaries, can make one squirm.

Let us imagine an analytic theorist "grandly" referring to a situation in which a human adult male is proceeding to a lower level on a slightly inclined passageway, by advancing each foot alternately, never having both feet off the ground at once, and by using the feet not as were their soles like the curves of rockers, but by abrupt shifts of stress from heel to toe, with corresponding motions of the arms also contributing to the maintenance of bodily balance, on a relatively smooth surface, hence not as when adjusting to randomly distributed impediments across a stony or briary field or through a stretch of timber. Then let's admit it! All that the analyst was saying adds up to this: "The man walked down the road."

Thus, consider when Mills cuts Parsons's "Grand Theory" down to size by "translating" an analytically bulky passage thus: "When people share the same values, they tend to behave in accordance with the way they expect one another to behave." Forget "socspeak." Just look up the definitions of all those terms (such as "share," "values," "tend"—above all, "tend," since so often "tend" *to do* is also entangled with "tend" *not to do*—"in accordance with," "expect," and "behave"), then analytically replace those words with their definitions from an ordinary dictionary—and the more exact you are, the "entangleder" your narrative becomes.

When confronting, as Parsons nearly always was doing, a "universe of discourse" which is being referred to partly in terms of specialized cant already "naturalized" within a given community of sociologists and partly being subjected to tentative analysis in catch-as-catch-can terms, the resultant descriptive nomenclature is but a kind of plodding. The analyst describes each *definiendum* as though for the first time, in order to help find out just what the situation is composed of.

And here's something that may surprise some readers who know something of Parsons's concerns with matters of social equilibrium. In my article "Dramatism" (*International Encyclopedia of the Social Sciences*) I refer to Albert Mathiez's *The French Revolution* as a book which traces step by step an ironic development whereby a succession of unintentionally wrong moves led to unwanted results. If one viewed this whole disorderly sequence as itself a species of order, then each of the stages in its advance could be interpreted as if "designed" to stabilize, in constantly changing circumstances, the underlying pattern of conditions favorable to the eventual outcome (namely, the kind of equilibrium that could be maintained only by a series of progressive developments leading into, through, and beyond the Terror).

I asked Parsons whether his concept of "equilibrium" could go along with that, and he said Yes. I remembered it in my state of gridlock because it reflects the very kind of speculative pliancy that Mills and his other foes would have denied him.

But the main point is this: Grand Theory or no Grand Theory, Parsons was a confirmed analyst, a true virtuoso at the art, which in its way is as much of an art as musical improvisation. The reports of students in his seminars give us grounds to believe that his "performances" along such lines were in effect "appreciated" as by an "audience." And he died a hero's death, being felled by a stroke in the very midst of an impromptu Parsonian unfolding, on the occasion of his being honored by the University of Heidelberg, where he had got a degree half a century before. (Last-minute revision: the rumor was inexact. But if history were still as limber in such matters as it once was, the rumor would have prevailed because it is so "true in principle.")

Obviously, things are on a different slope when aspects of order which Parsons deals with in terms of "institutionalization" get placed by *ATH* in terms of "bureaucratization." In his keen dislike of what he calls "the Bureaucratic Ethos," with its ideals of "human engineering," Mills calls the cult of factual research a "bureaucratization of social study." And thereby, since "social study" is his preferred term for "substantive" studies guided by the "sociological imagination," Mills's phrase comes close to paralleling this book's incongruously perspectival formula, "bureaucratization of the imaginative," except that the order supplied in the results of study would be by definition beyond suspicion.

For my term "bureaucratization" is "universal" in its application, not "factional." *Any* method would be a bureaucratization—and in the case of highly developed technological structures there is the paradoxical twist whereby obsolescence becomes a function of innovation. For new equipment designed to exploit a more efficient process can cause extensive expensive industrial plants to be scrapped or saddled with forbidding costs of "modernization" because in their present state their products cannot compete in the market for such goods. Or, insofar as they do "rebureaucratize" their plants and methods, they make such "re-industrialization" technologically inefficient as a whole, to the extent that the total worldwide productivity of the various competing plants would then amount to much greater expenditures than the market for such goods is able to dispose of. And that unwieldiness is further aggravated by shifts in the utilization of energy when a wholly competent plant designed for one fuel becomes comparatively inefficient if innovations make another fuel less costly. When the costs of wear and tear are added, the total expenditures for technological efficiency can amount to considerable inefficiency, though a bright investor who knows what to "phase in" and what to "phase out" can continue to pick monetary winners by the equivalent of an "imaginatively" artful dodging among the bureaucratic clutter, as experts in the "agribusiness" line can get and are getting profits in their market by demanding methods of "efficiency" in the use of the soil that earn them maximum immediate monetary yield at the long-run cost of depleting the soil (and at no cost to them, for they will have moved on, to "bureaucratize" their kind of pliancy by "efficiently" depleting the soil elsewhere). Nor should we forget the bureaucratizations of political rhetoric whereby all this is done (with extra subsidies at public expense) in the name of the family farm which their methods have all but obliterated. I go into this matter a bit because I would certainly have discussed it if I were writing *ATH* now.

But let's turn to Mills's rage against "Abstracted Empiricism," which involved him in differing strongly with Paul F. Lazarsfeld, who, he said, "is among the more sophisticated spokesmen of this school" and has greatly reduced the scope of technology to techniques of research characterized by Mills as "methodological inhibition." "The Method" of "Abstracted Empiricism" has no place for the kind of sociological imagination that "enables us to grasp history and biography and the relations between the two within society," a task and promise the recognition of which was "the mark of the classic social analyst," characteristic of Spencer, Ross, Comte, Durkheim, Mannheim, Veblen, Schumpeter, Lecky, "the quality of all that is intellectually excellent in Karl Marx," and "the profundity and clarity of Max Weber," who, "like so many other sociologists, developed much of his work in a dialogue with Karl Marx."

The great sweep of all this is gone, Mills charges, being replaced by "advertising and media research," public opinion polls, or studies of "voting behavior," a subject matter which is probably chosen because it lends itself so readily to statistical investigation; but "the thinness of the results is matched only by the elaborations of the method and the care employed." He would not deny that many of such findings can have considerable practical utility in helping an advertiser plan a sales drive or advising an administrator about the nature and distribution of whatever prejudices pro and con may have to be taken into account with regard to some specific issue. There has always been somewhat of a sociology along that line, whatever it may be called, whenever there have been administrators—and if this age were not so pervasively characterized by a technological psychosis, much that is now called by its advocates or practitioners a "science" of "hu-

man engineering" (with its ideals of "prediction and control")
might be viewed as an extension of classical rhetoric's observations on the "art" of persuasion.

But there again, acute gridlock looms. For I begin "recalling"
what I did in *The Rhetoric of Motives*, when viewing the "rhetorical" dimension in myth and ritual (and let us not lose sight
of what is going on when the officiants of a ritual implicitly
identify themselves as the special functionaries whose office performs a prime and necessary function in the procuring of whatever group benefits are expected to result from the ritualistic
practices).

Mills quotes as accurate these comments by Bernard Berelson
celebrating the sort of "revolutionary change" that "the Method"
has brought about: Whereas in the past public opinion had been
studied "not for itself but in broad historical, theoretical, and
philosophical terms" by learned writers who "wrote treatises"
on the subject, "the field has now become technical and quantitative, a-theoretical, segmentalized, and particularized, specialized and institutionalized, 'modernized' and 'groupized'—in
short, as a characteristic behavioral science, Americanized." Shortly thereafter, resenting how such a style of social science "is not
characterized by any substantive propositions or theories" nor
"based upon any new conception of the nature of society or of
man or any particular facts about them," Mills sums up his
charge thus: "This style of research, in brief, is accompanied by
an administrative demiurge which is relevant to the future of
social study and to its possible bureaucratization."

Gridlockwise, I found myself wanting to split the difference.
It seemed to me that the "sociologizing of sociology" would lead
us to expect that the forms of bureaucratization most relevant to
the "progress" of technological innovations and their particular
kinds of disruptive by-products would "naturally" provoke and
subsidize "segmentalized" research of that sort to do with Technology's "natural" contributions to its expanding realm of

Counter-Nature. (In *P&C* and *ATH*, prior to the Bomb and disclosures about the scope of chemical waste, without realizing the dreadfulness of the future in that direction, I wrote of "unwanted" or "unintended" by-products, though the phrases "side effects" and "unforeseen consequences" turned up from elsewhere and have better met the Darwinian tests of survival.)

When advocates of "the Method" envision an indeterminate number of "scientific" sociologies, micro-sociologies tailored to whatever particular "factual" data a given project is designed to research, they could all be classed under the general head of "Administrative" or "Bureaucratic" Sociologies (if we use the term "bureaucratic" as a less "censorial appellative" than Mills's title "The Bureaucratic Ethos"). The underlying sociological assumption would be that any mode of administration, be it progressive, reactionary, or somewhere in between, would seek trained researchers' advice to help in the task of "human engineering" as defined by the given case, be it the concern of a "political government" or a "business government" (a useful classification proposed by Thurman Arnold). This would be the kind of sociology most likely to get "funded," a "fundamental" need of the department.

As distinguished from that discipline there would be a kind of Meditative, Philosophic, Heuristic, Comparative, Historical, even at times "Eschatological" Sociology, given to a style of speculation, observation, "system-building," developed in the light of what Mills characterizes as the "Sociological Imagination," which is

the capacity to shift from one perspective to another—from the political to the psychological; from examination of a single family to comparative assessment of the national budgets of the world; from the theological school to the military establishment; from considerations of an oil industry to studies of contemporary poetry. It is the capacity to range from the most impersonal and remote

transformations to the most intimate features of the human self—
and to see the relations between the two. Back of its use there is
always the urge to know the social and historical meaning of the
individual in the society and in the period in which he has his
quality and his being.

That is quoted from his book's introductory chapter, "The
Promise." The appendix, "On Intellectual Craftsmanship," in
developing a point about "a variety of viewpoints," talks about
the kind of shifts I discuss in *P&C* with regard to Nietzsche and
the concept of "perspective by incongruity," which I propose as
the name for the hermeneutic principle implicit in the program
that Nietzsche entitles "the transvaluation of all values." And
that, in view of our present topic, could be translated as "the interpreting of attitudes in terms of an attitude which the term
being interpreted had automatically, spontaneously, *sua sponte*,
ruled out."

Yet the example Mills focuses on ("deliberately inverting your
sense of proportion" for heuristic purposes) is from a section of
P&C, "An Incongruous Assortment of Incongruities" (reprinted
in the *Theories of Society* compendium), which is more Berg-
sonian than Nietzschean; and it even allows for "an attitude of
playfulness" (Mills), skewing perspectives just for the sake of
it, since the very nature of language suggests such possibilities
(though with masters of the art, Lewis Carroll or Oscar Wilde,
for instance, the thought of such intellectual perversities sets a
Freudian to looking for purely personal motives).

As I noted in my afterword to *P&C*, a double provenience of
some sort is attested in my own work by the fact that the book
was launched under the aegis of reviews by Harold Rosenberg
(in *Poetry: A Magazine of Verse*) and by Louis Wirth (in *The
American Journal of Sociology*). And I have indicated why I
take it that *ATH* is in the same groove. Beyond all questions,
parts of my counter-gridlock reflected a return of even personal

motives I had repressed (by expressing them roundabout) in the mere act of writing the books at all. And I glimpse behind my willingness to settle for "two sociologies" a duality that is probably an inheritance from Flaubert's wholly *esthetic* ideals of "pure form" embodied in gritty subject matter that got him into the law courts. Or perhaps inherited from the word made flesh as per James Joyce's "epiphanies," secular analogues of the Christian Logology. Can we ever clearly know what a tangle came into the world when our ancestors began learning language, and thereby Story was born?

In any case, we can note this much: In developing the idea of "bureaucratization" as embodied in the accumulations made possible and inevitable by successive "generations" of Technology, with my concept of the "neo-Malthusian principle" I stumbled upon another line of implications to be tracked down, once you start talking about "populations" as concerning not "the proliferation of *people* to their physical limits, but the proliferation of *habits* to their physical limits." That got me to using the concept of "ecological balance" figuratively, when distinguishing between the cultural effect of business enterprise in an *emergent* stage and its effect at a time when it has "attained its full proliferation, or bureaucratization" (footnote, page 154). Hence (see pages 166–167) when on the subject of "imagination" and its "bureaucratic embodiment," I *figuratively* idealize: "A well-balanced ecology requires the symbiosis of the two."

But I had also (see footnote, page 150) begun using the term "ecological balance" *literally*. And in the process, when referring to the kind of "technological efficiency" that exports two-dollar wheat and gets in exchange a Dust Bowl (a disastrous kind of enterprise that has assumed further alarming manifestations), I happened to say, "Among the sciences, there is one little fellow named Ecology, and in time we shall pay him more attention."

That nearly got me some unearned increment. The February 1970 issue of *Fortune* published an expert news item, "Our New

Awareness of the Great Web," by William Bowen, quoting my prophecy of thirty-three years before, and observing that my "prediction came true." But the outcome was unfortunate. For though the article specified the date when my book was published, it kept the title a secret. So, whereas there had been a Beacon Paperback edition of *ATH* available since 1961, the pebble caused nary a ripple. The article also refers to three ecologists who view their subject as "subversive." I'd probably have gone along with that "thought-style" ten years ago. But since then I have shifted to the perspective in terms of which I look upon ecology as technology's self-criticism—and I feel better.

Incidentally, in going back over this subject matter I found, in a copy of the original two-volume New Republic edition of *ATH*, the duplicate of a letter I wrote when applying for support toward the writing of it. It struck me as a limber way of discussing the cumbersomeness implicit in the detailed analysis of "unintended by-products" or "unforeseen consequences."

> Suppose that a man was writing a book. And suppose that each word in this book was not merely a thin smudge of ink on a page, but was actually the size and weight of a brick. By the time he had got to chapter three, he would have a wholly new problem on his hands. He would be surrounded by a mountain of bricks. The bricks would be a mere by-product of his intentions. Their clutter would have arisen incidentally, while all his interest was centered on the writing of the book—but he would have to take them into account nonetheless.
>
> I think that the processes of history are somewhat like that. Our ideas as to what we should aim at lead us to attempt certain things—and while we attempt these things, other results arise as by-products. The writer, finding himself surrounded by the clutter of bricks, would have to change his ways of writing so as to take this heavy incidental accumulation into account. And so, at certain stages in history, we have to change our ideas of purpose in order

to take into account our efforts' by-products that have piled up incidentally while our attention was focused elsewhere.

A civilization successfully weathers such a test when its critics enable it to understand what kind of clutter has arisen, and what new system of motives must arise to handle this clutter satisfactorily. I wish to examine the documents of history with the particular purpose of looking for such moments and noting how they were met. And I am extremely grateful for the generosity of the Guggenheim Foundation in enabling me to undertake this work.

This item turned up unexpectedly and puzzles me somewhat, since it is a better fit for *ATH* than *P&C*; yet I received a grant for *P&C* but not for *ATH*. Apparently, "as one thing led to another," *P&C* charted a course of its own. In any case, it serves well to introduce my wind-up for these pages, which will end on a parting look at this book's title and its relation to the perspectival formula "bureaucratization of the imaginative."

"History" in one pair corresponds to "bureaucratization" in the other, each having connotations of bunglesome clutter—and that leaves us with "imaginative" as analogous to "attitude." That works out to near-perfection. For quite as "imaginative" is the word for incentive, so in *A Grammar of Motives* (the chapter " 'Incipient' and 'Delayed' Action"), citing such texts as I. A. Richards's (*Principles of Literary Criticism*) and George Herbert Mead's (*Philosophy of the Act*) I would stress the relation whereby an *attitude* leads to its *enactment* (which is an attitudinally "neutral" term for "bureaucratization"). And if you cared to, you could substitute a quite grandiose similitude for the bureaucratization-imaginative pair. On the slope of the "creatively imaginative" from out of the "Unconscious," there is motivationally a volcano's magma, the molten rocks of motivation from which, in its irruption, there flows a deposit of lava that grows cold and hardens. Or in more sober dialectics, there is, I think we have mentioned, the idealistic philosophers' design of a becoming (*Werden*) that congeals into the state of a having-become (*Gewordensein*).

In the natural biosphere, much such "dying" leads to kinds of "decomposition" which form the ground of new growth. But in the realm of Counter-Nature, made possible by the ingenious, symbol-guided resourcefulness of Technology's ever-expanding counter-natural domain that the human animal has carved out of the world as it was, much that comes into contact with the "half-life" of some thermo-nuclear residues will remain "hygienically sterilized" for, in all likelihood, a long time after any human offspring could possibly still be here. Yet this is but an exercise in gratuitous exercising that belongs better later. So let's first talk more about the matter of "attitudes" in general.

For a limbering approach to the subject, I'd like to say some words in behalf of a book that is as handy as could be for giving us the feel of the integral relation between act and attitude. It is the elusive translation of a French text by Georges Polti entitled *The Thirty-Six Dramatic Situations*, and I don't think it matters at all whether there are or are not exactly that many. For our purposes it is unforgettably useful in helping us to realize how basic the expressing and clashing of attitudes must be to the kind of exercising that marks the eventfulness of appeal in the realm of poetics. The mere *naming* of such "situations" makes the point obvious. For instance: supplication, deliverance, vengeance, pursuit, disaster, falling prey to cruelty or misfortune, revolt, enmity of kinsmen, remorse, loss of loved ones ("here all is mourning").

Whereas the arousing and fulfilling of attitudes purely for love of the art can be specified as the mark of purely poetic gratification, rhetoric is the use of devices that arouse in the audience the attitudes that lead to corresponding responses in the practical realm, such as voting, purchasing, or being persuaded to favor some moral judgments or policies rather than others.

The place of attitudes in the scientific realm is more difficult to pin down. Even the "reconnaissance" of a spy is scientifically "neutral" in the sense that the spy should size up the situation as accurately ("disinterestedly") as possible, regardless of any bias (attitude) local to his particular interests or sympathies. In mathematics and the physical sciences the attitudinal components of motivation would be more deeply embedded (implicit) in the particular choice of medium and *definienda* that marked the specialist's vocation. With regard to the social sciences, I have said why it seems to me that the sociologizing of sociology leads me to a not very heroic compromise whereby there would be what Mills called the "substantive" branch and the many micro-sociologies adapted to local "administrative" uses (with overlaps?).

Philosophically, with regard to a *Weltanschauung*, an ATTITUDE toward Life, I incline to take it that that aspect of my symbolizing is in the sign of Diogenes and his followers (in the style of *ridendo dicere verum*—what I was later to sloganize as "smiling hypochondriasis"). Yet even there we confront a perturbation, since that is a "comic" frame of reference which I would opt for. Yet recently I received some comments from a friendly colleague who classes my position as essentially "tragic." And it is so in the sense that the "comic" attitude, quite like the "tragic" attitude, subscribes to this basic view of life as an education: We learn by suffering. With regard to information, study, knowledge, surely pain is the sharpest of admonitions any organism learns to choose by and thus to live by. I have read of wretched fellows whose bones were broken again and again, for their bodies so lacked sufficient sense of pain that they could never learn to move about in ways whereby they didn't bump against things self-protectively. Tragi-comically I sometimes wonder to what extent Technology's vast increase in the range and variety of pain-killers confuses our ways of learning, as some element or process that causes a pain is not corrected, but is canceled by a medicament that silences the warning while continuing to be the source of the admonition (as many carefree subjects get lung cancer because our lungs do not have the kind of pain-cells equipped to make the gesture of inhaling tobacco smoke admonitorily painful).

But what of HISTORY? Looking back, I note that I didn't get around to asking myself the question until 1955, for the Hermes edition of 1959 (mostly a revision by omission). The statement in my belated introduction that "by 'history' is meant primarily man's life in political communities" seems fairly adequate as a rough approximate, if "political" is meant in the wider sense of the "socio-political."

But as I have indicated in these pages, the Story comprising the countless aspects of History dissolves into that Undefinable *Definiendum*, "the Universe," that Qualitative-Quantitative X we can articulately attitudinize toward only in terms of the perspectives local to our countless "universes of discourse" that shade indeterminately into one another. Ultimately this kind of indetermination is such that, not only are our attitudes shaped by whatever may be the *Definiendum* or *Definienda*, but also they are "creative" in their own right. For an affliction is a different affliction if it is thought of as a punishment by a Higher Power, a case of tough luck, the doings of a personal enemy, or the curse of a social system that could be remedied, etc.

All told, throughout the History (the Changing Story) of Acceptances and Rejections there broods the fantastic Maybe of the transformations (the restless "transvaluations of values," i.e., "perspectives") that have to do with the two modes of departure from the state of nature made possible ("inevitable"?) by our peculiarly human medium of expression, identification, communication. These come to a focus in extensions of the personal principle and the instrumentalist principle, which are variously in agreement and at odds, the one attaining its fulfillment in the Stories (the myths) of the Supernatural, the other driving toward completion in symbol-guided Technology's realm of Counter-Nature (each kind of departure having its own species of Eschatology).

Yet just when I thought I was through with the subject of attitudes, I came upon a text which, to my considerable consternation, asseverates: "The conception of a static world in which social change only appears to go on may seem strange, but it can be derived . . . from Kenneth Burke's attitudes toward history." (The observation is in *Structure, Consciousness, and History*, edited by Richard Harvey Brown and Stanford M. Lyman [Cambridge University Press, 1978], pp. 87–88, in an article by Lyman.) Later in the same article, on the subject of "another formalistic, mythic approach" that "derives from the world of Kenneth Burke" (p. 89) the reader is referred to the Beacon Press Edition of *ATH*. This time my troubles take a somewhat different turn.

> Ironically, the study of history as dramatic mode bids fair to become what Plato opposed—a kind of "cookery." Actual histories are the products of "recipes"—combinations, recombinations, remakes, and warmed over scraps of the same basic plots. The dramatistic approach that derives from Burke holds up "cookery" as a process-in-use by both historical actors, historians, and historiographers. As a form of structuralism, however, it suggests a comparative structure of basic plots and an ultimate reduction of all histories to a repertory of scenarios that are enacted and reenacted throughout the ages.

The reference to Plato is the only quotation in the several paragraphs (which amount to less than four pages), and I can't be sure whether *I* use such "cookery" or it simply "derives" from such an approach, but at least I have sent a note to Professor Lyman asking that he tell me where the passage is in Plato, for I don't quite get the drift of its application to *ATH* as *I* read it. So at this stage I am waiting for advice, but in the meantime I have decided that I had better take the writer's comments as an admonition that my attitudes toward history (lower cased) can suggest some wrong leads. It's particularly disturbing because the book itself has one section entitled "The Curve of History," which sums up our Western development in five stages thus: Christian Evangelism; Medieval Synthesis; Protestant Transition; Naive Capitalism; Emergent Collectivism. To this I added a section called "Comic Correctives"; and as I now see, I was here proposing a "comic frame of acceptance" that was not strictly "sociological" in the *scientific* sense, but had the makings of an ethical *philosophy*, perhaps in the same groove as a Diogenes. (Professor Lyman's answer has been received and is reproduced as a postscript to this Afterword.)

Though I could not say that my "curve of [Western] history" for the past two thousand years was very profound (and it couldn't be very thorough, since the whole section comprises but about sixty pages), I did think it could be called an outline of *history*. Yet have I in effect myself said that this "cookery" could be treated as "warmed over scraps" of an earlier position?

In a matter of this sort, one purely technical consideration should be taken into account. If your terms are at a sufficiently high level of generalization, they can be applied *mutatis mutandis* to a wide range and variety of situations. In that respect the attitudes of "acceptance" and "rejection" (with regard to whatever in a given society could be called the "symbols of authority") are "recurrent" quite in the sense that distinguishes Yes from No. And different situations (such as class struggle) in the course of historical development could be expected to modify the "recipe" ("combinations, recombinations, remakes"), the high level of generalization intrinsic to the terms making them "permanently" applicable to all such changes.

The readers of this book who read Lyman's account of its drift would not need to be told that, quite as the first section in *ATH* is entitled "Acceptance and Rejection," his whole essay is entitled "The Acceptance, Rejection, and Reconstruction of Histories: On Some Controversies in the Study of Social and Cultural Change." I take it that by the "Reconstruction of Histories" Lyman would mean what I dealt with in another term of high generalization: the "Neo-Malthusian Principle," which "designates not the proliferation of *people* to their physical limits, but the proliferation of *habits* to their physical limits." A similar notion got popularized in the name of "Parkinson's Law," a perfect example of what *ATH* would call bureaucratization. My ethical slant widens its scope, but specifically illustrates the point by reference to a particular historical "reconstruction" thus: "A given situation offers a related set of *possible* laxities. By the workings of the neo-Malthusian principle, for instance, the combination of capitalism and technology both *permitted* a proliferation of private-enterprise habits and *demanded* this proliferation. And the proliferation continues to the breaking point," a historical development which *ATH* would classify as "Emergent Collectivism."

Since the "curve" does obviously chart five notably different stages of Western history (which, mixing the nomenclature of *ATH* with that of Spengler, we could say has become bureaucratized to the point where it has ceased to be a culture and has become a megalopolitan civilization), the trouble must be that a formula such as the "Neo-Malthusian Principle" or concepts such as "Symbols of Authority" that may provoke attitudes of acceptance or rejection are at so high a level of generalization that they apply *mutatis mutandis* to all kinds of societies. I have explicitly said that Frazer's concepts of magic, religion, and science seemed too temporal as stages, whereas I had begun to feel that they were always being born anew. And in my "Dramatism" article (*International Encyclopedia of the Social Sciences*) I find it quite "natural" to look for "scapegoats" in the workings of Technology, though terms such as "purgation by victimage" are totally alien to the glossary of that rationale. In a sense, some kinds of sociologists might well suspect that my speculations on the subject of human motives are by definition anhistorical because they are based on the assumption that the *same* "old Adam" is in all of us. So at that point, to confront the issue as directly as I can, I revert to a statement of mine which no sociologist need ever have known of, yet which is best able to feature the ingredient of *permanence* that I take to motivate our kind of symbol-using organism while at the same time allowing for countless histories of change.

I have already referred to a kind of novel, or anti-novel, *Towards a Better Life: Being a Series of Epistles or Declamations* (1932; now available in a University of California Press paperback edition). In the first preface to that effort I wrote:

> By changing the proportions of a very average man, we can obtain a monster. . . . That is, a monstrous or inhuman character does not possess qualities not possessed by other men—he simply possesses them to a greater or less extent than other men. Fiction is precisely this altering of proportions. The fictions of science alter them by such classifications as Nordic, capitalistic, agrarian, hyperthyroid, extravert. The fictions of literature alter them by bringing out some trait or constellation of traits, some emotional pattern, and inventing a background to fit. So science and fiction alike make monsters, though adults have agreed not to call an anatomical chart morbid, confining their attacks to the monsters of art. These monsters are constructed partly in the interests of clarity (as is shown in classical drama, where the depiction of violence, disease, excess, coexists with the ideal of clarity, though

strongly unbalanced characters may more readily display the main-springs of conduct).*

*With regard to this matter of "proportion," at the very last I receive from the editor Guy Amirthanayagam a copy of the book *Asian and Western Writers in Dialogue: New Cultural Identities* (Macmillan, 1982), containing my essay "Realisms, Occidental Style." In it I am dealing with the many problems involved in trying to decide just how accurate even an intentionally "realistic" story is likely to be, as a record of the "reality" it is designed to portray. On page 41, I observe:

> Surely the most troublesome problem in trying to use literature as social document concerns the problems of "proportion." Whenever I think of this issue I recall a remark by a deceased friend and poet, an odd fellow, John Brooks Wheelwright, concerning the nature of ideas. He said that with people who do not have many ideas, an idea can be like the introduction of rabbits into Australia. Since it has no natural enemies, soon it is nearly everywhere. In evaluating traces of a motive, we must also ask of what cluster it is a part, since its effect is reinforced or constrained by the presence or absence and comparative intensity of other motives. That is to say, a motive is but one ingredient of a motivational recipe. The other ingredients may modify its implications.
>
> Consider, for example, a work such as Dante's *Divine Comedy*. Would it not represent a notably different cultural complex if there were but the *Inferno*, the appeal to fear and vengeance by accounts of eternal suffering without hope, as contrasted with the pity theme in the *Purgatorio* and the theme of blessedness in the *Paradiso?*
>
> One problem of proportion with regard to the nature of our society has to do with the disparity between our powers as physical organisms and our powers as magnified by the resources, both technical and organizational, of applied science. The horrors of Auschwitz derive from a few instructions given by authorities who never went near the place. An overwhelming amount of the damage done by our ingenious, spendthrift modern weaponry in Vietnam was made possible by humble, orderly, obedient, peacefully behaving job-holders, who raise their families in the quiet suburbs, and perhaps do not even spank their children. One bomb dropped, by the merest twitch of a finger, upon a target so far below as to be unseen, can, without the slightest physical effort, do more damage than could have been done by a whole raging horde of Genghis Khan's invaders exerting themselves like crazy. In such dissociation which, given the current state of technological development, is all about us, there is a kind of built-in schizophrenia. Its disorders also foment guerrilla movements, and I suspect sheer aimless vandalism among puzzled, spirited youths whose energies would otherwise be unemployed. . . .
>
> Though the Realism of literature does give us the *feel* of Reality, as non-

I have said much more about the use of characters in drama that serve to motivate the plot by carrying things to excess. But this is enough to bring out what *I* thought my "Dictionary of Pivotal Terms" in *ATH* was designed for. I thought of it as depicting a *comedy* of human relations, themselves embodying a "comic frame of acceptance," while the maladjustments due to the "bureaucratization of the imaginative" serve to provoke the historical developments (changes in time) that bring our human foibles to the fore, in varying proportions and "recombinations." Yet that very perspective by incongruity itself does not designate a specifically historical outcropping, but is intrinsic to our generic nature as the specifically symbol-using animal, intrinsically goaded by what I was later to call the "entelechial" principle, the symbol-guided tracking down of implications, going to the end of the line, the ways of fragmentary excess that attain their terrifying grandeur in the self-chosen victims of tragedy.

My "glossary" of terms was trying hard to be as mellow as it could at a time when a great nation, with many of the greatest citizens the world has ever known, went mad, and all about us there were such goadings from so many quarters, and they developed from the most trivial of interrelationships, as tragic victimage emerged from barter, mere trade, a giving ("sacrificing") of one item in exchange for another.

---

literary documents cannot, it can provide no assurance that the *verisimilitude* of a fiction is the same as the *truth*.

This last point leads into the most important and most elusive problem of all: the extent to which a given work adequately represents the *proportion* of a given motive, as modified by the *proportions* of other reinforcing or corrective motives. . . . But the very nature of literature as a bid for the readers' attention invites kinds of emphasis that are analogous to the function of headlines in the news.

Each element in the atmosphere, by itself, would kill us. But in their proper proportions (which Technology's cult of energy is ever at work to disrupt) they are miraculously wholesome.

Later, in an article entitled "Variations on 'Providence' " (*Notre Dame English Journal*, Summer 1981), I was to sum up the matter this way:

> Logology would have to propose an invidious distinction between Historiography, a noble calling, and Historicism, a kind of excess caused by a kind of insufficiency. Historicism would not be content with writing history; it would go further, and hold that we are *nothing but* the products of the particular age in which we happen to live (or, as Heidegger puts it, to be "thrown"). Logology, on the other hand, would start from a generic definition of our specific nature as human beings. What, then, is the "substrate" of which we are historical manifestations?

In the appendix "On Intellectual Craftsmanship," Mills's *The Sociological Imagination* takes that same position: "Always keep your eyes open to the image of man—the generic notion of his human nature— . . . and also to the image of history—your notion of how history is being made" (p. 225). And in the July 1982 issue of *The American Journal of Sociology*, the same magazine that flatteringly though not so tellingly launched *P&C* with the review by the editor Louis Wirth, there is an essay that, while saying that *The Rhetoric of Religion* "is almost entirely a structuralist and formalist treatment of language," sees it as "resting on the more sociological early writings," such books as *P&C* and *A Grammar of Motives*. By leaving out of account many aspects of my speculations, the article brings out all the more the "overwhelmingly sociological undercurrents" on which my Dramatistic theory of language as symbolic action treats "the symbolic in dialectical interaction with the socio-economic." It is entitled "Knowledge, Meaning, and Social Inequality in Kenneth Burke" and is by James G. Carrier, in the Department of Anthropology, University of Papua New Guinea. But though he refers to many of my books and articles, *ATH* is not even listed.

Since it has been for long out of print, he may not have seen it. I shall write and ask him whether he does know it, and if he does whether he finds any cause to read *ATH* as Lyman does.

True, even if *ATH* were as bluntly unhistorical in its thinking as Lyman would seem to believe, the "eschatological" dimension I have added "formally" since then would seem to introduce modifications of some sort. As I see the issue now, both the Marxist eschatology and my Logological brand assign a major role to Technology. If you put "technology" in place of "labor" in Engels's article, we are both saying what the third clause of my "Definition of [Hu] Man[s]," in *Language as Symbolic Action*, says: "separated from their natural condition by instruments of their own making." The next clause, "goaded by the spirit of hierarchy," includes the history of class struggle, but in my *Rhetoric of Motives* the symbols of authority identified with a ruling class would be more interested in the dialectic whereby the ruling class became "naturally" privileged, in keeping with the logic of the whole social structure, its status reinforced by the prevailing thought-style. Yet to say as much is to realize how essentially of Marxist provenience it is.

The difference in the two eschatologies enters where Marxism features the class-conflict aspect of the integral relationship between social upheaval and technological development, whereas Logological eschatology, my style, would feature the destiny of Technology itself. By the Marxist view of this social-instrumental duality, the resolution of the cultural disruptions due to the *social* side of this interwovenness will mean the end of the social problem. But the Logological view of this situation is that no political order has yet been envisaged, even on paper, adequate to control the *instrumental* powers of Technology. Even if you granted, for the sake of the argument, that ("come the Revolution") the utopia of a classless society becomes transformed from an ideality to a reality, there would remain the ever-mounting purely *instrumental* problems intrinsic to the realm of Counter-Nature as "progressively" developed by the symbol-guided "creativity" of technological prowess itself.

But hold! The "creativity" of words figures more radically here. (In *The Origin of the Family, Private Property, and the State in the Light of the Researches of Lewis H. Morgan*, the International Publishers edition with introduction and notes by Eleanor Burke Leacock, see the appendix, "The Part Played by Labor in the Transition from Ape to Man.") I shall quote from pages 260–61 concerning primitive cultural conditions long after our ancestors, as Engels explains it, had become clearly differentiated from their anthropoidal forbears. Logology would agree with Engels's Marxism in recognizing a basic dialectical relationship between tool using and speech whereby the development of each contributed to the development of the other. The prime economic emphasis of Marxist dialectical materialism leads him to favor the instrumental factor as motivationally primary in the interaction between speech and "labor." Logology's stress being, by the nature of its perspective, upon matters of *communication*, there is no need for it to choose a hypothetical "first." We but hold that speech makes possible the modes of attention and communication without which the technical innovations that have now "flowered" in high Technology (and quite frequently it does "labor" old-style out of a job) could not have been developed. *Language* makes possible the kinds of accountancy for such symbol-guided resources to be invented, modified, and accumulated, including devices for "implementing" the accountancy.

We might incidentally note: The Marxist choice of "labor" rather than Logology's choice of "Technology" as key term here implicitly enlists on its side moral connotations (akin to the so-called Protestant Ethic) that the strictly *instrumentalist* connotations of the term "Technology" do not so "naturally vibrate with." But above all we should call to the reader's attention what almost "magical" change takes place within the space of the two pages from which these excerpts are being lifted.

First: "All the planned action of all animals has never succeeded in impressing the stamp of their will upon the earth. . . . The animal merely *uses* its environment, and brings about changes in it simply by his presence; man by his changes makes it serve his ends, *masters* it. This is the final, essential distinction between man and other animals, and once again it is labor that brings about that distinction." Then enter the kinds of admonitions that contemporary Technology is beginning somewhat to deal with in the name of "environmental impact statements." "Let us not, however, flatter ourselves overmuch on account of our human victories over nature. For each such victory nature takes its revenge upon us," as with deforestation that causes torrential flooding. Engels makes one error here. He speaks of a potato diet as causing scrofula; yet not the potato but the *cooking* of it makes it scorbutic. In sum, each victory "in the first place brings about the results we expected," but in the end it can have "unforeseen effects." Then he added these untroubled words of over a hundred years ago: "With every day that passes, we are acquiring a better understanding of these laws and getting to perceive both the more immediate and the more remote consequences of our interference with the traditional course of nature." Finally, after giving the kind of evidence that leads Logology to call human "mastery" of nature a manmade realm of "Counter-Nature," Engels sums up: The more such progress continues, "the more will men not only feel but also know their oneness with nature, and the more impossible will become the senseless and unnatural idea of a contrast between mind and matter, man and nature, soul and body, such as arose after the decline of classical antiquity in Europe and obtained its highest elaboration in Christianity."

The various toxic waste dumps are *in* nature; all Counter-Nature (much of it advantageous) is *in* nature. It is "unnatural" only in the sense that, thanks to the symbol-guided "labors" of Technology, we have altered the nature of our environment as no other animal's mere "presence" in the world has been remotely able to do. Logology goes on hearing what Engels said the first time, and all the more so because, since his day, the "consequences of our interference with the traditional course of nature" has "mastered," among many other things, thermonuclear energy and the lore of recombinant DNA, a kind of "oneness with nature" that probably still does go on with the "Old Adam" in human nature's round of attitudinizings, but certainly not in the history and putative eschatology of technologically (instrumentally) still-evolving Counter-Nature.

Addendum by Way of Partial Recantation

The essay "Psychology and Form" in my earlier book *Counter-Statement* has a footnote which I should discuss because it bears so strongly upon my position in the afterwords to *P&C* and *ATH* with regard to the distinction between the artistically personal and the technologically instrumental:

> One of the most striking examples of the encroachment of scientific truth into art is the doctrine of "truth by distortion," whereby one aspect of an object is suppressed the better to emphasize some other aspect; this is, obviously, an attempt to *indicate* by art some fact of knowledge, to make some implicit aspect of an object as explicit as one can by means of the comparatively dumb method of art (dumb, as distinguished from the perfect ease with which science can indicate its discoveries). Yet science has already made discoveries in the realm of this "factual truth," this "truth by distortion" which must put to shame any artist who relies on such matter for his effects. Consider, for instance, the motion picture of a man vaulting. By photographing the process very rapidly, and running the reel very slowly, one has upon the screen the most striking set of factual truths to aid in our understanding of an athlete vaulting. Here, at our leisure, we can observe the contortions of four legs, a head and a butt. This squirm-

ing thing we saw upon the screen showed us an infinity of factual truths anent the balances of an athlete vaulting. We can, from this, observe the marvelous system of balancing which the body provides for itself in the adjustments of movement. Yet, so far as the æsthetic truth is concerned, this on the screen was not an athlete, but a squirming thing, a horror, displaying every fact of vaulting except the exhilaration of the act itself.

Obviously, my comments here on "truth by distortion" reflect the very *attitude* that was to be "substantively revised," with corresponding developments all along the line, when *P&C* (and thereby also *ATH*) get to tracking down the implications of the "re-evaluative" term "perspective by incongruity." Such a shift but parallels in miniature the Story of all History as shrewd storytellers recount it ("reconstruct" it) in the light of whatever perspective marks any Next Phase.

Nor should we forget here the (as though planned) incongruities whereby many of our great national enterprisers have become All-American Multinational Conglomerates for the Global Exportation of Jobs, thereby causing the citizens of our nation to buy from abroad parts that were once produced at home, but now entail an "unfavorable balance of trade," with corresponding inflation, and all for want of the explicit perspectives by incongruity that nail this racket down (and its twists whereby *our own government* is at the service of those Supernationalist Corporations' empires, even helping them cut down the taxes for those legal persons, which tax us doubly first by making us import what their parent companies began by producing domestically and next by having us pay for all our nation's administrative and military resources that reinforce their ways of prospering at our expense).

But that's an aside. Yet, also it's a real aspect of the situation that such "global" exploitation of our domestic resources by the multinational corporations is in its way "visionary." For Technology has decreed that this *is* One World. And there they are, seeing all *local* issues in terms of *global* opportunities, whereas laborers necessarily confront *global* issues in immediate *local* terms. Nor should we forget the logological fact that representatives of any union "naturally" have a divided allegiance, quite as a political party owes its first loyalty to itself, its second to its constituents—and where there are accumulated dues to be invested, Union's Insiders "naturally" do not consult the general membership, the "solidarity" of which is "naturally" not abreast of such matters. Yet to say as much is not by any means tantamount to saying that there are not also genuine interests in common. Surely you have heard a rank-and-file member say, when such possibilities lead to charges: "Let them get what they can. It's OK with me, as long as they help me get what I get."

But with regard to my complaints about the distortions of slow motion, the hardening of my position into a Totally Schizoid Dualism that confronts this realm of personal feeling with wholly feelingless meter-readings helps me realize how astounding is the mode of analytic demonstration made possible by this contribution from the realm of Counter-Nature which reveals to us, as a new form of *beauty*, say, a wing in *natural* flight. And slowed replays of moves in athletic contests are a veritable squandering of analytic prowess.

Yet there are also the many invitations to an attitude of glumness that might liken the whole Technologic Edifice to a vast grotesque Cathedral composed of nothing but gargoyles. They spurt not rain-water but a constant downpour of electronic and chemical pollutants which, it has been pointed out (long after all our ingenious inventions have succumbed to wear and tear and change of fashion and in all likelihood even after the whole human race is gone), will still go on, as our bequest to the future, insofar as the human race lets itself have one.

However, Technology has a kind of built-in hopefulness, not just with regard to the resources and corresponding resourceful-

ness of Technology itself, but even to hoping that a worldwide
political system adequate to control its uses and misuses can somehow be contrived.

Kenneth Burke

January 1983

POSTSCRIPT

Several times with my closing words about these companion
volumes *P&C* and *ATH*, theoretical comments turned into Story.
And so again this time. Professor Lyman wrote me an answer
to my inquiries, but when I came to discuss his reply in this Afterword I couldn't find it. My letter had been sent in February from
Emory University in Atlanta, and his answer was sent to me
there. But when I returned to my home in May, I found that my
study had suffered quite a plaster fall during the winter. The
work of repairing the damage added to the disorder, with the
result that I couldn't find his letter. In considerable embarrassment, I asked if he could without inconvenience send me another copy. I reproduce part of his answer. (I have since located
the first one. The accident was an advantage at least to the extent
that his present account gives several more important details of
explanation.)

> I hasten to write you in response to your letter of November 9. . . .
> Rather than search out from my files the original letter I wrote
> you in February, I am writing a new one. The issue is as you say
> a reference to my statement:
>
>> Yet another formalistic, mythic approach derives from the work of
>> Kenneth Burke. Just as Plato's *Republic* is a philosophico-political
>> utopia presented as a dramatic dialog, so Burke suggests that our
>> understanding of history seems to be a recounting of basic dra-
>> matic plots. Some of these dramas tell of the return of the prodigal
>> son, the death of the king, sibling rivalry, and so on, but are applied

to groups, societies, and nations that are anthropomorphized as persons. Ironically, the study of history as dramatic mode bids fair to become what Plato opposed—a kind of "cookery." Actual histories are the products of "recipes"—combinations, recombinations, remakes, and warmed over scraps of the same basic plots. The dramatistic approach that derives from Burke holds up "cookery" as a process-in-use by both historical actors, historians, and historiographers. As a form of structuralism, however, it suggests a comparative structure of basic plots and an ultimate reduction of all histories to a repertory of scenarios that are enacted and reenacted throughout the ages. (It is not the case, however, that a dramatistic sociology must necessarily avoid matters of history . . .)

Plato's discussion of cookery occurs in *Gorgias.* I am using the translation by W. C. Helmbold, published by the Library of Liberal Arts Press of New York in 1952. The relevant pages are 22–27 (or in the numbering system used by classical scholars, sections 462–466). . . .

As you correctly note, I say that "the conception of a static world in which social change only appears to go on may seem strange, but it can be derived from Kenneth Burke's attitude toward history." As you see, I do not attribute the conception of a static world to you but rather claim only that it is a possible derivation from your work and as I now understand, one that you yourself do not accept.

There is another issue here in my usage of the term "cookery." I am, in fact, engaged in a double metaphor and also a usage in which one metaphor desublimates and dialectically reverses the other. Yet all of this "methodology" is implicit and hidden behind the rather simple statement about cookery that appears in the published paper. What I mean to convey here is the following. I use the term "cookery" in derivation from Plato's usage in *Gorgias.* There Plato treats cookery as a knack to be distinguished from an art. Moreover, as a knack it bears a vulgar and destructive relationship to the art of medicine. Plato uses the knack/art, cookery/medicine analogy in order to criticize the argument of Polus that rhetoric is an art. According to Plato's spokesman, Socrates, rhetoric is a knack. Now all of this is contained in a larger discussion by Plato of the politics of power vs. the justice of the good Republic. Hence rhetoric as a knack is related to politics in a foul manner, as is cookery to medicine.

However, I am also using cookery in a quite different manner. Here it intends to refer indexically to the idea of "recipes-for-living" as developed by the philosopher/sociologist Alfred Schutz. In this sense no negative evaluation of cookery is intended and, indeed, this usage desublimates and dialectically reverses the negative image derived from Plato. All of this is intended to lead ultimately in my essay to my own positive consideration of Simmel's theory of history that I discuss in the final pages of the essay. From your very important letter I learn that my own intentional double metaphor might not be conveyed to the reader who does not see behind the printed word.

My response to the word "cookery" had been along these lines: Since the term was obviously being used in a bad sense, I took it that, more than two millennia ago, no less an authority than Plato, in his historic quarrels with the Sophists of his day, had applied an accusatory epithet to my (lower case) "attitudes toward history."

Feeling offended, I began to feel defensive; and accordingly, I asked what could be said in my behalf, once I knew precisely what that great philosopher's charge against me was. First there was the fact that Plato's attack on rhetoric in his *Gorgias* was more than canceled by his *Phaedrus*, a glowing presentation of what has been called the Socratic erotic says about "the possibility of a philosophic rhetoric" (I quote from Eduard Zeller's *Outlines of the History of Greek Philosophy*). And I recalled Aristotle's *Rhetoric*, in which he discusses the discipline as an "art." And through having written a *Rhetoric of Motives* and a

Rhetoric of Religion, I learned the hard way what a masterpiece that book is. I had had a big investment in the subject of rhetoric ever since my first book of criticism, *Counter-Statement.* Nay more, I felt rebellious enough to speak in praise of "cookery" as a highly civilized "art." But Professor Lyman shows how Plato's great art of analogizing is being applied to *bad* rhetoric. (The grandest possible address by a speaker attempting to *persuade* an audience would be, in Aristotle's terms, an act of rhetoric.)

But when Professor Lyman turns to "using cookery in a quite different manner," and so refers "to the idea of 'recipes-for-living' as developed by the philosopher/sociologist Alfred Schutz," all resistance vanishes in a flash. For that way is surely in the same groove with my essay entitled "Literature as Equipment for Living," reprinted in my collection of essays, *The Philosophy of Literary Form* (originally published in 1941, and now republished by the University of California Press).

My one problem is: it's an essay on proverbs, and I call it "a *sociological* criticism of literature." But though I was commenting on a *book* of proverbs, they were doubtless a medium that, in its beginning, made its way by word of mouth; and many must have been the bequeathments of illiterates. As I saw then, "there is no 'pure' literature here. Everything is 'medicine.' Proverbs are designed for consolation or vengeance, for admonition or exhortation, for foretelling. Or they name typical, recurrent situations."

And I ended by "sociologically" viewing all literature in that light:

> What would such sociological categories be like? They would consider works of art, I think, as strategies for selecting enemies and allies, for socializing losses, for warding off evil eye, for purification, propitiation, and desanctification, consolation and vengeance, admonition and exhortation, implicit commands or instructions of one sort or another. Art forms like "tragedy" or

"comedy" or "satire" would be treated as *equipments for living*, that size up situations in various ways and in keeping with correspondingly various attitudes. The typical ingredients of such forms would be sought. Their relation to typical situations would be stressed. Their comparative values would be considered, with the intention of formulating a "strategy of strategies," the "overall" strategy obtained by inspection of the lot.

I could have got Professor Lyman as wrong as he said I could be got wrong. And the issue does help bring out the philosophical/sociological (as vs. a would-be strictly "scientific") element in my book's dictionary of foibles and "attitudinizings," terms which I would class as "comic." In these mean days it's a great privilege to end on so mellow a slant.

Kenneth Burke